Australian
HEROES
of World War II

Dr Mark Johnston has established himself as one of the foremost authorities on the Australian Army in World War II. He was described in the Australian War Memorial's *Wartime* magazine as 'the leading historian on the experience of Australian soldiers during the war'. He is Head of History at Scotch College, Melbourne, and author of 12 books, including *Derrick VC in His Own Words* (2021) and *An Australian Band of Brothers* (2018) with NewSouth Publishing.

Australian HEROES of World War II

REMARKABLE STORIES OF
BATTLEFIELD COURAGE

MARK JOHNSTON

NEWSOUTH

UNSW Press acknowledges the Bedegal people, the Traditional Owners of the unceded territory on which the Randwick and Kensington campuses of UNSW are situated, and recognises the continuing connection to Country and culture. We pay our respects to Bedegal Elders past and present.

A NewSouth book

Published by
NewSouth Publishing
University of New South Wales Press Ltd
University of New South Wales
Sydney NSW 2052
AUSTRALIA
https://unsw.press/

Our authorised representative in the EU for product safety is Mare Nostrum Group B.V., Mauritskade 21D, 1091 GC Amsterdam, The Netherlands (gpsr@mare-nostrum.co.uk).

© Mark Johnston 2025
First published 2025

10 9 8 7 6 5 4 3 2 1

This book is copyright. Apart from any fair dealing for the purpose of private study, research, criticism or review, as permitted under the *Copyright Act*, no part of this book may be reproduced by any process without written permission. Inquiries should be addressed to the publisher.

 A catalogue record for this book is available from the National Library of Australia

ISBN   9781761170362 (paperback)
          9781761179303 (ebook)
          9781761178481 (ePDF)

Cover design Luke Causby, Blue Cork
Cover image Wounded in the chest and leg on Sykes, Tarakan, Sergeant Glyn Pope (right) receives assistance to safety from Private John Higgins. AWM 089473
Internal design and cartography Josephine Pajor-Markus
Printer Griffin Press

All reasonable efforts were taken to obtain permission to use copyright material reproduced in this book, but in some cases copyright could not be traced. The author welcomes information in this regard.

CONTENTS

List of maps		vii
Abbreviations		ix
Introduction		1
CHAPTER 1	Baptism at Bardia	12
CHAPTER 2	The advance to Benghazi	23
CHAPTER 3	Tobruk: Holding the thin Red Line (April–May 1941)	33
CHAPTER 4	Mission impossible: The campaign in Greece	46
CHAPTER 5	Island of doomed heroes: Crete	55
CHAPTER 6	Tobruk: Besieging the besiegers (May–October 1941)	70
INTERLUDE 1	THE LANGUAGE OF HEROISM	80
CHAPTER 7	The unsung heroes of the Syrian campaign	83
CHAPTER 8	The Japanese onslaught: Malaya and Singapore	102
CHAPTER 9	Doomed battalions: New Britain, Ambon, Timor and Java	125
CHAPTER 10	Return to the desert: Egypt	140
INTERLUDE 2	THE WARRIORS' WEAPONS	165
CHAPTER 11	Kokoda: The first clashes (July–August 1942)	169
CHAPTER 12	Milne Bay: Breaking the Japanese spell	175

CHAPTER 13	Kokoda: Fighting retreat, fighting return (August–November 1942)	185
CHAPTER 14	El Alamein: The decisive battle (October–November 1942)	199
CHAPTER 15	The Beachhead Battles: Gona, Buna and Sanananda	217
INTERLUDE 3	THE 'TYPICAL' HERO	244
CHAPTER 16	Wau–Salamaua: Heroism in the hills	247
CHAPTER 17	By air, sea and land: Lae and the Huon Peninsula	270
CHAPTER 18	To Sattelberg and Shaggy Ridge	288
CHAPTER 19	Bougainville: Through mud and blood to victory	317
INTERLUDE 4	HEROIC RESCUERS	342
CHAPTER 20	New Guinea: From Aitape to Wewak	344
CHAPTER 21	New Britain: The few imprison the many	376
CHAPTER 22	Borneo I: Tarakan and North Borneo	382
CHAPTER 23	Borneo II: Balikpapan	408
Conclusion		423
Acknowledgements		427
Bibliography		428
Notes		437
Index		447

LIST OF MAPS

Libya, 1941	13
Bardia	16
Siege of Tobruk, 1941	34
Greece, 1941	47
Crete	56
Retimo	58
Syria	84
Malaya and Singapore	103
Rabaul	126
Ambon	129
Timor	131
West Java	134
Alamein area, Egypt	141
Kokoda and the Papuan beachheads	170
Milne Bay	176
Wau and Salamaua	248
Lae and the Huon Peninsula	271
Markham and Ramu valleys	289
Shaggy Ridge area	302
Bougainville	318
Aitape–Wewak	345
New Britain	377
Borneo and Tarakan	383
Balikpapan	409

ABBREVIATIONS

AIB	Allied Intelligence Bureau
AIF	Australian Imperial Force
ANGAU	Australian New Guinea Administrative Unit
AT	anti-tank
DCM	Distinguished Conduct Medal
DSO	Distinguished Service Order
FOO	Forward Observation Officer
GM	George Medal
LMG	light machine gun
MC	Military Cross
MID	Mentioned in Despatches
MJC	Mark Johnston's Collection
MM	Military Medal
MMG	medium machine gun
NAA	National Archives of Australia
NCO	non-commissioned officer
PIB	Papuan Infantry Battalion
RMO	Regimental Medical Officer
SMG	submachine gun
TSMG	Thompson submachine gun
VC	Victoria Cross

INTRODUCTION

This book is about Australian soldiers whose courage made a difference at crucial points in World War II land battles. Most but not all of them received medals or other official recognition for their bravery. Many of their stories have never been published before or only in rare or specialised books. This is not an exhaustive account of every medal winner, for considering that there were well over 1700 medals awarded for bravery, writing such a book is virtually impossible.[1] Instead, the focus is on how some 700 individuals, from a wide range of units, risked their lives to bring victory on every front.

Men demonstrating physical courage have been considered an ideal in Western civilisation since the Greek stories of Achilles and Hector. That emphasis on warrior-heroes has diminished a little, though references to 'heroes' still abound in Australia, for example, on anniversaries of battles and on Anzac Day. Then, and on Remembrance Day, the concept of heroic self-sacrifice stops a nation. Every army needs its men to be courageous and promotes a military ethos designed to encourage bravery.

Australian soldiers often observed that the honours and awards system, which provided official rewards for bravery, was imperfect, especially as many courageous actions went unrecognised. The award winners who were most acknowledged were the Victoria Cross recipients, of whom there were 17 in the Australian Army in World War II. Numerous books have been written about these remarkable men, and I have chosen to concentrate on soldiers not so well known but outstanding in their way. I have woven their stories into a narrative of Australian land forces in World War II.

A problem inherent in writing history is harmonising different or downright contradictory accounts of the same event. Nowhere is the difficulty more apparent than when seeking the truth of brave men's deeds. I have often had to match up various accounts between memoirs, the Australian Army official histories, unit histories, war diaries and citations for medals. Sometimes, differences are irreconcilable. In such cases I have sought to give the account that seems most plausible rather than the most sensational.

Let's take one example of many. Corporal Allan Rose received a Military Medal for his actions in the Aitape–Wewak campaign in New Guinea. His citation, or official explanation of his award, says (with abbreviations written out in full):

> Corporal Rose is a section commander [of] 17 Platoon 2/6 Australian Infantry Battalion.
>
> On 25 April 1945 he commanded a patrol operating north of Maprik, which was ambushed and the leading scout, Private G. Ryan, wounded. Corporal Rose organized covering fire and, despite heavy enemy fire, succeeded in dragging Private Ryan to safety. He then attacked from the flank, causing the enemy to withdraw.
>
> On 17 June 1945 he led a patrol into the Yamil 2 village area, personally killing two enemy, when his brother, Private F.W. Rose was wounded, falling across the track and under enemy fire. Corporal Rose organised supporting fire, dashed at the enemy with fixed bayonet, and killed three causing the remainder to flee.[2]

This citation was written around 1 August 1945. Testimony from an earlier campaign also suggests that Rose was a courageous soldier, but did he do all that is described in the citation? These remarkable acts are not attested to in either the official Army history or the history of the 2/6th Battalion, even though the latter mentions both patrols. Moreover, the citation implies that Geoffrey Ryan was rescued, when officially he was 'killed in action'. The 2/6th Battalion's official war diary for 25 April mentions Ryan's death in the ambush and the mortal wounds inflicted on another Australian, but nothing about Rose's efforts. The diary's entry for 17 June does not refer to the action described in the citation, but the patrol led by Allan Rose in which his brother was wounded is described in the 16 June entry: enemy casualties are said to be 'two wounded', with no reference to three killed.[3] There seem to be no newspaper accounts of Rose's efforts. How to report such a story, where many of the details cannot be verified? In this case, I left out Rose's medal-winning efforts, but this example well illustrates typical issues with evidence. An important hindrance to accurate reporting is that many of the events described below occurred at high speed. As Andy Torrent observed when describing the action that earned him a Military Medal: 'It would be safe to say that the writing of the account of the action just mentioned took much longer than the action itself, as one does not dawdle over such things.'[4] This adds to the danger of misreporting. One problem particular to jungle warfare – where most of the awards recorded below were won – was that thick vegetation meant that acts of individual bravery were often not witnessed and recorded. Moreover, the chaotic nature of battle in every war ensures that many soldiers performed heroic deeds that went unobserved. In many cases, these deeds undoubtedly cost them their lives.

The point that the awards system was deeply flawed was made not only by individuals who themselves missed out but by innumerable other commentators, including men whose bravery was recognised. Many others deserved decorations too, and Alan Avery, a Military Medal winner, was only slightly exaggerating when he asserted of the Kokoda campaign: 'Everyone should have got a gong [medal] up there you know; they really should have. There were so many acts of bravery there.'[5]

Gordon Combe, who won a Military Cross in New Guinea, made a more general point in the history of the 2/43rd Battalion:

> It seems inevitable in war that many decorations other than those awarded are earned and many heroic deeds perforce go unrecognized – anybody who was in action with the battalion will be able to recall some outstanding feat of arms or example of inspirational leadership that merited a decoration but passed without due recognition.

He added that because of this fact, members of the battalion regarded decorations as representing the 'quality and spirit of the whole battalion'.[6]

That point can be applied to the entire Australian Army. War-making involves teamwork, and individual soldiers who were decorated, including Victoria Cross winners, generally achieved their great feats with the help of others. In a large postwar survey among Australian veterans, many medal winners stated that they were 'only the holders of what was won by their units'.[7] This attitude applied particularly among leaders – the non-commissioned officers (NCOs) or officers who, as is to be expected, often received awards. Platoon Sergeant Andy Torrent wrote in his memoirs that after he received the Military Medal for bravery near Lae, he was unhappy that his men were given little credit. He felt that every commander, no matter how small or large his unit, wanted recognition for his men, and gave as a further example his battalion commander, Colonel Hugh Norman, who on visiting him in hospital stated, 'They gave me another gong for the job you boys did in crossing the Busu river'.[8] Major Harry Harcourt, who received a US Silver Star serving with the 2/6th Australian Independent Company, once requested that his post-nominals not be used, as 'the men made it possible for me to win these awards'.[9] The existence of a rewards system encouraged singling people out and emphasising what they did on their own, but fighting was very much a joint activity. Success was usually possible only if men fought well as a group.

The decorations system caused ill feeling, guilt, resentment at injustice, envy and criticism both of units and of higher authority. Yet few Australians argued that there should be no awards at all.

Introduction

If certain commanders felt guilty about the awards they received, there were also officers who recommended others for awards that they probably did not deserve. This was inevitable, for commanders could obtain reflected glory if their subordinates received awards, thus encouraging unwarranted recommendations. This is not to say that obtaining an award for one's men was easy – recommendations had to be approved at several higher levels. Henry 'Jo' Gullett, a postwar politician and decorated soldier, wrote that he had certain knowledge that some politicians sought to obtain decorations for their friends and constituents, but failed, 'because that was not the way the system then worked'.[10] Instead, he said, awards 'often had to be earned two or three times' before deserving recipients received them.[11] The story of Owen O'Connor's Bougainville Distinguished Conduct Medal is illuminating. His citation, the official history and two newspaper articles all have slightly different versions of what happened, and his battalion history says that publicity given to O'Connor's feats at the time 'was not appreciated by Army Headquarters' and cost him a Victoria Cross.[12] Some commanders in the 6th Division, the first division to go overseas, played a perverse game of denying awards to their men. The historian of the division's 2/2nd Battalion boasted that the unit 'imposed its own standards; and those standards have been rigid to the degree of harshness'.[13] By mid-1945, the unit had not given a single Military Cross – the standard bravery award for officers – to its lieutenants in four campaigns! Little wonder that Gullett, a 6th Division veteran, asserted that many soldiers so resented this miserliness that they 'became opposed to the whole system of decorations'.[14] The official historian records a similar miserliness in the 2/13th Battalion, one of the 9th Division's best, compared to its World War I equivalent. British and New Zealand units reportedly received more decorations in the same or similar campaigns. This stinginess was surely counterproductive to unit morale and the image of the Army.[15] Gullett pointed out too that because the Australian model tended to give awards only for 'fairly spectacular' actions, many soldiers who fought consistently well and were the bulwark or helmsmen of their units in many engagements went unacknowledged.[16]

Although individuals were nearly always acting as part of a group, a common type of courageous action involved one Australian stepping forward when heavy casualties endangered the group's cohesion. This related to a factor essential to the success of Australian soldiers in both wars but often overlooked: unlike many of their enemies and allies, the vast majority of Australian frontline soldiers were volunteers. They had chosen to fight.

I originally set out to tell the story not only of the heroic deeds of individuals but also of the men's subsequent wartime service and postwar lives. Unfortunately, it soon became apparent that this would involve many not-very-illuminating stories of men staying with their units until war's end and receiving little or no advancement. Instead, I have opted to tell after-the-event career or life stories, but only if they are unusually interesting. It is worth noting that there was no guarantee that a man who was courageous in the heat of battle would make a fine leader of men if promoted.

If soldiers who feature in this book committed misdemeanours during their service, I have usually mentioned them. This is partly to give a fully rounded picture, and it is noteworthy that most Australians in the ranks probably had at least one blemish in their record, such as an instance of being Absent Without Leave (AWL). My interest in disciplinary breaches possibly owes something to the schoolteacher in me. A third reason relates to a fascinating quotation in Lee Kennett's excellent book about American soldiers in the war. He cites US Army psychiatrist Eli Ginzberg:

> Many of the outstanding combat soldiers were hostile, emotionally insecure, extremely unstable personalities who might well be termed clinically 'psychopaths,' whatever that may imply, who fully enjoyed the opportunity of taking out hostilities directly in a socially acceptable setting of warfare and who in the absence of such an outlet not infrequently end up in penitentiaries.[17]

I read this early in the writing process and initially considered it very simplistic, even though I had been surprised to find that one Distinguished Conduct Medal winner had gone to prison after the war. After reading Ginzberg's comment, though, I began looking out for signs of potential psychological issues in the men concerned and found more than I expected. Kennett argues that most Americans did not enjoy combat, and I sense that most Australians felt the same, even medal winners. William Dargie, a famed Australian artist, told an illuminating story about painting a portrait of Jim Gordon, who had won the Victoria Cross in Syria. During the sittings, Dargie was impressed by the Western Australian farmer's laconic and serious manner – 'Not the smiling, happy-go-lucky "Digger" of legend' – and his downplaying of heroism. 'No-one likes wars. It's just a matter of sticking with your friends', Gordon had said. One day, as they discussed Gordon's Victoria Cross–winning actions in Syria, Dargie noticed that Gordon was trembling. Interpreting this as a result of the strain of sitting too long, Dargie apologised. Gordon reassured him, saying, 'I always get like this when I think of that action'.[18] Another brave man troubled by his own actions was Horton McLachlan (DCM), a central figure in one of Australia's greatest war paintings. The man wielding a submachine gun as a club in Ivor Hele's classic *Operation Bulimba* wrote after the war that 'It's hard to forget putting the bayonet in one side of several men, and out the other, and bashing a fellow's brains out with a Tommy gun, which I had to do to stay alive and save the company from the machine guns'.[19]

Most individuals could not overcome fear and achieve such prodigies. Jack Atkinson, who won a Military Cross in New Guinea and a Commander-in-Chief's card in the Middle East, felt that an innate tolerance of danger allowed some to cope with fear better than others. He acknowledged that he too had been frightened to the core and that his teeth had chattered before and after close-quarters fighting. He saw the same in others but had the utmost respect for his fellow soldiers and their willingness to do their best.[20] By contrast, John Langtry, who as a sergeant won a Distinguished

Conduct Medal in Bougainville and became a senior officer and significant Australian military commentator after the war, wrote that US General SLA Marshall was correct to single out 'non-firing or deliberate failure to fire' as a central reality of human performance in combat. 'There are', he concluded, 'all too few fearless soldiers'.[21] This suggests that the brave few tend to carry the load of the others. There's an old saying that there's no 'I' in 'team', but there is no doubt that individuals did make special contributions in war.

For all its flaws, the British system of military decorations used in the Australian Army of World War II worked. Australian soldiers wanted these decorations and generally respected men wearing them.

As Max Hastings remarks, 'successful warriors have often been vain and uncultured men'.[22] Nevertheless, most of the men in this book, whether officially decorated or not, were not psychopaths or men on the make, but admirable. Some even come down to us in the record as saintly. Sergeant Ron Patrick, for example, who won a Military Medal in Tobruk, was said to be a pious, laconic teetotaller who only became aggressive when sent into No Man's Land. Then he led rather than ordered his men, whom he protected, taking on the most difficult jobs and ensuring that credit went to them rather than him. Little wonder that they loved him, only to lose him when he died during a raid at El Alamein.[23] Even in our era, when the constant use of hyperbole has devalued words such as 'hero', the term clearly applies to the vast majority of those described in the following pages. They contributed mightily to winning a war for a just cause. Many were badly wounded or died. The fact remains that most of their contributions involved killing other human beings, often in large numbers. In recounting these stories I was at times horrified at the thought of being an Italian, German, Vichy French or Japanese soldier facing the men described here, some of whom come across in their citations as merciless one-man armies. Most official accounts of why men received medals involve slaughter, but rarely did those accounts detail the carnage: when enemies were killed by the heroes' bullets or bayonets, very seldom are we told exactly where the projectiles or blades struck the victims.

Introduction

There is a certain bloodlessness about the official Australian accounts of bloody deeds, and inevitably that anaemia affects the evidence available for retelling them. Nevertheless, the following chapters should inform and astonish. In addition to narratives of all the main campaigns, I have provided four short 'interludes', or essays, on key elements of the topic: the language surrounding 'heroes', the warriors' weapons, the features of a 'typical' hero and the role of a rescuing hero.

Notes on style

Throughout the book, wherever a person has initials in brackets after his name, it refers to the decoration he received for the action being discussed. For instance, 'John Smith (MM) captured an enemy post' shows that Smith obtained the Military Medal for the action described. In some cases, men received additional awards on other occasions. For instance, Tom Derrick earned a Distinguished Conduct Medal in 1942 and a Victoria Cross in 1943. In each case, those initials will appear after his name on separate occasions. That may sound odd, but I think it works. If no initials appear in brackets after an individual's name, this means he received no official recognition for the action described. Unless stated otherwise, all individuals were aged in their twenties when they performed their remarkable deeds. Similarly, where no comment on the individual's later career is mentioned, it should be assumed that he stayed with his unit until the end of his service or of the war. Unless stated otherwise, all Australians discussed survived the war. Australian Army Victoria Cross winners are all mentioned, but briefly. Of all decorated Australians, their stories have already been told in the most detail.

Reference is sometimes made to 'recommendations' and 'citations'. A recommendation is a full statement, usually written by a commanding officer, of why an individual should be awarded a medal. A citation is a short official statement, taken from the recommendation, of why a medal was awarded. The main honours and awards were:

- *Victoria Cross (VC)*: The 'pre-eminent award for acts of bravery', awarded for 'most conspicuous gallantry, or daring or pre-eminent acts of valour or self-sacrifice or extreme devotion to duty in the presence of the enemy'. Available to all ranks.
- *Distinguished Service Order (DSO)*: Awarded to officers, usually above the rank of captain, for distinguished service, typically in combat.
- *Military Cross (MC)*: Awarded to warrant-officers and commissioned officers of the rank of captain and below for bravery on the battlefield.
- *Distinguished Conduct Medal (DCM)*: Awarded to personnel below the rank of warrant-officer for conspicuous bravery on the battlefield. Second only to the Victoria Cross for other ranks, that is, soldiers who are not commissioned officers.
- *George Medal (GM)*: An award for gallantry, especially for civilians, but also for deeds of military personnel not performed in the face of the enemy. For example, removing ammunition from nearby flames.
- *Military Medal (MM)*: Awarded to personnel of the British and Commonwealth armed forces below the rank of warrant-officer for bravery on the battlefield.
- *Mentioned in Despatches (MID)*: Awarded for gallantry or commendable service. In submitting reports on operations to their superiors, officers mentioned soldiers who performed noteworthy actions or showed gallantry. These reports were published in the *London Gazette*, meaning that any named soldier would be 'mentioned in despatches'. Recipients received a certificate and were entitled to wear a bronze oak leaf.
- *Bar to medal*: A bar worn on the riband or ribbon of a medal, indicating that a recipient has won it a second or subsequent time.

These honours and awards were not available in infinite quantities. There were quotas. These applied to 'immediate awards' given in each campaign and to 'periodic awards' given over an extended period. In

Introduction

1942 the former were supposed to be available at a rate of six per month for every 5000 troops on operations, the latter at a rate of one per 250 men every six months. The process was deliberately kept opaque but at times quotas were exceeded.[24]

As mentioned, many whose deeds are recorded here lost their lives in the war. Official posthumous recognition for bravery was possible only in the form of the Victoria Cross, of which eight of the 17 Army awards were posthumous, and the Mentioned in Despatches.

Units and ranks are referred to constantly in this book. This table should help readers unfamiliar with the terminology:

Military units and commanders

Component	No. of men	Commanded by
Army	60000–100000	General
Corps	30000–50000	Lieutenant-general
Division	16000–18800	Major-general
Brigade	3000–4000	Brigadier
Battalion	700–860	Lieutenant-colonel
Company	120–185	Captain
Platoon	32–40	Lieutenant
Section	8–11	Corporal

CHAPTER 1

BAPTISM AT BARDIA

The first Australian soldiers to fight in World War II were members of the 6th Australian Division, the first formation raised for overseas service in the war. Their baptism of fire, at Bardia, in Libya, was a long time coming, for while the division was formed in 1939, that battle was in January 1941. After arriving in the Middle East in early 1940, the all-volunteer 6th Division trained hard, despite lacking much equipment it needed to train and fight according to the British military manuals that the Australian Army followed. In Australia in 1939, some dubbed the early recruits 'economic conscripts', men forced to join by the tough economic times of the Great Depression. The 6th Division undoubtedly had more larrikin hard cases from the deprived and desperate in Australian society than the 7th, 8th and 9th divisions formed after the fall of France in mid-1940. Nevertheless, the recruits to those divisions also included many from the underprivileged and working class. The 6th derisively called them 'deep thinkers', men who waited too long to 'hear the bugle' and enlist.

So in January 1941, the 'first in' were going to be 'first to fight'. They were sent to the Middle East to complete their training, but when Italy entered the war on Germany's side in June 1940, North Africa became a potential theatre of operations. The Italian fascist leader, Mussolini, commanded large armies ensconced in Libya and Abyssinia and made no secret of his desire to expand Italy's empire. In September 1940, he cautiously invaded British-occupied Egypt, where he coveted the Suez Canal, key to Britain's connections to the Indian Ocean and the precious lands, resources and populations around it. By December 1940, eight Italian divisions were scattered

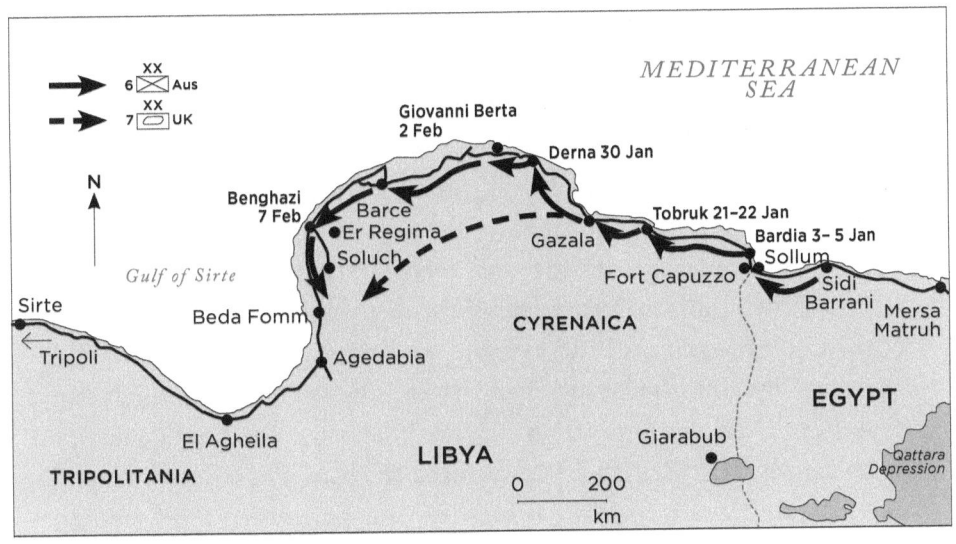

Libya, 1941

between Bardia, a large Italian base just inside the eastern Libyan frontier, and Sidi Barrani, in Egypt. That month, British General Richard O'Connor's Western Desert Force, comprising little more than one British and one Indian division, attacked the Italians at Sidi Barrani. Using new Matilda tanks, O'Connor's forces defeated the Italians and forced them back to Bardia. General Archibald Wavell, the overall British commander in the Middle East, decided to withdraw the Indian division for use against the Italians in Abyssinia and replaced them with the 6th Australian Division. Thus the Australians' first action would be against an Italian force in Bardia, which on 14 December was cut off from the rest of Libya when British tanks blocked the road leading west. The Italian position was not hopeless. The 40 000 Italians outnumbered their Australian and British besiegers. Moreover, Bardia town was surrounded by a 30-kilometre defensive line of underground concrete 'posts', all created at great expense, connected with deep belts of barbed wire and well provisioned with troops, weapons and supplies. Bardia's commander, General Annibale Bergonzoli, boasted to Mussolini that the fortress was 'impregnable'.

Into battle

Before dawn on 3 January 1941, Australians of the 16th Brigade (formed in New South Wales) marched across flat ground towards the enemy defences, widely dispersed to limit the effect of the expected Italian bombardment. They wore newly issued leather jerkins over their greatcoats and were heavily laden with arms, ammunition, tools and three days' rations. An issue of rum helped cope with the cold and the tension, and many sang while crossing the start-line marked with lengths of rifle-cleaning flannel tied together. Their singing was barely audible once the bombardment from nearly 100 British Commonwealth guns began at 5.30 am, concentrated on a narrow stretch of the perimeter. The leading Australian infantry battalion was the 2/1st, or Second First, so-called to differentiate it from the 1st Battalion of the militia back in Australia. The 2/1st captured a series of enemy posts and pushed right and left to widen the breach. By dawn, engineers had completed crossings of the anti-tank ditch and the 2/2nd Battalion, supported by British infantry tanks, advanced through the gap.

Groups of two or three tanks, each group with a platoon of 30 Australians, subdued one post after another, generally after 15 minutes of fighting. Italian artillery posed the main threat, especially several gun batteries, which could hit any Australians emerging from the gap in the wire. Captain Gordon Hendry (MC) commanded a company of the 2/2nd that was initially in reserve but was ordered to fill a gap that had developed between the leading companies. In doing so he and his men came under heavy fire, but despite this and a lack of tank support they pressed on and spread out, tackling outposts and guns, whose crews sometimes fought to the last or surrendered only as the Australians got close. Soon all three of Hendry's platoon commanders were dead or wounded and the company's main body was reduced from over 100 to just 20 men. Son of a minister, Hendry had been a schoolteacher at Scots College and Shore, and served as a lieutenant in the Sydney University Regiment. The official historian called him a 'resolute and always-thoughtful young leader', and now he proved it. When a group of four enemy guns and some machine guns fired on them, Hendry acted. After ordering three Bren light machine guns (LMGs) to give supporting fire, he personally led a bayonet charge and drove the Italians from the guns. By war's end, Hendry was a lieutenant-colonel commanding a battalion in Borneo, where he died in an accident in September 1945, aged just 32.

Private Bill Abbott (DCM) also charged the guns at Bardia. On seeing that one enemy post, covered by field guns and anti-tank guns, was holding up the 2/2nd advance, he volunteered to attack alone under covering machine-gun fire from the battalion's 'Bren carrier' vehicles. Assisted by a carrier crew he succeeded, capturing 120 prisoners and two light machine guns (LMGs) among continuing enemy bombardment. Thus began Abbott's eventful war. This farm labourer from Casino, NSW, was captured in Greece in April 1941 but made a lone escape by boat and reached Turkey before returning to Egypt. For this he was Mentioned in Despatches, but also caught malaria in this period and was often hospitalised. He broke his thumb in unarmed combat training in 1944 and did not rejoin his battalion until 1945, in New Guinea. During fighting there in March, he was wounded on successive days, receiving gunshot and grenade wounds to the thigh, foot and head before being evacuated. He was discharged on medical grounds. Guns and violence continued to be part of his postwar life. In 1951, he shot and killed a married teenage couple near Casino, before setting them and their property alight. The judge wondered aloud whether Abbott's military experiences contributed to his 'plight'. Abbott was sentenced to death, later commuted to life imprisonment. Newspapers likened him to Hercules and noted that he was wearing a jungle-green shirt and trousers when he committed his crimes.

By 9 am on 3 January 1941, the 16th Brigade's three battalions had opened a bridgehead more than six kilometres wide within Bardia's defences. Six Italian M11 medium tanks launched a counterattack, directed at the 2/3rd Battalion. A solid tank shell heralded their arrival, knocking the rifle from an Australian officer's

AUSTRALIAN HEROES OF WORLD WAR II

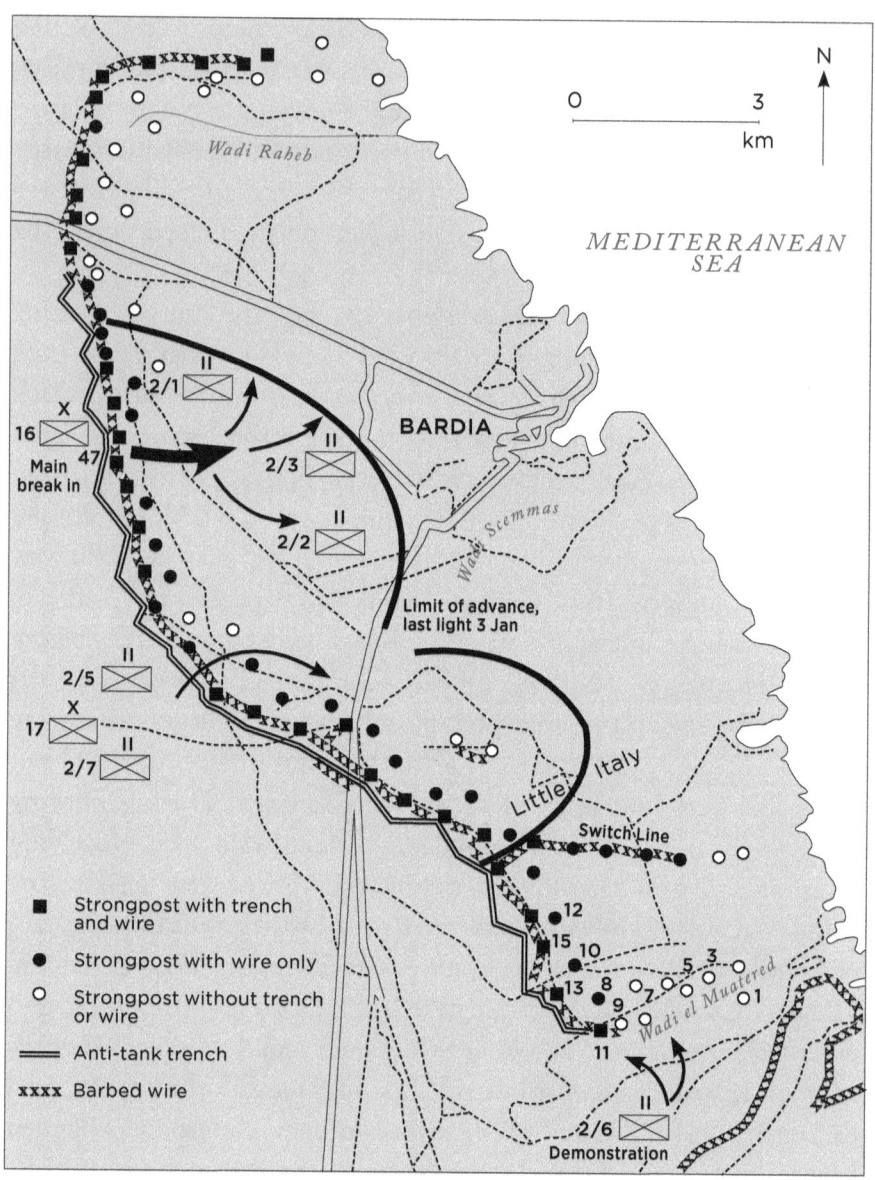

Bardia

hand and mortally wounding his runner. Private Harold Hergenhan bravely ran towards the M11s, only to be killed when his grenade exploded prematurely. A lieutenant emptied his revolver into the leading tank, but the vehicles moved off and freed 500 Italian prisoners. When two Australians rushed towards the tanks firing a Bren, the tanks departed. The prisoners were recaptured. The tanks now approached the 2/3rd headquarters, killing an officer who challenged them with an anti-tank rifle. The Australians' prospects looked grim until three 'portees' – anti-tank guns mounted on trucks – drove up. Corporal Arthur Pickett (DCM) brought his gun into action first and, firing at a range of under 200 metres in the open, quickly knocked out four tanks. The fifth tank fired back, blowing the crew off the portee: one was killed, another wounded. Pickett got the survivors firing again and the fifth tank was destroyed, only for the sixth tank to set Pickett's portee alight. The sixth tank was soon destroyed. The solid shots of the Australians' 2-pounders easily penetrated the tanks' thin armour before ricocheting around and inflicting carnage that shocked many of the unblooded Australians. Pickett, a painter from Arncliffe, NSW, was accidentally wounded in the backside several days later. His war service was punctuated with many illnesses, including a middle ear infection that had him evacuated from Greece before the campaign ended. He served in New Guinea before being discharged medically unfit in December 1943.

Private Ted Boland (DCM) began the day as a platoon orderly in the 2/2nd, but after his platoon commander was killed and the platoon sergeant wounded, he stepped forward to take command. He reorganised the platoon, then led it all day, capturing 16 Italian gun positions. He was immediately promoted to sergeant and retained command of the platoon for the following battle. Boland's courage was apparent again in the Kokoda campaign, where despite receiving a bad head wound at Eora Creek, he insisted on obtaining water for wounded comrades.

By midday the Australians had collected some 6000 Italian prisoners. Victorians of the 17th Brigade now entered the fray. They faced an unexpectedly tough test. Lacking tank and artillery support, with many already weary from a disturbed night and long marches, they came under intense artillery and machine-gun fire while advancing south. They incurred heavy losses and many became pinned on the flat ground. Within minutes of leaving a wadi (a low, dry watercourse), two forward platoons of the 2/5th Battalion lost every officer. About half their men were hit. Their company commander, Captain Charles Smith, took a Bren from one of his men and sought to fire back at enemy gunners who were engaging them 'over open sights'. Seeing this, Sergeant William Symington (MID) acted. Born in India as William Symington Brown, he was living in New Zealand when he enlisted for World War I in 1915. He won a Military Medal in 1916 and, after becoming an officer, the Military Cross in 1918 for capturing an enemy machine gun and killing its crew. On enlisting in early 1940, he gave his occupation as 'soldier' and his age as 39; in fact, he was 45. He shortened his name too. On the flat plain at Bardia, he lay with head, arm and leg wounds when he noticed Smith using the Bren. Symington crawled over to the 30-year-old farmer and insisted that Smith use his body for cover and as a gun rest. Soon after, a shell wounded both men again, and they were dragged to cover in a stone hut in the wadi. The battalion medical officer was attending them and other wounded when a shell struck the hut, killing Symington. Smith died some two weeks later.

For all their losses, the 2/5th and 2/7th battalions found a way forward. Captain William Griffiths (MC) pulled his company back to the wadi and, though still under fire, used its cover to advance along the flank of the enemy guns. Impatient at the slow progress of one platoon, he called on another platoon, under Sergeant Bill Morse (DCM), to join him.

Born in West Melbourne in 1905, Morse enlisted in October 1939, giving his occupation as 'labourer'. In fact, he was dependent on the dole, or 'susso', and perhaps fitted the stereotype of the 'economic conscript'. He was also a fine athlete – a prewar Victorian champion walker – and his superiors saw potential in him. He was soon promoted to corporal, attended schools on tactics and weapons in the

On his return to Australia in December 1942, Sergeant Bill Morse is greeted by his proud mother, who is admiring the Distinguished Conduct Medal ribbon on his chest.
AWM 137351

Middle East, and by the time of Bardia was a sergeant commanding a platoon. His superiors' judgment was now vindicated. He was directed by Griffiths and helped by a courageous corporal, Bob Shattock (MM), who led a charge against a gun position that resulted in 100 prisoners. With a force numbering no more than 20, Griffiths and Morse advanced further and further into the Italian lines. An Italian medical post, an Italian anti-aircraft battery and a group of field gunners all surrendered to them. Leaving two-man pickets to usher the prisoners back, the Australians pushed on until they found a group of enemy tanks, some with engines running. A few Bren rounds brought 200 more prisoners. The Australians then came upon an amphitheatre-like depression within the wadi, apparently empty until a shot from Morse brought out 75 surrendering Italians, part of an artillery headquarters who had been living in secure luxury with enamel baths, silk garments and cosmetics. Griffiths now drove an Italian car back to his own headquarters, but Morse was not finished. On seeing some Italian helmets above a wall some 500 metres away, he took one man and, firing as he went, called on the Italians to surrender. Another 200 did so. Morse became something of a celebrity for this feat, leading to him being dubbed 'The One-Man Army'. He served in Greece but was then downgraded medically and held base jobs for the rest of the war.

Australian engineers, or 'sappers', were vital at Bardia, where they blew gaps in the enemy wire, created crossings over an extensive anti-tank ditch and disabled mines. Lance-Sergeant Edward Peel (DCM) of the 2/2nd Field Company exemplified their work. After leading his subsection in making a crossing and cutting the wire, on his own initiative he led them forward and cleared an area of 'box-type' anti-tank mines under shell fire. Later, while probing forward again, he came across an enemy post that the infantry had missed, and with two others, advanced with his pistol and cleared the position. That night, while visiting his officer, he noticed a group of Australian infantrymen pinned down in front of Italian Post 16 and was able to direct reinforcements to their aid. This intrepid soldier, a Melbourne boot repairer, later joined the commandos and became an officer. Lieutenant Bill Cantelo (MC) of the same field company was responsible for building crossings over the anti-tank ditch at Post 39. After shell fragments wounded him in the face and neck he left instructions while being treated. As soon as he could he returned to his men, resumed command and led them on to Post 35, clearing mines under fire as they went. Then it was on to Post 31, supervising the construction of another crossing and disarming mines. Cantelo, a mining engineer, later commanded a field company and rose to lieutenant-colonel.

At the southern end of the Bardia front, the 2/6th Battalion made a diversionary manoeuvre, crossing a deep wadi and attacking the heavily armed and fortified Post 11. Intense fighting raged around this post, which was still holding out at the end of a day that cost its attackers nearly 60 casualties. Still, by then the Australians controlled about two-thirds of Bardia's perimeter and had penetrated nearly two kilometres into the 'fortress'.

Victory at Bardia

The key objective of the battle's second day was Bardia town, which sat partly on cliffs and partly on a beach below. The 16th Brigade advance, supported by tanks and the carriers of the 6th Division Cavalry, faced hard marching and some stiff opposition, especially shelling. The arrival of British tanks sealed the capture of Post 11. One of the last actions occurred at the Wadi Raheb, where light artillery and small arms fire from a large sangar – a walled defensive position built above the hard ground – pinned down an Australian platoon on open ground 150 metres away. The Australians' ranks were thinned due to the loss of men sent to escort prisoners and they were outnumbered five to one. A section comprising just four men under Corporal Don Rankin (DCM) of the 2/1st Battalion was closest to the sangar. Firing his Bren from the hip, Rankin charged to the post's right, followed by his three men. He set up his gun where he could enfilade the enemy, silencing the artillery and forcing them to surrender to his platoon, many of whom owed him their lives. Rankin was later captured in Crete.

The Australian artillery was important at Bardia, and their forward observation officers took particular risks. Captain Norman Vickery (MC) travelled the battlefield in a Bren carrier, acting as the only mobile forward observation officer (FOO) of the 2/1st Australian Field Regiment. At one point he found himself to the right of an enemy battery firing on Australian infantry and supported by an infantry garrison armed with machine guns and anti-tank rifles. Vickery and his driver made a daring attack. After receiving a few of the carrier's rounds, the battery and garrison surrendered, giving the Bren carrier a haul of about 1000 prisoners. This David and Goliath action embodied much of the battle of Bardia. By 1945 Vickery was a brigadier, receiving an MBE for superb work commanding naval bombardments in the Pacific.

Victory at Bardia naturally came at a cost. At the end of 4 January, the medical officer of the 2/1st Battalion, Captain Tom Selby (MID), was called to help Sergeant Allen 'Cracker' Craske who had been hit by a sniper at dusk. Craske, a charismatic, articulate and popular Tasmanian in an anti-tank company, had earlier arrived in the nick of time to protect 2/1st infantry from three tanks and had aided Selby in ministering to a casualty at the bottom of a deep wadi. When Selby found 'Cracker' dead in the back of an ambulance, the exhaustion and strain caught up with him and he wept quietly in the dark corner of his dugout. By the time the final mopping up of Bardia finished on 5 January, the dead Australians totalled 130. More than 300 were wounded. In his account of Bardia, decorated veteran Ken Clift described the 6th Division as 'magnificent soldiers' and concluded: 'I reckon their Anzac forefathers looked down on them with full approval'.

CHAPTER 2

THE ADVANCE TO BENGHAZI

Italian losses at Bardia were staggering, comprising 40 000 troops, 400 artillery pieces and 130 tanks. Yet many Italians still garrisoned Libya, including more than 25 000 in Tobruk, about 100 kilometres to the west. Even before Bardia fell, General O'Connor was planning an advance on Tobruk, and Australian troops reached it within three days of Bardia falling. Its defences were like Bardia's, including concrete posts protected by wire and an anti-tank ditch. At 45 kilometres, its perimeter was longer, and at either end were deep wadis.

Water was scarce, meals largely comprised tinned 'bully' beef and Army biscuits, and the Australians lived in shallow trenches. Their attack, supported by fewer than 20 British heavy tanks, commenced before dawn on 21 January 1941 and struck the eastern half of the fortress. Again, engineers blew gaps in the wire, disarmed mines and neutralised the anti-tank ditch. The 16th Brigade led the advance, this time with the 2/3rd Battalion and tanks punching a hole in the southern perimeter through which their sister battalions (2/1st and 2/2nd) marched. Signallers were vital to maintaining contact between the various headquarters, using both wireless sets and field telephones. For the latter, they laid nearly 200 kilometres of telephone cable at Bardia and another 250 at Tobruk. Several won decorations for bravery under fire, and on 21 January three took the initiative in the fighting. Signallers Ken Clift (DCM), 'Butts' McKeague (MM) and 'Tubby' Bruce (MM) were in a signals truck driving to where they expected to be able to lay cable for the 2/3rd Battalion. Instead, on topping a rise, they saw Italian troops barely 150 metres away across a wadi and realised they were well ahead of the front. The Italian defences here included a concrete pillbox, from which a machine gun was firing through a loophole at Australian infantry, while just 50 metres behind this emplacement the trio saw a battery of Italian artillery. Between them, the signallers had three pistols, two rifles and some grenades. Undaunted, they advanced across the wadi towards the pillbox. McKeague and Bruce used rifles to engage the emplacement's defenders, though the machine gun in the pillbox could not traverse to hit them. Clift managed to get behind the emplacement and throw a grenade into the pillbox. The result was, as he put it, '"minced" machine gunners!' The trio then turned to the artillery battery, which was still firing on the Australian infantry. Some rapid fire and the sight of Clift advancing with a grenade were enough to drive the gunners into the trenches behind the guns. They soon emerged carrying white flags. Some 60 surrendered to the trio and the arriving 2/3rd infantry. Clift, a 25-year-old draughtsman, ended the war a lieutenant in the Australian Parachute Battalion. He later wrote two war memoirs and a history of the 2/3rd Battalion. He played up the larrikin nature of the 6th Division, summing up his wartime memoirs as 'a story of adventure and frustration, of pride and disillusionment, of escapades and punishments, of love and heartbreak and, above all … of comradeship which only a soldier knows'.

When one company's commander fell wounded, the 2/3rd's Warrant-Officer Bruce MacDougal (DCM) took over and led it against Post 41. The defenders were firing fiercely, but the Australians shot back and MacDougal, shouting, led his new command in a 200-metre charge. The Italians resisted until the Australians reached the post, where MacDougal tossed grenades into the entrances from above.

At Bardia, the 19th Brigade had only fought on the last day, and Tobruk on 21 January provided its first real test. Backed by a heavy barrage, the men marched spread out towards an escarpment overlooking Tobruk's harbour. All went well until, on the left, the

2/8th Battalion struck posts grouped around the main road junction, set in an arc shielding Tobruk town and an Italian corps headquarters. The battalion came under fire from the twin machine guns of dug-in Italian tanks, as well as infantry and artillery posts that embodied the toughest Italian resistance. The Australian infantry got among the tanks – initially misidentified as machine-gun posts – before a planned artillery bombardment could be brought down, so it was infantry versus tanks. The Australians fired small arms and anti-tank rifles at the tanks' vision slits, though at least one, Sergeant Jim Burgess, jumped aboard with a grenade. He was mortally wounded by machine-gun fire but put the pin back before it could explode among his mates. Some 14 of the tank blockhouses had been neutralised when the crews of the remaining eight surrendered. Soon, 2/8th Battalion men were confronted with mobile medium tanks. A group of nine vehicles launched a counterattack, capturing one bunch of Australians.

Private 'Oz' Neall (DCM), a 31-year-old grazier from Lake Mandi, Victoria, now joined the action. His platoon's Boys anti-tank rifle had been damaged and its gunner wounded when Neall picked it up. Owing to ammunition shortages, he had in training only fired an anti-tank rifle once. Using a stone, he was able to repair the Boys sufficiently to feed and fire one round at a time and do what he later called 'some good work' against the tanks.

Soon the smoke of battle cleared enough for him to see another anti-tank rifle sitting on a rise some 200 metres away. Its owner had also been wounded, an indicator of the danger of the role, but Neall dodged machine-gun fire to reach it and bring it back. During a brief pause in the action, Neall was eating when a cry went up for his help. When he went forward, light tanks seemed to be everywhere. After he opened fire on them, all turned their guns on him. Nevertheless, he knocked out three. The remaining six eventually fled. Neall later went to Greece, where an observer likened him to Simpson and the donkey on seeing him load wounded men on donkeys and bring them down from high ground in the Vevi Pass under German fire. 'Oz' contracted a severe middle ear infection and was evacuated

In the assault on Tobruk on 21 January 1941, Warrant-Officer Bill Stenning led his platoon in capturing or knocking out eight tanks. He is pictured in May 1944, after receiving the Commander-in-Chief's baton as a cadet lieutenant at the Army Ordnance School, Broadmeadows, Victoria.
AWM 141154

from Crete before it fell. By war's end he was a lieutenant with an Australian Works Company.

Another 2/8th man who took on tanks was Warrant-Officer Bill 'Curly' Stenning (DCM). He was commanding a platoon when his company came under fire from a dug-in tank 300 metres away. The Australians moved to within 20 metres and lay in a semi-circle around the tank. One who approached with a grenade was shot dead. Stenning then fired an anti-tank rifle and penetrated the tank. A crewman emerged and was promptly shot. Stenning was credited with forcing the surrender of another four tanks. Later in the day, his platoon became separated from the company and was attacked by three medium tanks. Though Stenning was wounded in the shoulder, he and his men held their ground and knocked out all three tanks. Stenning served as a major in the postwar Australian Army.

In the centre of the 19th Brigade advance, Sergeant Harry Watts (DCM) and Private Stefan Broinowski (MID) of the 2/4th Battalion captured a machine-gun post firing at their company from the right. By nightfall, the Australians had taken almost the entire eastern half of the Tobruk fortress. It was exhausting work, for many had marched and fought over 30 kilometres of desert. All this effort was rewarded the following day as Italian resistance collapsed. While the infantry went around the perimeter collecting Italian prisoners, the divisional cavalry drove their carriers into the town to be met by thousands of Italian base troops and sailors waiting to surrender. The Australians had suffered just over 350 casualties, nearly a third of them from the 2/8th Battalion. In return they took 25 000 prisoners, gained a superb and undamaged port and huge amounts of equipment that would soon become very useful.

The dangerous road to Derna

The Italians had lost nine divisions since Sidi Barrani and had just one division and various smaller units left in Cyrenaica, the eastern part of Libya. These fled west, followed by the British 7th Armoured

Sergeant Vince McQuillan won the Distinguished Conduct Medal at Bardia, where he captured 60 prisoners using just a pistol. Near Derna on 27 January, he was commanding a Bren carrier when it was ambushed and hit a landmine. He died of his wounds in captivity.
AWM P03636.001

Division and two brigades of the 6th Australian Division. An Italian rearguard fought hard and well at Derna, which the 19th Brigade was tasked to capture. Sergeants Vince McQuillan (DCM) and George Mills (MID) had done great work in their Bren carriers in the previous battles. On the last day at Bardia, they had exchanged fire with an Italian emplacement, which McQuillan eventually marched into alone. Though armed only with a pistol, he emerged with 60 prisoners. Mills captured 40 prisoners on the road between Bardia and Tobruk where, on the last day of fighting, his carrier had been one of the first two into the town. Now at Derna on 27 January, they hit trouble.

McQuillan's carrier was ambushed by well-concealed Italian machine guns and anti-tank guns. As he turned to escape, the carrier detonated a mine, which killed his driver and broke McQuillan's arm. The troop's wirelesses were out, so other carriers that came forward to help got caught in the ambush. So did the doctor's truck, which was fired on. Italians captured McQuillan and three others. McQuillan died of his wounds in Italian captivity a few days later. George Mills was in a carrier that came up to help, but it ran over two mines, mortally wounding him. His driver was also killed as he sought to escape. Enemy artillery fire prevented all attempts to reach the destroyed carriers until the Italians retreated from Derna.

After dawn on 28 January, a 2/11th Battalion fighting patrol was returning to their lines having captured several abandoned enemy machine guns and artillery pieces. They knew that the area they were crossing, near the main road, had been mined, and though most were careful, one pointedly stood on the telltale disturbed ground, asserting that as anti-tank mines they would need 600 pounds of pressure to detonate them. He was unaware that the Italians had removed the pressure springs from some of these mines, and when one of them exploded he was killed instantly. The severe wounds among five other men included a punctured lung, severe facial damage and a broken femur. The Italians commenced shelling and machine-gunning the area, but Captain James 'Killer' Ryan (MC), the unit's doctor, came roaring down the road in a truck with his team of stretcher-bearers. The Italians respected the truck's white flag and allowed Ryan to undertake lifesaving work in peace. All the wounded survived. Because of his bravery at Derna, Ryan, a Queensland medical practitioner, became the first Australian medical officer to receive a Military Cross in World War II. He showed similar courage in Crete. With German paratroopers all around the battalion, he went forward three times with stretcher-bearers to collect the wounded, under a Red Cross flag, while pulling captured German light-wheeled stretchers. The Germans ceased firing while the casualties were collected. After Crete fell, Ryan sought to escape in a landing craft with a group of Allied soldiers but was captured when an Italian submarine stopped the vessel at sea. He was repatriated to Egypt in April 1942 and then returned to Australia. He served with various field ambulances and performed more lifesaving work as a surgeon in New Guinea. By war's end he was a lieutenant-colonel.

By 30 January, the Italians had abandoned Derna. During the advance along the main road towards the major Italian city of Benghazi, well-ensconced Italians firing machine guns from a high escarpment delayed the advancing Commonwealth troops on 31 January. A 2/8th Battalion company was ordered to clear the enemy that night. Climbing the steep escarpment in darkness, the lead group, under Lieutenant Colin Diffey (MC), surprised an Italian carrying a machine gun. When he made to call out to his comrades, Diffey grabbed him by the throat and struck him with his pistol, breaking the handle in the process. As the advance continued, Diffey touched a metal object with his foot and realised it was a landmine. With great courage he tested his theory that the mines strewn all around were anti-tank mines by stepping hard on two of them and surviving. There were more than 180 mines in the area. The group pressed on to the top of the escarpment, where they captured about 50 Italians. The next morning when Diffey led his platoon ahead in daylight, they soon encountered a dozen machine guns and two tanks, so he pulled them back. Artillery fire was called on this Italian rearguard, which soon abandoned its superb defensive position.

Diffey, a Victorian farmer, was a courageous leader in Greece and New Guinea, where as a major he was wounded in the shoulder by a sniper while reconnoitring an enemy position in May 1945.

On 6 February 1941, lead elements of the 6th Australian Division entered Benghazi. Meanwhile, British armoured forces crushed the remnants of the 10th Italian Army at Beda Fomm, forcing the Italians to evacuate Cyrenaica entirely. Had the British continued their advance and captured Tripoli, the Axis would have been unable to continue operations in North Africa. However, Churchill and his chiefs of staff considered the Libyan campaign a primarily defensive operation to safeguard the British base in Egypt. Their higher priority was preventing Greece from falling to the Axis, which would soon draw the Australians there.

Giarabub oasis

After the fall of Benghazi, the only remaining Italian stronghold in Cyrenaica was the Giarabub oasis, 230 kilometres south of Bardia on the edge of the Sahara Desert. Giarabub's garrison comprised 2000 men, with numerous field guns and automatic weapons, manning strongpoints protected by barbed wire. Since December 1940, most of the 6th Division Cavalry Regiment, mounted in trucks, had been besieging this garrison. Though greatly outnumbered, the Australians forced the enemy from his outposts into defences around the oasis itself. In mid-March 1941, Australian Brigadier George Wootten was ordered to capture Giarabub. There was transport enough to lift only one battalion (the 2/9th) and one company, and he would have neither tanks nor aircraft to help him. Rather than attack along the obvious route from the north, which would involve fighting through the Italians' main defences, Wootten proposed an approach across a rough track that ran through marshy ground east and south of the town. He ordered a reconnaissance in force to establish two lines south of Giarabub, the closest of them just 1000 metres away from the town. This reconnaissance, the battalion's first effort of the war, succeeded beyond all expectation, thanks mainly to the initiative of 30-year-old company commander Captain Bernard Berry (MC). Tall, thin and red-headed, his men had nicknamed him 'Berry the Bastard', though some knew how concerned this Adelaide civil engineer was for their welfare. He took his company right into the southern defences, where his men captured two posts before he withdrew to positions from which the main attack could be launched. The next day was marred by sandstorms, but there was enough visibility for Berry to take photographs. As he did so he reassured the men that the Italians 'cannot hit you', only for a bullet to go through his camera case. Apparently unperturbed, Berry continued to take photographs. The following night was the second in which they froze in shorts and shirts, but after they were joined by the main attack force, the assault went in on 21 March. Berry was wounded in the right arm and side early on, but his company played an important role in capturing the centre of the defences. By day's end, 94 Australians had been killed or wounded, while 250 Italians were killed and 1300 captured. Berry, whose reputation had skyrocketed among his men, would, after recovering from his wound and serving in the siege of Tobruk, rise to the rank of lieutenant-colonel, command three different militia battalions and serve in New Guinea and Bougainville.

The fall of Giarabub marked the end of the First Libyan Campaign. It left some unfinished business but was an astonishing success in ground gained and enemy forces destroyed. That success came at a surprisingly low cost in lives but required huge efforts from Australian units and troops.

CHAPTER 3

TOBRUK: HOLDING THE THIN RED LINE (APRIL–MAY 1941)

In March 1941, the 6th Division left Libya for Egypt and then Greece. General Wavell believed that the Germans would not risk sending forces to North Africa as this would depend on Italian naval support, and that even if they did so, such forces would not be ready to attack for months.

Thus he felt confident entrusting the defence of Cyrenaica to less than half of the 2nd British Armoured Division and to the untried 9th Australian Division, which was neither fully equipped nor fully trained. Contrary to his expectations, German forces began arriving in Libya, at Tripoli, in February. Before the end of March their aggressive commander, General Erwin Rommel, launched a full-scale invasion of Cyrenaica. The 2nd Armoured Division, nearest the frontier, was quickly overrun and thrown back. By 4 April, the Germans were in Benghazi. Not far to the east, on an escarpment, were the 9th Australian Division's 20th and 26th brigades, which were now ordered to withdraw to higher ground. The rearguard, tasked to hold a key pass on the escarpment at Er Regima, was the 2/13th Australian Battalion.

On 4 April 1941, the 2/13th fought the first Australian ground action of the war against Germany when German mobile forces attacked it. The fighting was confusing, but one man who stood out was 22-year-old Captain Ted Handley (MC). His company had to cover more than two kilometres of front, including the pass, which

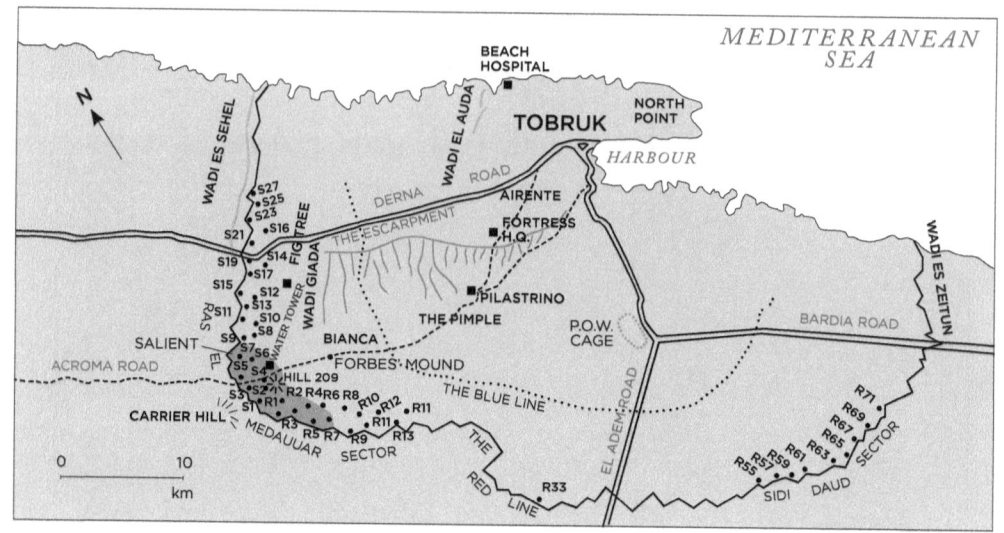

Siege of Tobruk, 1941

the Germans attacked with what the Australians estimated as 2000–3000 well-equipped infantry, 12 tanks and four armoured cars. With barely 100 men, Handley could not stop this force, but even with enemy tanks and infantry pouring past his headquarters, he remained in position, coolly directing his platoons. His citation called his effort 'an epic of personal courage', given the artillery, machine-gun and rifle fire directed at him and his men. Handley eventually withdrew his company in good order. The battalion sustained about 100 casualties at Er Regima, but it and supporting British artillery knocked out several enemy vehicles. Most of the defenders survived until dark, when transport arrived to whisk them away. Handley, a prewar truck salesman, rose to major with the 2/13th, but ill-health, especially tropical diseases, hampered his career and he retired from the Army in January 1945.

After the retreat from Er Regima, the 9th Division was ordered to withdraw by the coastal route towards Tobruk. They were harried all the way by enemy aircraft and fast-moving motorised columns that threatened to cut them off, and some unfortunate British and Australian troops were captured.

Wavell sent reinforcements to Tobruk, including the unusually well-trained and equipped 18th Australian Brigade, which now joined the 24th Brigade of the 9th Division. Wavell flew to Tobruk on 8 April with Australian Major-General John Lavarack, whom he appointed to command all British troops in Cyrenaica. The garrison must hold Tobruk for up to two months, he stated, after which British forces would advance from Egypt to relieve it. Lavarack arranged for the 9th Division's commander, Major-General Leslie Morshead, to bring the division inside the Tobruk perimeter. On 10 April, as the division took up position around the Red Line, or perimeter, advanced elements of the German forces approached along the coast road. They were thrown back by artillery fire, including rounds from Australian 'bush artillery', Italian guns manned by Australian infantrymen willing to improvise.

The siege begins

On 11 April, Axis forces completed their encirclement of Tobruk, and the siege began. Lavarack was called to Egypt, but before he left, the Germans used a tank regiment and a machine-gun battalion to assault the southern perimeter on 13/14 April. German infantry and tanks tried to infiltrate through gaps between the posts held by the Australian 2/17th Battalion. Some 30 Germans, supported by two light field guns, eight machine guns and several mortars, moved through the wire about 100 metres east of Post R33. A platoon of the 2/17th, under Lieutenant Austin Mackell (MC), held this post. Realising that the Germans intended to establish a bridgehead through which enemy tanks could advance, Mackell took six men to attack them. Supported by covering fire from R33, they outflanked and then launched a bayonet charge at the Germans. Mackell killed one with the bayonet and used his rifle butt to club another on the head. Two bullets hit Corporal Jack Edmondson (VC) before he reached the enemy, but he managed to bayonet at least five, two of whom were attacking Mackell. The Germans fled, leaving 12 dead and a prisoner. Edmondson's wounds proved fatal, but his extraordinary feat was recognised by the posthumous award of the Victoria Cross – the first awarded to the Second AIF. Other members of his platoon did outstanding work and were decorated. Lance-Corporal Alfred 'Shorty' Dunbar (MM), a six-foot-two-tall milk carter from Manly, had on the first day of the siege taken over a section of reinforcements who had only just reached the front and were nervous. When they first saw the enemy, only Dunbar opened fire, using the section Bren, but his example inspired them. When on 13 April the enemy began firing on R33 in preparation for their major assault, Dunbar ran 500 metres through enemy fire to the next post, R32, to inform company headquarters, and then returned. In the firefight on the morning of 14 April, his section – with him again on the Bren – knocked out six enemy machine guns.

Mackell later spoke of being surprised at the Germans being 'useless at close range' and how as they fled he had 'ended up laying into them with a big brick'. Before enlistment, this alert and cheerful officer was a commercial traveller selling ceramics. He remained in the postwar army, rising to lieutenant-colonel and receiving an OBE.

Mackell's successful clash with the group near Post R33 was only a preliminary to much hard fighting in this 'Easter Battle'. Hundreds of Germans soon poured through the gap in the wire and by 4 am enemy tanks had come through that bridgehead and assembled at R32. The company commander there, Captain John Balfe (MC), had orders to let the tanks through and concentrate on the following infantry. So they lay low and, once the leading tanks had headed off for Tobruk town, the Australians rose and opened fire on the groups of 15–20 Germans following or riding the Panzers. They pinned down the Germans, though some had manoeuvred behind the Australians. Rommel's men brought anti-tank and field guns forward, but Balfe had his men wait till they were close and then snipe the crews, all of whom were killed. Balfe also decided to deal with up to 150 Germans positioned in a house and stone sangars behind Post R32. In approaching the house, one platoon commander's hand was shattered, but Sergeant Bob McElroy (MM) eventually took that platoon to dead ground within 50 metres and then ordered a bayonet charge. The Australians threw grenades as they ran, and soon saw Germans running towards them from the house. Rather than attacking, they were begging for mercy. One of McElroy's sections went into the house and used the bayonet. The Australians took 18 prisoners, killed a similar number and saw the rest fleeing for the wire.

The German tanks that had broken through also came to grief when they entered the sights of British field guns. Eventually the Panzers fled, for the first time ever. They headed for the gap in the wire, where many of their infantry Kameraden were captured, or killed by Australian small arms or British artillery fire. The Easter Battle was a remarkable Allied victory, and as General Lavarack handed over the defence of Tobruk to General Morshead, he congratulated all the defenders on a wonderful day's work. Unfortunately, months of fighting lay ahead. Balfe later commanded another 9th Division battalion, the 2/32nd, and was wounded twice at Alamein. McElroy was promoted to lieutenant but was first wounded and then killed at El Alamein in 1942.

On 15 April, Rommel switched his focus from the southern to the western sector, where he directed mainly Italian forces to capture the dominant feature, called Hill 209 or Ras el Medauuar. Machine-gun and British artillery fire often broke up these attacks from a distance, but Australian patrols also went out to cause havoc: one 23-man patrol under Lieutenant Claude Jenkins captured 75 Italians on 15 April while a seven-man patrol under Corporal Vincent McBroom brought in 63 the following day. Both Jenkins and McBroom were killed later in the siege. On 16 April, more than 800 Italians, an entire battalion, found themselves trapped between fierce enemy fire from Australians in front, and heavy British shelling falling behind them. When a small group of Australian Bren carriers under Lieutenant Zac Isaksson approached, there was a brief fight, including some fire on the Italians from German tanks following them. One German officer and more than 800 Italians surrendered.

On 21 April, reconnoitring Bren carriers spotted nearly 50 Italian vehicles and many infantry gathering in a wadi behind Carrier Hill, a feature more than a kilometre from Australian lines. A raid was planned for the following day, to be led by Captain Bill Forbes (DSO). The red-headed Adelaide schoolteacher was a devout Christian, slight of stature but reputedly fearless. Three British tanks and five Australian carriers were to support him and his understrength company. The plan was to move behind Carrier Hill and attack it from the rear. The operation began badly on 22 April when the three leading British tanks advanced into the dawn mist and did not reappear until after the raid. Undaunted, Forbes personally led the attack in a carrier driven by Isaksson. When the Australians got close, enemy infantry opened fire with mortars and small arms, pinning them to the ground. Forbes, though, jumped out of his carrier and, waving a rifle and bayonet in the air, yelled, 'Come on, you bastards!' His men followed. One carrier, under Sergeant Len Batty (DCM), was already circling and firing on an Italian gun battery. The Italians turned heavy machine guns and artillery pieces on the little carriers and the infantry, but most of their fire was wild. Eventually, an anti-tank round stopped Batty's carrier, wounding the brave sergeant. His Bren gunner, Ron Daniels (MM), kept firing until he too was wounded, at which point the driver Jack Spavin (MM) took over until Australian infantry arrived. When those footsoldiers were 200 metres from the Italians, they launched a bayonet charge, some firing rifles or Brens from the hip. The Italians facing them bolted or surrendered, as did those nearby facing carriers and infantry. For the loss of three dead and six wounded, the Australians took nearly 370 prisoners, as well as anti-tank guns, machine guns and documents. This action was immortalised by the great Australian war artist Ivor Hele in his painting *Raid on Carrier Hill*. Spavin, who received not only a Military Medal but also a prestigious Commander-in-Chief's Card, was killed in 1942 at Tel el Eisa.

To support the 2/48th raid on 22 April, the 2/23rd Battalion also raided Italian positions, employing two forces totalling 130 men. One force captured 40 Italians and sustained only two wounded.

Tobruk: Holding the thin Red Line (April–May 1941)

From left to right, Private Jack Spavin, Private Ron Daniels and Sergeant Len Batty lean on their Bren carrier on 20 April 1941, two days before the 2/48th Battalion's successful raid at Tobruk that would see each of them win a medal, and Batty sustain a wound.
AWM P02688.001

The other force, under Lieutenant Alan Hutchinson (DSO), met uncharacteristically stiff resistance and eventually its lead group was reduced from over 20 men to just six. They were close, though, to their original objective, a group of field guns, and when Hutchinson asked his men if they wanted to go on, they said yes. They dashed between shell bursts, palls of smoke providing their only cover. But the Italians stuck to their guns. Jumping up from the lip of the wadi where the guns were, Corporal Bill Crummey ran forward with a grenade, only to be shot down. Hutchinson followed him, forcing the Italians to flee their pit, and then lay beside Crummey to check his wounds. Crummey was still holding his grenade, which only now exploded. Crummey was killed, Hutchinson severely wounded in the leg. Sergeant Jack Barnard (DCM) took charge. Ignoring a shoulder wound from an explosive bullet, he ordered two anti-aircraft guns destroyed with hand grenades and, after trying unsuccessfully to extricate Hutchinson, led the small group as they fought their way out, driving prisoners before them. Barnard had risen through the ranks and was later commissioned before dying at Alamein. Bill Crummey's brother John died there too, in July 1942.

On the night of 24/25 April, a 56-strong fighting patrol of the 2/43rd Battalion went beyond the eastern perimeter in search of enemy defences. They demonstrated their inexperience, with some groups becoming lost, and the raid ending with a retreat under fire and two men killed. However, Corporal Bill Curren (MM) emerged as a superb fighting soldier. When a machine-gun post halted his group, he closed to within ten metres and hurled in grenades that silenced the gun and killed the crew. Gathering more grenades, he then attacked an enemy trench, inflicting casualties on the German riflemen firing from it. Curren, a labourer from Winkie, South Australia, was the first 2/43rd man decorated for bravery. He would be killed by enemy shelling on 28 July 1942, receiving a posthumous Commendation Card for Gallantry in Action.

The 'May Show'

Rommel had not lost the initiative. On 30 April, he followed up a powerful and terrifying aerial bombardment by sending two German divisions, including the recently arrived 15th Panzer, to attack the western perimeter near Ras el Medauuar. As in the Easter Battle, he sent troops to infiltrate between the Australian positions at night, preparatory to the main assault the following morning. Engineers removed mines from in front of the perimeter, while Panzers used grappling irons to remove the wire, leaving the defenders with little more than small arms for defence. The 2/24th Battalion bore the brunt of the fierce attack that on the morning of 1 May enveloped an area extending six kilometres. It was just a matter of time before each post surrendered, but wherever possible, the Australians fought back. In post R5, tanks blew the weapon pits 'sky high'. Bren gunner Corporal Lou Gazzard stood outside his pit so he could fire down on Germans advancing along a ditch. The official history called this young schoolteacher 'a living symbol of utmost valour'. Eventually he was shot through the forehead, the only fatality in the post before its garrison surrendered that afternoon. Sergeant Gordon Poidevin, commanding the post, believed that Gazzard should have received a posthumous Victoria Cross. A platoon under Lieutenant John Rosel (MC) occupied posts S10, S11 and S11a on the far right flank. One of his men remembered 'huge tanks everywhere, and swarms of Dagoes and Jerrys, the noise was terrific, and bullets and shrapnel were flying'. Rosel took control of the company after the commander was captured. In a famous message to his 2/23rd neighbours, he set out the enemy dispositions, his own weapon and ammunition strengths, and requested that his message be passed on to higher command. In the midst of this message, he declared, 'Viva la batallion [sic]'.

Whenever German tanks came into range of the few anti-tank guns in the area, the Australian and British gunners fought on bravely, often with captured Italian guns, until their weapons were knocked out. From behind Forbes' Mound, Corporal Fred Edmonds of the 26th Anti-Tank Company commanded a gun that achieved several hits, stopping two tanks. Even after return fire tore pieces off the gun, Edmonds kept firing until he was hit and fell mortally wounded. Corporal Felix Aston's crew set two tanks alight, including a Panzer III, and was set upon by a dozen more tanks. Aston's captured Italian gun had no shield and soon two crewmen were hit. Aston and the remaining gunners knocked out a third tank before a Panzer shell destroyed their gun. Aston, an optical mechanic, was a member of the 24th Anti-Tank Company. His Military Medal was one of seven medals and commendations won by the 80-strong unit in May. More than half of the company became casualties at Tobruk.

The siege of Tobruk hung in the balance that day. A German attempt to push further was halted on a minefield at a second line of defences. The 2/48th launched a counterattack that was doomed in its attempt to recapture ground, but which forced Rommel to go onto the defensive. Morshead was able to re-form the perimeter line around the breach. Thus was created the 'Salient', the deadliest ground at Tobruk. The attacks of 30 April – 1 May killed or captured about one-half of the 2/24th Battalion, but these Australians achieved much.

The Axis attackers suffered significant losses in tanks and men, mainly due to British artillery. Most importantly, although Rommel captured Ras el Medauuar, he did not achieve a decisive breakthrough. The position around the Salient was unstable for days.

Morshead ordered his reserve brigade, the 18th, to drive the Germans out of the Salient on the night of 3/4 May. Carried out in almost pitch dark by troops with little knowledge of the ground and flimsy support, the task was ill-conceived and essentially impossible. Two platoons of the 2/10th Battalion, in the centre, were ordered to mop up advanced enemy positions several hundred metres away. Nearly 400 metres out, the right-hand platoon, stretched out on a 150-metre-wide front under Lieutenant Frank Cook (MC), came under heavy machine-gun fire from a flank. Cook led his platoon in a bayonet charge and, after throwing grenades as they approached, captured enemy trenches without suffering a single casualty to an estimated six enemy machine guns. Cook's height – 6 feet 2 inches – probably gave him a menacing air as he advanced. He then led a

Tobruk: Holding the thin Red Line (April–May 1941)

Gunner Ted Courtney won a Military Medal for standing by this captured Italian anti-aircraft gun during two dive-bombing attacks on Tobruk.
AWM 020589

section against other trenches, capturing two prisoners, an anti-tank gun and several machine guns. Cook's father had earned a Military Cross too with the British Army in World War I. As a captain, Cook would earn a Distinguished Service Order for leading a company in a daring attack at Sanananda in 1943. As a major, he would be Mentioned in Despatches for bravery at Balikpapan in 1945.

The platoon moving alongside Cook's at Tobruk became pinned, sustaining serious casualties. Cook sent Lance-Corporal Alexander Taylor (DCM) to locate this platoon. Three times Taylor crossed fire-swept ground in a vain attempt to find them in the dark. However, during one foray he came across an enemy machine-gun position and on his own initiative attacked, killing all six occupants with his Tommy gun. Though wounded, when his platoon retreated, he remained behind with Cook to cover the withdrawal.

In the 2/9th Battalion advance, Lieutenant Bill Noyes (MC) could not find an enemy-held post, R8, that according to the map was left of the road but was in fact right of it. His platoon pushed on through the darkness, fighting the enemies they encountered. With bayonets and grenades they charged one group of up to 80 Italians taking cover behind a pile of stones. Many defenders were killed; the rest ran. When three Italian light tanks drove up, Noyes, Sergeant Bob Hobson (DCM) and three other men sneaked up behind them, forcibly opened the turret lids and dropped in grenades. After one crew member escaped, Hobson sat on the hatches of the other two until the grenades exploded. All three tanks caught fire. Hobson, a fair-haired 31-year-old clerk from Cunnamulla, Queensland, received a serious arm wound that day but would rise to lieutenant by 1945. Noyes, a Sydney car salesman, would receive an MBE for his work on the 19th Brigade staff in 1945. Now, in the Salient, Noyes and his platoon pushed on, capturing more ground until, numbering just six men, they rejoined their company, discovering R8 on the way. Ironically, the enemy had not even occupied it. The Italian garrison facing the Australians in this area lost 100 of its 150 men.

Most of the defenders here were well-entrenched Germans and ultimately the Australian brigade withdrew. Nevertheless, the aggression of the Salient's Australian defenders convinced Rommel that he needed some of his best troops holding this bulge rather than attacking on the Egyptian frontier. The Australian defenders' main job was now to strengthen their defences, especially around the Salient.

One notorious strain on Tobruk's defenders was innumerable enemy air attacks. The Axis enjoyed complete air superiority, though anti-aircraft gunners fought back bravely against the daily bombardments. Gunner Ted Courtney (MM) of the 8th Light Anti-Aircraft Battery manned a captured 20mm Breda anti-aircraft gun. On 25 April, his detachment was under a dive-bombing attack from 40 aircraft when the gun sustained a serious stoppage. The rest of the detachment took cover but Courtney freed the stoppage and enabled his comrades to re-engage the enemy aircraft. On 7 May, during a dive-bombing attack on nearby heavy artillery, the Breda had another stoppage. Three enemy Me-110 aircraft fired on the gun pit, narrowly missing Courtney, but the 31-year-old cleared the gun and the fight resumed.

CHAPTER 4
MISSION IMPOSSIBLE: THE CAMPAIGN IN GREECE

When the Germans invaded Greece on 6 April 1941, only one Australian brigade, the 16th, was in the forward area. The rest of the 6th Division was in Greece or on its way, but the only other Commonwealth forces there were the New Zealand Division, a British armoured brigade and the headquarters of I Australian Corps. Designated 'Lustre Force', they and the brave but ill-equipped Greek Army could not possibly halt the 14 divisions the Germans used to invade Greece and southern Yugoslavia. After seizing Salonica, German forces threatened to outflank the remaining Allied troops in north-eastern Greece by attacking not just from the east but also from the rear through the Monastir Gap. It was decided that the Greek-British force would retreat to a new defensive line, the Olympus–Aliakmon line. In the meantime, a rearguard named 'Mackay Force' after its Australian leader and comprising Australian, New Zealand and British elements would delay the threatened German outflanking manoeuvre for long enough to allow the transport-strapped Greeks to join the British forces in the new positions. Already exhausted from camping on exposed snow-clad ground, Australians of the 2/4th and 2/8th battalions did just enough against pressure from German infantry and tanks, including those of the SS Adolf Hitler Brigade, to enable them and the Greeks to retreat to the new defence line. Among the Australians

Mission impossible: The campaign in Greece

Greece, 1941

who died in this fighting was the 2/8th Battalion's Lieutenant Tom Oldfield. He commanded the foremost platoon in frozen positions on the mountain overlooking Vevi when the SS troops attacked in tight-packed formations early on 12 April. All but six members of Oldfield's platoon were killed or wounded. Oldfield fought with his service revolver in one hand, a captured Italian Beretta pistol in the other, and reportedly accounted for several enemy soldiers before he was himself killed. Born in Albury in 1921, Oldfield put his age up three years at enlistment, when he was just 18. As one of his Albury mates was marched off as a prisoner, he saw 'the Boss' lying still, blood pouring from a bullet hole in his forehead.

Sergeant Wally Duncan (DCM) was ordered to take his platoon to the area where Oldfield's had been overrun. Showing great courage and calm, Duncan led his men forward through heavy fire to the vital ground, which they held for some hours. Duncan had been wounded at Tobruk, where he had already shown outstanding leadership and, unbeknown to him and his unit, he had been promoted to lieutenant in February. By war's end, this deputy shire clerk from Corowa would be a captain.

Commonwealth artillery kept firing until the enemy neared. The anti-tank gunners lost 16 guns to the enemy. Captain George Killey (MC) of the 2/3rd Field Regiment had, as a forward observer on 11 April, called down fire that blew off the road several German motorcyclists in the vanguard. On 12 April he was among the last men out, leaving only when nearly surrounded and calling down fire on his own position as he and his signaller departed on foot. As they fled they jumped over a bank and into a limestone pit, which acted like quicksand: fortunately, someone was there to pull them out, covered in white lime to their chests.

When the 2/3rd Field Regiment was ordered to withdraw, its officers and men had to heave and sweat to pull their guns out of muddy ground. They only got away because one gun 'held off the Hun', as one officer put it. That gun was commanded by Sergeant Doug Russell (DCM), a Darwin labourer, who remained in action until enemy infantry was just 550 metres away and firing machine guns at his crew. His gun and nine others were saved, with just two left behind in the morass.

A new Anzac Corps

On 14 April, the British overall command decided that the Olympus–Aliakmon line was too vulnerable and that another retreat was necessary. The Commonwealth forces would fall back 130 kilometres to a 'Thermopylae Line' between the famed pass and Delphi. This represented an abandonment of Greek-British cooperation, as the Greeks did not have the transport to keep up with the relatively well-equipped British force. Control of the withdrawal went to General Sir Thomas Blamey, commander of the AIF, who renamed his force the 'Anzac Corps' in memory of the 1915 one. Many of the troops did not learn of that new name until the campaign was over, but Australians spoke proudly of being part of the Anzac tradition. Their ability to fight and to cooperate was tested in a series of withdrawals on the Aliakmon line, in the Olympus passes and especially at the Pinios Gorge. Holding that gorge was necessary to allow Commonwealth forces to escape through a bottleneck at Larissa. On 18 April, the Germans launched a major assault across the Pinios River. The 2/2nd Battalion carrier platoon was sent to a flank to thwart the German advance there, but it soon lost its commander and five men killed or wounded by mortar fire. In reply, two Australians silenced one mortar crew with Bren guns, while Corporal Allan Lacey (MM) deliberately exposed himself to the enemy's fire, thus enabling the wounded to be pulled to safety. In 1942 Lacey was wounded in the Kokoda campaign and was promoted to lieutenant, but he struggled with mental health problems. He went AWL for five months in early 1943 and was discharged medically unfit in 1944.

At the Pinios River, two mortars under Sergeant Geoff 'Punchy' Coyle (MID) used extra primary charges to propel their 3-inch mortar bombs beyond their normal range, knocking out several enemy mortars in the morning, then landing 350 bombs in 90 minutes among the Germans crossing on rafts and seeking cover in rushes on the southern bank. Twenty-year-old Coyle, a former labourer from Newcastle, ended the war a captain. His corporal and fellow Novocastrian, Frank Evans (MM), demonstrated outstanding accuracy, ignoring enemy machine-gun and sniper fire while coolly changing targets and observing the results of his shooting. This mortar fire helped to break the German infantry attack in their sector but could not stop tanks. When Panzers approached, Coyle had just six bombs remaining. While he and his men continued the fight with rifles, he sent the mortars back in a truck, which was soon destroyed by tank fire.

German tanks and aircraft proved decisive. At one point, 15 men from the 2/2nd Battalion surrounded a tank that, impervious to their bullets, ran over two Australians. The survivors and other Australians retreated.

On 18 April, 6th Division artillerymen further north, at Elasson, performed expertly alongside New Zealand and British artillery in holding off German tanks and infantry. This allowed a night withdrawal so that by 19 April, all but the troops in the hills at Pinios Gorge had made it south of Larissa.

Wherever Commonwealth troops travelled during daylight hours, they were now subject to air attack. Unsung heroes at this time were the military policemen, or provosts, who directed and supervised convoys. Sergeant Frank Harris (BEM), of the 7th Division Provost Company, distinguished himself, especially on 17 April when he and two other men were responsible for getting a large convoy of troops on the move again after they had taken shelter from a severe air attack on the road between Lamia and the Brallos Pass. By 'sheer strength of character and personal courage', ran Harris's citation, he inspired his own men and 'his conduct was such that the men in the Convoy, who had taken cover during the attack, immediately returned to their vehicles and at his direction continued their journey' in an area where a blockage could have created serious trouble.

Henry Killalea won the Military Medal with the Light Horse at Beersheba in 1917. In 1941 he earned the Distinguished Conduct Medal for saving lives and equipment in Greece. On being medically discharged in 1943, he gave his age as 47. He was one of Australia's oldest men to win a decoration for bravery.
AWM 020937

The air attacks on convoys put a strain on all drivers, another largely unsung group. Many became so exhausted that whenever their very long convoys halted, they fought a losing battle to stay awake. Among these hard-working and courageous men, Private Felix Craig (MID) showed extraordinary valour at Pharsala on 18 April when a convoy came under attack from about 12 dive-bombers. The Australian Army Service Corps (AASC) history says 'Craig continued to respond with a machine gun, making himself a target until killed, providing a diversion which allowed most vehicles to get away'. The AASC's historian wrote angrily of the 'vacillation' that deprived Craig and the AASC of a first Victoria Cross. Craig, an accountant and auditor from Ararat, Victoria, was a gifted young man, a scholarship-winning student, dux of his school and a fine athlete. Felix's family raised a stained-glass window to his memory at Ararat.

A member of the Corps of Signals brought attention to himself on 20 April. Lance-Sergeant Henry Killalea (DCM) was about 45 years old when, at a rail siding at Levadia, he saw that three trains had been set alight by enemy aircraft. Ammunition was exploding and senior officers considered it too dangerous to attempt salvage among the trains, which were loaded with petrol, ammunition and anti-tank mines. Killalea, who had served at Gallipoli and won a Military Medal at Beersheba, took the initiative with a New Zealander, Driver McDonald. Though ignorant of how to drive a locomotive, they managed to get one working and save 28 trucks by shunting down the line to a safe position. They also loaded oil onto supply vehicles and salvaged ammunition and mines stacked a few metres from blazing trucks where heavy-calibre ammunition was exploding.

Gun duel at Brallos Pass

By 21 April, the Anzac Corps was sitting on the Thermopylae Line, named for a historic defensive position familiar to many of them. A key position for Australians on that line was the Brallos Pass. Here,

Lieutenant John Anderson (MC) of the 2/2nd Field Regiment was ordered to site two 25-pounder guns so they could prevent the Germans from crossing the Sperkhios River via a demolished bridge on the plain below. To be within range on the escarpment that his regiment was holding, Anderson had to place the guns on a ledge at the side of the road, some 4.5 metres apart. Late that day, German vehicles were seen coming down the road from Lamia towards the bridge. From nearly 10 kilometres away, Anderson's guns put the first vehicle out of action. Accurate fire from his guns through the night ensured that by morning the bridge was still unrepaired.

On 22 April, the Germans tried to locate Anderson's guns, especially by aerial reconnaissance. A British-manned Breda anti-aircraft gun located to protect his guns forced one of these aircraft to land on the plain, where Anderson's guns inflicted further damage on it. However, the Germans brought forward their own long-range guns, bigger than the 25-pounders, into position in distant woods. Anderson's guns again interfered with German vehicles coming down the road, but now the enemy guns fired back at them, getting closer all the time and eventually landing rounds just five metres from the gun pits. Anderson used unorthodox methods to gain an extra 500 metres. Instead of employing charge bags 1, 2 and 3, he used charges 1, 3 and 3 again, despite the danger of bursting the gun. Still, his rounds fell short of the enemy guns, and every time he fired one of his 25-pounder rounds (88mm calibre), German 150mm guns retaliated. Anderson later noticed that German infantry had reached the foot of the pass in some 20 trucks. One of his guns was damaged and out of action, but he and his men lifted the trail of the other gun onto the edge of its pit to allow it to fire down the face of the hill. The crew fired some 60 rounds into the dismounting infantry. The German medium guns then fired numerous rounds, including airburst, at Anderson's ledge, and the Australian gunners took cover. On returning, they found the second gun damaged. By now the duel with the enemy medium guns had lasted eight hours. More than 160 rounds had exploded near Anderson's guns, destroying trucks and some of his own shells, but miraculously none of the men on that ledge had been hit. Anderson sent half his men away to safety with parts of the first gun, while the remainder worked on repairing the second. But now their luck ended: devastating German rounds landed among them, killing six and wounding four. Anderson carried some casualties to help and returned later to disable the gun. Anderson began the war as a humble gunner but finished it a captain.

Evacuation

As early as 15 April, the senior British commanders in the Middle East had determined that Lustre Force would have to be evacuated altogether from Greece. So on 24 and 25 April, evacuation of the Commonwealth forces began from two main areas, around Athens and in the Peloponnese, protected by rearguards that again included Australian artillery and infantry. A German paratroop landing near the Corinth Canal on 26 April forced all evacuations to be shifted to the Athens area, but this went relatively smoothly.

The Australians' fighting withdrawal over nearly 500 kilometres ended in defeat but not catastrophe. The Australians lost some 320 killed, nearly 500 wounded and over 2000 captured. Much equipment had to be abandoned too, and this loss would soon be felt on Crete.

CHAPTER 5

ISLAND OF DOOMED HEROES: CRETE

About half of the 6th Division was evacuated to Crete rather than Egypt and around 2000 unarmed men of this contingent were later removed to Egypt. But on the eve of the German attack, there were 6500 Australians, 15 000 British troops and 7750 New Zealanders on the island, together with 10 200 poorly armed and largely untrained Greek troops. New Zealand General Bernard Freyberg commanded this multinational group, called 'Creforce'. Freyberg received intelligence that the Germans planned to invade the island with airborne troops. He deployed his troops to defend the three key airfields, at Maleme, Retimo and Heraklion, as well as the major port at Suda Bay. Australians would fight in all four sectors. Capturing one or more airfields was critical to the Germans' plans. All three were near the coast, linked by a single road, and north of a rugged chain of mountains. German aircraft, which dominated the skies, soon made the airstrips unusable for Allied aircraft.

The German invasion began spectacularly on 20 May. Some Germans landed in gliders, but most arrived by parachute, scattered among the Allied positions. This made for vicious no-quarter fighting, and at least two Australian battalions ordered their men to take no prisoners on the first day. The ruthlessness of some German paratroops towards prisoners became apparent at the 2/7th Field Ambulance's Advanced Dressing Station at Retimo. Private Edgar Randolph was treating about 40 badly wounded Australians when

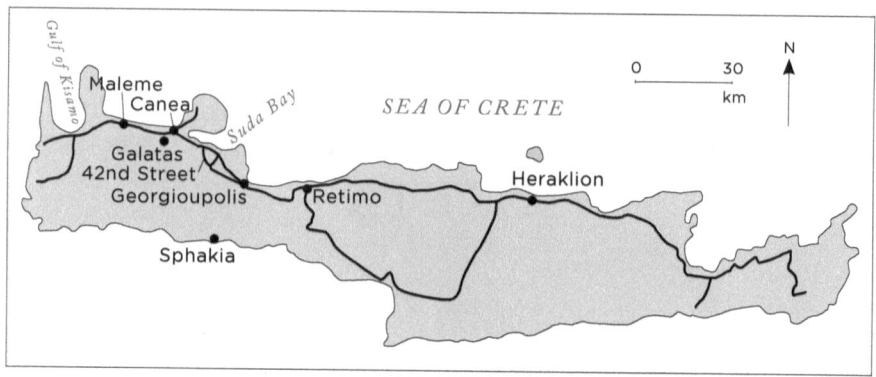

Crete

he heard automatic gunfire and saw a menacing line of 30 paratroops approaching. The German officer in charge ordered the wounded gathered together, then all other Australians but the doctors lined up, including stretcher-bearers wearing red and white brassards. The German told Major Bert Palandri (MID), the senior Australian officer, that while the doctors and wounded would remain unharmed, he could not take prisoners along and would shoot the lined-up Australians. Palandri protested, apparently undaunted even when the angry German thrust a pistol under his chin. The perilous situation was resolved when a group of Australian bearers arrived carrying a wounded German, who reported that he had received excellent, even preferential treatment. The German commander apologised and left Palandri all his men.

One Australian battalion with a 'no prisoners' order on the first day was the 2/4th, based in Heraklion alongside three British battalions and Greek troops. The Germans started badly there: for example, in the battalion area, 90 paratroops died for the loss of three Australians. The position was similar at Retimo, where most of the Commonwealth defenders were Australians of the 2/1st and 2/11th battalions. The 2/11th had a no-prisoner order but actually took 88 prisoners on 20 May. Many more Germans were killed as they descended or landed.

The critical ground at Retimo was the airfield, in the 2/1st Battalion's area. Both sides recognised the importance of Hill A, which overlooked the airfield. Captain George Killey, whom we saw in Greece, was an artillery officer in an observation post slit trench on the hill. This bank officer, one of the first Western Australians to enlist, shook hands with his signaller as transports flew over Retimo and said: 'We may have five or six minutes to live but we will get a few before we die'. In the ensuing few minutes, he killed three Germans with his revolver. Many paratroopers died or were captured on the lower ground below, but other Germans established a foothold on Hill A. The Australians of the two battalions fought back eagerly, for example, in a successful bayonet charge by the 2/1st's Transport Section, a unit normally kept away from the fighting. By the end of 20 May, the Germans controlled most of Hill A, were scattered among the vineyards and about 500 survivors had gathered at nearby Perivolia village. The Germans made little ground elsewhere that day, but fatefully they gained footholds near the Maleme airfield to the water. They consolidated their hold on the Maleme strip the following day, and Freyberg ordered a counterattack to recapture it on the night of 21–22 May. Delays prevented the counterattack from succeeding. A troop of four captured Italian 75mm guns under Captain Bill Laybourne Smith (MC) made a valuable Australian contribution, hitting at least five and perhaps as many as 17 German aircraft on the airstrip, as well as two enemy artillery pieces and a motorcycle. Siting the guns so that enemy aircraft could not spot them was difficult. Laybourne Smith's skill in siting his guns here and over the following 11 days during the retreat across Crete kept his troop's casualties low. It also brought heartfelt thanks from the New Zealanders they supported throughout. On the night of 22 May, intense German pressure forced Freyberg to withdraw about 4 kilometres east, thus abandoning Maleme airfield.

This effectively ensured German victory in Crete. Reinforced by mountain troops, the Germans continued advancing over the next few days, despite the Australian gunners' disruptive fire.

The 2/7th and 2/8th battalions were allotted a line covering

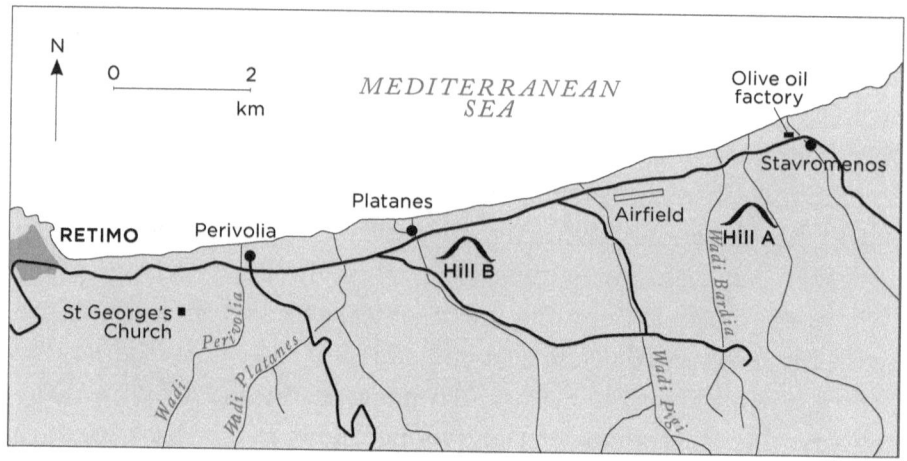

Retimo

Canea and Suda Bay. By 26 May they were on the right of a new line east of Canea, along a north-south dirt road nicknamed '42nd Street'. At about 11 am on 27 May, some 400 Germans approached the 2/7th positions and raided an abandoned depot. The two forward Australian companies were ordered to attack. There was a close-range exchange of fire, and as the firing intensified, Private Mick Baxter (MM) stood up, declaring he could not see 'a bloody thing'. On walking forward, this Melbourne labourer found himself under machine-gun fire, but instead of taking cover he trotted on, then ran, firing his Tommy gun from the hip. He put to flight a group of Germans defending a wadi. According to Reg Saunders, an Aboriginal soldier destined to become famous, 'It was then we charged – more to save Mick, I suppose, than anything else'. The two companies launched a bayonet charge, and the Māori battalion on their right did the same. In the words of an eyewitness account, the Germans 'dropped everything and ran'. Tired Australians were galvanised into action and soon drove the Germans back more than a kilometre, leaving behind several hundred dead.

A participant called this charge 'one of the epics of this war'. The Germans later investigated whether Australians killed surrendering men, an accusation the Australians rejected. They lost 10 killed and

28 wounded, including Sergeant 'Blue' Reiter (MM), who led his platoon despite a head wound. He remembered that in the charge 'All the frustration of months of bombing and strafing was taken out on the Germans'. Reiter, a labourer from Kardella, Victoria, was an outstanding soldier.

Evacuation and rearguards

On the day of the 42nd Street charge, Freyberg received orders to evacuate Crete. He ordered a withdrawal over the mountain road to the south-coast village of Sphakia. Nearly 15 000 men assembled near the end of the tarred road, which trailed into a steep goat track down to the beaches. A rearguard, comprising the 2/7th and 2/8th battalions, a British battalion and Laybourne Smith's two remaining guns, did exceptional work. They ambushed and slaughtered the German advance guards on 30 May. Late on 31 May, the last unit, the 2/7th, was still holding its ground under enemy shelling, despite appalling strain and on pitiful rations, when it was ordered to the beach. Sergeant Harry Thomas (DCM), of the 2/7th's Intelligence Section, performed prodigies over five days of strenuous fighting and marching. He helped innumerable fatigued men, some of whom he carried. On hearing that an exhausted group had fallen behind, Thomas ignored his own torn feet to return and bring in 11 men. In the final stages, he guided two companies through dangerously rough high ground to the beach in pitch darkness. Yet as he put it, the 'nightmare trip down the cliffs was all in vain'. The 2/7th's retreat to the beach was too late, and most of the battalion was captured. Thomas, who would rise to major and be Mentioned in Despatches for his later work, was one of just 16 who escaped.

In the meantime, the fighting at Heraklion and Retimo was over. In both places German paratroopers quickly isolated the defenders by blocking the road to the east and west, but in neither place could they capture the airfield. At Heraklion, a notable fight occurred at Apex Hill, a 300-metre-high feature with superb views of the distant airfield and surrounding area. It was outside the Heraklion defensive perimeter, so the Australian reinforced platoon sent to occupy it on 23 May had to use a lamp to communicate with 2/4th Battalion headquarters. Inevitably, the Germans recognised this ground's value, and early on 26 May several hundred of them approached Apex Hill from three sides. The defenders were under Lieutenant Ken 'Pluto' Kesteven, who had earned a Military Cross in Greece when he led his company after the commander and second-in-command became casualties. Now, on Apex Hill, he coolly calculated that his men would have to fight their way out. The groups approaching from south and west of Apex Hill were 200 and 500 strong respectively, so it would be best to go north where the enemy force looked to be about 50 strong, and where the Australians could use cover from a rocky outcrop and then a wheatfield. Kesteven's men moved unscathed through the rocky outcrop, but on emerging came under intense fire. Kesteven had just removed the pin from a grenade when he was hit. His arm paralysed, the young sales statistician said politely to the private beside him, 'Get rid of this will you – and mind out – it has no pin'. With Kesteven out of action, Sergeant Ted Swanson (DCM) took command. A prewar regular soldier, Swanson was one of several veterans attached to the group sent to Apex Hill and was Kesteven's platoon sergeant. He now threw a grenade and, waving his rifle in the air and yelling madly, charged. Twenty metres behind him followed the other Australians, firing rifles, Brens and Tommy guns. Another who distinguished himself was Private Selby Dean (DCM), a signaller who had performed wonders as Kesteven's signaller on Apex Hill, maintaining communications with Battalion HQ. Taking their wounded with them, the charging Australians reached the safety of the lines of the Black Watch, killing up to 30 Germans in the process. After the charge, Dean was shocked to find bullet holes in the front and rear of his helmet. The Germans occupied Apex Hill, but it conferred no decisive advantage. The following day, the British and Australian garrison received an order to evacuate Heraklion, and on 28 May, they left by sea.

Holding on at Retimo

The evacuation order did not reach Retimo, where the fight continued. By dawn on the second day, the only Australians remaining on the critical Hill A were a section under Corporal Herbert Johnston (DCM), a Sydney plumber's apprentice. In their post halfway up the vine-covered slopes they were surrounded, and under continuous mortar, grenade and small arms fire from Germans creeping close to their positions. They thwarted every attack, though, until relieved on 21 May. Johnston, who had been wounded at Tobruk in January, would later be captured and remain a prisoner until repatriated in 1944.

On 21 May, Lieutenant-Colonel Ian Campbell (DSO), commanding the 2/1st Battalion and the Retimo Sector, ordered Captain Boyd Moriarty of the 2/1st to recapture the entire hill. Moriarty organised a force, scrambling between positions to give them orders and narrowly avoiding bullets that ricocheted off rocks whenever he became momentarily visible. His force comprised men from all the battalion's companies, including drivers. Their dashing attack succeeded brilliantly, recapturing the hill and leaving only scattered Germans between it and the village of Perivolia to the west. To the east, the Germans blocked the road at the Olive Oil Factory, which Campbell sent Moriarty to capture on 22 May. As he raised his head to look between the forks of a tree while reconnoitring, the man the official historian called 'the gallant Moriarty' was shot dead. The 34-year-old department manager had in 1926 lost his father to a war injury received in 1917. The Australians eventually recaptured the Olive Oil Factory on 26 May.

Just as German occupation of the Olive Oil Factory blocked the road to the east, so their possession of Perivolia blocked western access. The 2/11th Battalion and their Greek allies tried repeatedly to capture the village, dominated by St George's Church and its surrounding stone wall. Dozens of Australians were killed or wounded trying to cross open ground and take the village. One leader here was Captain Ralph Honner, a Western Australian solicitor. He had earned the

Military Cross in Greece, and in his citation his commanding officer called him 'the best Company Commander I have known in this or the last War'.

Private Henry 'Slim' Johnson (MM) was a Bren gunner in a dangerously forward position at Perivolia where, on 23 May, the Germans launched a counterattack, supported by up to 40 low-flying aircraft. Johnson and his No. 2, Fred Symmons, were both wounded, but despite this and crops burning around them, they stayed at their gun. When his section commander was hit, Johnson took over the platoon and the German attack was beaten off. Symmons died of his wounds. Johnson, a Kalgoorlie carpenter, was captured.

There were two Matilda tanks at Retimo. Both became bogged on 20 May when their British crews were killed or captured. After recapturing Hill A, the Australians recovered the tanks on 24 May and got them both working. Crewed by Australian infantrymen and artillerymen, the two vehicles suffered repeated mishaps, especially jammed guns. The British crews were rescued at the Olive Oil Factory but were not up to resuming work. So when the tanks supported an ill-fated Australian attack on Perivolia on 27 May, their crews were all-Australian, commanded by Lieutenants Pat Lawry (MC) of the 2/1st Battalion and Jack Bedells (MID) of the 2/11th Battalion. Lawry had been prominent in the successful defence of Retimo airfield and now his self-confidence and nonchalance – based partly on driving a captured Italian tank at Bardia – were vital in prompting the tank attack. He and Bedells drove into the enemy lines, but their ill-starred vehicles soon struck trouble. An anti-tank round penetrated Lawry's tank, killing the gunner. While bailing out, the remaining crewmen were badly burned. Lieutenant Bedells' tank drove near the edge of the beach and in the dim light initially fired on friendly troops. A German satchel bomb stopped the vehicle. Then a mortar bomb struck the cupola and as Bedells sought to extricate himself, enemy fire cut off several fingers. Australian infantry repulsed Germans who tried to capture the tank. At dark, the crewmen – all wounded – escaped. Their freedom would not last long. Lawry had a broken leg and burns to his chest, hands and face so severe that he required months of treatment, much of it while covered in a plaster cast and most as a prisoner. His paratrooper captors treated him compassionately and the German doctors he encountered in Athens 'couldn't have been better, they were first class'.

A German parachute officer captured by the 2/11th Battalion early in the fight expressed admiration for the marksmanship of an Australian who from 600 metres had broken up an attack. Late in the fight around Perivolia, other Australian marksmen came to official notice. Largely to counter the Germans' mortar fire, Warrant-Officer Charles Mitchell (MM) was ordered to create a sniping squad. Mitchell and Private Andy Mulgrave (MM) were each issued a captured German sniper rifle, with telescopic sights. One sniping post they used, setting up before dawn and leaving after dark, was near two small buildings some 800 metres from the German right flank. Mitchell wrote later that the two snipers 'had some good sport getting about ten Jerries a day'. Enemy soldiers who went to recover supplies dropped by an aircraft into No Man's Land suffered heavily. Mulgrave's citation said that operating at an average of 950 yards, he scored 19 kills witnessed by the Australians and a further 11 confirmed by the Greeks, whose morale was said to have been powerfully boosted by 'the amazing accuracy and persistence of his marksmanship'. He looked and was said to have been much younger than his official age of 21.

By 29 May, German reinforcements, including artillery and tanks, were approaching Retimo from east and west. Campbell realised that defeat at Retimo was imminent. Considering the losses he anticipated if his men tried to escape and the potential cost in civilian lives, he chose to surrender. He telephoned this news to Lieutenant-Colonel Ray Sandover (MID), the 2/11th commander, who ordered his men to destroy their arms and escape through the hills. A brave 2/11th rearguard enabled some men crucial time to escape. Fifty-two officers and men of the 2/11th reached Egypt, while 16 of the 2/1st did so.

The battle for Crete was over. 'Blue' Reiter later wrote that he and everyone else who managed to escape was bitter 'and our tolerance

AUSTRALIAN HEROES OF WORLD WAR II

Private Andy Mulgrave cleans his Lee-Enfield rifle. On Crete he was issued a captured German rifle with telescopic sights and won a Military Medal for his 'courage, calmness and deadly ability as a killer'. He was captured but had a series of extraordinary adventures, ending the war fighting alongside the American Army in Germany. He was twice Mentioned in Despatches.
COURTESY OF THE MULGRAVE FAMILY

of the powers that be, unless they were very bloody good, was never the same'. General Freyberg, one of 'the powers that be' but also, as a Victoria Cross winner, a man who knew much about courage, summed up the efforts of the Australians on Crete when he sent a message to Campbell on 23 May: 'You have done magnificently'.

Escapes from Greece and Crete

Some Australians left behind after the evacuation of Greece and Crete sought to evade capture and find their own way back to their forces in Palestine or Egypt. Some of the 5000 Australians who were captured there also made escape attempts. A few of their stories follow.

After his capture in April, Lieutenant Max Derbyshire (MC) of the 2/2nd Battalion was transported to Corinth. Conditions were rough and the motor trimmer from Wagga fell ill. He was in hospital when in late June he was told he would be flown to Germany. Determined to escape, he mingled with a large group of other ranks in the cookhouse at mealtime, pretending to be supervising, and then hid in a nearby storeroom. Three officers joined him and they sought to escape that night. Following an abortive attempt when they were shot at, they climbed a wall at midnight and escaped. After procuring clothes from sympathetic civilians, Derbyshire entered Athens with another officer, who was eventually captured. Derbyshire moved about, but for roughly a year he stayed with one family in Athens until December 1942, when the local resistance helped him reach Turkey by boat. Derbyshire returned to the 2/2nd and, as a captain in 1945, received a Bar to his Military Cross. His skill and courage were exemplified when he personally led a bayonet charge against strong Japanese positions near Dagua, New Guinea. Several officers given higher roles later in the war were among those who made hazardous escapes from Greece, including future commanders of the 18th Brigade (Fred Chilton) and these battalions: the 2/1st

(Paul Cullen), 2/11th (Charles Green), 2/28th (Don Jackson), 2/31st (Jim Miller) and 2/1st Pioneer (Adrian Buckley).

Although by 1 June the Germans had clearly won in Crete, thousands of British Commonwealth troops remained at large there, and about 600 of them returned to Egypt in vessels as diverse as barges, submarines and fishing boats.

Private Harry Richards (DCM) of the 2/11th Battalion recovered a motor landing craft left behind at Sphakia. Richards had earlier assisted and carried a hospital patient, Sergeant Kilpatrick, from Retimo to Sphakia and refused an opportunity to be evacuated. After hiding this landing craft in a cave, the 32-year-old Perth farm hand decided that it had enough fuel to reach the African coast via the island of Gavdos. He collected a party of 60, including two British Marine officers who accepted his command. When the MV *Leaving*, as Richards dubbed the vessel, noisily left the cave on 1 June, two German machine guns fired at it, but Richards and his crew picked up sufficient speed to get out of sight. On reaching Gavdos, Richards realised that his fuel and food were insufficient for all on board to continue. After ten volunteers agreed to stay on the island, Richards and 51 others (including newcomers with supplies) resumed the voyage. On the 3rd, with all petrol gone, they were still 160 kilometres from Egypt. Richards constructed a sail from four blankets and eked out the rations over the next five days. On 8 June he wrote in his log of all men being weak, the sea flat and how he had to address the moaners 'in words I cannot write'. After a religious service into which all put their heart and soul, land was sighted. Fourteen hours later they landed near Sidi Barrani. A fellow escaper praised Richards' command as masterly and inspirational, his care for the others 'beyond description'. Richards' subsequent career was sad. Poor health, including 'anxiety state', led to him being classified as B and later D class and transferred to various base units. He was frequently in trouble with his superiors, to whom he often used bad language. He was court-martialled in early 1944 and found guilty of 'conduct to the prejudice of good order and military discipline'. He was discharged later that year.

Captain John Fitzhardinge (MBE) of the 2/3rd Field Regiment commanded another landing craft. He had skilfully directed captured Italian and German guns at Retimo, and in the retreat led a party across Crete to Timbaki Bay. Fitzhardinge energetically organised a working party to salvage a supposedly unusable landing craft and get it running. On 2 June he led 11 officers and about 70 men leaving for Mersa Matruh. The following day at about 3 am, an Italian submarine intercepted the boat, ordered them to stop and called for the officer in charge. Fitzhardinge swam to the submarine and explained that the barge was carrying unarmed men, including sick and wounded. The Italian commander agreed to let the men go if the officers swam to the submarine, as POWs. Fitzhardinge ordered the officers to surrender, though one drowned in the attempt. The barge drove on to safety, while Fitzhardinge and his fellow officers were taken to Italy and imprisoned.

One man aboard a third landing barge to escape was wearing pyjamas! When the Germans landed on 20 May, Corporal Ron Bradfield (DCM) of the 2/11th was in hospital near Canea with dysentery. The hospital was bombed and strafed, then overrun by paratroopers who used the occupants (Bradfield estimated they numbered 300-400) as a human shield while advancing on a nearby hill. New Zealand troops rescued the patients, who were eventually moved to a transit camp at 42nd Street. Still in his hospital pyjamas, Bradfield now took up a rifle and webbing and fought alongside the 2/3rd Field Regiment for four days. Though separated from them at Sphakia, he escaped on a landing barge commanded by a British lieutenant. When the barge ran out of fuel, the lieutenant and other men left for help on a smaller boat. An Australian, Private Ivan Hansen, took over and got the barge to North Africa. Most of those on board had to be hospitalised, having been without food for six days, but Bradfield cheerfully went straight back to his battalion. The former farmhand later served as a lieutenant in the 2/3rd Pioneer Battalion in New Guinea. By late 1944 he was diagnosed as medically unfit with 'anxiety state' and his appointment was terminated.

During the fighting at Retimo, Lieutenant George Greenway

Corporal Ron Bradfield. Rescued from a hospital during the Cretan campaign, he took up a rifle and fought on in his pyjamas till the retreat, after which he boarded a barge and escaped to Egypt. After six days without food, most of his fellow travellers had to be hospitalised on arrival, but Bradfield went straight back to his unit!
AWM 008530

(MC) of the 2/11th Battalion took a turn commanding one of the Matilda tanks, but he was forced to stop when a German shell struck the turret, stunning and temporarily deafening him on 26 May. When Crete fell on 1 June, Greenway and 14 others made their way south, looking to escape. They spent two months in the hills until a British submarine rescued them on 29 August. Greenway, a 37-year-old station overseer from Western Australia, then volunteered to return to Greece to help others escape. From December 1941 to March 1942, he and a small team of volunteers travelled the Greek islands establishing lines of communication with Turkey. Despite bad weather and some obstruction from the Turks, they organised seven food and supply dumps and gained much valuable information. They could only travel at night as Italian vessels and aircraft were constantly patrolling the islands. Greenway lived on a 7-ton Greek caique for over 70 consecutive days, without a break. At one point, commanding a Greek fishing trawler, he carried 77 Greek refugees from Turkey to safety in Cyprus. By 1945, Greenway was a captain in the 2/11th.

The young sniper, Andy Mulgrave, was captured at Retimo on 30 May but escaped after assisting to kill three guards. He was recaptured late in June. He twice attempted to escape on the Greek mainland and in 1942 twice escaped from German camps for one and two weeks. In April 1945 he escaped again, this time from Stalag XIIIC at Hammelburg, Germany. He joined US forces in the last stages of the fighting in Bavaria. His adventures there included capturing three Germans single-handed, receiving life-threatening injuries when he attempted to capture another three and was surrounded by more than 20 SS men, and accepting the surrender of 15 Germans when he was being treated for his wounds in a private house in Kleinwenkheim.

CHAPTER 6

TOBRUK: BESIEGING THE BESIEGERS (MAY–OCTOBER 1941)

On 15 May 1941, the British launched 'Operation Brevity', an attack across the Egyptian frontier designed to relieve Tobruk. To dissuade Rommel from withdrawing forces from Tobruk, the Australians undertook aggressive patrols and advances, especially in the Salient. In what a British war diary called 'the boldest patrol since the occupation of the fortress', on the dark night of 15/16 May, the 2/15th Battalion sent 68 men into a raid on enemy transport near Carrier Hill and Ras el Medauuar. On arriving they found the transport had moved, but they inflicted casualties before returning home. Corporal Gordon Smithers (DCM) and his section were ordered to destroy a medium tank. Positioning his Bren gunners under a nearby truck, Smithers led the attack, personally throwing four ST 'sticky' grenades at the tank. The crew quickly abandoned the vehicle, which caught fire, but soon enemy infantry were all around. Using grenades, Smithers silenced two machine-gun posts. While attacking the second post, a burst struck his arm. He and his section covered the 15 kilometres home with one man missing and three wounded. Smithers' left arm was later amputated.

The Australians' 15–16 May attacks proved unnecessary as Operation Brevity failed. The Germans counterattacked in Tobruk and reportedly captured Salient posts S8 and S9. The 2/23rd Battalion was ordered to recapture these and several other German positions. It

Lieutenant John Rosel of the 2/24th Battalion is pictured sitting in a Tobruk dugout at centre. On the right, the flamboyant Captain Ian Malloch, MC; on the left, Lieutenant GG Anderson, who was killed on Trig 33 in July 1942.
COURTESY OF MIKE ROSEL

later emerged that the 'lost' posts were still in Australian hands, but the counterattack went ahead on 17 May. The Australians and assigned British tanks made no preliminary practice or even discussion, so when the tanks accidentally opened fire on the Australians, the latter had no established means of communication. In a smoke-shrouded fight against German tanks, artillery and entrenched machine guns, the Australians suffered 163 casualties in four hours. Captain Ian Malloch (MC), a 35-year-old company director from Toorak, won universal praise that day. When 40 Germans had infiltrated his company's positions on 30 April/1 May, the confident and capable Malloch had fired flares, gathered his company and killed or captured all the infiltrators. The following night, he and his company had advanced through machine-gun and anti-tank fire, and in hand-to-hand fighting recaptured one post, freed its captured garrison, then relieved the surviving defenders of another post. Malloch, a prewar militia officer, had been conspicuous, waving his arms around in the advance, especially with a 'wind-up' signal calling his men to push on. He once struck a captured German officer for his arrogance, then apologised. Another time he risked his life to save a German in No Man's Land whose hands had been blown off. After enemy fire drove him back three times, he ordered machine gunners to end the man's misery.

When the daunting 17 May attack commenced, Malloch seemed to one eyewitness 'as though he were on a hiking tour'. Though wounded, Malloch continued to push his men forward against the enemy's positions, which sat on an escarpment some 20 metres high. Eventually he set up a headquarters from where he directed his unit. Thunderclaps of airburst, fired by German 88mm guns, exploded 15 metres overhead and scattered shrapnel below. By the time he ordered a withdrawal, Malloch had sustained five wounds: to the arm, head, knee, thigh and hand. He was brought to the regimental medical officer (RMO), who had a syringe primed to ease Malloch's pain, only for the latter to threaten to 'drop' him if he used the injection on him before he had reported to the commanding officer. Malloch survived his wounds, but they were serious enough to force his return to Australia. He re-enlisted in 1942 and rose to lieutenant-colonel postwar, but his frontline days were over.

Other casualties owed much to stretcher-bearers, such as Private James Kelly (MM), who repeatedly went out under fire from a pipeline near S8 to rescue casualties. The Scots-born 36-year-old brought in seven and attended them under fire for an hour.

Dangerous and damaging patrols

The endless stressful routine of patrolling continued. A consistently brave and energetic practitioner was Lieutenant Ron Beer (MC) of the 2/48th Battalion. At the end of May, he took a patrol eight kilometres out – part of it in a captured car – and, with five men, laid mines on a dusty track that many enemy trucks used. The mines knocked out two lorries the following day. In July, Beer took a small patrol 2200 metres out, then led them in attacking a much larger Italian force. His men inflicted many casualties and, despite heavy fire, brought back a prisoner. The 2/48th Battalion history notes that he was an Italian 'who, like many of his countrymen, was not averse to talking'.

Corporal Jack Weston (DCM), another fine patroller, gained near-legendary status within the 2/48th Battalion. By 31 May he had led or accompanied 23 patrols. He was highly skilled at night patrolling, whether for reconnaissance or fighting patrols. His nickname was 'Tex', supposedly because he put a notch on his Tommy gun for each new kill. The official historian singled out Weston as a man who could even patrol in the Salient, with its enemy posts close together, protected by booby traps and alert German machine gunners.

Acting Sergeant Neil Russell (DCM) of the 2/12th Battalion led a 19-man fighting patrol on 11/12 July that won praise from General Morshead. Russell's task was to attack earthworks three kilometres from the perimeter. He led his men past booby traps and anti-tank mines that protected the position, then tripped a booby trap that wounded him. He continued, though, leading the patrollers in close-quarter fighting – with bayonet, grenade and SMG – around nine Italian sangars. Though wounded again by grenade splinters, he and his men secured three prisoners. The raid occurred in moonlight and enemy machine-gun fire came from the flanks. Acting Corporal Francis Lynch (MM) single-handedly attacked one machine gun, silencing its crew with his Tommy gun. As the patrol headed home, Russell realised one man was missing. He turned around, taking a stretcher-bearer (probably Private Oliver James). They located the wounded man and though he was moribund, tried to move him to safety. Russell only gave up the attempt when the stretcher-bearer was also mortally wounded. Russell's own wounds affected his left leg, right eye and right big toe. This Brisbane clerk ended the war a captain.

Morshead also praised 'a particularly good effort' by a 2/43rd night patrol in late July, when there was an urgent need to obtain a prisoner from the Salient. While guiding the patrol, Sergeant Jim Cawthorne (MM) detected a German working party coming down a road some 1400 metres from the Australian lines. When the Germans were just 10 metres off, Cawthorne stood up and called on them to surrender. Instead, they opened fire, wounding him in two places. The Australians now fired, and the few German survivors fled. Cawthorne ran after them, killing one and capturing another. His prisoner gave valuable information on Tobruk's Salient. Cawthorne continued his patrol duties while his group eluded another large enemy party. He added a Bar to his Military Medal at Alamein, where he proved an inspirational leader. For example, he and an officer once went out and rescued a casualty lost on patrol. Cawthorne himself was later commissioned. This model soldier was lucky to have been accepted into the Army. Standing just 5 feet 4 inches tall, he was initially rejected on medical grounds, but had tried again, changing his name from Leslie to that of a deceased brother, Cecil, though his comrades called him 'Jim'. An Adelaide physiotherapist in civilian life, Cawthorne gave his occupation as 'railway employee'.

Fighting to reduce the Salient

When the 2/13th Battalion entered the right side of the Salient in June, it advanced its positions. The new ground was covered in booby traps and 'S' mines, which leapt out of the ground and could cut a man in half. Corporal Geoff Hunt (DCM) and another member of the unit's Pioneer Platoon patrolled forward and located many of these deadly devices before returning with a larger party to clear them. Enemy mortar bombs soon fell among them, killing two and wounding three. Hunt coolly extricated the wounded and returned with another party. They continued working the following night, despite more casualties. On the left of the Salient he did the same, while also placing barbed wire in front. It was impossible to complete that task silently, and again Hunt remained steadfast under fire. This short-statured lionheart, who also guided patrols through booby traps and minefields in No Man's Land, was killed in the siege's last days.

On 3 August, Morshead sent single companies of the 2/28th and 2/43rd battalions into attacks on the shoulders of the Salient. The forces were inadequate for their assaults on thoroughly prepared enemy positions. The 2/28th attack was directed at Posts S6 and S7. By the time Lieutenant John Head's platoon reached S6, only one member remained unscathed; he himself was injured in the neck and both legs. He wisely ordered a retreat. Lieutenant Harold Coppock's platoon passed through some German outposts unnoticed while approaching S7 from the flank, but then came under sustained fire. Lance-Corporal Kitchener 'Kitch' Anderson (MID), a 25-year-old Fremantle shop assistant, was wounded in the advance, but he continued firing his Bren from a position he set up to take on Germans shooting at Coppock's group as they assaulted S7. Though wounded a second time, he kept fighting for 20 minutes until Coppock dragged him into S7, where he died. Coppock and as few as two others took S7, killing four and capturing six Germans. Coppock sustained a gunshot wound to the neck and a growing black eye. He reached for his Very flare pistol to send the success signal and call for reinforcements, only to find it had disappeared: a bullet had cut the belt to which the pistol was attached. Reinforcements eventually arrived, only to be forced to surrender the following night. In this fight, the 2/28th Battalion suffered 88 casualties, and the 2/43rd Battalion 106, including all officers and 70 per cent of other ranks. Captain Lew McCarter (MC) commanded the 2/43rd assault forces, whom he inspired with great confidence. Though twice wounded, he urged his men on, but when the situation's hopelessness became apparent, ordered a withdrawal. He remained at the wire in front of the battalion, ensuring that all who could came through, and was among the last to leave. His men considered him outstanding, as did his superiors: within a year he was commanding the 2/28th Battalion.

One of McCarter's platoon commanders on 3 August was Warrant-Officer Bob Quinn (MM), well known in the battalion as an outstanding prewar Australian Rules footballer. His task was to take R7, a heavily defended concrete post surrounded by mines and covered by enemy artillery and mortars. Though wounded at the outset, Quinn led the platoon into close-quarter fighting. Mortar fire wiped out an entire section silhouetted by flares. The platoon lost more men crossing a minefield to the edge of the anti-tank ditch, which was booby-trapped and unbridged. They took cover in it, but only three men survived the ensuing grenade fight. On emerging from the ditch with grenade fragments in both legs, Quinn was wounded again, in the face. He was wiping off the blood with his hand when one of his men observed, 'Hell, Bob, half your face is blown away.' Quinn replied, 'Any — change would be an improvement, Harold.' Quinn would be wounded again in New Guinea, as a lieutenant, but would return to league football after the war.

Sergeant Wally Tuit (MID) of the 2/43rd Battalion commanded the stretcher-bearers in the attack, which started at 3.30 am. He helped to evacuate casualties through heavy mortar and shell fire. At 7 am, after the attack had failed, Tuit, the battalion chaplain, Padre Gard, and several others stood holding a large Red Cross flag on the bonnet of an ambulance as it drove slowly towards the scene of the battle. One observer called it 'as brave and daring a thing as I ever saw done'. The Germans ordered the truck to halt 300 metres short of R7. The Australians debussed, walked forward and met a German officer under a Red Cross flag. Tuit and his bearers were permitted to pick up all their wounded. Chivalrous German engineers devitalised part of a minefield. After the wounded were removed, all the dead were brought in, Tuit supervising continuously until 5 pm, some 14 hours after moving up for the attack. Hoping that the Germans would show compassion on their side of the Salient, the 2/28th Battalion's Sergeant Ken Lyall took out a truck showing a Red Cross flag to collect the many wounded, but when he and others tried to leave the truck, German fire forced them back.

An engineer, Sergeant Keith Young (DCM), was active on 3 August, just as he had been continuously in the Salient since its creation. A section sergeant in the 2/13th Field Company, much of his work involved supervising the disarming of mines and booby traps in No Man's Land so that patrols could proceed safely. As this area was constantly under mortar and machine-gun fire, most of the disarming work was done on moonless nights. As Young's recommendation stated, it would be hard to exaggerate the risk involved in this work, and the endorsements of five battalion commanders were included. This Queensland builder's labourer performed brilliantly in the attack on R7 on 3 August and especially the withdrawal of the 2/43rd Battalion, during which he was wounded in the chest.

Last days in Tobruk

Just holding the Salient continued to be nerve-racking. From July, General Blamey, with Australian government support, urged that the Australian garrison of Tobruk be relieved. He was worried about the physical impact of months of poor food and strain. The 18th Brigade was withdrawn in August, but Churchill and the British commanders did not want any more Australians removed. Germany had invaded the Soviet Union in June and was sweeping all before it. Yet while Tobruk held, the Axis could not advance into Egypt and threaten Suez and the oilfields of the Middle East. Changing the

Tobruk garrison might endanger that rare bright spot. The Australian government insisted and in September–October, the 70th British Division replaced the 9th Australian Division, which was gradually withdrawn by sea. On the last night, the relief convoy proceeding to Tobruk had a destroyer sunk and had to turn back. Consequently, the 2/13th Battalion was left behind. It was still there in November when the British launched an offensive to relieve Tobruk. A series of tank and infantry battles followed around the high ground at Sidi Rezegh, Belhamed and Ed Duda. The 2/13th Battalion was part of a force that sortied from Tobruk and joined this fighting from 29 November to 1 December. Indeed, it made a crucial contribution, recapturing Ed Duda in a night attack, and then holding it while the Germans took Sidi Rezegh and Belhamed. Sergeant John Searle (DCM), a bank officer from Cudal, NSW, was leading five men in the night charge when they noticed a group of Germans. When called on to capitulate, the Germans went to ground and opened fire. Searle and his party charged straight into that fire, causing the enemy to panic and surrender. The Australians prodded two men in an adjacent pit with their bayonets, only to hear the response 'O.K. Bill – it's me – Perkins!' This was Les Perkins (MM), a 35-year-old 2/13th Battalion stretcher-bearer who on 3 August had on his own initiative risked his life to go repeatedly to the aid of the wounded of the nearby 2/43rd Battalion. This 'small grazier and labourer' had been twice wounded in April and would be again at El Alamein. He had been captured by the men now made prisoners by Searle, who ended the war a captain.

On the other flank of the 2/13th attack, Bren gunner Private Bert Ferres (MM) noticed an enemy position that could enfilade the whole advance. With three mates he strode towards the post, firing from the hip and calling on the Germans to surrender. They fired back, but Ferres and his comrades were soon among them, clearing out the position and taking 25 prisoners. After delivering the prisoners to the reserve company, he returned to the fight. The Australians took 167 prisoners that night while suffering seven casualties. The 2/13th Battalion men knew well that they had been 'first in' against the Germans at Er Regima on 4 April, and that they were last out of Tobruk in December 1941.

Few words are as evocative of the Australian military tradition as 'Tobruk'. It suggests stubborn defence against great odds. That is accurate, but the 'Rats of Tobruk' also followed Morshead's instruction to 'besiege the besiegers' and take the fight to the enemy whenever they could. This required initiative and self-sacrifice.

INTERLUDE 1
THE LANGUAGE OF HEROISM

Ken Clift, who won a Distinguished Conduct Medal at the capture of Tobruk, asserted in his battalion history that 'Australians have no desire to be depicted in heroic mould'. He justified this on the basis that 'they are probably the most unsentimental and irreverent soldiers the world has ever seen'.[1] Clift was prone to exaggeration but was right in that Australians frowned upon playing up brave deeds, especially their own. The term 'hero' was in much less use among Australians of the World War II generation than one might imagine. A search for the word 'hero', and the related 'heroism' or 'heroic', in the seven-volume official history of the Australian Army in World War II reveals the following number of uses concerning Australian soldiers: 0 in volume 1 (*To Benghazi*), 0 in volume 2 (*Greece, Crete and Syria*), 3 in volume 3 (*Tobruk and El Alamein*), 2 in volume 4 (*The Japanese Thrust*), 3 in volume 5 (*South-West Pacific Area*), 1 in volume 6 (*The New Guinea Offensives*), and 0 in volume 7 (*The Final Campaigns*). Fewer than ten! All but two of these books are over 600 pages in length, each recounting dozens or hundreds of acts of bravery. The words 'courage' and 'brave' are more common, but in Long's *Final Campaigns*, for example, which covers a huge amount of fighting, 'courage' or its derivatives are used just seven times about Australians (twice for Tom Derrick) and 'brave' just once! The totals for 'courage' and 'brave' for Australian individuals or groups in the other official Army volumes, including quotations from other sources are: 2 and 0 (volume 1), 7 and 3 (volume 2), 7 and 5 (volume 3), 8 and 2 (volume 4), 25 and 60 plus in *South-West Pacific Area* (volume 5), 20 and 7 (volume 6).

The numerous battalion histories show similar attitudes to these words, which today seem entirely appropriate. A search for 'hero' in ten battalion histories reveals that only one – Russell's *Second Fourteenth Battalion* – used the word ten times or more. 'Brave' was more common, but only reached double figures in five of the books, while 'courage' appeared over ten times in all books, and nearly 50 in Russell. Even 'courage' was not bandied about, though. A few days before the end of the war, General Morshead spoke to the 26th Brigade Group at Tarakan about factors crucial to the winning of battles. Above all, he said, was 'courage', but he added that courage was something 'which we call "guts"'.[2]

Tom 'Diver' Derrick VC, DCM, one of Australia's bravest soldiers, used 'courage' only three times in his lengthy diaries: once for a dead German, once for fellow soldier 'Snowy' Ranford at his death, and a third time for the courage required of his platoon during his Victoria Cross–winning actions at Sattelberg. Derrick does not seem to have used the term 'hero' once in his diaries. He used 'brave' only in quoting a poem, and indeed that is how other Australian authors tended to use the term 'hero'. They also used it in reference to men rescuing the wounded – something seen as especially honourable – the dead and, humorously, with tongue-in-cheek, when describing men coming home from campaigns or leave who 'felt like heroes' or 'acted like heroes'.

Humour was often connected with courage. The official history described Captain Jack McNamara MC, a legendary figure within the 2/24th Battalion, as a man of 'courage and riotous good humour'.[3] Clift argued that among Australian soldiers 'a very peculiar sense of humour' replaced 'heroics'.[4] Men such as Derrick, McNamara and Clift all had a strong sense of humour, which helped mask their deeper feelings and pride in their achievements. Men who had achieved great deeds were generally reluctant or reticent heroes, not least because immodesty was heartily disliked among Australian troops. Like ancient Spartan warriors, the ideal was to be brave and laconic. So while bravery was the stock in trade of frontline Australian soldiers, the attendant adjectives were not part of their everyday language. They did praise their units, and to a lesser degree their mates – especially the dead ones – but generally their ethos required them to make their actions speak louder than their words. In the Australian Army, 'courage' and 'bravery' (let alone 'gallantry') were words generally confined to the official language of citations for honours and awards. Looking back now it seems necessary and desirable to use those terms when describing the actions of Australians, bearing in mind the need to avoid the hyperbole that cheapens and flattens the extraordinary.

CHAPTER 7

THE UNSUNG HEROES OF THE SYRIAN CAMPAIGN

The Syrian campaign, as the 1941 campaign in Syria and Lebanon was called then and since, is little known. After France fell in 1940, the pro-German Vichy regime took control of Syria and Lebanon. Their position close to British-occupied Palestine and the Suez Canal troubled the British government, which became alarmed in May 1941 when German aircraft used Syrian airfields to support a revolt against British forces in Iraq. Under pressure from Free French leaders who believed that they could swiftly topple the Vichy regime in Syria, Churchill insisted that Wavell send troops there.

The hard-pressed Wavell's main available force was the unblooded 7th Australian Division, though one of its three brigades was in Tobruk. He also had one Indian and two understrength Free French brigades. Opposing them would be the equivalent of two-and-a-half divisions: 35 000 regulars, 8000 of them Frenchmen and the remainder African. The predominantly Australian invasion force had few tanks, whereas the French had 90. Wavell and Blamey warned their respective governments that the invasion was a 'gamble'. Hopes that the Vichy French would be caught by surprise or welcome the attackers proved unfounded.

The British commander, General 'Jumbo' Wilson, planned a three-pronged advance along the main routes from Palestine into Syria. One brigade would follow each route until it captured an important town. The reinforced 21st Australian Brigade would travel

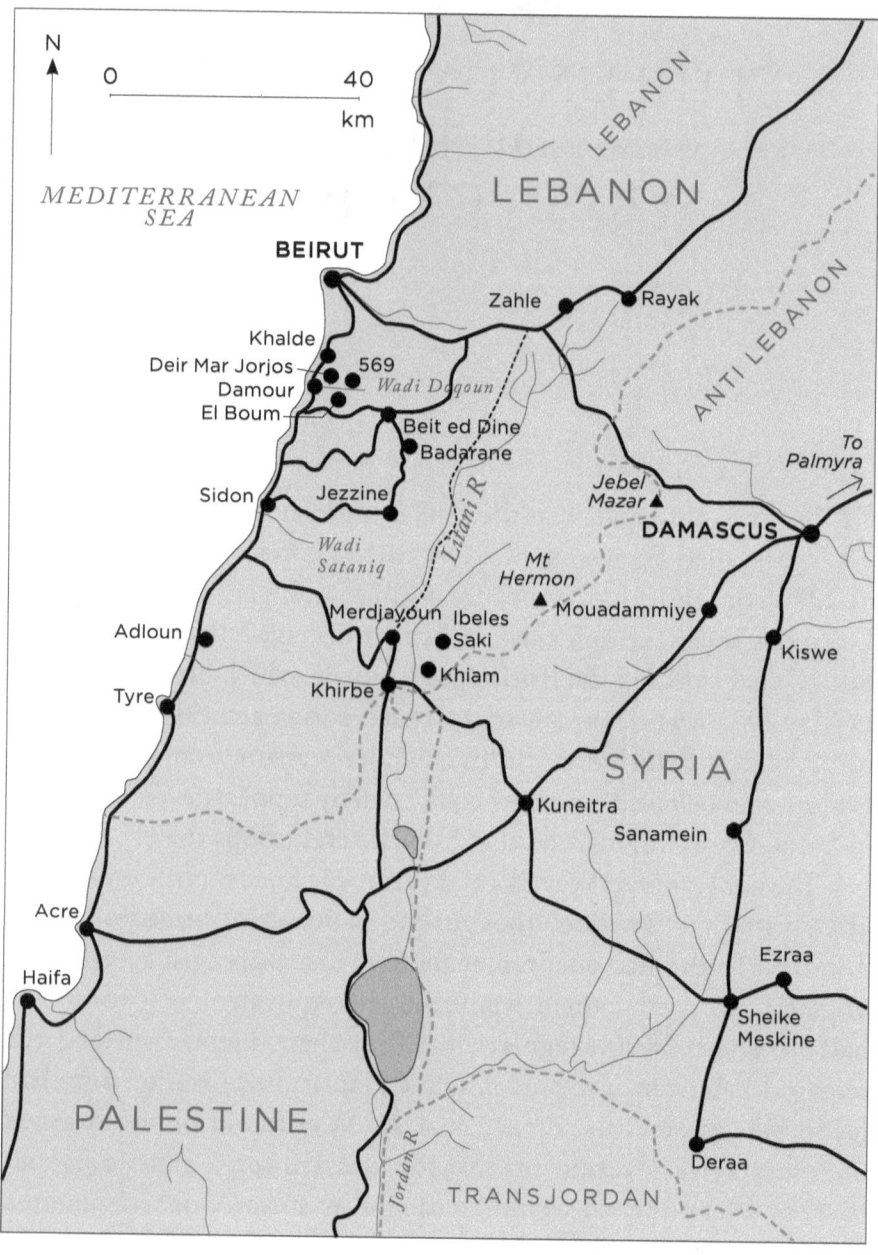

Syria

the narrow coastal plain to Beirut, seat of administration in Syria. In the centre, the reinforced 25th Australian Brigade would push along winding mountain roads between the Lebanon and Anti-Lebanon ranges to Rayak airfield. On the right, desert flank, Indian and Free French forces would advance to Damascus. The invasion commenced at 2 am on 8 June.

Coastal advance to Sidon

The Vichy troops defending the Syrian border posts resisted, but Australians overcame them in brisk fights. By nightfall on 8 June, the two Australian columns on the coastal advance had contacted the enemy's main defensive line, on the Litani River. Vichy forces demolished the crucial Litani bridge on 9 June, just as the 2/16th Battalion was approaching. The battalion had boats, but the river was too fast to paddle them across. Captain Ben Hearman ordered ropes from the boats and telephone wires from the road to be knotted into long cables. Corporal Alan Haddy (MID) tied a cable around his body and dived into the Litani. When he surfaced, a mortar bomb fragment struck him in the chest, but he reached the far bank and tied the cable to a tree. Eight Kalgoorlie cobbers then manned a boat and, using the rope, passed through mortar and machine-gun fire to reach the opposite bank unscathed. The company commander was killed and Hearman wounded on the south bank. The few men who got across fought aggressively, but their position became precarious when two French destroyers came close inshore and fired on the Australians.

Six 25-pounder guns of the 2/4th Field Regiment fired high-explosive and armoured piercing shells at the ships, which then departed. The gunners now turned on the Vichy forces across the Litani, thus helping the Australians expand the bridgehead. That night the last defenders retreated. By morning Australian engineers and infantry had constructed a pontoon bridge over the Litani. During the fighting, Sergeant Barry Bracegirdle (DCM) commanded a platoon pinned down by a machine-gun nest. Braving fire from it and snipers, Bracegirdle advanced 800 metres on his own and silenced the crew with grenades.

The 2/27th Battalion attacked the next defence line, at Adloun, on 10 June. Its men were exhausted after three days with little food, drink or sleep and much fighting and marching. The supporting artillerymen were tired too, and the 2/4th Field Regiment commanding officer, Major Walter Rau (DSO), was in pyjamas when called out after 3 am. Throwing on a greatcoat, he led forward a 25-pounder and, in an unusual move for a regimental commander, personally directed close-range fire that dispersed enemy tanks, knocked out some transport vehicles and killed the stubborn defenders of a building.

With the gunners' support, the 2/27th attacked Adloun's well-prepared Vichy defenders, including two companies of the French Foreign Legion. French close-range fire and explosions were causing casualties and fear all around, but Captain Duncan McPhee distinguished himself. Although wounded in the head by a sniper's bullet, the 33-year-old seemed to be everywhere, using his deep voice to encourage and direct men who even the battalion history called 'badly shell-shocked and shaken'. By war's end, McPhee was a lieutenant-colonel with an OBE.

Less conventional than McPhee was Lance-Corporal Richard Howes (MM). He had put up his age from 15 to 29 in World War I, enlisted in 1916, and was twice wounded on the Western Front. On trying to re-enlist in 1939, the widower with a young family was initially rejected on account of age (40) and height (5 feet 4 inches). 'Personally I think the 2nd A.I.F. has lost a good man', he wrote in a letter to the authorities. In May 1940, with requirements lowered, this Adelaide engine driver was accepted and sent to the 2/27th. During the advance on Adloun, he was 'absent without leave' from his job at battalion headquarters but turned up at a forward company. When machine-gun fire pinned down the company that night, Howes took it upon himself to find the enemy gun. He crawled 150 metres under fire, engaging the enemy with his rifle as he did so.

Lance-Corporal Richard Howes, who won the Military Medal while AWL in Syria. At the time he was 41 years old.
NATIONAL ARCHIVES B883 SX3404

He shot one soldier attempting to man a powerful 25mm gun. When close enough to the MMG post, he called upon the gunners, in broken French, to surrender. They continued to fire for a while before capitulating. Howes was warned not to go AWL again.

The advance resumed on 11 June until French tanks and anti-tank guns halted the vanguard, centred on Lieutenant Tom Mills' 13 Bren carriers of the 6th Division Cavalry. Mills went forward on foot with three other carrier men. Together they silenced French anti-tank guns, forced off some light tanks and, although his Tommy gun jammed, they captured 45 well-armed Foreign Legionnaires. For this, Mills, a 33-year-old NSW tin miner, received a Bar to the Military Cross he had won at Bardia. By 1945, a lieutenant-colonel, he commanded the 2/4th Armoured Regiment.

The Australians overcame steep terrain, enemy infantry, artillery, aircraft and tanks to reach Sidon by 15 June.

Advance to Merdjayoun

In the 25th Brigade sector, the 2/31st Battalion was to take Merdjayoun, while the 2/33rd advanced through Khiam. Stiff enemy resistance, especially from artillery, delayed the Australians' progress on the first day, but 21-year-old Lieutenant George Connor led a patrol of four men that seized a key bridge at 4 am before it could be blown by the dozen French troops that they drove off. Later that morning, men of the 2/33rd made an extraordinary effort against Fort Khiam. The 1925-built fort sat some 425 metres high, and its defenders, numbering nearly 100, could observe anyone approaching through the cleared country surrounding it. It reminded many of the Foreign Legion fort in the film *Beau Geste*. When the foremost Australians were within 300 metres of the fort, enemy artillery, mortar and machine-gun rounds pounded them. Those not hit ducked for cover. Connor again took the initiative. Under covering fire he approached the wall of the fort alone. After throwing grenades through a loophole, he climbed a drainpipe and entered the building.

He broke down the door of a long barrack room and shot up the occupants with his Tommy gun. After doing the same at another barracks, he captured two medical orderlies and possibly silenced a Hotchkiss machine gun that was harassing his comrades outside. Four other Australians then tried to join Connor, and although one was badly wounded, three others – Sergeant Arthur Sweetapple, Corporal Ross Campbell and Private Jack Wayte – made it inside. A French soldier was captured: one source says he was an NCO who wanted to surrender, another that he was a fighting officer. By now the garrison was fully alert and the Australians took cover in a room for four hours. Connor called on his comrades outside by shouting through a firing slit. Eventually his party escaped, taking at least one prisoner, through a hole they and others outside had made in the wall. Their company retired, determined to attack again at dawn.

The following morning, the Australians found the fort abandoned. For his efforts at Khiam, in 1944 Connor was awarded the Russian Order of the Patriotic War 1st Class. Neither he nor the three men who supported him received any Australian decoration. One, Ross Campbell, lost his brother Kenneth in the initial attack on the fort. Wayte later died in New Guinea.

After capturing Khirbe, the 2/31st found Merdjayoun abandoned on 11 June. The divisional commander, General Lavarack, then decided to switch the 25th Brigade to support the coastal advance, which was progressing even faster. The 25th would capture Jezzine, connected by road to nearby Sidon.

The Australian column was alternately welcomed and fired upon. Lieutenant-Colonel Selwyn Porter (DSO, MID), inspirational commander of the 2/31st, was wounded in the buttock by a sniper's bullet but remained on duty until ordered to hospital two weeks later. French machine guns on Green Hill, overlooking Jezzine, inflicted casualties on the Australians, whose Vickers guns silenced most. Private Percy Luff of the 2/31st worked his way to the rear of one machine gun and killed five Frenchmen around it with a rifle and bayonet. Luff, a 35-year-old Brisbane labourer, was only about 5 feet tall. At Badarane, on 9 July, he used a Bren to silence an enemy machine gun that had his undermanned company pinned down. On breaking cover to take on another enemy post, he was struck by machine-gun fire. Though severely wounded in the side, he kept firing until he ran out of bullets. He lay in the open for seven hours. When his mates finally got to him, he was unable to walk, so they made a makeshift stretcher of rifles and pullovers. It took five hours to carry him to an ambulance. 'Luffy' made not a single complaint, but on being transferred to the ambulance vehicle, said, 'I will never forget my mates for all they have done for me'. He died of his wounds on 12 July. Jezzine fell to the Australians on 14 June, thanks to a bold attack that involved men swinging down a cliff face while grabbing vines and tree branches.

Landmines constituted a threat throughout the campaign. During the advance on Khirbe, Sergeant Arthur Giles (DCM) of the 2/5th Field Company and four others removed mines and roadblocks while under fire to enable Bren carriers to continue the advance, and then cleared obstacles in front of those vehicles all the way to the outskirts of Merdjayoun. By 13 June, Giles had supervised the removal of some 800 French anti-tank mines. Later in the campaign he and his men laid mines and a huge charge of ammonal, while intermittently under fire. Giles was later commissioned and became a lieutenant-colonel in the postwar regular Army.

The French counterattack

On 15 June, the Vichy French counterattacked in the eastern and central sectors. They hit the Australians at Merdjayoun with artillery, cavalry, infantry and, most tellingly, tanks. The infantry defending the routes to Merdjayoun, primarily the 2/33rd and 2/5th battalions, had no effective anti-tank weapons of their own, so they depended for protection on the cavalry's light tanks and the artillery's field and anti-tank guns. After French tanks and infantry overran the forward defences, Lieutenant Viv Thomas (MC) of the 2/2nd Australian Anti-Tank Regiment took forward his troop of 2-pounder guns and sited them in a defile. There they engaged 11 enemy tanks, which eventually fell back. Vichy infantry advancing along the ridges on the flanks later poured down small arms fire on the gunners from close range. Only then did Thomas order a withdrawal, gun by gun, all the time maintaining a duel with the advancing tanks. The latter fired their 40mm guns and machine guns. Thomas's troop hit eight tanks, putting at least five *hors de combat*. During this furious 45-minute-long action, the nearby Australian infantry disengaged without loss. Between them, the Australian anti-tank gunners knocked out 13 tanks that day. When ordered forward to extricate two guns, Lieutenant David Bolton (MC) took a motorcycle down the road, coming under machine-gun and rifle fire from the surrounding ridges. Eventually he had to leave the bike and, still under fire, reached the guns on foot. The Australian infantry had now retreated, and it was vital to withdraw the guns. Bolton had just ordered the crews to do this when enemy tanks appeared on the road. Bolton immediately ordered the guns to engage. They knocked out three tanks and forced the rest to retreat. By now French forces were between the gunners and the Australian infantry, whose transport vehicles were riddled with bullets and useless. Bolton spiked the guns, and then, under cover of darkness, led the crews back to the Australian lines. Vichy forces reoccupied Merdjayoun that night. They briefly regained Fort Khiam, too, though in hand-to-hand fighting, a 2/33rd Battalion company recaptured it. Lieutenant Connor, who had been chiefly responsible for its original capture, was himself captured that night. He would return following the armistice, but only after spending time as a captive in Greece, Germany and France.

The French counterattack eventually faltered, but it dislocated Allied plans for some days.

The advance resumes

Australian troops played a crucial role on the third axis of advance: the inland road to Damascus. About 400 men of the 2/3rd Battalion, still recovering from Greece and Crete, were now sent into another exhausting operation. Their trip to the front, eight kilometres south-west of Damascus, included a train crash and a truck journey in which two vehicles overturned. Attached to the 5th Indian Brigade on 20 June, they soon came under shellfire. The Australians' commander, Lieutenant-Colonel Donald Lamb, was ordered to send one company to cut the Damascus–Beirut road, and the remainder of his battalion to capture heights overlooking this road. Seven stone forts sat atop these heights. The Australians quickly occupied two, but a numerically superior French outflanking force recaptured one fort and many soldiers, including Lamb. Mistaking the surrendering Australians for Frenchmen, an Indian carrier crew fired, killing two and wounding Lamb, who was deposited in the Vichy Fort Weygand.

Captain Philip Parbury (MC) commanded the company sent to cut the Beirut–Damascus road. After a skirmish with enemy troops, he scouted ahead, found the road and called his men forward. They cut down two telegraph poles, put them across the road and hid. French vehicles arriving from Damascus and Beirut halted in the darkness and were captured. Parbury soon had 86 prisoners. Hearing fire from the ridge above, Parbury sent this message to brigade: 'Water rations and ammo almost depleted and troops becoming exhausted. Enemy on high ground dominate this position from both sides of the road and at dawn position will become untenable. I intend to attack.' Leaving a platoon at the roadblock, he led the rest on a two-hour climb up the cliff. There they joined a fight going on for the forts.

The foremost was Fort Goybet. British artillery fire fell on it but stopped 10 minutes early according to the Australians' wristwatches. The advance began hesitantly. Corporal Wal Morgan (MM) and two other men got within 30 metres of the walls and, braving enemy machine-gun fire, sought to throw grenades through the firing slits. Private Walter Scott Orr, a 44-year-old World War I veteran, was killed manning a Bren gun at the foot of a wall. Morgan's group fell back, but as the Australians prepared another assault, the defenders raised a white flag.

The original plan was for the main body of Australians to turn now on Fort Weygand, but it had already fallen to an amazing feat of arms. Staff-Sergeant Carlyle Smith (MM) was a company quartermaster-sergeant, whose usual job was accommodating and supplying the troops. His enterprising nature had brought him the nickname 'Beau Geste', which he now vindicated. On his own initiative, he organised a four-man patrol, armed entirely with submachine guns, and drove forward in a kitchen truck. Inspired by the plight of their battalion headquarters, the patrollers crept towards the fort on their own. They shot the sentries guarding a party of Australians outside the walls. These freed Australians were under Lieutenant John Gall (MC), who soon organised a party of five, including Smith, to attack the fort itself. Smith threw grenades and again distinguished himself. Gall's little band captured the fort, inflicting 35 casualties, taking eight prisoners and freeing the captured Australians inside, including the battalion commander. 'Beau Geste' Smith, a labourer from Marrickville, was also Mentioned in Despatches in 1942. He died of war-related tuberculosis in 1946, aged 35.

On 21 June, during the fight for the forts, the platoon that Parbury left at the roadblock was also in action. It comprised just nine Australians and three Free French under Lieutenant Murray Murdoch. He put eight men on the left of the road facing Beirut, while he and Sergeant Jim Copeman (MM) took up positions on steep slopes to the right. Enemy tanks and armoured cars with infantry support tried intermittently for 12 hours to break through, but somehow Murdoch's band held them off, killing seven, firing at the vehicles' weapon slits and hurling grenades and mortar bombs. By the time Indian reinforcements arrived with Major John Stevenson, acting commander of the 2/3rd Battalion, the battle for Damascus was over, mainly because the presence of the Australians' roadblock had persuaded the Vichy commander to abandon the city.

After one night's rest, the 2/3rd was ordered to join the advance down the Beirut–Damascus road, attached to the 16th (British) Brigade. Fire from high ground threatened the Australians' advance, but Private Tim Donoghue (MM), an expert Bren gunner, took the initiative. Working his way forward, from 450 metres he shot the crews of three French machine guns and accounted for two snipers. Donoghue later won a Military Cross as a platoon commander in New Guinea, where he led his men up steep terrain and behind stubborn Japanese defences near Numoikum. In a charge he led against their rear, eight Japanese were killed, but he was shot in the groin. He continued to direct the action from the ground and was not evacuated for 14 hours.

In Syria, the advance next reached the foot of the 490-metre-high Jebel Mazar. British Brigadier Lomax, believing it unoccupied, ordered the 2/3rd to send a company to hold this vital feature. Finding it occupied, Stevenson sent in two attacks that failed, largely because a local guide initially took the Australians to the wrong peak. Lomax ordered a withdrawal, but Stevenson persuaded him to let the 2/3rd make a third attempt. After repulsing a strong French counterattack, Captain Allan Murchison led some 140 men in the advance. A strong wind muffled the sound of their approach. On spotting enemy sentries on two steep knolls, Murchison, who had won a Military Cross at Bardia, sent one platoon towards each knoll. Bayonets were crossed in the subsequent melee. Though the Frenchmen were above them, the Australians could see the Vichy silhouettes against the sky. Corporal Frank Barnes grabbed one Frenchman's rifle and pulled him down the slope. Eventually the sentries surrendered. Leaving 16 valuable soldiers to guard the 30 prisoners, Murchison pushed on. The ground was so steep that men had to sling their rifles and use both hands to ascend. In the darkness and howling wind, they soon became separated. During a 10-minute halt, most fell asleep on this second night of fighting. When the advance recommenced, the climbers spotted and attacked a Vichy machine-gun position silhouetted against the sky. They skirted around and seized one machine gun, but a second opened fire when the attackers were just 30 metres distant. Murchison advanced on it, pistol in hand, but then Private Maurice Melvaine (DCM) ran forward with fixed bayonet. Melvaine, a prospector from Uralla and tuba player with the battalion band, seemed doomed when the gun traversed towards him and its tracers went to his right and left.

Instead, he reached the gun unharmed and captured it: his citation states he killed the crew, while the official history says the lone gunner fled. The Australians reached the summit without further loss and, in a bayonet charge, dispersed or captured Jebel Mazar's remaining defenders. Blunders denied the Australians promised artillery support, so they had to beat off repeated attacks. An enemy Hotchkiss machine gun pinned down one platoon for three hours. When an Australian section sought to outflank the gun, a sniper shot one Australian in the head. This seemed to inflame Private Clarence Atkinson (DCM), an Indigenous Australian. Taking a haversack of grenades and hurling them as he went, he dashed forward among the rocks and enemy fire until he had cleared the area and captured the Hotchkiss. His citation calls his courage 'amazing'. Atkinson was often in trouble with the military authorities, usually for going AWL. For being 'an illegal absentee' from his unit, he spent several months in a military prison in 1944. He faced hard times after the war too, with a Sydney newspaper headline reading 'Winner of DCM sleeps in street'. Despite Atkinson's heroics on Jebel Mazar, the Australians withdrew.

Meanwhile, in the central sector, the Australians fought to regain ground lost in the Vichy counterattack. Two attempts to recapture Merdjayoun failed, despite the remarkable efforts of artillery observation officer Lieutenant Roden Cutler (VC) and 79 casualties to the 2/25th Battalion. Fort Khiam was recaptured without a fight on 20 June. On 23 June, a depleted company of the 2/33rd Battalion fought an epic hand-to-hand battle to gain and hold a ridge, the 'Little Pimple', north of Khiam. Grenades were thrown and returned, men were killed with bayonets, a French 37mm gun twice changed hands, and four French counterattacks were repelled. Sergeant Neil Henderson entered a French 37mm gun position, killed two crewmen and turned the artillery piece on an enemy machine gun that was inflicting casualties. As he fired his second shot, a bullet to the head killed the 34-year-old grazier. Private Bill Gesch (MM) contributed vitally to holding off counterattacks despite a serious head wound that rendered him temporarily unconscious. Gesch had frequently been in trouble for going AWL and breaking out of barracks, and in early 1941 had been in a detention barracks in England. This Toowoomba stockman would be wounded again in New Guinea. The 2/2nd Pioneer Battalion found Merdjayoun abandoned on 24 June.

Meanwhile, there was heavy fighting north of Jezzine. Hills 1284 and 1332 overlooked Jezzine and the surrounding roads and many Australians were killed or wounded trying to capture them. The 2/31st Battalion sent a strong fighting patrol against Hill 1284 on 22/23 June, but on reaching the summit came under blistering fire from concealed posts and artillery. Atop Hill 1284 sat a 40-metre-wide fortress, surrounded by a two-metre-high rock wall bristling with machine guns. As the 2/31st men withdrew, Private Murray Groundwater (MM), who had recently distinguished himself by taking seven prisoners, covered his comrades with his Bren. Firing from as close as 15 metres, and despite being attacked with grenades, he was credited with killing at least six enemy soldiers. Lance-Corporal Bill 'Inky' Ferguson (MM) contributed to this rearguard too, throwing at least 30 French grenades he found in an enemy post.

The 2/14th Battalion, recently arrived from fighting on the coast, and further tired by the long journey and high altitude at Jezzine, was ordered to capture Hills 1284 and 1332. On 24 June, two 2/14th companies crossed gullies and sheer rock faces in a frontal attack, based on little or no reconnaissance. Inevitably, it failed, at a cost of ten killed and 31 wounded. A platoon under Lieutenant Gerald O'Day was sent into another suicidal attack on Hill 1284 from a different direction. They climbed for over an hour, mostly on ground so steep that they were hidden from the enemy's view. Eventually they were spotted and an hour-long close-range firefight began, Australians versus Foreign Legionnaires. These aggressive French troops sent out several parties to attack with grenades. One French group lost six men shot down and the rest withdrew, but ten Australians were wounded in these grenade attacks. O'Day's platoon was low on ammunition too, and eventually withdrew. Privates Alan Avery (MM) and Leo Deeley (MM) were outstanding here. Avery, a Melbourne nurseryman, had been in trouble with Army authorities five times since enlisting in May 1940, but now inspired his platoon. Though wounded in the back and buttocks by grenade splinters, he moved coolly among the rocks while using his Tommy gun to keep a 16-strong enemy bombing squad at bay. He shot four before running out of ammunition, upon which he seized a rifle and kept enemy heads down until wounded again and evacuated. This outstanding fighting soldier would be a lieutenant by 1944, but that year was court-martialled for stealing a truck and giving a false name. Leo Deeley, a 19-year-old Bren gunner, silenced an enemy machine gun on 24 June. He too was twice wounded and took up a rifle once his Bren was damaged. Deeley was killed on the Kokoda Track the following year.

O'Day's platoon extricated itself with only one dead and 11 wounded. By the end of 1943, the platoon would have collected a further three Military Medals, as well as a Victoria Cross and a Distinguished Conduct Medal. The losses in the attacks of 24 June were not entirely futile: years afterwards, a former French Foreign Legion officer at Jezzine told O'Day that the heavy French casualties against the 'incomparable' Australians had led to their withdrawal from Hills 1284 and 1332 a few days later.

On 26 June, General Lavarack, now commanding all Syrian operations, chose to replace the Australians at Merdjayoun with British forces and to concentrate the Australian forces on the coast. For these operations, the 7th Australian Division would include the 6th Division's 17th Brigade, temporarily comprising the 2/3rd and 2/5th Infantry and the 2/2nd Pioneer battalions. The 300 weary men now constituting the 2/3rd would be transferred from the Jebel Mazar area.

The battle for Damour

Capturing Beirut would probably clinch the campaign, but first the enemy's defences would have to be overcome at the Damour River, which ran through a great ravine. The Australians attacked from south, east and north, intending to surround the main Vichy force. The hard-fought battle of Damour lasted four days. In a frontal assault on 6 July, the 2/16th Battalion took key ground to the south. On crossing the river, Alan Haddy threw grenades into one enemy post and directed fire at it. He was calling the enemy to come out and fight when a sniper's bullet struck him in the face, passing through both cheeks and damaging his mouth. The Vichy command estimated that the Australians sent four battalions to attack El Atiqa ridge, the main defensive position overlooking the Damour River. In fact, just 263 men of the depleted 2/16th were involved. About 40 per cent of those 263 were killed or wounded in close-quarter fighting. Sergeant Jack McVeigh (MM) used his Bren to devastating effect, contributing to his company taking 90 prisoners and killing 50 enemy troops. Lieutenant Roden Cutler accompanied the 2/16th advance as a FOO and contributed more heroics until seriously wounded. Only after 26 hours was it possible to rescue him. He lost his leg, but won the Victoria Cross, becoming the only Australian artilleryman to do so. The 2/16th frontal attack against the French Foreign Legion at El Atiqa was on ground that the divisional report later described as 'well-nigh impossible', but by the end of 6 July, the battalion had gained a foothold. The following day, while the 2/16th edged forward, the 2/2nd Pioneer Battalion advanced into the coastal area to clear enemy posts among dense banana plantations. Forty-one-year-old Corporal Tom Shannon (MM) demonstrated 'courage, determination and physical endurance' leading his section on this and the following day, until wounded in the shoulder. After returning to his unit, this farmer from Tallangatta, Victoria, was captured in Java in March 1942. Two years later, Shannon drowned when a US submarine sank the Japanese transport *Tamahoko Maru*, a so-called 'hell ship' he was travelling in.

While the southern attack proceeded, the 2/14th and 2/27th made flanking movements to the east, designed to prevent enemy counterattacks from Beit ed Dine. The 2/14th established a roadblock on the Beit ed Dine road and captured one of two commanding hills. The enemy thwarted the first attempt to gain the other feature,

Hill 567, by rolling grenades down the steep slopes. Vichy armoured cars and infantry came down the Beit ed Dine road but were repulsed by anti-tank rifle, Bren and mortar fire. Mortars were not designed to take on vehicles, but Corporal Bert Sargent ingeniously held a 3-inch mortar in his hands to achieve the necessary low trajectory. Later in the war he invented a 'Sargent adaptor', which involved attaching grenades to mortar bombs to enable them to fire airbursts above enemy positions. Commissioned in October 1942, he joined 'Z' Special Force in 1943. The prewar driver from Wangaratta was captured during a raid on Singapore Harbour (Operation Rimau) and beheaded by his Japanese captors in July 1945. Sargent's mortar detachment now offered valuable fire support as the riflemen made another attempt on Hill 567. Private Jim Jeffrey (MM) led the section that captured the peak and carried out a wounded man under fire. Jeffrey was later wounded on the Kokoda Track and became a lieutenant. Captain Bill Russell (MID) commanded the 57-strong force that took this feature and prevented enemy reinforcement of Damour along the road.

The 2/14th's actions protected the 2/27th's advance further west. After Lieutenant Charlie Sims (MC) and three men spent 36 dangerous hours finding a potential crossing of the Damour, on the night of 5/6 July, he and his platoon led the successful crossing to El Boum. Heavy shelling killed or wounded all but one officer in one company and caused the men to disperse. Lieutenant Mert Lee (MC) brought up his company and took over, seizing a key objective. Lee's fine leadership and mountain-fighting skills would later be tested on the Kokoda Track. Sims would be there too and become a major by 1945.

The 2/27th successfully established a corridor through which the 17th Brigade could advance to put the lid on Damour. The 2/3rd and 2/5th battalions were each about 300 strong, with many 2/3rd men suffering from exposure, malnutrition and other ill-effects of the Damascus fighting. The men carried heavy loads over hills that exceeded 500 metres in places. The 2/5th not only captured their objective, Deir Mar Jorjos, but also four artillery pieces, eight machine guns and a Foreign Legion colonel. The 2/3rd, on the right, captured two well-defended hills in daring attacks on 8–9 July. Parbury and MacDougal again took leading roles, as did section leader Private Hector Mackay. His service record says Mackay was born in Scotland in 1905, but he was reputed to be aged over 60 and was clearly an expert rifleman. He died of illness in December 1945.

On 9 July, the 2/2nd Pioneers continued pushing through the plantation against strong defences, including artillery and tanks, in a concrete drain or gully. Sergeant Charlie Warburton (MM) was prominent. The 44-year-old had been a corporal in the First AIF, and when his platoon commander was wounded on 25 June, he took over near Merdjayoun. While extricating the platoon from danger there he carried a badly wounded man 100 metres.

Now he led that platoon in destroying key enemy positions. Eventually, a French machine-gun bullet struck him in the chest, forcing his evacuation. Corporal Albert 'Taffy' Stokes (MM) took over from Warburton and led the platoon right through the plantation. Company commander Captain Clive Nason (MC) was also outstanding in this advance. Like Stokes and Shannon, he was captured in Java in March 1942. His devotion to duty in imprisonment earned him an MBE.

The 2/2nd Pioneers and 6th Division Cavalry entered Damour on 9 July, followed by other Australian units from east and west. The French had withdrawn. Nevertheless, the 2/5th Battalion could not rest, being ordered instead to push north. A roadblock near Khalde held them up on 10 July. When machine guns north of a nearby orchard fired on his platoon, Lance-Corporal John Smith (MM) volunteered to lead his section against them. He took the section through the orchard, cleared the enemy in the vicinity and entered a building near the roadblock. From the roof he spotted four enemy posts and used his Bren to force the occupants back. He later crossed the road under fire and attacked enemy positions on the beach with another weapon. According to his citation, 'by a great feat with a "Tommy gun" firing from the left hand, [he] cleared the posts'.

During the fighting for Damour, the 6th British Division, still including some Australians, continued pushing towards the Jebel Mazar, while the 25th Brigade progressed in high ground north of Jezzine. On the night of 9/10 July, the 2/31st advanced on daunting heights overlooking Amatour and Badarane. Supported by artillery concentrations of nearly 5000 rounds, the exhausted men eventually got within range of the enemy and fired while continuing to climb. One post's resolute defenders held up the advance on the right. Private Jim Gordon (VC) crept forward until close enough to charge, then bayoneted the post's four occupants.

On 11 July, the Vichy French agreed to an armistice. Australian soldiers were understandably annoyed that their efforts were largely kept quiet in the press, not least because their casualties – some 1600, including more than 400 dead – had been higher than the combined total of the British, Free French and Indians. Moreover, the operations were mostly fought under an Australian general. Despite this lack of publicity, the decorations for bravery awarded to the Australians reflected their courage and efforts, totalling nearly 80. The two Victoria Crosses were the most famous, but an Australian ambulanceman could say with genuine admiration in a letter home that 'it was nearly impossible country and every one of the lads deserved the V.C.'.

CHAPTER 8
THE JAPANESE ONSLAUGHT: MALAYA AND SINGAPORE

In 1920, Australian military experts identified Japan as the only major threat to Australia's future security. Despite accepting this, Australian governments of the interwar period neglected the armed forces. The reasons for this included a hatred for war after 1914–1918, the restraints imposed by the Great Depression and complacency about Japanese fighting qualities. Australians were also confident in Britain's ability to defeat any Japanese aggression, and specifically in the capacity of a British fleet at Singapore to prevent an invasion of Australia. Only in 1937, with Japan's invasion of China and Germany's new aggressiveness, did governments begin to increase military spending drastically and expand the home defence force (militia). A recruiting drive for the militia brought 80 000 volunteers by September 1939. When war with Germany broke out that month, there was no prospect of fully arming that force, which was raised to operate solely on Australian soil. The first Australian soldiers to fight the Japanese in World War II would meet them overseas, supporting the Singapore Strategy in Malaya.

Germany's early successes meant Britain's fleet and air force became fully committed to the war against Hitler. In September 1940, Japan formed a military alliance with Germany and Italy, and Japanese troops marched into French Indochina.

Britain was still determined to hang on to Singapore and Malaya. Australia offered to help. By August 1941, the 8th Australian

The Japanese onslaught: Malaya and Singapore

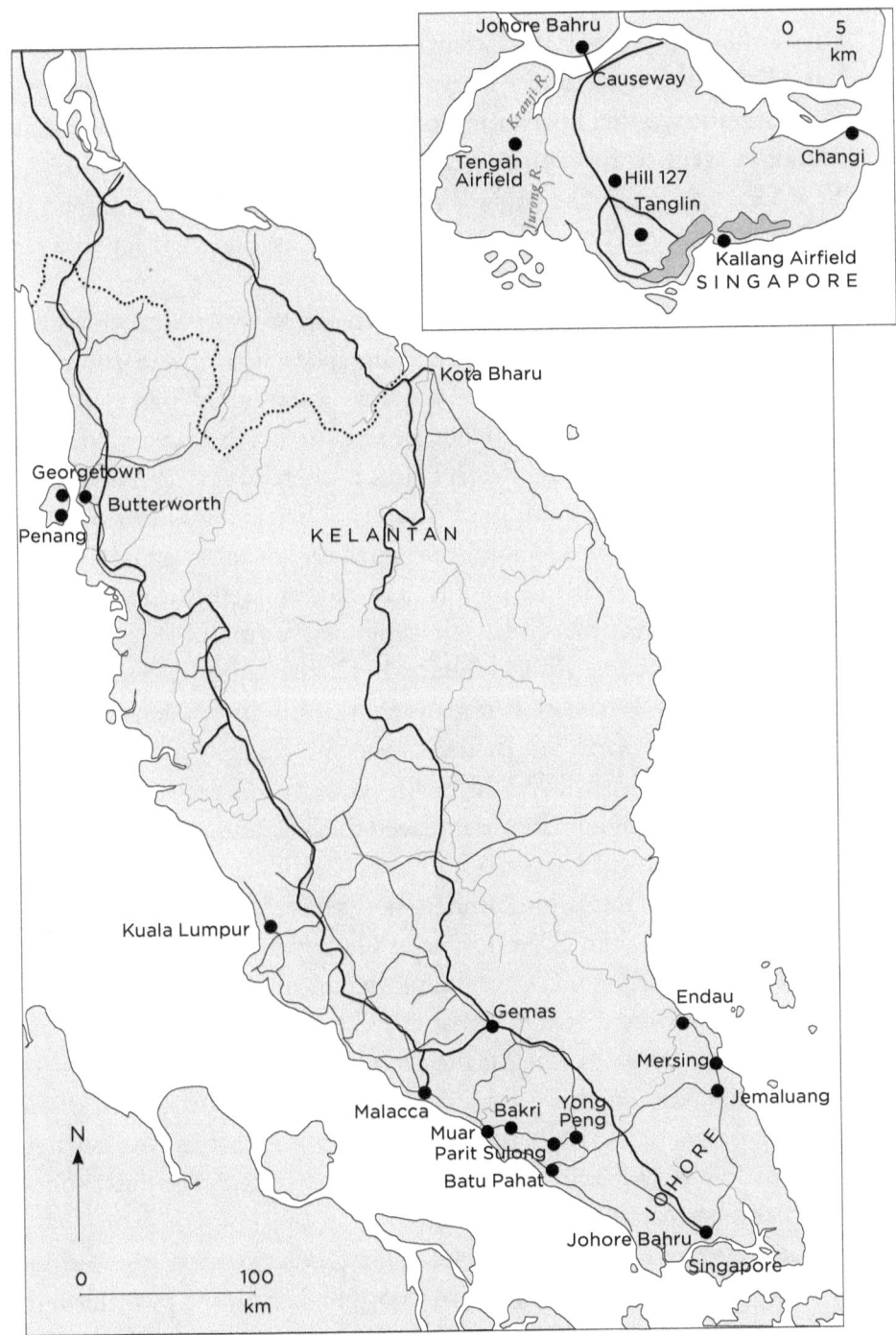

Malaya and Singapore

Division's headquarters and two of its three brigades as well as several RAAF squadrons were in Malaya with British forces. The division's third brigade was held back for protection closer to home: the 2/22nd Battalion went to Rabaul, the capital of the Mandated Territory of New Guinea, while the brigade's other two battalions remained in Australia, waiting to be sent to the Dutch East Indies if Japan went to war.

On 7 December 1941, Japan attacked across a vast area stretching from Burma to the North Pacific. Singapore was one of the main objectives of its combined operations assaults. When Japanese battalions began landing at Kota Bharu, in north-eastern Malaya, just before the attack on Pearl Harbor, there were no Australian troops to oppose the landing as the 8th Division was stationed in southern Malaya. Once ashore, the Japanese advanced rapidly down the peninsula. The British and Indian troops facing them had no answer to the Japanese tanks, air superiority, amphibious landings and encircling tactics. By 14 January 1942, the Japanese had entered Johore. The 8th Division commander, the highly credentialed but abrasive General Gordon Bennett, was in charge of 'Westforce', comprising all British forces in north-western Johore, including his 27th Australian Brigade. Bennett placed this brigade astride the trunk road, the main axis of Japanese advance. At its head, near Gemas, was the 2/30th Battalion, under the severe Lieutenant-Colonel 'Black Jack' Galleghan (DSO). One of Galleghan's companies, under Captain Des Duffy (MC), was deployed in an ambush position in thick jungle beyond a bridge across the Gemencheh River. Lots were drawn for the honour of being the ambush company, and the rest of the battalion envied the company chosen but knew too that if the Japanese suspected a trick and sent out flanking parties, the isolated company – nearly 5 kilometres ahead of the rest of the battalion – would almost certainly be annihilated.

Late in the afternoon of 14 January, Duffy's men allowed an advance party of 200–300 Japanese troops on bicycles to pass through their position, but when another 700–800 cyclists appeared after an interval, the Australians blew charges they had laid on the bridge.

The Japanese onslaught: Malaya and Singapore

Bodies, timber and bikes were thrown skyward. The Australians threw grenades and fired their small arms into the startled enemy, of whom they later claimed to have killed 600. The ambush company then withdrew through the area now held by the Japanese who had been let through before the ambush. The Japanese main body was close behind. There was hand-to-hand fighting in the withdrawal, which led to the company being separated into two groups. Duffy, a 31-year-old staff supervisor from Sydney, brought his group in after 39 hours in the enemy-occupied area. He was recommended for a Bar to his Military Cross a week later when he personally led his company in a bayonet charge that rescued another hard-pressed company. Like many recommendations for bravery in this campaign, it was unsuccessful.

Others who fought bravely in the withdrawal from the Gemas ambush included Private Ray Brown. When confronted by four screaming Japanese, he stabbed one in the back, and another in the shoulder, where his bayonet got stuck. The other two jumped on him. Brown managed to free the bayonet of one Japanese, who was strangling him, and use it to kill his attacker. The other Japanese used his bayonet to stab Brown 22 times and fracture his skull before leaving him for dead. Brown survived and was carried to safety. Lieutenant Harry Head, who was nearby, killed a sword-wielding enemy officer but was himself badly wounded. He and up to 90 others were then guided to safety by Sergeant Amos Doolan, who later died as a POW. Two sections under Corporal Neil Huntley (MID) served as the company's rearguard. Six never returned – they were last seen assuring others 'We'll pin them down – you get back'. It later emerged that this little group held off two Japanese attacks before heading into the jungle. A Japanese patrol captured the six on 2 February. After initially treating them well, the Japanese tied the hands of Privates Robert Bland, John Cochrane, Fred Collett, Ernest Sams, Terence Trevor and Lance-Corporal Clive Mulligan and machine-gunned them at Muar on 3 February. All but Sams and Trevor died immediately or that night. Sams died of wounds five days later. Trevor was unhurt but fell with those machine-gunned around him. The Japanese machine gunner left the scene after a second round of shots. Trevor cut his bonds with his teeth and after further trials reached his battalion comrades in imprisonment.

Six hours after the Gemencheh Bridge was blown, the Japanese had repaired it. Further down the road, the main body of the 2/30th was still unaware of the outcome of the ambush and was somewhat mystified when Japanese tanks approached on the morning of 15 January. Two anti-tank guns of the 2/4th Anti-Tank Regiment were in position with the 2/30th Battalion, although Galleghan had initially dismissed them as an unnecessary nuisance. The 2-pounder anti-tank guns knocked out at least four tanks and delayed the Japanese advance till the afternoon. Captain William Melville (MID) led a company counterattack against the advancing Japanese infantry. Close to the objective he was wounded, but kept directing his company until he was evacuated to hospital in a car. Enemy aircraft attacked, holing the vehicle about 20 times. Melville was at the time holding a severed neck vein in another soldier, thereby saving the man's life. Melville was evacuated to Australia and as a lieutenant-colonel later commanded the 11th Battalion. Eventually the counterattack came up against Japanese tanks and halted. Corporal Frank Abbotts, a 40-year-old timber carrier, was seriously wounded in the chest while attacking a machine-gun post but later carried another casualty to treatment.

Using trees for cover against the Australian anti-tank guns, Japanese tanks and infantry attacked again in the afternoon. The Australians fired small arms and threw grenades, and Private Fred Breese took up a forward position with his anti-tank rifle. An unsuccessful recommendation for a Military Medal said he quickly fired off 50 accurate rounds, stopping one tank (apparently after 30 hits!) and causing another to veer off. The tanks eventually withdrew. Breese's hearing was seriously affected, contributing to a spell in hospital before he returned to his unit in Singapore.

That afternoon of 15 January, Galleghan withdrew the 2/30th. The battalion had not held the Japanese as long as hoped, but its courage was undeniable. Of this action, Japanese Lieutenant-Colonel Tsuji later wrote: 'The 8th Australian Division ... fought with a bravery we had not previously seen'. Warrant-Officer Arthur Purdon (DCM) stayed on the battlefield until, in the teeth of close-range fire, he brought out the last of the wounded. Throughout this campaign, he also ensured that rations went to the foremost troops, irrespective of bombing and shelling.

On 16 January, the elite Japanese Guards Division smashed into the inexperienced 45th Indian Brigade on the west coast near the Muar River. The next day, Lieutenant-General Arthur Percival (the overall British commander in Malaya) sent forward British reinforcements and ordered that the 22nd Australian Brigade's 2/19th Battalion be relieved from Eastforce and sent to Muar, where Bennett also sent the 2/29th Battalion. On arriving at Bakri that afternoon, the 2/29th unexpectedly found that nothing lay between it and the enemy, and in a nocturnal clash wiped out a Japanese patrol. Attached to the 2/29th were four 2-pounder guns and crews from the 2/4th Anti-Tank Regiment. The 2/29th commanding officer, Lieutenant-Colonel John Robertson, shunned the gunners, excluding their commander, Lieutenant Bill McCure, from his briefings. On his own initiative, McCure set up two guns and ignored Robertson's sole order to him: to keep the guns away from the 2/29th's forward troops. On the morning of 18 January, five Japanese light Type 95 tanks came down the road towards those forward troops. After cresting a rise, they drove downhill towards a cutting. Two guns lay in wait for them, one under Lance-Sergeant Clarrie Thornton (MID), concealed behind a mound among rubber trees and covering a bend in the road, the other some 400 metres back under Sergeant Charlie Parsons (DCM) on the edge of the cutting. Waiting until the tanks were side-on, Thornton's detachment fired armour-piercing shells at the first two. The shells passed right through the tanks, which, amazingly, rolled on. Thornton's shells were similarly ineffective against the fourth and fifth tanks in the column, but when the gunners changed to high-explosive shells, they were able to knock out those two vehicles. Further down the road, Parsons changed to the same ammunition and knocked out the first two tanks. The third tank, trapped between the four burning wrecks, was destroyed when an Indian officer threw grenades down the open hatch. McCure and his batman, 'Tich' Morley, carried high-explosive ammunition to the gunners, who seemed to be enjoying the action immensely. Thornton later wrote that for each of the 70 shells his crew fired, the men followed a ritual born of their ribbing of an officer in Australia. The loader, Lance Gilbert, gave each shell a kiss and called out 'Tally Ho', whereupon the gun layer, Claud Brown, responded 'There the bastard goes' as he depressed the firing pedal. Thornton had been slightly wounded in the hip and was glad of a breather before three more tanks came into view and took on his 2-pounder in a close-range gun duel. Tank six fired but missed, and Thornton's return shot blew it up. Tank seven tried to outflank him by entering the jungle about 200 metres away. It opened fire on the Australians, but Thornton ordered the gun to switch targets and was able to silence it. However, Japanese infantry climbed into this tank and opened fire again. By now, Thornton was firing on tank eight, which was itself shooting through a smoke shroud and narrowly missed the gun. Thornton was quickly able to set it alight, though, and turning on tank seven, put it out of action for good.

Instead of making a frontal assault, the Japanese infantry, who had offered little support to their tanks, used their well-tried tactics of firing at the Australians in front of them and thus fixing them in place, while sending troops through the jungle to cut the road behind their enemy. Realising this, Lieutenant-Colonel Robertson bravely took the risk of riding pillion on a motorbike to report to brigade headquarters down the road. He had himself won a Military Cross in 1917. On the way back, he and his despatch rider were fired on and hit. Mortally wounded and lying on a stretcher, Robertson apologised to McCure later in the day, saying, 'I'm so sorry … only for your persistence in defying my orders and positioning your guns where you did, there would have been wholesale slaughter'. McCure had an extraordinary war. Unlike most of his comrades, he would not be killed or captured. He fought alongside British and Communist Chinese guerrillas until the end of the war, an ordeal that involved great hardship and loneliness. He received no recognition for his

Sergeant Charlie Parsons (centre), with Gunner Len Coutts and Gunner Ken Daniels, standing against their anti-tank gun in a clearing near a roadblock at Bakri, Malaya. Parsons was awarded the Distinguished Conduct Medal for his crew's role in destroying Japanese tanks.
AWM 011309

efforts. Similarly, Thornton, a farmer from Berrigan, New South Wales, received scant reward for his extraordinary bravery.

Japanese infantry came forward after the destruction of their tanks, and their machine gunners soon pinned down a company under Captain Bill Bowring (MC). Sergeant Victor Wedlick (DCM) brought up his Bren carrier in response to a request. He was unaware that some Japanese had climbed the trees, and as he sought to eliminate a Japanese machine-gun post, he was wounded in the neck, back and jaw. He only withdrew when his guns jammed, and then returned with two more carriers, which together forced the enemy machine gunners to retreat. Nearly all the carrier crewmen were wounded in this action. Wedlick, a Bendigo butcher, would not be admitted to hospital for six days, in the meantime showing 'conspicuous gallantry' by driving in close to an enemy machine-gun post and thereby allowing two trucks containing wounded men to be withdrawn. He also contributed to an attack on an enemy roadblock.

The Japanese who ambushed Lieutenant-Colonel Robertson were part of a roadblock behind the 2/29th Battalion, and when the 2/19th arrived that day, its men routed this Japanese force and cleared the road.

On 19 January, the 2/19th was preparing to relieve an isolated Indian battalion on the Muar when it was itself attacked. Here, the commanding officer, Lieutenant-Colonel Charles Anderson (VC), first showed his tactical acumen by employing methods previously well exploited by the Japanese: he sent one platoon into a frontal attack to pin the enemy, a second on a flank attack and a company to circle behind and strike the Japanese rear. These manoeuvres, expertly effected by the Australians in their first action, so confused the Japanese that an eyewitness said they 'literally ran round in circles', leaving 140 dead at a cost of ten Australian deaths. Lieutenant Pat Reynolds led the attack, his men employing bayonets and grenades. At one stage he was pinned down among a group of dead Japanese, when suddenly a 'corpse' propped himself up on his left hand and made to throw a grenade with his right. Reynolds fired his pistol and the grenade exploded, blowing half the man's head off. A grenade fragment struck Reynolds in the head, and he fell into a gutter. There, a wounded Japanese slowly raised his rifle to shoot Reynolds, who tried firing his pistol again with his unwounded arm. He was out of bullets, but his batman, Les Truscott, despatched the Japanese. He then bound up Reynolds' wounds and walked towards the platoon. Two unarmed Japanese rushed him, but he shot both dead. Truscott, a 23-year-old hotel groom from Tumut, died in action two days later.

The 2/19th had no time to savour their victory. A wounded sergeant brought news that 400 Japanese had attacked the 2/19th transport two miles back and set up roadblocks. That morning, Japanese aircraft hit the 45th Brigade Headquarters, which was in temporary command of the 2/19th and 2/29th. The many casualties included the severely concussed brigade commander and nearly all his staff and many already wounded 2/29th men in a parked truck. At the brigade major's invitation, Lieutenant-Colonel Anderson took command of the brigade. He was an ideal choice. He had experienced jungle warfare in East Africa in World War I. In training his battalion he had emphasised aggression, especially use of the bayonet, and gave the impression that he would be personally involved in any fighting. For example, he always carried several hand grenades. He was compassionate, but also calm and realistic about the necessity of risking lives to achieve military objectives. Now out of communication with Westforce, which was retreating, he had to make decisions on his own.

Grim glory on the road to Parit Sulong

On 20 January, Anderson's Australian-Indian force began a desperate fighting withdrawal to Parit Sulong village, eight kilometres away. After this force set out, the Japanese occupied Parit Sulong, thus cutting off the escape route. The subsequent three-day ordeal of Anderson's force is an epic of Australian history. At the first roadblock, 36-year-old Lieutenant Alan Ibbott and six of his men were killed as their bayonet charge took them right into enemy trenches.

Following Anderson's suggestion, Captain Frank Beverley had his company enthusiastically singing 'Waltzing Matilda' as they made a flank attack. With the roadblock still standing, Anderson ordered the leading platoon to make an all-out attack while he personally attacked two machine-gun posts that were holding up the advance. He crept up on the posts and destroyed them with grenades. He also used his pistol to shoot one Japanese dead. This action inspired his men. While Anderson's leadership was critical, so was the willingness of his men to fight. As General Percival later commented: 'The award of the Victoria Cross to Lieutenant Colonel Anderson of the AIF was a fitting tribute both to his own prowess and the valour of his men'. That valour was apparent on many occasions. Private Arthur Williams (MM) was a conspicuously brave stretcher-bearer, who accompanied one of the bayonet charges on 20 January, aiding and recovering many wounded under machine-gun fire in the open. He was listed as missing, presumed dead, on 22 January. Captain Victor Brand (MC), a 26-year-old Jewish doctor from St Kilda, was RMO of the 2/29th Battalion. When the enemy shelled and mortared the bunched-up Australians in front of a roadblock, he left the safety of the slit trenches in which many were sheltering and attended wounded Australians and Indians wherever he found them. When the time came to break out in small groups, Brand remained with the walking wounded rather than leave them to the Japanese, who murdered the wounded who had to be left behind. Short in stature, Brand had tremendous courage and compassion, as became obvious too in his work in captivity as a doctor on the Burma Railway.

Captain Bowring was the only company commander of the 2/29th Battalion to survive the Malayan fighting. On 20 January, when artillery fire forced the evacuation of one sector of the front, he personally led a bayonet charge that recaptured the ground. He later led another such charge, and at Parit Sulong advanced and engaged enemy tanks with an anti-tank rifle. He would be wounded in the neck, calves and back while stalking a sniper on Singapore.

General Bennett assigned just one artillery battery, the newly formed 65th Battery of the 2/15th Australian Field Regiment, to the

45th Brigade before the fighting began in Johore. They did sterling work, firing 6519 rounds between Muar and Parit Sulong and also engaging in infantry fighting. After their commander, Major William Julius, was killed in the air attack on 45th Brigade HQ on 19 January, Lieutenant John Ross (MC) took over. On 21 January, when Japanese tanks approached the rear of Anderson's force in the dark, Ross and Sergeant Bertie Tate (DCM) ran back to a gun they had set up in an anti-tank role. They used grenades and their 25-pounder to set alight a tank. In an example of the uncertainties that can surround such actions, gunner and author Russell Braddon claimed that the credit should have gone to Gunner Jack Menzies. The 65th Battery war diary states simply that 'Sgt Tate's gun engaged and destroyed an enemy tank'. Tate died as a prisoner of war when the ship in which the 38-year-old Bondi barman was travelling, the 'hell ship' *Rakuyo Maru*, was sunk in September 1944. The 65th Battery and 2/4th Anti-Tank Regiment suffered grievous losses in the Parit Sulong retreat.

During that retreat, Corporal Geoffrey Bingham (MM) and Signalman Max Benoit (MM) maintained wireless communications from the back of an open truck in the column. Benoit, an electrical testman often in trouble with authorities, continued his vital work, even though he was wounded three times and suffered severely. He died in Thailand in 1943.

Anderson's bloodied force approached Parit Sulong on 21 January, but when a British relief attack was abandoned on 22 January, their fate as an organised force was sealed. Anderson ordered the men to withdraw east in small parties. Only 130 men of the 2/29th and 271 of the 2/19th reached Yong Peng and relative safety.

Lieutenant Ben Hackney of the 2/29th was severely wounded in the leg before the retreat to Parit Sulong, which he endured in a truck filled with wounded. He witnessed horrific sights, including men killed by enemy fire entering the vehicle. Eventually the truck had no driver, and he took over, using his one good leg. He was wounded in that leg too, and the back, while taking a break outside the truck, but he still dragged himself into the seat and drove on. When the order came for everyone to try to escape, he stayed with the truck, using a Bren to discourage the surrounding enemy from approaching. Ultimately, the group of about 110 torn and bloodied Australians and 40 Indians surrendered. They were forced to strip and sit in a circle. The Japanese seemed to take pleasure in repeatedly kicking prisoners' open wounds. The prisoners' clothes were returned, but they were brutally forced into two obscenely crowded buildings. At one point, water and cigarettes were brought towards them, only to be thrown away after the Japanese took photographs. At sunset, the Japanese roped or wired together all the prisoners except those left for dead, including Hackney. The fettered troops were brutally led away, shot by a firing squad, doused with petrol and ignited. This was the notorious Parit Sulong massacre. After crawling away at night, Hackney later found Sergeant Ron Croft, among other petrol-soaked survivors who had not been tied up during the shooting. Though weak and exhibiting great strain, Croft carried a wounded man to cover and then did the same for the 14-stone Hackney. Hackney attributed this amazing feat not to Croft's physical strength but to 'his wish and willingness to help; courage, guts and manliness'. Croft, a married salesman from Richmond, Victoria, died in captivity that April. Hackney evaded capture for 36 days, after which he was beaten again. He had lost five stone in weight but survived the war.

Many who reached Yong Peng were helped by two Lanchester armoured cars acquired by the 2/30th Battalion in December 1941 and now commanded by Sergeant George Christoff (DCM). On about 21 January, Christoff was ordered to take his armoured car forward to ascertain Anderson Force's position. He did this with great daring, driving through Japanese rear positions, interrogating locals and only turning around when stopped at a roadblock. Thirty-year-old Christoff did not find the 2/19th or 2/29th battalions, but the next day went out again, locating and ferrying back 20 Australians. He made the same dangerous journey three more times that day, engaging Japanese forces with his Vickers machine guns each time. On 30 January, Christoff and his armoured car killed several members of a Japanese patrol, including an officer whose sword was taken to

Australia. Soon afterwards, four Japanese 'Nate' aircraft attacked the armoured car. After a long chase, they reportedly dropped eight bombs, a fragment of which killed Christoff. He was buried nearby but his body was never recovered.

The fighting at Mersing

After the 2/19th Battalion had left Eastforce to help in the west, the 2/18th and 2/20th battalions had gradually withdrawn from the Endau area to north of Mersing. On 22 January, two Japanese battalions attacked the main bridge on the Mersing River. Australian mortar, machine-gun and artillery fire repelled them. When the main Japanese body moved west to find another river crossing, an Australian section that had been pulled out the night before was ordered to reoccupy their former positions astride the northern approaches to the bridge. Their platoon commander questioned the order, to no avail, and the section crossed in boats in daylight. About 100 metres from their former post they came under heavy fire. One man was killed, two wounded. When the section commander was badly wounded, believed killed, Private Francis 'Joe' Wilson (DCM), took command. He had a bullet wound in the arm and shrapnel wounds in the back but made effective use of a bag of grenades. Most of the Japanese occupying nearby trenches were killed, thus enabling the Australians to recapture their section post. When the section's ammunition ran low, 39-year-old Wilson ordered a withdrawal to the river, though on learning that his section commander was still alive, he went and rescued him. All survivors made it across the river. Wilson's wounds were being dressed when he observed, 'Let me get back there – those Japs couldn't hit a bag of shit at a hundred yards'. Strong words from a prewar school headmaster!

The 2/10th Field Regiment's 25-pounders proved effective at Mersing. Gunner Charles Easton (MM) was praised for his work with what his citation called 'an AA LMG', probably a Bren. Though continually under attack from dive-bombers, he kept firing at them, officially for some seven days. The 30-year-old horse trainer from Thargomindah, Queensland, used his LMG to protect the field guns, at one stage destroying an enemy machine-gun section.

General Percival now ordered the establishment of a new defence line, running from Jemaluang in the east to Batu Pahat in the west, but he already had a contingency plan for a retreat to Singapore. In the east, the 2/18th Battalion took up a strong ambush position on the Nithsdale and Joo Lye estates on the road to Jemaluang. Japanese troops arrived sooner than expected, on the night of 26/27 January. The Australians underwent a baptism of fire and showed impressive battle discipline. A Japanese source called the subsequent fight 'an appalling hand-to-hand battle'. Private Colin 'Col' Spence (DCM) took over his section when the commander was wounded. During a firefight with a Japanese machine gun, he took cover behind a tree to dodge a grenade. Suddenly, a Japanese officer, unseen in the dark, approached Spence from behind and slashed him across the back with a sword. Spence later likened the feeling to being struck with a length of bamboo. Turning to his left, he fired his rifle at the officer from the hip. He later recalled thinking at the time of doing the same to a wallaby at home. When the Japanese fell face forward, Spence bayonetted him repeatedly in the neck. He later recalled saying with each thrust: 'Fuck you, fuck you, fuck you and fuck you!' Spence then directed his men's fire and movement and drove off the attackers, before stretcher-bearers evacuated him. His wound, running from his right shoulder to his left waist, required 150 stitches. He was evacuated from Singapore shortly before it fell. The wound led to his discharge from the Army in October 1942, when he resumed his work as a primary school teacher. At the Nithsdale estate, the 2/18th lost 83 killed, but probably inflicted heavier casualties. Afterwards, the 22nd Brigade of which it was part fell back to Jemaluang.

On 27 January, General Percival decided that the danger of an enemy flanking move in the west necessitated a general withdrawal to Singapore. While retreating along the trunk road the Australians showed that they were improving tactically. On 29 January, the 2/26th Battalion's last day of fighting on the mainland, Australians

Private Colin Spence, a former primary school teacher who was slashed across the back with a Japanese sword in Malaya. He killed the sword-bearer and directed his section in driving off the Japanese attackers. He later received 150 stitches. He was awarded the Distinguished Conduct Medal.
AWM P04154.005

ambushed a party of Japanese on bicycles. A lull followed when the Japanese occupied the peak of a hill, without pushing to the reverse slope, which an Australian company occupied. The company commander sent a platoon under Lieutenant Ron Magarry (MC) to attack, if possible clearing the Japanese from the hill. Magarry led the platoon in an extended line. They first threw 34 grenades and then charged with the bayonet. The grenades wrought devastation, although some wounded Japanese attempted to fight on, usually as the Australians stepped over or past them. After stepping over a Japanese soldier with a terrible thigh wound, Magarry heard a shot just behind him. He turned to see one of his men, Private Terry Parker (DCM), reloading his rifle. Magarry gave him an accusing look for killing a wounded man, but Parker yelled, 'He was about to shoot you in the back'. Magarry thanked him, dealt with a similarly suicidal Japanese in front of him, and then found himself confronted by several Japanese approaching him in single file. Magarry's men were preoccupied elsewhere, so he used 'bayonet, rifle butt, bullets and boot, plus a lot of luck' to dispose of them all. A firefight soon developed, with a concealed machine gun a particular threat. Parker now unscrewed the cap of a bakelite grenade and threw it high and accurately into the enemy position 30 metres away. Magarry reported that the explosion lifted the enemy gun and two gunners more than three metres into the air, although Parker's citation says he made a lone charge and followed up the explosion with the bayonet. Magarry spotted two more Japanese setting up a machine gun in high grass to his rear, but before they could fire, he charged towards them and, from cover, fired into their surprised faces from just two feet away. Magarry killed 12 Japanese in this action and covered the withdrawal until all the wounded were evacuated. He calculated that the enemy dead lying around the feature numbered 250 to 300. Parker, a labourer from Atherton, later shocked his comrades when, after the withdrawal, a Japanese LMG suddenly opened fire in their midst. It emerged that Parker was firing it, to give the enemy some of their own medicine, but he took Magarry's 'advice' never to do so again. One of Magarry's men, Norman Derrington, later said of this action, 'The boss got an MC, Terry Parker got a DCM and I got a bloody stammer', referring to an impediment he developed after this fight. Derrington, who later served in Korea, also stated that he thought Magarry should have received a Victoria Cross. The 2/26th Battalion did much more fighting that day, ably supported by the 2/15th Field Regiment, which helped destroy Japanese forces forming up to attack in full view of the Australians. A Japanese account of this battle described how Australian 'warriors continued their suicidal resistance like wounded boars'. The Japanese eventually withdrew, enabling the Australians to continue their retreat unmolested.

The Australian withdrawal to Singapore Island was complete by 31 January. Some 35 000 Japanese had defeated 60 000 Indian, Australian and British troops on the Malayan mainland. The Australians won more credit than most in a campaign with few Allied high points.

The fall of Singapore

Partly because the Australians fought well in Malaya, General Percival placed their depleted battalions – most at half-strength – in the key north-western sector of Singapore, where the straits between Malaya and the island were narrowest. The island's defenders were reinforced in late January and early February 1942, but many Australian reinforcements were raw recruits, unacclimatised to the Army and the tropics. The two Australian brigades had excessively long frontages to defend: 5 kilometres for the 27th Brigade, 15 kilometres for the 22nd Brigade. Lieutenants Darrell 'Dal' Ottley of the 2/19th and Roy Homer of the 2/20th bravely led three- and five-man patrols to the mainland opposite their battalions and, on the night of 7/8 February, indicated that large numbers of Japanese were concentrating there. Over the next few days, Ottley and his two fellow patrollers would be killed and Homer mortally wounded in the Singapore fighting.

Following intense artillery and aerial bombardment, the Japanese landed in 260 landing craft on the 22nd Brigade's sector after 10 pm on 8 February. The Australians directed machine-gun and mortar fire at the 13 to 16 battalions involved. Lieutenant Eric Wankey (MC) of the recently arrived 2/4th Machine Gun Battalion set up his three Vickers guns – each provided with 20 000 rounds of ammunition – along a 60-centimetre-high stone wall at a jetty well suited for a landing. The Japanese bombarded the area from 10 am and continued until 11 pm. A direct hit knocked out one gun position and its crew. When the landings began at 9.30 pm, with barges attempting to land at 10–15-minute intervals, Wankey's guns held them off with close-range fire, which sank and capsized barges. For an hour Wankey fired a Vickers, with assistance from Private Jimmy Loller, until a Japanese mortar round, shot from a barge, landed in their pit, wounding both men severely in the legs. Nevertheless, Wankey remained at his post, controlling the guns until at least 1.30 am. The gunners used rifles, bayonets and grenades, as well as their Vickers, before enemy pressure forced them to withdraw. Wankey and Loller were evacuated to hospital, where Wankey had his leg amputated above the right knee. Loller lost his left leg. Fellow prisoners at Changi made artificial limbs for both, which served them throughout the war.

Sergeant Harry Dumas of the 2/20th distinguished himself the day the Japanese landed. His efforts to cover the withdrawal of his platoon with a Bren and a bag of grenades are mentioned in the official history and resulted in an unsuccessful recommendation for a DCM. Dumas, a bespectacled Sydney clerk, reportedly only passed the eye test on enlistment by memorising the chart. He went missing on 10 February, presumed dead, and was last seen groping for his glasses in the dark.

On the 2/18th's front, a platoon under Lieutenant Jack Vernon (MC) was well forward on a small hill that became an island as the tide rose. After a 15-hour bombardment, including 67 shells in 10 minutes, 80 Japanese landed on the island. Vernon and his men killed or dispersed the wave. Japanese mortar fire covered the second wave, inflicting 13 casualties on Vernon's force. His platoon exacted heavy losses again, but in the end Vernon decided they must withdraw. Some of his men were wounded and others were non-swimmers, but he ingeniously tied rifle slings together and, fastening them to objects on the island and mainland, enabled the non-swimmers and casualties to cross. The 34-year-old station hand personally swam the channel between his island and the main island numerous times to assist. Vernon's promotion to captain was in the works days before the battle for Singapore.

On 8 February, failure of communication prevented effective use of Australian artillery. This was not for lack of heroic effort on the signallers' part. The 2/26th Battalion commander saw an unnamed signaller lying in the open under severe shelling and transmitting messages on a phone.

Japanese numbers and tactics enabled them to establish a beachhead. On 9 February, the Australians withdrew to the vicinity of Tengah Airfield. By 10.30 am, the 2/20th had lost seven officers killed, three wounded and one captured. Many more of its other ranks were casualties. At one point the battalion commander, Lieutenant-Colonel Assheton (MID), called three of his Bren gunners to a small knoll to cover the withdrawal of the wounded. While moving between the gunners, Assheton was hit and killed, as was a gunner. A second gunner, Corporal Doug Phillips (MM), sustained a leg wound but continued to fire until struck in the head. The third gunner, Laurie Stewart, kept firing. Assheton, a 40-year-old civil engineer, and his gunners had with their sacrifice enabled his force to disengage and move to safer ground. Phillips was left for dead but recovered consciousness after a while. He lay doggo all day, hoping not to be bayonetted. The following day he was wounded a third time but survived. Percival committed reinforcements on 9 February, but not troops capable of launching the desperately needed counterattack. By 10 February, a new defensive line was being formed between the Jurong and Kranji Rivers. The 22nd Brigade was in the centre, flanked by the 12th and 44th Indian brigades.

On the night of 9 February, further Japanese landings began

in the 27th Brigade sector near the causeway. After hand-to-hand fighting, the Australians fell back. Percival sought to stabilise a new perimeter on 10 February, but Japanese pressure forced retreats. Percival ordered Bennett to regain the perimeter with a counterattack, but Japanese assaults cut communications and disrupted Bennett's plans. Two improvised Australian battalions, X Battalion and Merrett Force, went forward to counterattack, but the former was virtually annihilated, the latter savaged. Another improvised Australian unit heavily involved throughout the fighting was the 'Special Reserve Battalion', comprising surplus base troops and 2/4th Machine Gun Battalion reinforcements. By 11 February it had only about 220 men. Some made a bayonet charge that day, but after hours of fighting, they were withdrawing when Australian, Indian and British troops were caught in a bloody ambush. Major Albert Saggers, commanding the Special Battalion, recorded two remarkable instances of courage. Lieutenant Jimmy Till, a Western Australian regular soldier, received a shoulder wound before rushing a Japanese light artillery section and killing its entire crew of six with an automatic weapon. Saggers and a burial party found Till's remains ten months later. Like Till and Saggers, Lieutenant Vic Mentiplay was in the 2/4th Machine Gun Battalion before being assigned to the Special Battalion. After the Japanese ambush on 11 February, he was hiding in scrub when he saw a Japanese soldier bayoneting Indian wounded. This incensed Mentiplay, who charged the Japanese with his own bayonet. The Japanese, on higher ground, saw him coming and positioned his bayonet so that Mentiplay rushed on to its point, which entered his throat and came out the back of his neck. The point missed the Australian's jugular, and Mentiplay threw himself back onto the ground. Drawing his revolver, he shot the Japanese and then rushed at other nearby enemies. He killed five more before throwing the empty pistol at a machine-gun crew. Mistaking the gun for a grenade, they ran. Mentiplay then took cover under overhanging foliage in a pond. After the scene of battle moved on, he found and put on 'native clothes' and at dusk returned to his own lines, where he collapsed.

The Japanese onslaught: Malaya and Singapore

A crucial feature that day was Hill 127. Of 71 men under the 2/18th's Captain Ray Griffin who occupied the hill, only 22 emerged from the fighting. One was Private Eric Beresford (MM), No. 1 on a Bren. No fewer than five men acting as No. 2 on the gun became casualties that day, but Beresford continued firing the Bren until enemy fire destroyed it.

That night, a 2/29th Battalion patrol comprising Lieutenant Tom Oldfield, Corporal Harold Reid (MM) and four others delivered a message to brigade headquarters at Holland Road. On the way back, Lieutenant Oldfield left the group to investigate a light, with Reid following. On crossing the road, Oldfield was set upon and shot dead by up to six Japanese. Rather than flee, Reid stood his ground and shot all but one of the Japanese, who ran. Before Reid could recover Oldfield's body, more Japanese arrived. Reid retired, downing another three enemy as he did so, and then led the patrol to safety. Neither the official history nor his battalion history mention this 34-year-old Ararat drover's deeds.

Corporal Geoffrey Bingham, mentioned above for maintaining communications near Parit Sulong, was at 22 Brigade Headquarters when it became practically surrounded. He led several men in a charge until seriously wounded, but in doing so helped to liberate the headquarters.

The 22nd Brigade was forced back on 12 February. Australian and British nurses were evacuated on 10–12 February, while on the 13th, 1800 soldiers and 1200 civilians were embarked on small boats. By 14 February, with the defence line on the outskirts of smoke-wreathed Singapore, the AIF were together in the Tanglin area. The water supply to Singapore was compromised and unlikely to last another day. On 15 February, with surrender or slaughter the only options, General Percival chose capitulation. In Australia's greatest military disaster, 15 000 Australians went into captivity.

After Singapore fell, a British report blamed the loss of the fortress on the Australians, and some British writers have agreed. There was some very undisciplined Australian behaviour in the last days of the siege, attributable largely to the recently arrived reinforcements.

However, just seven of the 42 infantry battalions defending Singapore were Australian. More than 800 Australians were killed in that defence. To blame the Australians for the loss of the island and the failure of Britain's Singapore Strategy was unfair.

CHAPTER 9

DOOMED BATTALIONS: NEW BRITAIN, AMBON, TIMOR AND JAVA

Like those defending Singapore, Australian garrisons sent to other islands north of Australia faced grim fates. The Japanese allocated formidable air, naval and land forces to overcome them. The impossible odds were summed up by an RAAF officer at Rabaul, who sent to base the classic gladiators' cry: 'Those who are about to die, salute you!'

New Britain: Resist then retreat

The great natural harbour of Rabaul in New Britain was a key Japanese objective in late January 1942. 'Lark Force', the garrison of this isolated station, comprised the 2/22nd Battalion and other small detachments, all under Colonel John Scanlan.

On 20 January, more than 100 Japanese aircraft attacked Rabaul. Sweeping aside the few aircraft that opposed them, they bombed and strafed airfields and harbours at will. At Vunakanau airfield, 37-year-old Captain Ernest 'Pip' Appel (MC) commanded the company allotted to defend the airstrip. He encouraged his men to fire back at the Japanese aircraft with their rifles and World War I–era Lewis guns. Between raids, his men dug out dud bombs on and around the runway.

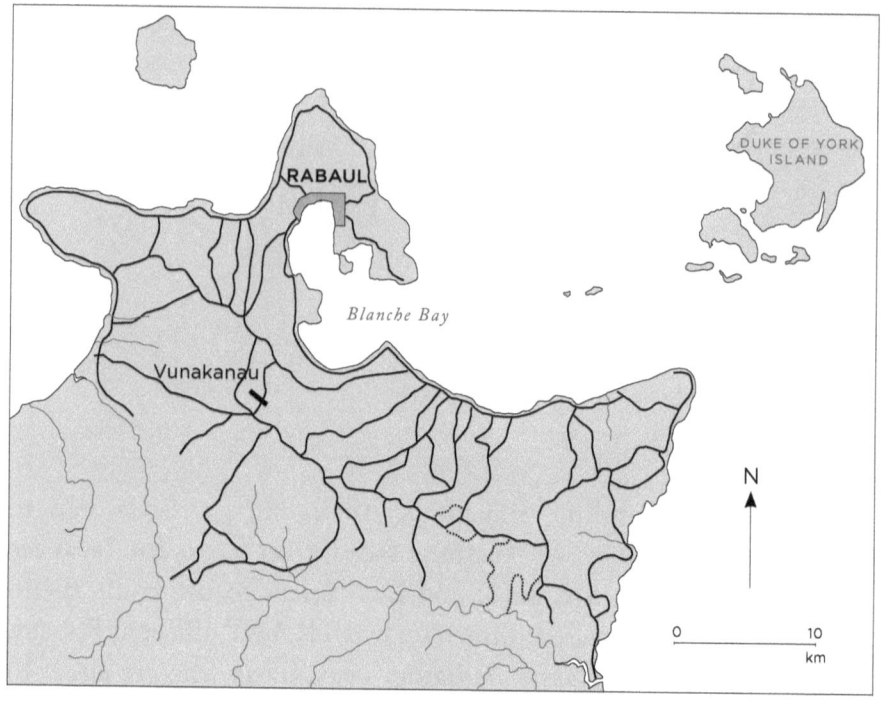

Rabaul

On 21 January, an approaching enemy convoy of warships and transports was sighted. Scanlan withdrew troops from scattered positions to southern Blanche Bay. Appel's company remained at the airfield, preparing demolitions. As day broke on 22 January, 50 Japanese carrier aircraft arrived overhead and, unperturbed by the Australians' small arms fire, dropped 180 bombs around the airfield. Only one man was wounded, but air raids on the coastal guns killed 11, and demolition work inadvertently set off an explosion that silenced the main wireless connection with the outside world.

Soon after midnight on 22/23 January, Japanese landing craft entered the harbour, where Australians heard and saw the Japanese troops laughing, talking confidently and lighting matches or shining torches. Once most of the invaders had disembarked, the defenders opened fire. Their firepower, however, included nothing more potent than mortars and Vickers machine guns.

The defenders frustrated several assaults, but although the Australians were still in position at dawn, Japanese troops were on their flanks and they were under air attack. At 7 am the Australians withdrew in good order. Appel's company at Vunakanau had been dive-bombed and strafed all morning, and his personal disregard of the danger inspired those around him.

Overwhelming Japanese strength made the defence of Rabaul hopeless. Appel was told to hold a road junction until all withdrawing transport had passed through. It was the last message he received, and he obeyed it. Only in mid-afternoon did he fall back to a bivouac established by his second-in-command, Captain Allan Cameron, deep in the jungle. There he found some 160 men – a number that increased over subsequent days – without food or supplies. Many groups of Australians were now moving west, and the Japanese sought to capture them. Some of those captured were executed on the spot, although Appel and his men were unaware of large-scale massacres at Tol and Waitavalo.

Appel now came into his own. He organised the men into groups that could find and carry food. Sensing falling morale, he gathered 285 men and appealed to them not to surrender, but instead to go to camps he intended to establish in the hills where he would prepare them to fight again. They responded positively, but a week later it became increasingly difficult to keep up their spirits, and only the departure of Japanese from a nearby harbour prevented a mass surrender. Appel's skill as a pharmacist enabled him to help the many sick men – on average 60 dressings per day. The Japanese sent messages urging Australians to surrender, and Appel covered 160 kilometres in five days, riding, walking and swimming to visit his scattered parties and urge them to persevere. It paid off. On 21 February, news of an evacuation plan arrived. After further westward movement, involving canoes, a pinnace, brave local administrators and Appel's perpetual encouragement, 400 Australians had been evacuated to safety by late March. The organisation, care and encouragement Appel gave his men during their arduous journey through mountain and jungle saved many lives.

He later rose to lieutenant-colonel, serving with RAAF aerodrome defence and the 29th/46th Battalion, but suffered much ill-health.

Another 2/22nd Battalion man recognised for bravery was Lance-Corporal Henry Mitchell (MM). With communications knocked out on 23 January, he acted as a motorcycle despatch rider between the area commander and the 2/22nd. Enemy fighters strafed him on each of his six journeys that day. He had to swerve across the road several times and had his motorcycle shot from under him. He repaired it and continued. Mitchell escaped the island and served with a motor transport workshop. He was discharged to war industry in December 1943, never having fired a shot in anger.

Horror and 'desperate resistance' on Ambon

'Gull Force', designated to defend Ambon and its airfield, revolved around the 2/21st Battalion. It lacked heavy weapons for the island's defence, but when the commanding officer, Lieutenant-Colonel Leonard Roach, complained to Army Headquarters in Melbourne, he was told ominously that Gull Force's role was 'to put up the best defence possible'. Roach calculated that the garrison could not hold Ambon for more than a day or two against the huge Japanese force then operating in the Dutch East Indies and urged its evacuation. He was subsequently replaced by Major William Scott.

After a discussion with Lieutenant-Colonel Kapitz, the Dutch officer commanding all forces on Ambon, the Australians accepted the roles of defending Laha airfield and the south-western portion of the Laitimor Peninsula, in the island's south.

On the night of 30/31 January, more than 6000 Japanese landed in three locations. One Australian private recorded that the defenders fought back fiercely but also wondered how long they had to live.

Dutch resistance at Paso was quickly broken. The Australians on the Laitimor Peninsula were pushed back and pinned at Eri by the end of the first day. The Japanese also attacked the two Australian companies at Laha and had to fight hard to overcome them.

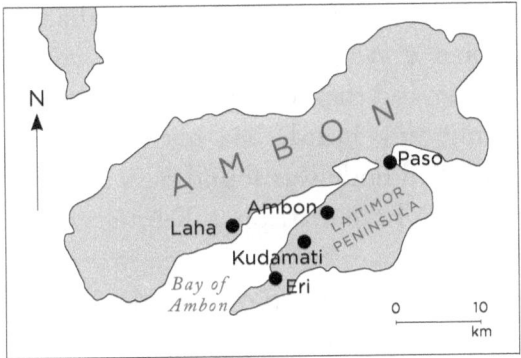

Ambon

A wartime Japanese article about the capture of Ambon called the Australians 'impudent' and 'suicidal', but acknowledged that the 'desperate resistance of the Australians after the breakthrough was not to be despised'.

No medals were awarded for that fighting, but there were heroic acts. After training as a rifleman for 18 months, Private Alan Murnane was told on 17 January that he was to become a stretcher-bearer. While accompanying a patrol that day, he heard a call for a bearer. His officer warned him and the other bearers they would be going 'at their own risk', but they did not hesitate. 'There was a hell of a lot of shooting going on around us', Murnane recalled, 'but we couldn't be worried about that'. After single-handedly helping a casualty to an aid post, Murnane and a fellow-bearer went into a pillbox, in which three terribly wounded men lay in a pool of blood. The bearers had no time to consider the horror of the wounds or the bullets and bombs whistling around, but got on with applying bandages. They marvelled at the stoicism of the wounded, whom Murnane called 'the gamest crew I've ever seen'.

The best-known acts of individual Australian bravery on Ambon were those of Driver William Thomas ('Bill' or 'Tom') Doolan, a motor driver married with two children in prewar Hawthorn. Accounts differ as to what he did, and the official history does not mention him. It does describe the Transport Platoon under Lieutenant Denis

Smith doing fine defensive work. An Australian War Memorial account says Doolan, a member of this platoon, volunteered to join a patrol on 1 February and then to remain behind to cover the party's withdrawal. Firing was heard, but his fate remained unknown until his bullet-riddled body was found days later. All accounts say that near the road at Kudamati on 1 February, he inflicted heavy casualties – one source says 80 – on as many as three truckloads of Japanese. He used a machine gun or grenades, a rifle and a revolver before he was killed. His lone action is perpetuated in an Ambonese Malay song, one line of which says, 'The Australian soldier Doolan killed many Japanese'. Locals tended his grave throughout the war.

On 3 February, Major Scott decided that further resistance by his depleted, exhausted and outnumbered force was pointless, and surrendered. Fifteen Gull Force men died in the fighting. A further 309 were massacred at Laha in February as reprisals for Japanese deaths following the sinking of a minesweeper on a mine in Ambon Bay.

Fighting against the odds on Timor

The next Japanese target was Timor. The garrison of Dutch Timor, 'Sparrow Force', comprised the 2/40th Battalion and attached troops under Lieutenant-Colonel William Leggatt, and several hundred Dutch troops. The 2/40th was deployed around Koepang, including one company at Penfui field where No. 2 Squadron RAAF was based. After the aircrew flew out of Penfui on 19 February, Leggatt asked headquarters in Darwin the purpose of Sparrow Force but received no reply. Darwin was heavily bombed that day.

The following day, 20 February, the Japanese invaded Timor. A landing at an undefended coastal area south of Koepang threatened the rear of the Australians, while a Japanese paratroop landing astride the main road to the north-east cut them off from their ammunition dumps and supplies at Champlong. At nearby Babau, two members of the 2/1st Fortress Engineers, Sappers Kenneth

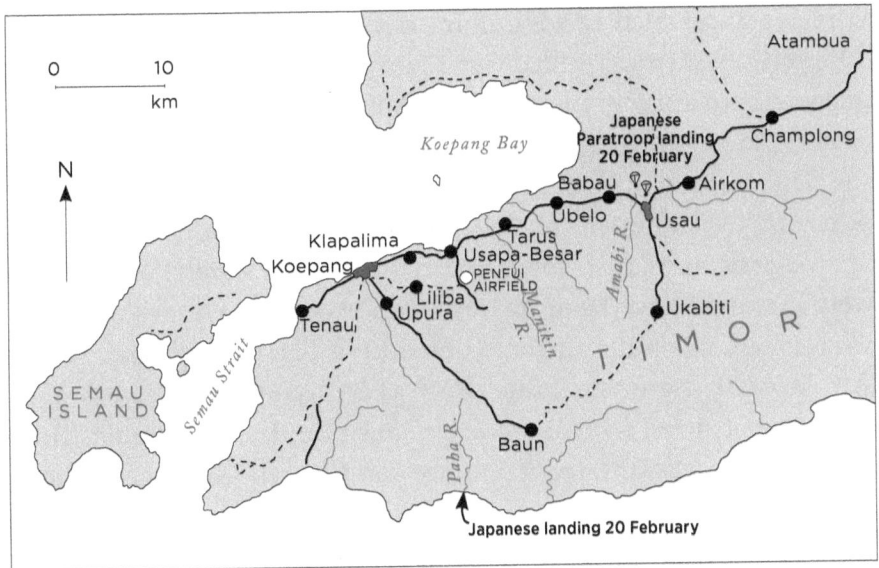

Timor

Hickey (MM) and Malcolm Livingstone (MM) did remarkable work. For two and a quarter hours they manned a Bren, inflicting an estimated 75 casualties on the paratroopers, and preventing the Japanese from crossing the road through Babau. Their Bren, the only Australian automatic weapon in action, enabled infantry reserves to be brought up, though Babau fell that afternoon. Hickey, aged 19, and Livingstone had enlisted at Paddington on the same day in July 1941.

Meanwhile, Japanese bombers destroyed the Australian coastal guns and the Australians withdrew from the beaches. The next day, Leggatt decided to concentrate his forces to recapture Babau before obtaining supplies for a guerrilla campaign. Captain Norman Roff's company flanked the Japanese, clearing paratroops from the adjacent maize fields, and recaptured Babau: the official historian calls this 'a brilliant success', considering the enemy strength. Roff was wounded, but with the help of two men, captured a building – probably a headquarters – and killed the ten paratroopers inside.

Using an antiquated Lewis gun in another building, Corporal James 'Dummy' Armstrong killed five more Japanese and drove off their party. Armstrong, a Launceston labourer, was killed by Japanese captors in 1943. Leggatt unsuccessfully recommended him for the Distinguished Conduct Medal, but in 2019, Armstrong was posthumously awarded the Australian Medal for Gallantry.

Leggatt moved his force into Babau, where several Australians were found to have been tortured and executed. He pushed on to Champlong but was confronted by dug-in Japanese at Usau Ridge. An Australian grenade killed Roff as he led his men across open ground, but fierce fighting took the position. On enlistment, Roff, aged 38, was headmaster of Launceston Church Grammar School. A Japanese machine gun on Usau Ridge pinned down one company, but Warrant-Officer Reg Hay (MM) led a party from another company in a bayonet charge across open ground and annihilated the enemy post. The grocer from Wynyard, who married two months after enlisting, proved a superb leader in imprisonment too, including the Burma Railway. He was the only member of the 2/40th singled out for a decoration until recognition was given by the Australian government in 2017 and 2019. Those awarded at that time included Warrant-Officer Basil Billet, who Leggatt recommended for a Distinguished Conduct Medal for courage and leadership of a platoon in the intense fighting at Usau, where he led his men though twice wounded, only collapsing after the fighting ceased. Captain Peter Maddern, who received an MBE for his leadership in captivity, received a Distinguished Service Medal for his 'distinguished leadership of "R Company"', comprising raw reinforcements who had enlisted in December 1941.

After leaving Usau Ridge and advancing on Champlong, the column of exhausted Australians was soon surrounded. When the Japanese demanded surrender on 23 February, Leggatt chose to yield rather than face annihilation. The Australians had lost 84 killed and 132 wounded. They claimed more than 600 Japanese troops killed.

Early on 20 February, Japanese troops landed in Portuguese Timor. They advanced towards Dili airfield, where Lieutenant

Charles McKenzie (MC) commanded a 20-man section of the 2/2nd Independent Company. Though supposed to wait for orders from the Dutch HQ for the airfield's destruction, communications were out and McKenzie gave the demolition order on his own initiative. His force was being surrounded, so McKenzie ordered an attack on a small bridge across which the Japanese were approaching the strip. This was to coincide with the demolition of the airstrip. In the ensuing fighting, the Australians inflicted heavy casualties, McKenzie bringing down several Japanese with his own rifle. The Australians escaped using the dust caused by the demolitions as a screen. In March, when strong Japanese forces moved inland, the company retreated further into the hills, where some 250 Australians from Dutch Timor joined them. From the hills, this force waged a successful harassing campaign for 12 months. Captain Bernard Callinan (MC) led many reconnaissance patrols and ambushes and oversaw a skilful evacuation of the island without loss. By war's end he was commanding the 26th Battalion on Bougainville. Another extraordinary soldier was Private Mervyn 'Doc' Wheatley, a Western Australian truck driver and kangaroo shooter. When on Anzac Day 1942 five commandos ambushed a Japanese truck near Villa Maria, Wheatley was credited with eight of the 12 Japanese killed. He was later celebrated in the press for 25–27 confirmed kills on Timor and up to 22 more. Twelve of them were said to have been inflicted in just 12 shots, over 15 minutes. Wheatley was one of seven brothers who served.

Java: Defiance and captivity

Control of Java on the eve of the Japanese invasion lay with the Dutch. There were some 25 000 Dutch troops on the island, as well as 3500 British, about 2800 Australians and an American artillery unit. Australian Brigadier Arthur Blackburn VC commanded an improvised brigade in the Buitenzorg area, south of Batavia, in western Java.

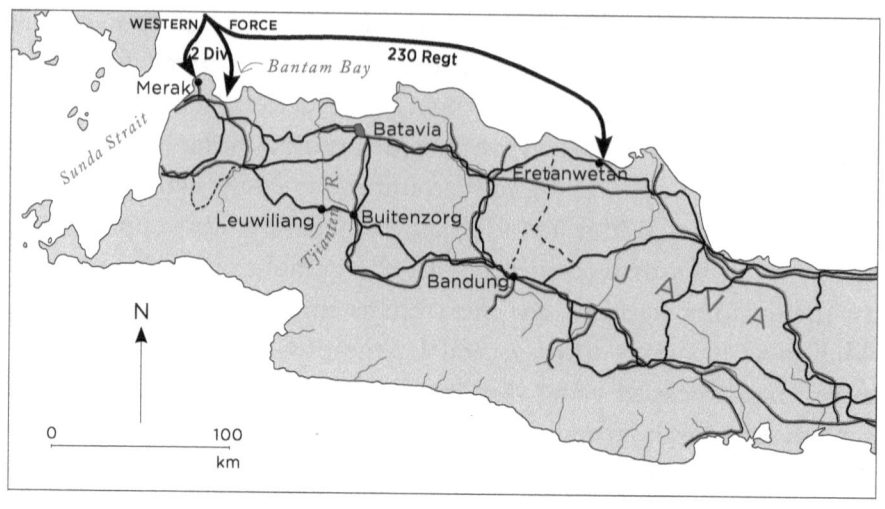

West Java

On 28 February, two Japanese divisions and part of a third landed in western, central and eastern Java and advanced rapidly. At Blackburn's suggestion, 'Blackforce' set out to counterattack the force advancing from the west. The blowing of a crucial bridge prevented the counterattack, but Blackforce, now including some British tanks and American artillery, held its ground bravely at Leuwiliang, some 24 kilometres from the key base at Buitenzorg. Blackburn had read notes on Japanese tactics and developed his own effective counter. He deployed two companies in depth on the road, but held most of his force in reserve, to respond to the inevitable Japanese encircling moves with his own counter-encirclement. His artillery would hold fire until maximum surprise and damage could be achieved. These tactics achieved results, but the courage of his men was tested. Throughout 3 and 4 March, Sergeant Clem White (MM) of the 2/2nd Pioneer Battalion moved among his sections as they came under intense mortar fire. Some were blasted out of their positions, but he rallied them. On 4 March, he saw one of his men lying severely wounded. Disregarding the heavy fire, he went to the casualty and, helped by others, brought him in. At this point, White sustained severe wounds, including a lost finger. The 32-year-old Melbourne insurance salesman had already suffered much misfortune in the war. He had sustained a foot injury during the fighting in Syria, necessitating two weeks' hospitalisation. That September his wife had died. He would soon go into captivity. His service file contains a poignant note from captivity to his young son. White survived the war, remarried and received his medal at Victoria's Parliament House in 1947. His happy ending was quite different to that of the man who took over his platoon at Leuwiliang, Sergeant William Ryan (MM). The 31-year-old continued White's work moving among the men, helping to resite their posts if they were destroyed. After his capture, Ryan drowned in the torpedoing of the *Rakuyo Maru* 'hell ship' in September 1944. At Leuwiliang, there were no signal communications from the companies to 2/2nd Pioneer HQ. Private Frank 'Spike' Edmondson (MM) made numerous journeys with reports to headquarters, five times taking a shortcut across waterlogged rice fields under fire rather than a longer, covered route. Edmondson had frequently been in trouble, missing most of the Syrian Campaign in a detention barracks.

On 4 March, Corporal Joe Richards (MM) of the same battalion was patrolling down a single-lane track in one of the garrison's light armoured cars when he contacted enemy forces. He opened fire with his Bren, but almost immediately the Japanese answered with anti-tank shells that disabled the armoured car and killed another crewman. Richards dismounted from the car and kept firing at the advancing Japanese. Another armoured car came forward to help but was hit by four shells, which wounded most of the crew. Richards kept up his lone stand until two platoons of Australians launched a counterattack that pushed back the Japanese.

Corporal Alan Graham (MM) commanded a section that held its ground at Leuwiliang from 2 to 5 March. For 36 hours they were under mortar, machine-gun and rifle fire. He ensured that his section replied with rifle fire and countered enemy infiltration attempts. When orders came to withdraw, the 32-year-old's section was reportedly last to leave, with him manning an anti-tank rifle and remaining until all his men had safely withdrawn. Graham died in the sinking of the *Tamahoko Maru* in 1944.

Early on 4 March, General Wijbrandus Schilling, Dutch commander in western Java, informed Blackburn that all forces were retreating to Bandung, and asked him to hold the vital road junction of Buitenzorg for another 24 hours. Blackburn agreed, retreating that night to a position covering Buitenzorg. Here, Lieutenant Tim Brettingham-Moore (MC) of the 2/3rd Machine Gun Battalion distinguished himself. After his company commander and all other company officers were wounded or captured in the fighting, the 21-year-old Tasmanian law student took over the company, organising and personally leading counterattacks against Japanese forces that were continually trying to outflank his men. After the war, Brettingham-Moore became a judge in the Supreme Court of Tasmania.

Blackforce held the roads into Buitenzorg until the afternoon of 5 March. For the loss of about 100 men killed or wounded, Blackforce held off about one-third of a Japanese division for three days. Eventually, Blackburn was ordered to withdraw from Bandung.

Dutch capitulation on Java was imminent, but Blackburn hoped to continue resistance or be evacuated. However, with Dutch advice that the hostility of the Indonesians would make guerrilla warfare impractical, no communications with Australia and a prospect of a medical disaster, he chose to join the other Allies in surrendering on 12 March. More than one-quarter of the 2796 captured would die as prisoners.

At Bandung, No. 1 Allied General Hospital was under the command of Temporary Lieutenant-Colonel Edward 'Weary' Dunlop (OBE). He later told of a group of wounded, one of whom had a broken femur. When Dunlop approached him, the man urged Dunlop to leave him and help others who could be saved. Dunlop often witnessed this self-sacrificing heroism of the wounded and sick in the years of captivity that lay ahead. He would be transported to Singapore and then, in January 1943, to Thailand, where he worked as a medical officer on the Burma Railway for the rest of the war.

He not only treated many wounded with remarkable efficiency and success but also spoke up for them to the Japanese. When Billy Griffiths, a British POW, had been blinded and lost both hands in a booby trap explosion, the Japanese wanted to kill him. Dunlop, who had operated on and saved Griffiths, stood in front of the bayonets and refused to move, saying: 'You will need to put those bayonets through me first'. The Japanese commander was not prepared to bear the consequences of killing Dunlop, so Griffiths was spared. In his memoir of working on the Burma Railway in 1943, Tim Brettingham-Moore wrote that Dunlop, running the hospital and camp, often 'personally intervened in a dispute with the Japanese staff and by sheer courage and personality got what he wanted'. Dunlop is one of Australian history's most heroic figures. At Dunlop's funeral in 1993, Sir Ninian Stephen described him as having 'a lone eminence of sustained heroism and superb achievement'.

By the second week of March 1942, Japan had occupied a perimeter that had been the objective of its huge offensives launched in December 1941. For relatively few losses, it had achieved in three months what it had planned to do in six. Its armed forces were now perilously close to Australia.

Escapes and attempted escapes from the Japanese

Japanese treatment of prisoners of war was notoriously brutal and led directly to the deaths of about one-third of the Australians captured in the Far East up to March 1942. No Australian soldiers captured by the Japanese in later campaigns seem to have survived. Unlike prisoners of the Germans and Italians, Australians who attempted to escape the Japanese and were caught usually faced death. Private James O'Dea enlisted in Sydney on 11 December 1941 and left for Singapore less than a month later. The labourer and accomplished boxer was fined for misbehaviour on the ship, but arrived in Singapore on 26 January 1942, just in time to join the 2/20th Battalion in the catastrophic battle there. Captured on 15 February, he was determined to escape. On 16 March, he and five other Australians from various units escaped from Changi POW camp and stole a boat. While wading ashore on the Malay side of the Johore Strait, they were recaptured. The Japanese executed all six men the following day. In the 21st century, the Australian government officially recognised the courage of these and dozens of other Australian prisoners who died trying to escape or were executed afterwards, awarding them the Commendation for Gallantry (equivalent to being Mentioned in Despatches).

In June 1943, Lieutenant Charles Wagner planned an escape with six others being held at Berhala Island camp, near Sandakan on Borneo. Wagner had earned the Distinguished Conduct Medal as the 2/18th Battalion's Intelligence sergeant in January 1942 and had been commissioned in the field. With help from locals and led by Captain Ray Steele (MID), they escaped through latrines that emptied to the shoreline. Soon dubbed 'the Berhala Eight', they joined American-led Filipino guerrilla forces on Tawi-Tawi Island. They trained the guerrillas and caused havoc among the Japanese, who by the time the Australians departed for Mindanao in October had sent 2000 troops in unsuccessful attempts to subdue the guerrillas. By December, the Australians were fighting a major Japanese anti-guerrilla offensive on Mindanao, and Wagner's charmed life was ended by a sniper. Some of the group returned to Australia by submarine, but other outstanding soldiers remained behind.

Robert McLaren (MC) enlisted as a private in April 1941, and though initially trained as a fitter and sent to armoured units, was transferred to the 2/10th Ordnance Workshops on 31 December 1941. The 39-year-old arrived in Singapore late in January and was captured when the island fell. Days later he and two other Australians escaped. Locals betrayed them in Malaya, and the Japanese put the Australians before a firing squad six mornings in succession before returning them to Changi. McLaren was sent to Borneo, where he met Lieutenant Rex Blow of the 2/10th Field Regiment. Both joined Captain Steele's escape party and remained behind when the party's other survivors returned to Australia. By December 1944, McLaren was a temporary captain, commanding an armed whaleboat. He used it to damage or sink three Japanese small craft in daylight raids on Parang harbour that month and against Japanese coastal defences and vessels in 1945. Ordered home in April 1945, this man of 'cheerful imperturbability' parachuted behind enemy lines in a five-man reconnaissance mission before the Australian landings at Balikpapan in July 1945. Despite mishaps, he reported successfully, earning a Bar to his Military Cross. His life ended prematurely in 1956 in a motor accident. Rex Blow ended the war a major in 'Z' Special Unit, receiving the Distinguished Service Order and an American Silver Star for his work in the Philippines. Wagner and Sergeant Rex Butler, one of the 'Eight' also killed in action, were posthumously Mentioned in Despatches and awarded US Silver Stars.

CHAPTER 10
RETURN TO THE DESERT: EGYPT

While the 6th and 7th divisions returned to the Far East in early 1942, the 9th remained in Syria. When Rommel finally took Tobruk on 21 June 1942, the 9th Division was recalled to the Western Desert. Its first action there in 1942 occurred on the night of 7/8 July, in a company-size raid under Captain Mervyn Jeanes (MC) of the 2/43rd Battalion. Jeanes took a 'fighting patrol' of four officers and 64 other ranks of his company, together with six battalion stretcher-bearers and 20 sappers of the 2/7th Field Company, to destroy enemy guns, vehicles and troops on a ridge about 2 kilometres from the British front. Jeanes prepared painstakingly, reportedly hiding in a wrecked tank for much of the previous day to observe the area of the proposed attack. The raiders were brilliantly successful, destroying four German anti-tank guns, six to eight vehicles, and one field gun. They inflicted about 50 casualties while sustaining eight. Private Derrick 'Red' Franklin (MM) returned driving a recaptured Bren carrier loaded with German prisoners and valuable maps. In a gunfight for the carrier, Franklin used his submachine gun to shoot several Germans, killing two. Franklin reportedly drove to the Regimental Aid Post (RAP) a German he had shot in the stomach. Despite medical treatment, the German died. One of Franklin's friends noted that 'Red was awarded the Military Medal, but as I heard it, would have preferred that his prisoner had lived'. A knee wound Franklin received in New Guinea effectively ended his war service. The main credit for the raid went to Jeanes, for his

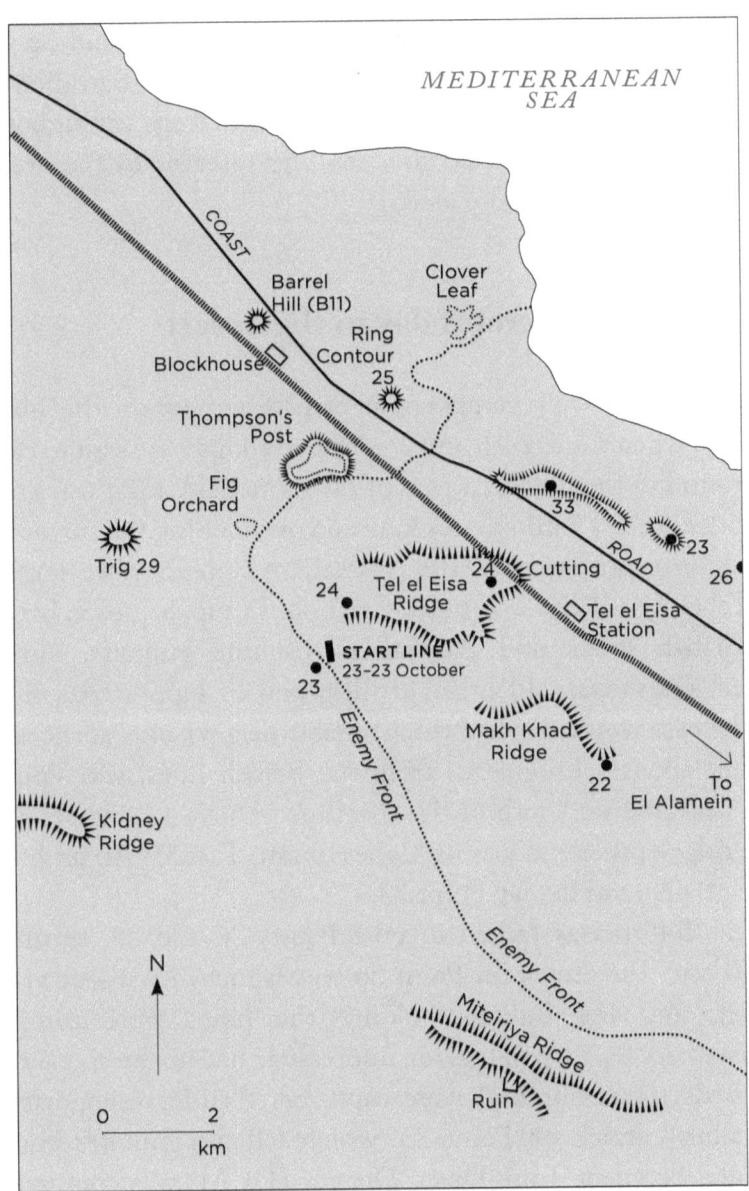

Alamein area, Egypt

planning, organisation and cool leadership. By war's end he would be a lieutenant-colonel, commanding the 2/43rd Battalion with distinction. The 7/8 July raid brought tributes from throughout the 8th Army. Rommel reacted too, sending reserves to the area and ordering troops to be more alert.

A fateful day in the desert

The Australians' July campaign began in earnest on the night of 9/10 July, when the 2/24th and 2/48th battalions were sent to capture key ground in the northern part of the battlefield. First was an east-west ridge, nearly 5 kilometres long and overlooking the surrounding area. After capturing that, the Australians were to move south and take Tel el Eisa Ridge and railway station. In support, each battalion had British tanks and Australian machine gunners, anti-tank gunners and sappers. Plentiful artillery and air support was on hand too. The east-west ridge had three notable heights: one, at the eastern end and about 3 kilometres from the British lines, was Point 26, some 1200 metres south of the coastline. About 4 kilometres away at the ridge's other end was its highest point, Trig 33. About halfway between, on a saddle, lay Point 23.

The 2/48th was tasked to take Points 26 and 23, setting out at 3.40 am. The attack on Point 26 was launched without artillery support, and the Italians holding the point were completely surprised: some, in pyjamas or undressed, had to be roused from their beds. Four hundred were captured. Artillery supported the Australians' attack on Point 23, which fell five minutes ahead of schedule. Sergeant Tom 'Diver' Derrick (DCM) was credited with capturing, through 'his own personal courage and leadership', three Fiat machine-gun nests and 100 Italians. It was the first noteworthy action of a remarkable career.

In the meantime, the 2/24th launched their assault, aimed at taking Trig 33. Advancing via sand dunes near the coast, they too surprised pyjama-clad men, but enemy resistance gradually stiffened.

A lone platoon sent ahead to clear the dunes met severe opposition. Lance-Corporal Jack Holman (MM) and his section captured four machine guns and their crews. This South Australian farmer was killed in the battle of El Alamein that October. The battalion's Bren carriers, armed with an unorthodox assortment of anti-tank guns and machine guns, used their mobility superbly and captured two troops of anti-tank guns in a daring assault. Here, Sergeant Errol Hewitt (MM) directed his section brilliantly and, after the death of one officer and the evacuation of another, commanded the platoon during later defensive fighting.

The 2/24th achieved a remarkable coup in these sand dunes: the capture of a highly efficient and important German unit, Intercept and Intelligence Company 621, which was camped there. Its commander was mortally wounded and some 70 men and their equipment captured. While detached Australians consolidated in the dunes, the 2/24th's main body swung left towards Trig 33, which they captured easily by 7.45 am.

Half an hour earlier, the 2/48th's men set off from Point 26 for their next objective, the Tel el Eisa station area. As they did so, enemy field guns near the station opened fire from close range. Following orders to silence these guns, Sergeant Weston, who won a Distinguished Conduct Medal at Tobruk, led his platoon across open ground, supported only by mortar fire. When close enough they charged, bayonets fixed. They sustained casualties from the guns but, largely because of Weston's inspiring courage, captured the crews. Corporal Jim 'Spud' Hinson (DCM) and his section braved point-blank fire to charge and take two guns and their crews at bayonet point. Thus, one platoon captured 106 men (reportedly mostly Germans) and at least four guns. Hinson, an English-born car trimmer, had barely begun to fight.

The 2/48th advance reached and occupied Tel el Eisa station and ground further east. The Australians came under heavy shelling but could dig only a few centimetres into the hard ground. British tanks and Australian machine gunners and anti-tank men joined them, though their tanks were soon forced back. An enterprising

2/24th officer, recently commissioned Lieutenant Ted Bell (MC), took out his platoon from Trig 33 and captured four siege guns and 100 Italians. Later that day he attacked enemy tanks with anti-tank grenades. On 22 July, a week before his 30th birthday, this South Australian tractor driver sustained a serious wound that cost him his left leg.

As 10 July drew on, Rommel's determination to recapture the ground from the Australians became increasingly obvious. Air attacks hit the east-west ridge, and the Australians repulsed probing infantry and tank attacks on Trig 33.

The first truly menacing attack came at 2.30 pm when ten tanks advanced towards the forward 2/48th companies south of Trig 33. The Panzers emerged through the artillery fire and reached the foremost Australians near the station. Unprotected by anti-tank mines, the men had to 'lie doggo' while the tanks ran over their slit trenches, crushing one man's shoulder.

The Australians fought back, though, using 'sticky' anti-tank grenades. Sergeant Bob Haynes jumped from his trench and placed a sticky bomb on one Panzer, which caught fire in the explosion. Its crew were shot down as they emerged. Haynes himself fell from a gunshot wound to the left chest but survived to fight again. In 1943 he received a Commendation Card. Opposition from Haynes and other infantrymen, as well as the anti-tank guns and field guns, forced the tanks back.

Later that afternoon, approximately 30 tanks advanced on Trig 33. Australian anti-tank guns picked off many, including some that became bogged in a saltmarsh. Gunner James McMahon (DCM) was outstanding as No. 1 on his gun, probably a 2-pounder, which he towed forward of the other guns. Three other crew members were wounded, as was he in the leg and hand (two fingers injured by the gun's recoil), but he fought on, destroying two enemy tanks. The commanding officer of the nearby 2/24th reported of McMahon: 'During the enemy counterattack I saw him well forward of the other A Tk gun positions continue to operate his gun though wounded and in pain. He had to be forcibly evacuated to the RAP and refused to leave while the action was on.' The tank and infantry attack was repulsed. McMahon was a regimental 'character'.

That afternoon, intense artillery fire fell on the two forward 2/48th companies near Tel el Eisa station. Communications between them were cut, and Signalman Dick Ramsdale (MM) of 9th Division Signals was sent forward to connect an alternative line. Under enemy fire and observation, he walked and crawled at least 1000 metres, and worked for two-and-a-half hours to provide this critical link. He then volunteered to provide another line and did so with raw and bleeding hands. The farm labourer from South Australia was later wounded at Alamein.

The enemy sent a seemingly overwhelming force to recapture the railway station from a 2/48th company not yet fully dug in. The Australians held on thanks largely to the leadership of Captain Col Williams (MC). He was killed 12 days later, without hearing of his award.

Ramsdale's connecting work was timely, for the heavy German shelling foreshadowed another attack on the two forward companies. With no anti-tank mines protecting the Australians, tanks drove among them at will. Company commander Captain Don Bryant (MC) remained in communication with battalion headquarters, calling in artillery fire and giving a running commentary. When asked about the situation, he replied coolly, 'She's sweet', a comment that entered battalion folklore. Having led the company on to Point 26, he now inspired them to hold on against the tanks. Bryant was later badly wounded at Alamein, but remained in the Army, receiving an MBE and retiring as a lieutenant-colonel.

While German tanks drove across trenches, calling on the Australians to surrender, Jim Hinson leapt from cover. This fine athlete raced to a Panzer and, after placing a sticky bomb, slid into a nearby trench and heard it explode. When an anti-tank shell hit another tank and set it alight, Hinson again left cover despite heavy shelling, this time chasing down and capturing the crew.

Amidst the German tanks and shelling, Sergeant Weston moved among his sections, instructing and encouraging. Like Hinson, he captured the escaping crew of a destroyed tank. For his efforts on this day, Weston added a Military Medal to his Distinguished Conduct Medal, but a tank ran over the Tommy gun that had helped him win the earlier decoration. This tall, well-built 30-year-old tractor driver would be severely wounded at Alamein, but still carry a wounded comrade more than a kilometre to a dressing station. He would serve in New Guinea and participate in the Australian contingent of the Victory march in London. Hinson would get to wear his Distinguished Conduct Medal ribbon, but die at Alamein in October.

Tanks attacked an Australian machine-gun platoon near the station, deliberately trying to crush them by making sudden turns and dropping the tracks into the trenches. One tank track scraped Sergeant John Cockram's back, crushed his water bottle and mess tin and bent his rifle barrel. After the war it emerged that the tank had broken three of his vertebrae, but now Cockram (MID) sought revenge: he chased the tank and stuck an anti-tank grenade on it, only to realise, when no explosion followed, that he had not pulled the pin. When his platoon commander was mortally wounded, Cockram took over.

Another machine gunner, Sergeant Gus Longhurst (MM), likewise ignored bullets from Panzer machine guns and calls for surrender and, jumping from his trench, chased a tank for 50 metres. Though a fine rugby player, he could not reach it. Yet as the tanks headed towards the station, anti-tank guns knocked out several and he brought his Vickers machine gun to bear on one escaping crew. They took cover in a trench, but, in a remarkable feat of strength, Longhurst lifted the 43-kilogram weight of the entire gun and tripod and, with the help of Private Bill Selmes, fired about 150 rounds at them. The crew surrendered. Longhurst's bravery inspired those around him, but the devout Christian impressed them too when, changing from avenger to Samaritan, he used his field dressing to treat the most seriously wounded German. In April 1945, then a lieutenant with the 24th Battalion, 27-year-old Longhurst was killed in action on Bougainville.

Corporal Jim Hinson is congratulated by his commanding officer on his Distinguished Conduct Medal in Egypt in August 1942. Another winner, Sergeant Jack 'Tex' Weston, is waiting to add his congratulations.
AWM 024750

At about 7.30 pm, the Germans sent in a really determined tank and infantry attack. They pushed one 2/48th company back, but a resolute counterattack by another of the battalion's companies, shouting, 'Come on, Australianos!', forced a German retreat to their starting positions. Sergeant Derrick damaged two German tanks with sticky grenades.

Thus ended 10 July 1942, a day of great achievement for the 9th Australian Division, which had captured important ground and a key intelligence unit, inflicted more than 1000 casualties at a cost of fewer than 100, and destroyed up to 22 tanks.

Hard fighting for Tel el Eisa

Early on 11 July, the 2/24th, supported by anti-tank gunners and machine gunners, captured East Point 24 on Tel el Eisa Ridge and 260 prisoners. Both sides had artillery observation over this ridge, and Australian casualties mounted during the day. Three Australian and two Commonwealth artillery regiments drove off several German assaults. The 2/8th Australian Field Regiment, fighting its first battle, gave crucial support, largely because of its forward observers near East Point 24 and the railway cutting. When one FOO was wounded, his assistant, Gunner Alan Kinghorn (DCM), took over. Kinghorn had no experience shooting with live ammunition, but 'shot' his troop and battery for four hours, until relieved by Lieutenant Tom Smith. Thirty minutes later, shrapnel knocked Smith unconscious, and Kinghorn again took charge, this time for three hours. All day this 36-year-old Hobart office worker played a vital part in holding off enemy tank and infantry attacks.

Late that day, a 2/23rd Battalion company took position on Trig 33's forward slopes, and on 12 July, faced the full brunt of German artillery, followed by up to 2000 infantrymen of the 21st Panzer Division. The company Bren gunners forced enemy infantry to ground, but took great risks: Private Ted Buckingham (MID) had two Brens shot from his hands in succession but continued with a third. A major German attack on Trig 33 late in the afternoon was repelled, costing Rommel some 600 dead. Australian artillery contributed substantially, as did a platoon from the 2/2nd Machine Gun Battalion. On 10 July, Corporal Vic Knight (DCM) and his section of two guns had carried their Vickers across Trig 33 under fire, set them up on the surface and provided invaluable support. Now, while covering the ridge's southern slopes, news came of enemy advancing on the right. Knight moved his section over the ridge, through intense enemy artillery, mortar and machine-gun fire. On arrival, they had no time to dig in, but set up their guns (initially two, later three) in the open and fired bursts of 100–150 rounds at German infantry emerging from half-tracks. Closely packed and advancing in waves, they presented a fine target, though mortars, artillery, tank guns and small arms supported them. Knight's men were never pinpointed, for whenever enemy fire got too close, he moved the guns backwards or forwards. Knight displayed inspiring nonchalance, standing and directing the deadly fire of his machine gunners, which hit targets as distant as 5000 metres. They used oil, water, soup and urine to keep the guns sufficiently lubricated and cooled to keep going for several hours. At nightfall, Knight and the gun crews – apart from two wounded men, one of whom Knight carried out – could finally dig in. His platoon's four guns fired 80 000 rounds that day. Knight, an English immigrant who once worked as a butler in NSW, later blamed a personality clash with an officer for preventing him from gaining a commission. Knight had left Australia a sergeant and returned in 1943 a corporal. He later served as a warrant-officer in Korea.

Australian gunners of the 2/3rd Anti-Tank Regiment showed cold-blooded courage in waiting for enemy tanks to drive within range. Tanks with 75mm and 50mm guns were more powerful than the Australians' 2-pounders (40mm) and 6-pounders (57mm), and they always carried machine guns that could inflict havoc among the gunners, whose only protection comprised gun shields and whatever concealment and cover they could find in the desert. On 13 July, when Panzers and infantry approached Tel el Eisa from the south-west, Bombardier Richard Cotterill (DCM) and his 6-pounder anti-tank gun crew knocked out four tanks. On the evening of 14 July, during another powerful attack, three of Cotterill's crew were killed or wounded, but they destroyed three tanks before the remaining gunner was killed and their gun disabled. Though wounded, Cotterill attached himself to the nearest infantry unit and acted as a runner to the company commander until the attack was repulsed.

Sergeant Reg Roberts (DCM) commanded an anti-tank gun, but when enemy infantry attacked without tank support on 13 and 14 July, he repeatedly took up a Bren and assisted the Australian infantry. He also directed his anti-tank gun when from an exposed position on 14 July it knocked out two German light field guns. When a 'tanks alert' sounded that evening, he again took charge as his crew destroyed two tanks. By nightfall, his gun was damaged but he and another sergeant beat off a lone tank that had broken through. When a withdrawal was ordered, Roberts extricated his men safely. He was wounded later in July, but by 1945 was a captain in the Far East Liaison Office. Roberts received an MBE for meritorious service, including intelligence patrols behind enemy lines in New Guinea, the Moluccas and Borneo.

The 2/3rd Anti-Tank Regiment suffered more than 100 casualties in the July fighting. The dead included Gunner Cecil Spittle, a gun layer who knocked out three tanks with three rounds from his 2-pounder on 14 July. A fourth tank then scored a direct hit on the gun, killing Spittle and wounding the other crewmen. For all the gunners' heroics, by day's end, the Australians had abandoned Point 24, withdrawing to Trig 33.

Early on 15 July, a German column comprising a tank and three vehicles mounting anti-aircraft or anti-tank guns approached the 2/48th positions near Tel el Eisa station. In the confusion of battle, Tom Derrick ventured out and placed a sticky grenade on the rearmost vehicle, which exploded with a blast so powerful that it knocked 'Diver' over.

A huge volume of shelling, mortar and machine-gun fire fell on the forward slopes of Trig 33 that morning, and at one stage, a section of 13 Australian machine gunners were almost the only Australians still there. Four were killed, three wounded and three later evacuated with shock. After six German tanks approached within 400 metres and opened fire with machine guns, the Australian gunners withdrew. Lance-Corporal Eric Brandrick (MM) returned through this fire to rescue a seriously wounded man and then made a second trip to save another. When the unaccompanied German tanks withdrew, the Australians reoccupied the forward slopes.

On 16 July, two 2/23rd companies and five British tanks were sent to recapture East and West Points 24 of Tel el Eisa Ridge. When close-range fire from an enemy post at the Cutting pinned down the foremost platoon, Lance-Corporal John Bell (MM) led the reserve section to a flank. He leapt over an embankment into the Cutting and, while his comrades threw grenades, inflicted heavy casualties with his Tommy gun. The platoon captured 30 Germans. By 6.30 am, one company had taken East Point 24. Captain Keith Neuendorf (MID) now led the second company towards West Point 24. Intense enemy fire was inflicting casualties, but Neuendorf coolly directed return fire. While pressing the bell on a tank to communicate with the commander, his hand was shot away. Undaunted, he pulled out a bootlace and, helped by his runner, tied it as a tourniquet. Taking an Italian pistol from one of his wounded officers, he was inspiring, one moment calling his men on, the next ordering them to ground, while he remained standing. Though wounded a second time, Neuendorf pushed on.

Enemy troops began surrendering in large numbers. By 7.43 am, the Australians were occupying West Point 24. While digging in they were deluged by shelling and machine-gun fire. Neuendorf walked through it, directing the tanks. The Australians destroyed more resistance nests and took more prisoners, but as Neuendorf walked back after helping a wounded man, a salvo of shells killed him. His body was found days later, pistol still in hand. He was recommended for a posthumous Victoria Cross. The initial recommendation was rejected as inadequately written and entered on the wrong application form, but Morshead then approved it. However, the recommendation seems then to have effectively been lost, for it was not considered again until 1945. Only in 1946 was Neuendorf posthumously awarded a Mention in Despatches. By the time Neuendorf fell, the Australians had taken 601 prisoners, but the 2/23rd commander, Lieutenant-Colonel Evans, decided that the newly won ground was untenable and pulled them back. Ninety of the 200 Australian participants in the attack were killed or wounded.

Fighting for Makh Khad and Miteiriya ridges

On the night of 16/17 July, the 24th Australian Brigade was sent to maintain pressure on Rommel by attacking south and taking Trig 22 on Makh Khad Ridge, and Miteiriya or 'Ruin' Ridge. British tanks and artillery provided support. The 2/32nd Battalion captured, lost and recaptured Trig 22 in heavy fighting. A squadron of the 9th Division Cavalry Regiment, operating seven Crusader tanks and 15 Bren carriers, contributed substantially. This force, under Captain Henry Fyffe (MC), was, according to his citation, fighting the 'first Tank action ever fought by an Australian Unit' (though Australian light tanks had fought in Libya and Syria), and much depended on him. It also depended on his tank crews, like Trooper Bill Masterson (MM), a gunner in a Crusader. During the advance, this tank suddenly came upon a well-concealed anti-tank gun just 30 metres distant. Masterson opened fire with his Besa machine gun, which killed two enemy crewmen but then jammed. He calmly tried to clear it, but could not, and as the remaining enemy gunners were bringing their gun to bear on the tank, he fired the 2-pounder gun. This scored a direct hit, knocking out the anti-tank gun. Fyffe's squadron eliminated several other anti-tank and machine-gun posts. Under intense shelling, Fyffe cheerfully directed the disposition of his vehicles, often on foot. He personally organised the evacuation of the wounded.

The 2/43rd passed through Trig 22 at about 6 am, then set off to cover the 5 kilometres to Ruin Ridge. It was daylight and they immediately came under extremely heavy shell fire, including airburst shells exploding overhead. Captain John Gordon (MC) and his company on the left met stiff resistance from Italians confronting them. In the section on the far left, all but Private Hollister Dean (MM) were hit. Dean fought back with his Bren, wiping out an enemy machine-gun post and keeping the flank secure. A butcher in civil life, Dean was killed in New Guinea the following year, aged 35. Gordon, aged just 23, led his company on to the objective, taking 400 prisoners en route. He then personally led them against enemy artillery batteries that were firing at close range. His men captured the gun positions and took another 150 prisoners, but soon massing enemy tanks and infantry menaced the whole battalion. Lacking anti-tank guns and low on ammunition, the 2/43rd withdrew to Makh Khad Ridge.

There the pressure intensified on the 2/32nd Battalion. At 10 am, tanks and armoured cars attacked the Australians. The anti-tank guns that forced them back included an unusual one. Corporal 'Curly' Leeson (DCM) of the 2/32nd had developed a reputation in Tobruk as a fearless patroller. The Queensland electrician's labourer had got a captured 20mm Breda anti-aircraft gun working and received permission to use it. During this counterattack, he came under machine-gun, anti-tank and mortar fire, but managed to knock out two and probably three enemy vehicles. Eventually, an enemy anti-tank shell struck his gun and threw him out of the gun pit with a face wound. Undaunted, he repaired the gun and resumed firing. He later left the pit to rescue a man lying exposed under fire. In doing so Leeson was wounded more seriously, in the hip, but returned to the gun and used it against enemy aircraft. This irrepressible soldier would be killed on 31 October in the Alamein battle. On 17 July he helped to consolidate the gains near Trig 22, where Private Tom Langford (MM), a stretcher-bearer, had just brought in a casualty. The medical officer said to him 'I'll be with you in a moment or two' – but found he was talking to thin air, as Langford was darting off in the distance after the next casualty. By day's end he had rescued 14 men.

On 17 July, the 24th Brigade took over 700 Italian prisoners and prompted Rommel to commit German tanks to prevent the loss of more ground. In the late afternoon, some of these tanks attacked again, overrunning several platoons and pushing the Australians back more than a kilometre. The situation was stabilised, partly due to the skill and courage of anti-tank gunner Lance-Sergeant Dan Daley (DCM). The tall station hand kept his gun working despite wounds in the wrist, upper arm and forehead. His gun knocked out six Panzer III tanks. Daley survived the war but died in an accident in 1949. He was driving a car that left the road near Moree at speed, killing him and four passengers. Daley was the fourth anti-tank gunner to earn a Distinguished Conduct Medal between 10 and 17 July.

Attempting the impossible

When General Sir Claude Auchinleck – who had succeeded Wavell – launched a series of 8th Army offensives on 21–22 July, Australian troops were among those committed. In the north, the 26th Australian Brigade was ordered to secure the right flank by capturing Tel el Eisa, and also Ring Contour 25, a position on the coast road that led to Rommel's main command and supply base on the Alamein front. Considering the meagre forces allotted, these were impossible tasks. The 2/24th and 2/48th had to continue holding their current positions, so could only spare two companies each for their attacks. The 2/23rd would attack too. The 2/24th's companies came under machine-gun fire as soon as they advanced, but Captain Bill Mollard's (MID) company secured Ring Contour 25 with light casualties. However, as they began digging holes in the open rocky ground, heavy machine-gun fire swept their positions, while German troops seemed to be arriving from all sides. Seven of the company's eight corporals were killed or wounded. Sergeant Bill Hughes (DCM) fought back. The platoon he commanded was on the objective, but pinned down by two German machine guns, 100 metres away. Hughes crawled forward, though still under fire, to a position where he could shoot. With two rifle shots, the 34-year-old dairy farmer disabled the No. 1 of each gun. Although these gunners were replaced by their No. 2s, he also despatched them, with two more shots. Nevertheless, the platoon had to withdraw. As they did so, Hughes heard cries for help from Corporal Bob Beecroft, some 150 metres away. Hughes went back and carried Beecroft until Beecroft was hit again and killed outright. Later, at Alamein, Hughes would be badly wounded in both knees and the left arm. This ended his frontline career. Mollard's men tried to hang on and maintain contact with the other company, which was also suffering. Its commander and second-in-command were both wounded and evacuated, leaving Lieutenant Albert 'Bunny' Austin (MC) in charge. Austin, a 23-year-old schoolteacher from Murtoa, was a recent arrival and barely knew the men. However, aided by the lone surviving NCO, Sergeant Gordon Annear (MID), he held the scattered unit together. When a withdrawal order came, Austin told Annear to assemble the able-bodied and accompany them back, while he stayed to gather and evacuate the wounded. Austin was now himself wounded in the leg but survived. The 22 July fighting reduced the two companies involved to just 74 men between them. The battalion estimated that they had inflicted 250 casualties.

Like the 2/24th, the 2/23rd met fierce resistance. Nevertheless, they took East Point 24. That feature was then shrouded in smoke from enemy artillery as German infantry fought to recapture it. After taking forward a mortar detachment in his Bren carrier, Corporal John McCluskey picked up wounded and took them back. He then collected and delivered ammunition, and on his own initiative established contact between the company commanders, who had been out of communication. McCluskey loaded his vehicle with wounded again, but his carrier was hit and he was thrown clear. After coming to, he repaired the carrier under fire and continued. Private Ron Claffey (MM) drove a truck over the battlefield and rescued more than 30 casualties in his bullet-riddled and shrapnel-damaged vehicle. Three times he insisted on going through seemingly impassable fire, despite attempts to restrain him.

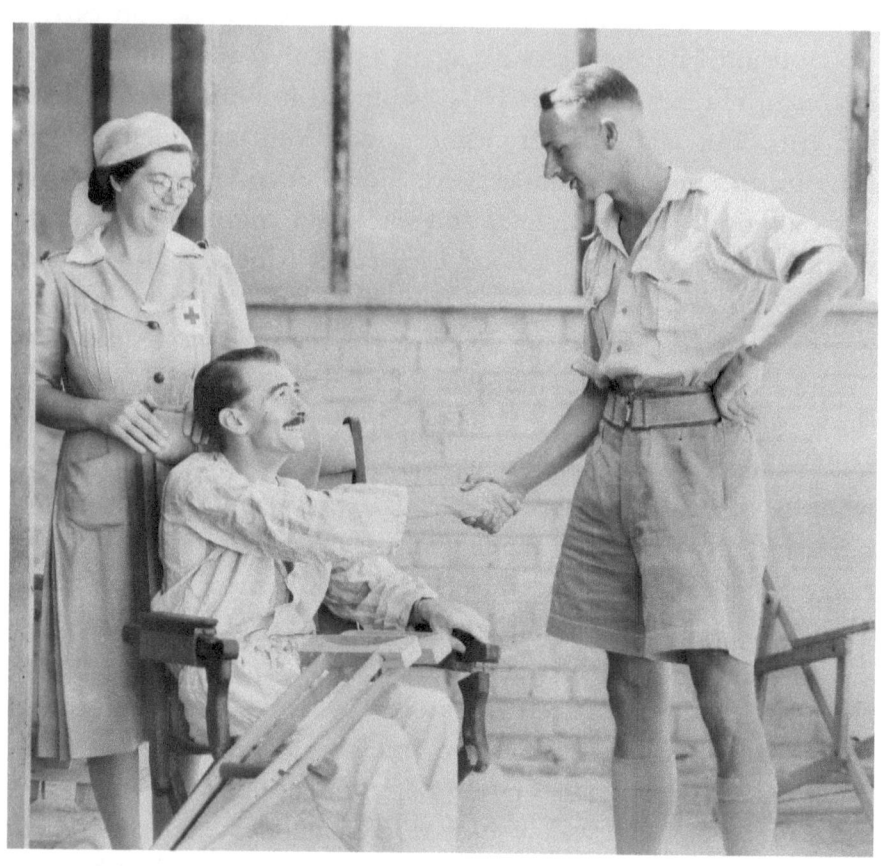

Lieutenant Albert 'Bunny' Austin, MC, in pyjamas, recovering from wounds received on 22 July 1942. The 23-year-old schoolteacher from Murtoa, Victoria had only just arrived at the 2/24th Battalion when he had to take command of a decimated company and lead its men to safety.
AWM 024865

One 2/23rd company advanced on the right after seeing the 2/24th's success signal from Ring Contour 25. Mollard observed them struggling forward under fire so heavy that all but one officer and half the company were soon dead or wounded. The lone officer on his feet, Lieutenant Ken Clarke (MC), was wounded in the ankle almost as soon as he came forward. A sniper shot away the wireless aerial, but eventually someone crawled out and called down smoke. By the time the company could withdraw through the smoke, Clarke was unable to walk. He and other casualties lay in the sun all day, but a patrol rescued them at night. In the week leading to 22 July, all of the 2/23rd's company commanders were killed and their replacements became casualties too.

While the 2/23rd fought for East Point 24, the 2/48th's two companies advanced on West Point 24. Both radios were soon out of commission, and they met intense artillery and mortar fire. Three of B Company's four officers were soon hit, and the sole survivor was out of communication on a flank. Sergeant Wally Pryor (DCM) took charge. He led the company into position and then, despite lacking maps, directed the defence until 8 pm. At dusk, with enemies moving in to surround them, he ordered the company to withdraw, taking along their wounded. On getting back, B Company comprised just 15 men. Pryor, a builder's labourer, finished the war a captain.

The other 2/48th company was pinned down by machine-gun fire and artillery too, just 100 metres short of the enemy positions. In an astonishing act of initiative, Private Stan Gurney (VC) stood up and charged the nearest machine gun. After hurling a grenade from just metres away, he bayoneted a German who emerged and confronted him. He and a comrade then ran into the post and together bayoneted another two Germans. Gurney then charged into the second post, where he bayoneted two more Germans and sent another out as a prisoner. As he charged a third post, an exploding grenade knocked him off his feet. Undeterred, he got up, grabbed his rifle, and entered another post, where he was last seen vigorously using the bayonet. Gurney's action, later recognised by a posthumous Victoria Cross, enabled his company to approach to within 150 metres of their objective, but again they became pinned down. The soldier who accompanied Gurney was Private Ivan Hanel, a 32-year-old metal polisher from Adelaide. He had often been in trouble with the military authorities, especially for being AWL. Like Gurney, he was killed in the fighting on 22 July. Private Herb Ashby (DCM), of the same company, commanded a section that became separated early on. He did not retreat despite intense enemy fire from in front and on the flanks. In the late afternoon, a British Valentine tank was knocked out nearby and Germans captured its crew and two of Ashby's men. On Ashby's orders, his remaining men opened fire on these Germans, killing them and rescuing the prisoners. For at least 14 hours he and his section inflicted casualties. In the entire action, the 2/48th sustained 115 casualties. The positive outcome was that the Germans abandoned both Points 24.

On 22 July, the 24th Brigade advanced again towards Trig 22 and Ruin Ridge. The 2/32nd took Trig 22 again, despite heavy losses. The 2/28th was ordered to take Ruin Ridge but stopped short of their objective thanks to misidentification of the ridge's location and misunderstandings with supporting British armour. One 2/43rd Battalion company supported the 2/32nd advance and was guided to its start-line by Lance-Corporal Jim Maddocks (MM) of the 2/43rd Intelligence Section. The company commander was soon mortally wounded and the leading platoon pinned down. On his own initiative, Maddocks went forward and found the platoon. It was under fire from in front and a machine-gun post just 25 metres away to the right. Acting alone, Maddocks grabbed the muzzle of an abandoned 88mm gun and swung it around until it pointed at the machine-gun post. Bluffed, the strongpoint's 15 Germans surrendered. Maddocks then brought up machine gunners who helped to consolidate the position.

Lieutenant Richard 'Darky' Cameron (DSO) took forward 13 machine gunners of the 2/2nd Machine Gun Battalion at dawn to support the 2/32nd's advance. He headed for the crest of a ridge allotted to them in planning but found it more than 300 metres from the nearest Australian infantry. Moreover, German machine gunners had got there first, and enemy mortars were firing on them from the ridge's reverse slope. Cameron had no time to dig in so ordered his two Vickers guns to set up in the open. On coming into action, they silenced all but one German machine gun, which inflicted two casualties. Cameron crawled forward to a position where he could fire his pistol at the lone German gunner some 75 metres away. Cameron then stood up and ran at the German, who was shot down by another Australian. Cameron grabbed the MG34 and turned it on the German mortar and anti-tank crews on the reverse slope. The gun soon jammed, though, and he ran back to his section through enemy fire. The Vickers gunners fired all morning, but with enemy airburst seeking them out, they eventually pulled back. Machine-gun fire hit George Hoskins in the shoulder, forcing him to drop a Vickers tripod, but his No. 2, Ron 'Jockey' McGregor (MM), went to him while carrying the gun and helped him back, despite being wounded in the shoulder himself en route. Then, without the tripod, McGregor set up the Vickers on a rock to fire it. By the time Cameron returned to the group after liaising with nearby infantry, only five of his men were still upright. He reorganised them into two gun teams and, taking his own turn on the gun, kept them operating for the following 24 hours. For four hours his unit was well in front of the nearest Australians. All but four of the 13 men who went out in his section became casualties. Apart from Cameron, whose Distinguished Service Order was a rare award to a subaltern, and McGregor, seven others received recognition: one Mentioned in Despatches and six Commander-in-Chief's Commendation cards.

Tragedy on Ruin Ridge

The 2/28th was sent south again on the night of 27/28 July to take Ruin Ridge. This time they reached the objective but became cut off and surrounded. At 7.30 am, intense fire pushed back the platoon on the battalion's left flank. Jumping from his weapon pit, Warrant-Officer Class 2 Fred Holding (DCM) ordered the men not to withdraw beyond the ridge and instead personally led them forward to their previous positions. His survival seemed almost miraculous as he moved continuously around the company area, ignoring intense machine-gun, mortar and artillery fire.

Gunner Athol Manning (MM) went forward in the initial advance with a 2/7th Field Regiment FOO, Captain Arthur Fielding. After the battalion wireless truck was blown up in a minefield, Fielding's Bren carrier contained the only functioning wireless on the ridge. When static made the wireless unworkable, the 2/28th commanding officer asked Fielding to go back to brigade headquarters, make contact and bring back much-needed ammunition. Manning accordingly drove the carrier through heavy fire, despite twice being challenged and fired upon by enemy patrols. Fielding urged Manning on as they approached burning vehicles in the minefield gap but was killed in an exchange of fire. The carrier then ran onto a mine. Manning risked his life to crawl through the minefield, still under fire. He reached brigade headquarters and delivered the message he had overheard Fielding receive. Staff-Sergeant Ken Lyall (MM) of the 2/28th was a company quartermaster-sergeant with the task of getting his vehicles with crucial supplies through to his company. They negotiated the minefield and enemy artillery fire to make it. Later, despite knowing the battalion was surrounded, Lyall volunteered to drive a truck back to brigade headquarters with a message about the state of communications, equipment and ammunition. While crossing the minefield, Lyall's truck was hit by an enemy shell and forced onto a mine. He and his driver, Laurie Pilmer, were thrown clear in the explosion but escaped to 2/43rd Battalion HQ, where Lyall delivered his message.

Despite these brave acts, the fate of the surrounded men was sealed when British tanks could not reach them. Instead, German tanks forced the survivors to surrender. Warrant-Officer Alan McIlrick (MID) of the 2/3rd Anti-Tank Regiment served a 6-pounder anti-tank gun until the gun was knocked out and he was killed. Four months later, when the ground was recaptured, the gun was surrounded by 19 used 6-pounder shells and six knocked-out tanks. McIlrick had won the Military Medal in May 1941 due to his courageous leadership commanding a gun in a rearguard action against 50 enemy tanks at Khireigat, Egypt. This ironworker's body was never found. The 2/28th suffered more than 500 casualties at Ruin Ridge.

Patrols and raids

The Ruin Ridge fighting marked the end of the July battles. The next large-scale fighting at Alamein occurred in October, but there was much patrolling in the intervening months. One outstanding patroller was the 2/15th Battalion's Captain Bill Cobb (Bar to MC). Cobb's fine patrolling and leadership in Tobruk earned him a Military Cross and helped establish the unit's esprit de corps. At Alamein on 4/5 August 1942, he led a 13-strong fighting patrol tasked with identifying the German unit facing them. Some 2700 metres out, the patrol was challenged. They went to ground and waited 20 minutes in silence. Cobb realised that the enemy suspected their presence but was determined to complete his mission. Hearing the bolt of a German machine gun pulled back in a post just 15 metres away, he decided to attack. He led the assault, throwing a 69 grenade that silenced the 'Spandau', but not before a burst wounded him in the leg and hit two other patrollers. The survivors pushed on, killing six. Corporal Alick Else (MM) took a prisoner. Cobb ordered a withdrawal and went to help subdue the uncooperative prisoner. Germans in nearby posts were firing, and a short-range submachine-gun burst killed the prisoner and struck Cobb's arm. Cobb shot the submachine gunner with his pistol and, ignoring enemy fire, searched the dead prisoner's body and cut off his shoulder straps. These and the man's paybook helped to identify the enemy unit.

As the patrol withdrew, Cobb blacked out due to his wound. Else took command and, after giving orders, took Cobb on his back. When Cobb came to and told Else he could stumble along, Else replied that he would carry Cobb even if he were 'bloody well dead'.

Other men helped and eventually they found a stretcher, while Else made numerous direction changes to ensure that the party evaded enemy fire. Cobb, a tall Queensland grazier, was killed on the first night of the battle of El Alamein, mourned by a company who loved him for his courage and sympathetic leadership. Else, another Queensland farmer, would win a Bar to his Military Medal the following year in New Guinea, where as a sergeant he led his platoon in a close-quarters attack at Kumawa. It was a poignant award for Alick, whose younger brother Cyril was killed in the same attack.

On 1 September, the 2/15th was sent with British tank support to capture West Point 23, a strongly defended position south-west of Tel el Eisa. This ambitious attack, codenamed 'Bulimba', was officially a diversion. Two companies led the advance that morning. The right-hand company was under Captain Lance Bode, who had won a Military Cross for leading a superbly successful raid in Tobruk and whom Morshead considered one of the division's best soldiers. After making some progress, this company became pinned down and Bode was killed, as was Lieutenant Ron Patrick, who as a sergeant had won the Military Medal in the same raid as Bode, personally killing four Italians. The left-hand company, following close behind the supporting artillery barrage, was more successful. Captain Len Snell (MC) led the men with dash, carrying a rifle and bayonet, and together they crossed the minefield and overcame a series of enemy posts before reaching the objective. One section was mopping up behind two others, but as they went through the outer wire of German defences, the section commander was killed and just four men were left standing. Private Reg Bambling (DCM) took command and led them through the inner wire where he could see an enemy post firing at the forward troops who had unknowingly bypassed it. Firing his Bren from the hip and calling the men on, Bambling charged this post, killing five Germans and capturing an officer and ten men. After detailing a man to escort these prisoners back, Bambling and his two remaining soldiers attacked another post 50 metres away. Again he fired from the hip, but went down on being shot in the back and left shoulder. As he lay in the open, mortar fire lacerated his legs. A British tank appeared and Bambling pointed out the enemy post to its commander and asked him to fire at it. The tank did so, killing and forcing the surrender of more enemy. Bambling was credited with ten enemy killed, 35 captured, and silencing four Spandaus and five submachine guns. The two brave men who accompanied him, unnamed in the records, carried him out. Bambling's three wounds were serious but he survived, finishing the war a lance-sergeant.

Corporal Horton McLachlan (DCM) led another section in Bulimba. As he attacked German posts on the assault's southern boundary, grenade fragments blinded his platoon commander, Lieutenant Dave Weir. 'Kill that German', Weir urged McLachlan, who obeyed by putting a bayonet through the enemy soldier. McLachlan paused briefly to take stock, then circled behind a German machine-gun crew firing from the left. He bayoneted the two gunners and then, as he moved back to his section, bayoneted another German who confronted him. He next swapped his rifle and bayonet for a Tommy gun from a wounded man and, after trying unsuccessfully to obtain more men from his officer to tackle two machine-gun posts on a ridge 200 metres up ahead and to the right, 'decided that I would have a go myself'. Using his submachine gun to keep their heads down, he saw two Germans dash from their weapon pit, where their machine gun had jammed, into the other pit. When he was just 20 metres away, all four occupants of the pit jumped out and ran for another dugout. With one burst, McLachlan killed all four. He then reached that dugout and killed its sole occupant. After moving on to yet another dugout and shooting its three defenders, he was out of ammunition and headed back over the ridge. As he crossed a partly covered dugout, a German grabbed him by the leg. McLachlan kicked him into the bunker and, when another German emerged, knocked his helmet off and clubbed him to death with his Tommy gun. One of his men passed him a grenade, which McLachlan threw into the dugout, killing all inside. McLachlan and others then sheltered in dugouts from enemy fire for about an hour, after which orders for withdrawal came. Only Snell and McLachlan made it out from that group. Ivor Hele portrayed McLachlan and Bambling in a memorable painting titled *Operation Bulimba*. A gunshot wound fractured McLachlan's wrist at Alamein in October, ending the frontline service of this station hand from Boggabilla, New South Wales. Sadly, while their actions were outstanding, the raid was largely a failure.

The commanding officer of the 2/15th was badly wounded and the commander of the tank squadron killed. Australian engineers assisted the British tanks. Once gaps had been made in the enemy minefield, Lance-Corporal Harold Baggaley (MM) was ordered to remain at one and ensure the safety of tanks passing through. When other nearby sappers were hit, Baggaley's area of responsibility widened and for two-and-a-half hours he guided tanks and kept them off unmarked minefields. He walked in front of several tanks to direct them and was knocked over when he ran in front of one to prevent it from running on a mine. Hurt but not seriously injured, he dared not leave the post for assistance. When the order to withdraw came he again assisted the tanks through the minefields and was among the last to leave.

By the time the 2/15th retreated, it had suffered 59 dead, two captured and 125 wounded. The unit captured 140 Germans and estimated that they killed 150.

INTERLUDE 2
THE WARRIORS' WEAPONS

Most of the heroic actions in this book involved men using weapons and, more particularly, small arms. The single weapon employed most often by the medal winners was probably the Bren light machine gun. Over 100 individuals named on these pages were Bren gunners or used Bren guns in an impromptu way while performing their notable deeds. Other unnamed Bren gunners feature here too. The most famous named ones were the six who won the Victoria Cross using a Bren – Kingsbury, Kelliher, Rattey, Partridge, Kenna and Starcevich. That's six out of 17 Army Victoria Cross winners in the war. Similarly, nearly a quarter of the men named here as winning Distinguished Conduct Medals and Military Medals did so using a Bren. The firepower of the Bren was the pivot around which Australian small unit tactics revolved. They were not perfect weapons, with many jams and malfunctions throughout the war. Apart from this problem, the Bren weighed more than twice as much as a rifle, and gunners were prime targets for enemy fire. Nevertheless, the gun had a unique appeal among Australian infantry weapons. Firing it in training impressed most users. An astute Australian veteran recalled that even though 'Bren gunner' was a perilous occupation 'nearly every infantry private wanted to be one'.[1] Those who became gunners (and they operated in two-man crews) were often remarkably attached to their Brens. Some were said to nurse them like babies, others to kiss them before going into action, and one war correspondent asserted that 'a Bren gunner in New Guinea would sooner mortgage his life insurance than part with his Bren'.[2]

There are several reasons why Bren gunners did so well. Many able and brave soldiers were attracted to and selected for such a responsible position, which in turn motivated men to perform. Moreover, for all the occasions it failed its gunners, it was probably still the best and most reliable LMG then in use, as the users' attachment to it suggests.

That dynamic was probably at work in the case of Bren gunner Harry Clout. An NCO recalled 'as a parade ground soldier I don't think there would be an NCO or officer in A Company that had not been caused many heart aches by Harry'. The same NCO paid tribute to him, though, as proving himself 'a brave and fearless soldier' in the Owen Stanley campaign. Clout was killed on 21 November 1942.[3]

The submachine gun, another weapon prominent in this book, was not available in large numbers in the early 1941 campaigns, and carrying one came with responsibility. In Malaya, after Japanese troops had seized one private's Tommy gun as he feigned death, the man said, 'I was glad to see the last of the bloody thing. Ever since I've had it I've been in for all the crook jobs.'[4] This attitude was unusual. Submachine guns were usually distributed first to NCOs, for whom it was in part a mark of status, but it was also a weapon, like the Bren, that inspired men to show themselves worthy of it. Submachine guns were ideal for patrolling and close-range work in desert and jungle. The Tommy gun was integral to Australian efforts in the Middle East, Malaya and Papua, as was the Owen gun that replaced it in the course of 1943. Over 80 soldiers mentioned in this book used submachine guns in their noteworthy actions, more than 50 of them with the Australian-designed Owen. Jimmy Anderson and Jimmy Jackson are two examples of many, while two of the Victoria Cross winners – Chowne and Mackey – used submachine guns on the days they died and earned their awards.

Mackey also used a rifle, the standard weapon for most Australian soldiers. More particularly, the great majority used the Short Magazine Lee-Enfield Rifle No 1 Mark III* (SMLE). Indeed, Mackey used his rifle with a bayonet, and he was one of four Victoria Cross winners who used that stabbing weapon. Australians had a high reputation with the bayonet among their allies and enemies, and this weapon, rightly associated with hand-to-hand fighting, features in many of the deeds in the book: some 26 cases in which men used the bayonet themselves, and 27 in which men led bayonet charges (three led charges and used the bayonet). McLachlan and Berry at El Alamein are two examples of many.

Of course, many more men fired rifles than used the attached bayonets. There are numerous stories here of fine marksmen, such as Mulgrave on Crete, Bingham at El Alamein, Plater at Gona, Exton at Wau-Salamaua and 'Hawkeye' Hawke at Wewak. German accounts often acknowledged the accuracy of Australian shooting. Among bolt-action rifles, the SMLE was very good, but it did not fire as fast as the American Garand semi-automatic, let alone a submachine gun, and its limitations were most apparent in the close conditions of jungle fighting. There, automatic weapons and grenades were most useful. Grenades are mentioned hundreds of times here, especially in the jungle, where they were arguably the single most important Australian weapon. The standard Australian 36M grenade was markedly more effective than Japanese and Italian grenades. Prominent among a long list of men whose grenade-throwing made a difference were Clift at the capture of Tobruk, Curren during the siege, Clarence Atkinson in Syria, Wilson in Malaya, Pyke, Simonson, Maidment and Hurrell on the Kokoda Track, Kotz and Ludlow at Milne Bay, Haddy, Plater and Ellis at Gona, Hudson at Buna, Gullett, Watt and Naismith at Wau-Salamaua, Dawes in the Lae campaign, O'Brien at Shaggy Ridge, Hedderman, Stubbs and Warren at Aitape-Wewak and Waters on Tarakan. Some brave men attacked tanks with 'sticky grenades': they included Smithers in Tobruk, Bell, Haynes and Derrick at

Tel el Eisa, and Albrecht and Joyce at Alamein. Kimberley used a blast grenade at Buna, while Gartner, Torrent and Symons used rifle grenades effectively.

Some men showed initiative in turning captured weapons on their erstwhile owners: including Cameron and Davidson at Alamein, Reeve at Wau and Weir on Long Ridge, New Guinea.

A notoriously difficult weapon to use effectively in action was a handgun, but some soldiers managed it. McQuillan captured 60 Italians with one at Bardia, Oldfield killed some Germans with an Italian Beretta in Greece, Cobb killed a submachine gunner who had wounded him in Tobruk, Bingham shot a German machine gunner at Alamein and Healey killed three Japanese at Knife Ford, New Guinea, with his pistol.

Whatever they used, the Australians discussed here made deadly use of the weapons at hand.

CHAPTER 11

KOKODA: THE FIRST CLASHES (JULY–AUGUST 1942)

In New Guinea, the Japanese occupied the strategically important bases at Lae and Salamaua in March 1942. Central to their plans of safeguarding their newly won gains was to capture Port Moresby, with its deep harbour and airfields. They sent an invasion force from Rabaul to take Port Moresby in May, but it was intercepted and forced to retreat in the naval battle of the Coral Sea. However, the Japanese retained naval and air supremacy in the South-West Pacific Area (which included Australia). American General Douglas MacArthur, commanding Allied forces in the area, was still unable to take the initiative. The only conventional Allied fighting forces in New Guinea at the time, and until mid-1942, were poorly equipped and trained Citizen Military Forces (CMF or militia). Australia effectively had two armies at the time, one comprising the volunteers of the AIF, the other the militia – part-volunteer, part-conscript – which was allowed to fight only in defence of Australian soil, including Papua. Soldiers within the militia units could transfer to the AIF, thus acquiring an 'X' service number of the type given to all members of AIF units.

General Blamey, commanding the Australian Army and nominally in charge of Allied Land Forces, advised MacArthur that guerrilla operations were currently the only means of taking the land fight to the Japanese. In April, the 2/5th Independent Company was sent to Port Moresby and, combined with the local militia-type unit,

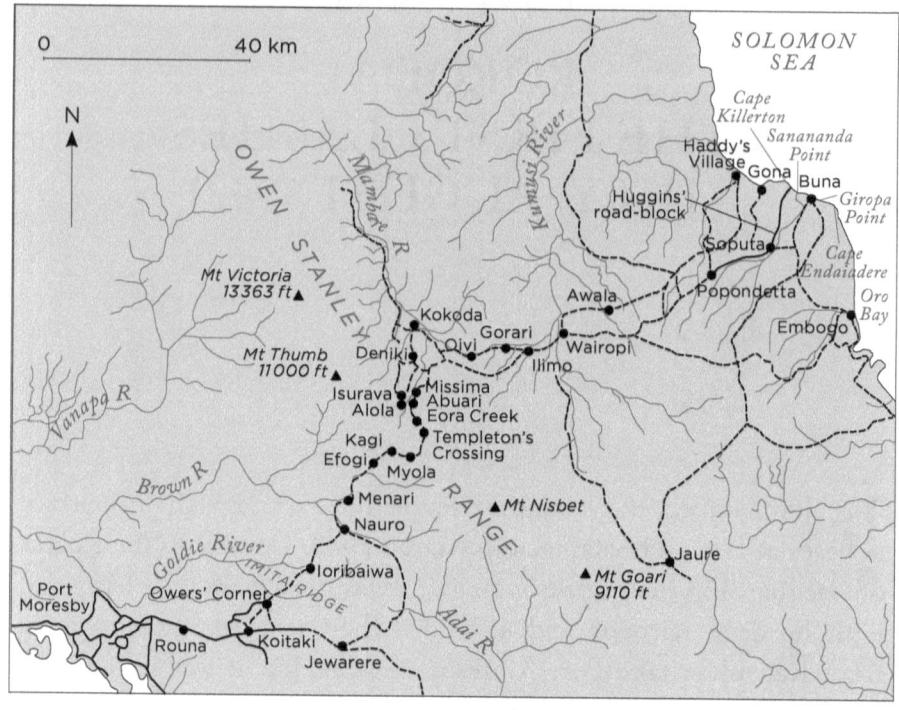

Kokoda and the Papuan beachheads

the New Guinea Volunteer Rifles, comprised 'Kanga Force'. In June–July they made effective attacks behind enemy lines at Salamaua and Heath's Plantation on the Markham River. The commandos' exceptionally dangerous work is exemplified in a night raid later in the year at Mubo. Sergeant Bill O'Neill (DCM) was in a party of three tasked with protecting the rear of the main assault party of 20. When 50 Japanese approached from an unexpected direction, headed by a sword-wielding officer, O'Neill opened fire with his Tommy gun from cover, less than 10 metres away, killing the officer and about a dozen others and scattering the rest. The main Australian party withdrew and O'Neill acted as rearguard at a bridge that was the sole escape route. Only when all other troops were clear and he was out of ammunition did he fall back.

The Kokoda campaign begins

On 21 July, about 2000 Japanese began landing around Gona, on the north coast of Papua, and marched inland to test a track that ran to the village of Kokoda, site of the only airfield in the mountainous surrounding country, and then over the Owen Stanley Range to their ultimate objective, Port Moresby. At the time, the only Australian troops in the area were the 300-strong Papuan Infantry Battalion (PIB), essentially a reconnaissance unit of local troops with white officers and NCOs, and forward elements of the militia 39th Battalion. The local people would be a major factor in this campaign. Some sought to help the Japanese, but most aided the Allies, albeit often with an element of compulsion. They did wonderful work helping the wounded and bringing forward supplies, but increasingly, the Australians recognised their value as jungle soldiers. One of the first 'native' soldiers to gain notice was Acting Sergeant Katue (MM). During the night of 22/23 July, he went alone through enemy lines and several kilometres beyond and, after obtaining valuable information on Japanese strength and dispositions, returned to the PIB headquarters. Katue made two similar forays in subsequent days. In an October 1942 caption on a painting of Katue, official artist William Dargie noted that on his shoulders and arms he wore the rank badges of four of 26 Japanese he had killed on his latest patrol.

From 23 July, the Japanese pushed back the small groups of militiamen and Papuans facing them. An early clash occurred at Oivi on 26 July. Lieutenant Doug McClean (MC) and his platoon of the 39th were brought to Kokoda that day in the only two serviceable aircraft available. McClean had changed his status to AIF on 13 July. Eager to fight, he rushed the first group forward to the front to join two 39th Battalion platoons under Captain Sam Templeton and a few Papuan Infantry. The Australians were eventually forced back to the Oivi plateau, where for hours they defended a perimeter some 50 metres wide. Templeton, a great organiser, left late in the day to find McClean's second group, but after a burst of fire in the jungle was never seen again. At dusk the Japanese encircled and massed to storm the Australians, calling on them in English. McClean and Corporal Charles Pyke (MM) took a pile of grenades and advanced to within 10 metres of the enemy, who reportedly had 20 'Nambu' LMGs. The two Australians each threw five grenades, which were effective judging by the groans and screams they elicited. In the resulting confusion, the Australian defenders retreated, helped by a remarkable Papuan policeman, Lance-Corporal Sanopa (Loyal Service Medal). By war's end, McClean was a major in the Parachute Battalion.

The Japanese pushed the Australians back to Kokoda, then captured it in a confused night battle on 29 July. In the moonlight, the Australians' brave commander, Lieutenant-Colonel William Owen, was throwing grenades from the foremost defences when a bullet struck him above the right eye, mortally wounding him. The 37-year-old bank teller from Victoria was posthumously awarded the American Distinguished Service Cross, the first Australian to receive that honour.

As some of his men carried Owen back, the battalion gradually retired. Private 'Snowy' Parr, a 20-year-old Bren gunner, held on as long as possible, blasting 20–30 Japanese who appeared in a clearing. He calculated that he got 15 of them, though Japanese records suggest that Australians often made exaggerated claims of casualties in this campaign.

The youthful 39th Battalion was somewhat dispirited on reassembling at Deniki, but the arrival of more 39th men, a new commander, Major Allan Cameron (DSO), and a few days' rest revitalised them. On 8 August they returned to Kokoda, determined to recapture it. Sanopa, rifle in one hand and grenade in the other, had reconnoitred a route into Kokoda from the east. Preceded by bombing and strafing American Airacobra aircraft, Captain Noel Symington (MC) led his company along this track and into Kokoda against negligible resistance. The two other 39th companies faced determined resistance and were largely pushed back towards Deniki. Sanopa brought news on 9 August that Symington's men were gradually being surrounded at Kokoda and needed food and ammunition. After intermittent firing at infiltrating Japanese, Symington's group faced hand-to-hand fighting late in the day. Two Australians guarding a forward position had their throats cut. One section had every man killed or wounded, including its Bren crew: Privates Ron Dridan (MM), wounded in the head, and Vic Smythe (MM), hit in the right arm. With another member of the section – probably Lance-Corporal Alex Lochhead (MM) – Smythe and Dridan continued fighting, knowing that losing the Bren would doom them. Together they repelled seven Japanese attacks over 24 hours, during which they were without food and water. Smythe, a labourer from Merbein, Victoria, was often in trouble for misdemeanours later in the war but finished as a corporal. Nineteen-year-old militiaman Dridan never joined the AIF and left the Army in 1944.

Eventually, Symington's men were forced back towards Deniki. Staff-Sergeant Jim Cowey was among the last to leave, and his five-man rearguard wiped out three Japanese who tried to block them. When a Japanese 'Woodpecker' medium machine gun suddenly opened fire, Cowey carefully leaned against a tree, held his breath and shot first the machine gunner, and then a succession of replacements. Later, he coolly ordered his men out and moved casually. Cowey, who typically wore his slouch hat turned down, had served at Gallipoli in 1915 and, as a lieutenant, been twice recommended for a Military Cross (once successfully) on the Western Front in 1918. The 52-year-old surely deserved a decoration at Kokoda too. Don McKay, who did receive a Military Medal for holding three key posts with his decimated section on 9 August, nominated Cowey as his lifetime hero. By his own admission, Cowey was now 'buggered', and within weeks would be evacuated with 'overage debility'.

When a strong Japanese force attacked towards Deniki on 13 August, three Australian companies faced them. The main assault, comprising waves of mushroom-helmeted Japanese advancing four or five abreast, came in on the left, where a platoon under Lieutenant Don Simonson (MC) was credited with repelling it with submachine guns and grenades. During a lull, Simonson crept towards the sound of rattling mess tins and threw well-aimed grenades that knocked out two troublesome machine guns and up to eight men. Simonson, a 22-year-old, would be wounded in the thigh within two weeks but recover. The next day, the Australians fell back hastily from Deniki, and, though without spades, dug in at Isurava.

On 16 August, Lieutenant-Colonel Ralph Honner (DSO) arrived to take over the 39th Battalion. His outstanding efforts in Greece and Crete were mentioned earlier, but Kokoda would be his finest hour. When he arrived, so did forward troops of another militia battalion, the 53rd, now part of Maroubra Force, the Australian force on the Kokoda frontline. On 23 August, Brigadier Arnold Potts, commanding the 7th Division's 21st Brigade, arrived to take over Maroubra Force. Two of his battalions, the 2/14th and 2/16th, were following him up the track, soon to win fame at great cost.

In the meantime, dramatic developments elsewhere in Papua were about to push Australians of the militia and AIF to the limits of their endurance and fighting ability. A formidable force of Japanese naval infantry, backed by tanks, aircraft and warships, was headed for Milne Bay, a key Allied base on the eastern tip of Papua.

CHAPTER 12

MILNE BAY: BREAKING THE JAPANESE SPELL

On 25 August 1942, Japanese marines landed at Milne Bay in eastern Papua. Since June, the Allies had been building a base and several airfields there, amidst torrential rains, thick mud and malarial mosquitoes. A narrow strip of shore between sea and mountains now became the scene of vicious fighting. Australian aircraft based at the one completed airstrip (No. 1 Strip) had already been fighting air battles over Milne Bay and continued to play a key role above the land battle. Major-General Cyril Clowes commanded Milne Force, comprising primarily the 7th and 18th Australian brigades. On the night of 25/26 August, Japanese transport ships landed their troops around Ahioma, east of KB Mission. There they encountered a company of the 61st Battalion, a militia unit. The Australians found themselves engaged in night fighting against superior numbers, eventually including a light tank. The 61st had no anti-tank weapons, but the next morning, when the tank commander stood up in his turret to negotiate a log bridge over a creek, Lieutenant Bert Robinson (MID), a leader of the defence, shot him dead from about 150 metres away. The tank rolled down the bank and was bogged for the rest of the day. Robinson, a six-foot-tall saw sharpener from Queensland, would die in action in 1945 on Bougainville.

From just after dawn on 26 August, Australian aircraft strafed the Japanese landing craft and destroyed Japanese petrol dumps.

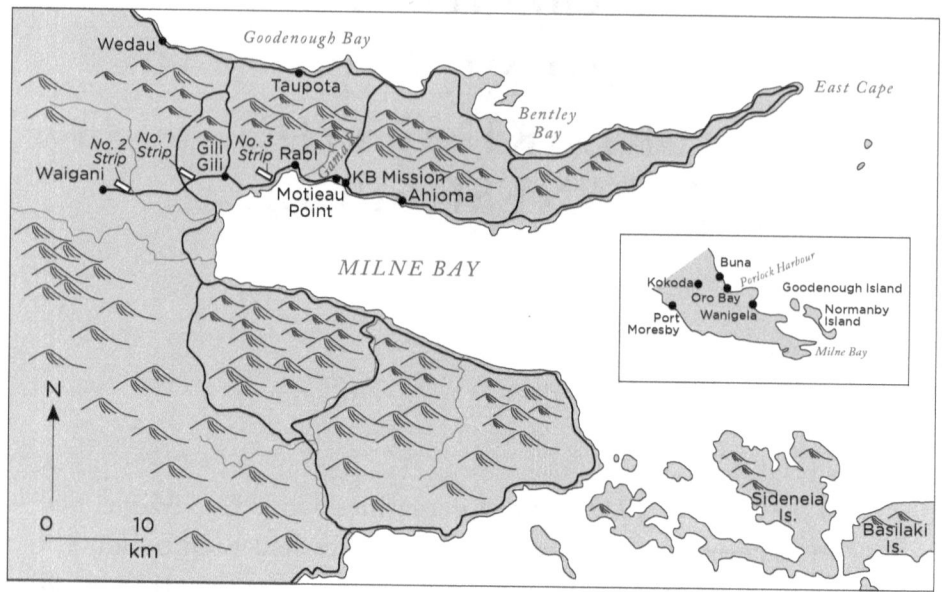

Milne Bay

Several hundred Australians of the 61st and 25th battalions went to the front, though the Japanese did not reappear. Late in the day, the Australians pushed the Japanese out of KB Mission. Robinson scored another notable kill when, on patrol deep behind enemy lines, he shot dead the tall leader of an approaching enemy patrol. As one 25th Battalion company advanced beyond KB Mission, a platoon under Sergeant Stan Steele (MM) became cut off. Corporal John Warren (MM) saw this happening on his right and ordered his section to help. Concussion from an enemy grenade blew him down a creek bank, but he rejoined his men and threw his own grenades. Even when shrapnel from a mortar struck the back of his head, Warren continued to lead the section in releasing Steele's platoon. Warren's own section was later surrounded until he led them out. He was awarded the 25th Battalion's first Military Medal since 1918. Steele later received the same award.

At 10 pm, the Japanese attacked near the KB Mission, drawing Australians into another bitter and confusing night fight. At 4.30 am, with casualties mounting and the Japanese outflanking them, the Australians withdraw, hoping to use the Gama River as an obstacle to the two Japanese tanks now operating.

The 61st had been fighting for two days and nights and welcomed relief when the veteran 2/10th Battalion arrived on 27 August. The South Australian unit reached the KB Mission without hindrance but had been unable to dig in before nightfall, when Japanese infantry and tanks attacked. The 2/10th had come forward lightly armed, with more Tommy guns and sticky grenades than usual but fewer Brens and anti-tank rifles. The sticky bombs failed to stick to the tanks, which alongside the aggressive Japanese infantry exerted great pressure. For more than four hours Captain Geoffrey Miethke (MC) led his company's defence, on the left flank, against these tanks and infantry firing from 100–200 metres away. Their fire, generally inaccurate, concentrated on the Australians' Brens, so Miethke had these passed around positions, but never for more than a few minutes at a time. Nevertheless, three men had been wounded serving one Bren by the time it reached Private Jim Kotz (MM), who advanced with it single-handedly and silenced an enemy post. He later killed three Japanese with a grenade, and though severely wounded in the chest, he survived. Miethke's men beat off four attacks by midnight and were sometimes surrounded, but when the pressure became overwhelming, fell back. That was at about 12.30 am, the same time that five Japanese bullets struck another Bren gunner, Private Bert Abraham (DCM), in the ankle and knee. As Miethke's company withdrew, his comrades did not notice Abraham's absence, but whenever he was conscious, he fought on. A tank tried repeatedly to run him over in the dark, but he rolled away each time. By the time a patrol went out and found him the next morning, Abraham had killed several members of a Japanese patrol, which the Australians dispersed. Carrying Abraham to help took several days, and he faced many operations.

Lieutenant Bert Robinson is slinging his rifle second from left at the back with his 61st Battalion platoon. He was prominent at Milne Bay in August 1942 and was killed in action on Bougainville in February 1945.
AWM 055562

Battle for the airstrip

Meanwhile, at the Gama River, numerous determined Japanese troops and their tanks bypassed 2/10th men defending the creek and pushed on towards an airfield, No. 3 Strip. Some 25th Battalion men became caught up in the retreat, but two NCOs led a defence east of the strip that was to prove important. Sergeant Stan Steele had earlier cleared a field of fire from the road to the coast, and his 16-strong platoon was joined by Sergeant Joffre Ludlow (MM) and 15 men. The group had not slept for three nights and Ludlow, seeing his men falling asleep over their weapons, rotated them through watches just five minutes long. At 5 am they heard Japanese coming down the road. The Australians held their fire until the enemy were just 20 metres off, then blasted one group after another as they tried to cross the cleared ground. A Vickers gun firing from the airstrip complemented the Australians' Brens. Tracers from a Woodpecker MMG were at one point just clearing the Australians' heads, hitting one man's pack, but Ludlow, an unassuming Queensland orchardist, seized the initiative. With fire support from Privates Ron Finney and Bob Wyatt, he used grenades to destroy the three-man Japanese crew. Later, the Japanese brought forward a mortar. Ludlow eliminated its five-man crew with grenades, sending a Japanese helmet flying. Steele and Ludlow held on for three hours, thus preventing the Japanese from rushing the airstrip. No Australians were killed, while the Japanese left approximately 50 dead and discontinued their attacks for that night.

By the end of the next day, 28 August, the 25th and 61st battalions were in defensive positions at the airstrip. The expected attack did not eventuate that night, or on 29 or 30 August. On the latter day, Australian patrollers found evidence of Japanese atrocities in the form of dead compatriots tied up and bayoneted or shot at close range. Lieutenant Aub Schindler (MC), commanding the 25th's Mortar Platoon, was sent on a patrol to blow up the two abandoned Japanese tanks. This was 3000 metres forward of the frontline, and like many others, Schindler was suffering from raw feet, a product of constant mud and water. Nevertheless, the patrollers disabled the tanks with gelignite on the tracks and engines. Then they returned to their two shallow mortar pits, which together contained about 100 bombs, and which were dug much closer than normal to the infantry in the jungle positions. So that night (30/31 August), when flares revealed the enemy gathering on the eastern edge of the airstrip, the mortarmen were only about 300 metres away. Schindler ordered 'Rapid fire!' and their bombs had a devastating effect on the enemy for three hours, during which the mortars were resupplied by men who ran a gauntlet of Japanese fire. The flash from the mortars attracted much enemy fire, but Private 'Hammy' Hamilton maintained communication between the guns and an observation post manned by Lieutenant Keith Acreman (MC) of the 101st Anti-Tank Regiment. Some 162 Japanese dead were found in the area where the mortar bombs had fallen. From the time the Japanese launched their ill-fated attacks at 3 am, many others fell to Australian and American fire, much of it from Robinson's indefatigable platoon. Lieutenant Schindler later joined the Australian New Guinea Administrative Unit (ANGAU), working at an Agricultural Station in New Guinea's Eastern Highlands producing quinine.

The Australians attack

While Australian militiamen were halting the Japanese attacks on the airstrip, AIF men of the 2/12th Battalion were advancing, wading through mud and killing some 70 Japanese as they pushed beyond the airstrip. The leading company engaged the organised Japanese resistance in front of them, but, with speed at a premium, inevitably left in its wake large numbers of Japanese, who were hiding in the undergrowth and trees. For seven hours the battalion was continuously sniped. Behind the leading company came the battalion headquarters and the other companies. Corporal Richard Holmyard (DCM) commanded a section of a recently formed 'Commando Platoon', tasked with protecting battalion headquarters. That protection involved dealing with Japanese snipers in palm trees at the eastern edge of the airstrip and wherever encountered in succeeding days. Holmyard personally 'beat the jungle', coolly clearing Japanese troops from the roadside. His actions came to a head on 3 September when he and another man sought out a Japanese Nambu LMG that had flanked the platoon. Armed with a grenade, he rushed the post across 30 metres of open ground, killing three. Richard, named for an uncle killed in World War I, had been 21, unemployed and living in Launceston when he enlisted in October 1939. He was often in trouble with the authorities, even being court-martialled in 1943. He would lose his medals on Anzac Day 1972 while drinking on the wharf at Hobart.

Captain Colin Kirk (MC) commanded the company behind the headquarters, and he too risked all in organising the beating of the jungle. His orderly was killed working beside him. Kirk's company eliminated at least 40 snipers. On the first night of the 2/12th's advance (31 August – 1 September), Kirk's company halted at the Gama River and helped to thwart a determined Japanese counterattack. Kirk, a Toowoomba bank clerk, died in action four months later. Two companies of the 9th Battalion assisted the 2/12th in frustrating the Gama River counterattack.

Private Lionel Baumann (MM) was a 9th Battalion Bren gunner whose section held the road at Motieau. Strong enemy patrols attacked his section hourly from three sides, but he drove off each one. During one enemy frontal attack, this Queensland farmer advanced on the Japanese, firing from the hip and dispersing them.

On 1 September, the 2/12th occupied KB Mission. The 2/9th Battalion joined them the following day and continued to advance. Lieutenant Colin Fogg's platoon of the 2/9th attacked across a stream, inflicting 34 casualties. Fogg received a head wound and fell into the creek, where he was initially left for dead. However, his batman, Private Cedric Reid, pulled him out of the water and bandaged his wound, persisting even when a bullet shattered his own right arm. Reid's courage was not officially recognised, and neither was that of Lance-Corporal John Ball, a giant soldier whose body was found later near the muzzle of Japanese machine guns where he had advanced beyond all his mates, none of whom had seen him die. His commanding officer reportedly recommended Ball, unsuccessfully, for the Victoria Cross. Ball's story is reminiscent of those Australians (including the original 9th Battalion) who advanced beyond all others at Gallipoli on 25 April 1915 and whose deeds were never recorded.

On 3 September, when Kirk's company and the commandos pressed along the shore, they encountered prepared Japanese defences. Private Archie Johnston (MM) and a mate attacked one defiant post. When his companion's Tommy gun jammed, Johnston continued alone, bayonetting the post's occupants and capturing their machine gun. He then stood guard over another comrade who lay wounded by sniper fire until the snipers had been dealt with. When another platoon lost their officer and sergeant wounded, Corporal Jack Gordon (MID) took over the platoon and personally killed some six enemies, including one with whom he fought a duel at about five metres' distance, each firing from behind a tree. Gordon, a 34-year-old Queensland grazier, died in action that December when a bullet detonated a grenade on his belt.

The 2/9th Battalion led the advance again on 4 September. Sergeant Roy de Vantier (MM) was leading a few men when they encountered five Japanese, including two carrying Nambus. Undaunted, de Vantier killed all five with his Thompson submachine gun. After ordering his section to cover, Corporal Jack French (VC) made a lone advance in which he destroyed two machine-gun posts with grenades and a third with a submachine gun. His men found him dead in front of the third pit. De Vantier, a 24-year-old schoolteacher from Gympie, would die in action soon too, as a lieutenant.

By 6 September, when the 2/9th and 2/12th reached the remnants of the Japanese main base, the battalions had sustained some 200 casualties in the six-day advance. Japanese intentions remained obscure, and Japanese ships came in nightly to bombard the shore. However, by 8 September, organised fighting was over. The victory, won mainly by Australian soldiers and airmen, lifted Allied spirits everywhere. Sir William Slim, commander of the British 14th Army in Burma, declared that the news of the Japanese defeat at Milne Bay was a great morale booster to his troops, who acknowledged that 'of all the Allies it was Australian soldiers who first broke the spell of the invincibility of the Japanese Army'.

In a postscript to the Milne Bay battle, a grim fight occurred on nearby Goodenough Island, where RAAF fighters destroyed seven Japanese barges on 25 August. The 350 troops they carried were thus marooned on the island, and in October, the 2/12th Battalion was sent to eliminate them. There was sharp fighting in rough terrain on 23–24 October, before Japanese vessels arrived and evacuated their surviving compatriots. The 2/12th sustained over 30 casualties, and men attached to the unit from the 2/5th Field Ambulance risked their lives to bring in 13 wounded. Two of these brave ambulancemen were killed by mortar fire. A third ambulanceman was Private Roy Marriott (DCM), a Melbourne labourer who since enlisting had often been in trouble for being AWL. Now he raised the spirits of the soldiers around him by going straight to the aid of men hit by machine-gun fire. He was himself hit in the back twice but continued to help the orderlies in the RAP. Indeed, he had to be restrained from going out to bring in more wounded. On 24 October, Marriott was the only Medical Corps man aboard the two-masted motor vessel *McLaren King* when it left Goodenough Island with casualties. Three enemy aircraft appeared and strafed the vessel for 20 minutes. Four casualties sustained second wounds, and two crew members were hit. Marriott distinguished himself again by going to the aid of these men. Hampered by his own bullet wounds and exhausted from their haemorrhaging, Marriott used improvised splints on a crew member's fractured leg. When, several hours later, the ship reached Gili Gili wharf at Milne Bay, Marriott insisted on all other wounded men being treated before going to hospital himself for treatment. He was later briefly a lance-corporal, but ill-health, including eye problems, led to him being medically downgraded.

Goodenough Island was the scene of another unusual and extraordinary act of bravery on 10 March 1943. By then, the 47th Battalion was garrisoning the island, where that morning a landing craft disembarked 22 Japanese near Vivigani. Lance-Corporal Ted Cook (MM), leading a nearby patrol of four men, sent two to report to battalion headquarters. The enemy approached, seizing Cook from behind and laying out his companion, Private John King, with a boat paddle. Cook was 36, but the Queensland truck driver was also 6 feet tall and weighed 84 kilograms. He pushed away one of the Japanese holding him, felled a second with his fist and opened fire with his Owen, first at those around King and then at his own assailants. Eight fell dead and another escaped, while Cook and King held the remaining 13 as prisoners until help arrived.

CHAPTER 13
KOKODA: FIGHTING RETREAT, FIGHTING RETURN (AUGUST–NOVEMBER 1942)

On 26 August, while the Australians at Isurava waited for much-needed reinforcements, the Japanese resumed their advance. Brigadier Potts sent the recently arrived 53rd Battalion to counterattack towards Missima, on a branch track east of the main track. Inadequately trained and equipped and lacking the enthusiasm of AIF units, this battalion became a scapegoat. Many of its men sacrificed all for the cause, such as Private Donald MacGraw, a forward scout killed on patrol on 24 August, while others fought well, including Private Bert Bostock, the second scout on that patrol, who killed four Japanese moving towards MacGraw's body. On 26 August, Japanese fire dispersed the battalion's companies at Missima, and the commanding officer was killed.

On 27 and 28 August, the newly arrived 2/14th Battalion and depleted 39th Battalion engaged in intense fighting for Isurava. At a memorial built there in 2002, one of four pillars commemorates the 'courage' of all the Australians and Papua New Guineans who fought on the Kokoda Track. The most famous of these soldiers is Private Bruce Kingsbury, who won a posthumous Victoria Cross for advancing with a Bren, firing from the hip and preventing his battalion headquarters from being overrun. It was the first Australian Victoria Cross won on Australian territory. Beside him was his mate Alan Avery, who had won the Military Medal in Syria. Private Charlie McCallum (DCM), a 35-year-old farmer from Tarra Valley, Victoria, might also have won the Victoria Cross. This log-chopping champion was strong and determined, although he had been hospitalised three times since enlisting – for rubella, jaundice and mumps. On 29 August, McCallum was the dominant figure in his platoon as, against great odds, it held its allotted area, slightly elevated ground overlooking the battalion line of communication. Four times it was pushed off the ground, but each time counterattacked and recaptured it. When a final retreat became necessary at about 5.30 pm, McCallum covered the platoon's withdrawal. Though wounded in the forehead, leg and arm, he continued firing his Bren and a Tommy gun acquired from a wounded mate. When the magazine of one ran out, he used the other to check the enemy's rushes while reloading the first. During one attack, a Japanese tore McCallum's utility pouches off, but the Australian wrenched himself away and killed his assailant. When his mates called out that they were all clear, at about 6.00 pm, he pulled out, bringing both weapons. His citation estimated that he personally killed at least 25 Japanese. His mates put it at closer to 40. He won a Distinguished Conduct Medal rather than the Victoria Cross, for which he was recommended. McCallum died in fighting on 8 September. His mother carried her only son's medal with her for the rest of her life.

Lieutenant Harold 'Butch' Bisset and his platoon thwarted repeated attacks until he was mortally wounded. Lieutenant 'Mokka' Treacy (MC), a Mildura shop assistant, took over another hard-pressed platoon astride the track after its commander was killed. On 29 August, Treacy directed a skilful defence. When withdrawal became necessary, he and his platoon held the track so platoons on their right could escape. He called forward stretcher-bearers to evacuate casualties, helped construct stretchers and placed a rearguard on the track that enabled the whole platoon to escape. Treacy saved many lives but lost his own to a sniper later that year at Gona, where his strong physique, encouragement and direction made him a target.

Private Tom Fletcher (MM) was a stretcher-bearer who carried out wounded under heavy machine-gun fire at Isurava on 29 August. On hearing that a 39th Battalion casualty lay in the open and could not be rescued, Fletcher evaded enemy fire to bring him in, tended him, constructed a stretcher and had him evacuated. This 41-year-old farm hand did the same for some 13 wounded on 30 August, when the battalion again suffered heavily. On the night of 30/31 August, Fletcher was with 40 retreating Australians who became cut off. Eight were wounded, and for the next three weeks, Fletcher accompanied them behind enemy lines. Eventually, the stretcher-bearers became too weak physically to carry the casualties any further, but Fletcher volunteered to stay behind with five wounded and two sick in a village. By the time relief arrived, Fletcher and his charges had been massacred. He was recommended for a Distinguished Conduct Medal, a recommendation supported at brigade and divisional headquarters but not the higher headquarters.

The 2/16th Battalion covered the 2/14th's withdrawal. Both battalions were attacked on 30 August as the Japanese seized high ground on the flanks. The 2/16th repeatedly launched counterattacks up a steep wooded slope against camouflaged Japanese defences on the right, on Abuari ridge. During an ambush, machine-gun fire killed section leader Corporal Michael Clarke. Private George Maidment (DCM) then came forward. His real name was Alexander Thornton, a 28-year-old Sydney labourer, whose service record was full of entries about illness, including hospitalisations for influenza, rubella and fever in Australia, and epilepsy, sandfly fever and skin rashes in the Middle East. There were also an extraordinary number of disciplinary breaches: in 1942 alone he was fined the large sum of 5 pounds and confined to barracks for 14 days in April, fined the same amount for drunkenness, using insulting language to an officer and refusing to obey an order in May, and 3 pounds and seven days' detention for being AWL for eight days in June! But Maidment had another side, already apparent in Syria, and he now gathered Clarke's grenades and advanced on the enemy machine-gun posts, which sat above a waterfall. Though almost immediately wounded in the chest and lung, he pressed on, destroying several posts and stopping only when out of grenades and ordered to rejoin his platoon. The Japanese pushed forward, prompting Maidment to pick up Clarke's TSMG.

Spurning any cover, he delayed the attackers with accurate fire while the rest of the platoon retreated. Only when out of ammunition did he join them. He was bloody and exhausted but refused assistance walking to the RAP, where he collapsed and was stretchered out. He later died of wounds. Maidment was recommended for the Victoria Cross by commanders all the way up to division but received the Distinguished Conduct Medal instead.

Self-sacrifice for their men: Efogi to Ioribaiwa

From 30 August, Japanese forces repeatedly threatened to surround the Australians. By 5 September, Maroubra Force, now including fresh 2/27th Battalion troops, was at Efogi. Fierce Japanese attacks endangered even Potts' headquarters and on 8 September all three battalions retreated. The 2/27th lost contact with Maroubra Force and was temporarily out of the fight, while by 10 September the 2/14th and 2/16th together totalled just 307 men. That day, Brigadier Porter took over Maroubra Force and pulled it back to the crucial Ioribaiwa Ridge.

Lieutenant George Pearce (MC), a 32-year-old orchardist from Shepparton, had led his 2/14th Battalion platoon in a successful counter-attack on 28 August and remained on duty despite a gunshot wound to the penis. He held his platoon together in dense jungle against numerous attacks the following day, when he also led a fighting patrol that inflicted casualties. When part of his company withdrew, he reorganised the remainder into a defensive perimeter, which held out until early 1 September, when he ordered them to break into groups and fight their way back to the main body. He brought a party of 11 back after four days in the bush. Pearce was wounded again, in the left leg, on 11 September. A third wound, at Gona on 6 December, proved fatal. Pearce was short, wore an oversized hat, and was a self-taught intellectual of exceptional endurance, courage and initiative.

Warrant-Officer Ron Preece (MM) of ANGAU exercised another

kind of invaluable leadership. On 4 September, this plantation manager from Papua and some 30 'natives' set up a stretcher-relay post close to the frontline near Templeton's Crossing. Heavy fighting soon erupted and Preece led the increasingly anxious locals to a safer location. At dawn, his men overcame their fear, collected the stretchers and evacuated the wounded. Preece's citation called his efforts here 'superhuman'. He was a valuable guide for Australian troops and won great credit with the 2/27th's stretcher-bearers. Those who paid tribute to Preece included Corporal John Burns (MM), who commanded a group of seven stretcher cases, nine walking wounded and sick left behind by the 2/27th's main body in a yam garden east of Nauro on 19 September. Burns had already spent ten hard days helping move the stretchers. At the garden they were ordered to wait for rescue, but in the meantime, Burns and 6-foot-tall stretcher-bearer Private Alf Zanker (MID), both of whom volunteered to remain with the casualties, had with them just ten dressings, one morphia bottle and one syringe. They built shelters but the nights were cold, the heat and flies tormenting. Burns and Zanker washed the men, all of whom used Burns' shaving gear and toothbrush. The two ministering angels spent entire days and nights with the sickest men. The work was so demanding that both experienced blackouts. Following an outbreak of diarrhoea, Burns and Zanker had to lift men for 24 hours. When, despite all their attention, Burns' close mate Len Williams died, Burns and Zanker dug a grave using a helmet and a machete. Most wounds became flyblown. Burns and Zanker, who often slept two hours or less at night, read the New Testament and ran discussions to keep the men occupied. Burns and Zanker also foraged for and cooked food for the men whose pain they were constantly trying to minimise, despite their own hardships. Burns later wondered why they did not all die of exposure. On 2 October, Preece and his bearers rescued them. It still took another five days' travelling for Burns' party to reach medical treatment. As Burns left the hospital, 25 kilograms lighter, the other survivors gave him a huge cheer. A sniper shot him in the hand at Gona, where carrying a wireless set made him a priority target. He also contracted scrub typhus. He later edited and wrote most of the 2/27th Battalion history. His father, George, had won the Military Medal in 1916.

Captain Mert Lee earned a Bar to the Military Cross he won in Syria. His company covered the withdrawal from Efogi, and he directed it in dispersing enemy attacks from as close as 20 metres away. When the company withdrew, Lee and two others were last to leave, with empty magazines. Acting Corporal 'Blue' Moloney (MM) became a section leader in the 2/16th during the fighting and proved a natural leader. With a Bren he held off attackers on 29–30 August, he enabled the evacuation of wounded at Efogi and was credited, alongside Private William Walker (MID), with killing at least 20 Japanese in a watering place ambush. Like his friend 'Diver' Derrick, Moloney was a young man of Irish extraction, a jokester sometimes in trouble with authority, but he too would lose his life as an officer in May 1945.

Turning point at Imita Ridge

On 14 September, the fresh 2/31st and 2/33rd battalions of the 25th Brigade arrived and relieved the 21st Brigade. In subsequent days, the 2/27th and large parties of the 2/14th returned after long and debilitating marches around the Japanese flanks.

The Japanese were tiring too, but they struck the Australians hard before the newly arrived battalions could consolidate on Ioribaiwa Ridge. Brigadier Ken Eather pulled back to Imita Ridge and was told by his superiors that he must retreat no further. By 17 September he had five battalions in firm position.

Within a week the Australians were advancing cautiously, now with artillery support. On 28 September, they found Ioribaiwa Ridge abandoned. The exhausted Japanese were heading back to the coast, but it would be a fighting withdrawal. Lieutenant Arch Barnett (MC), who had been wounded and captured in Syria but repatriated after the armistice, was prominent in the 2/25th Battalion's advance.

He received a chest wound while leading an attack on a Japanese machine-gun post near Myola. Corporal 'Os' Stanley (MM), a medical orderly, went forward under perilous conditions and stitched Barnett's gaping wound on the spot. The battalion's medical officer later declared Stanley's lifesaving dressing of this wound equal to the work of a surgeon. In civilian life, Stanley was a Rockhampton clerk.

On 13 October, Lieutenant Kevin Power (MC), a regular soldier, led a 50-strong patrol of the 2/33rd in a brilliant and innovative surprise attack on the Japanese rearguard. He divided the patrol into nine groups of five men, each under an NCO. They eliminated a Woodpecker MMG and killed up to 30 Japanese for one Australian killed and four wounded. When the enemy reacted and threatened to overwhelm the patrollers, Power led three separate attacks that rescued wounded men. He and Corporal 'Bluey' Bogan coolly acted as rearguard until the others withdrew safely. Power showed near-incredible bravery again as a captain in October 1943 when for 15 minutes he fought like a one-man army. While using an Owen gun and pistol to take on Japanese holding a knoll, he carried out two wounded men as fire hit his pouches, and then employed a Bren to combat Japanese on another knoll.

Lance-Corporal Phillip O'Keefe (MM), a 30-year-old stretcher-bearer with the 2/33rd, was credited with evacuating 17 casualties between 12 and 14 October, several on his back while crawling through undergrowth under heavy fire.

The 3rd Battalion CMF had been fighting since early September. On 17 October, during an attack on strong defences at Templeton's Crossing, Sergeant Bede Tongs (MM) took over a platoon when its commander was wounded. He then crawled along the fire lane of an enemy machine gun and threw a grenade into the gun pit. When the explosion threw the two occupants out of the pit, the sight of them lying dead inspired Tongs' men. Whooping and yelling, they seized the ridge, where they captured valuable documents and equipment. Tongs, a carpenter, ended the war a captain in the 2/3rd Battalion.

On 20 October, the 6th Division's 16th Brigade took over the advance from the 25th, which in the past month had sustained over

200 battle casualties and 771 men evacuated sick. After a brief and bloody fight at Templeton's Crossing, the 16th advanced to Eora Creek, where the Japanese were dug in on a steep ridge. Their defences were like a castle keep, some 300 metres wide.

On 22 October, the 2/3rd Battalion occupied Eora Creek village on the creek's eastern bank. The Japanese could see them, and soon inflicted casualties. Sergeant Arthur Carson (MM), who as a stretcher-bearer won a Distinguished Conduct Medal at Bullecourt in 1917, brought forward members of his Pioneer Platoon. They evacuated the wounded, losing one pioneer dead, another wounded. Carson received a Military Medal, giving the 49-year-old the rare distinction of winning a decoration for bravery in both world wars.

The strength of the Japanese positions was not yet apparent, but two companies of the 2/1st Battalion were sent across a ford to outflank them. The scrub was thick and a waterfall obstructed their path, so when an attack went in on 23 October, it included only Captain Alex Sanderson (MID) and Lieutenant Keith Johnston's 17-man platoon. Japanese soon surrounded the Australians and killed 11, including both officers. Sanderson had a captured German machine pistol from the Middle East, and when the 34-year-old accountant's body was discovered, it was reportedly ringed with more than 300 spent shells and some 30 dead or dying Japanese.

By 22 October, most of the 16th Brigade occupied ground overlooking Eora Creek, but also under Japanese observation. Artillery, mortar and machine-gun fire soon fell among the unsuspecting Australians. A mountain-gun shell struck the joint RAP of the 2/1st and 2/3rd battalions, killing three and wounding the 2/3rd medical officer, Captain Goldman. Captain John Connell (MC), lanky RMO of the 2/1st, had been stooping down to pick up his case when the shell arrived. A mountain-gun had seriously wounded the first battle casualty he ever treated, just two days earlier. Connell, a Melbourne doctor, saved that man's life and now found himself treating 16 more casualties. Still under enemy fire, Connell was assisted by Lance-Sergeant John Doran (MM), a Sydney labourer who continued working despite a painful foot wound. In December, Doran would walk back to Port Moresby for medical treatment. Connell became a revered figure in the 2/1st.

That night, the Australians sought to capture two bridges over Eora Creek. A Japanese machine gun inflicted casualties on the first patrol that attempted to cross, but it had gone when Lieutenant-Colonel Paul Cullen (DSO) and his adjutant bravely crawled across the body-strewn bridge to reconnoitre beyond. Cullen then ordered Captain Peter Barclay (MID) to take his company across preparatory to an attack the following morning. Most of Barclay's platoons negotiated the two bridges in the moonlight before the enemy opened fire and halted the crossing. Once across, the platoons became separated.

In daylight, Lieutenant Bill Pollitt's platoon found themselves trapped in a cul-de-sac, with Japanese dropping grenades on them from rocks above. All but seven of Pollitt's men became casualties here. One, Lance-Corporal John Hunt (MID), found a way around the flank, climbed the slope, and stalked and killed the grenade-throwers. Hunt, a 30-year-old Bathurst labourer, was killed later that day.

Others in Barclay's company got further forward, but Barclay – a cheerful station manager who had risen from the ranks – was killed that morning. Lieutenant Jim McCloy (MC) took over, commanding two platoons but unable to advance on the relatively open ground. They cleared the way though for the following company under Captain Basil Catterns (MC). Catterns' men linked up with some survivors but were soon digging in to avoid fire from the cliffs. By nightfall on 23 October, the 2/1st across the creek were just 30 metres from the enemy and pinned. For days the Japanese could fire and roll grenades down on Catterns' men. One grenade bruised Catterns. Though often sniped at, he frequently visited his men.

While waiting for reinforcements to outflank the Japanese right, Cullen sent his 18-strong Pioneer Platoon that way under Lieutenant Gordon Leaney (MC). After two hours' climbing, Leaney split his force into two and sent them through rainfall to reconnoitre left and right. The left-hand group found nothing, but the right came upon a clearing with a blockhouse beyond it. Corporal James Stewart (MID) crossed the clearing to investigate. Peering inside, he saw two Japanese machine gunners about to eat a meal and shot them with his Tommy gun. Alerted, nearby Japanese attacked, twice wounding Stewart and, during a 10-minute firefight, killing or wounding all but two others in his section. Leaney joined Stewart with the rest of the platoon, which dug in, a thorn in the Japanese side.

The stalemate at Eora Creek would only be broken on 28 October, when 2/3rd Battalion forces managed a wide flanking movement around the Japanese right. Australian forward scouts fell but their compatriots pushed on, moving from tree to tree. Corporal Lester 'Tarzan' Pett (MM) was leading his section when he noticed that machine-gun fire had halted the platoon to his right. He immediately charged the source of that fire, shooting a Bren from the hip and eliminating two posts. He then brought up his section, which cleared the neighbouring platoon's remaining obstacles. Published sources, but not his citation, say he personally knocked out four posts. They say, too, that he was 'five feet of dynamite', while his service record indicates he was at least 4 inches taller than that. Pett died of wounds several weeks later. Sergeant Gilbert Cory (DCM) led a platoon attack on high ground west of the creek. With many of his NCOs hit, he moved continuously between the sections, directing them even when so severely wounded in the face that he was temporarily blinded. He later required extensive plastic surgery. Cory experienced an unsettled life before the war and was occasionally in trouble in the Army, but his brilliance as a combat soldier was undeniable, and by February 1945, the 38-year-old motor car salesman was a lieutenant.

When the enemy finally broke, abandoning posts, weapons and over 50 dead, the 16th Brigade saw Japanese running away for the first time. Making this possible cost the Australian formation nearly 300 casualties.

That day, General George Vasey replaced General 'Tubby' Allen as commander of the 7th Division, which MacArthur and Blamey had criticised as moving too slowly. Pursuit of the retreating

Japanese began immediately. On 2 November, the 25th Brigade occupied Kokoda, where the airstrip provided a supply point and a place for evacuating the wounded. As the Australian flag was raised, a stretcher-bearer recorded that 'tribute was paid to all who had died along the track for the Victory that had taken place here'. Vasey ordered the 16th Brigade, under his command, to push on to Oivi and the Kumusi River. Sunnier weather, more open terrain and better rations improved the troops' morale. Nevertheless, the Japanese held high ground near Oivi village, and from log bunkers and trenches managed, aided by two mountain guns, to halt the Australians. Vasey sent the 25th Brigade south of the Japanese – numbering some 2800 in the area – towards Gorari, where it could cut off the enemy's retreat. This manoeuvre resulted in fierce fighting as the Japanese tried to escape the trap. Lieutenant Morrie O'Donnell (MC), of the 2/31st, and his platoon charged up a bank, down across a creek and up the opposite bank, using bayonets, TSMGs and grenades. O'Donnell reached a group of weapon pits first. He killed a Japanese in one pit, but a point-blank shot from the second pit struck his jaw, exited through his neck and felled him. He stood up and continued to lead until he collapsed. O'Donnell survived to serve as a captain in the postwar British Commonwealth Occupation Force in Japan. Captain Lloyd Hurrell (MC), of the 2/31st, estimated that his battalion killed hundreds of 'crazed' Japanese trying to break out day and night. On 11 November, he and two NCOs were firing from behind a large ficus tree when a Japanese officer thrust a Taisho pistol into a gap in the above-ground tree roots and shot Hurrell's sergeant in the hip and then Hurrell in the forearm. Enraged, Hurrell rushed the officer, now kneeling and reloading, and fatally bayonetted him above the collarbone. Heeding his men's warnings to take cover, he called them to pass him grenades. Several were rolled to him, and according to his citation, he eliminated a machine-gun position with 'a remarkable throw'. Silence followed and he led his men forward. The officer beside him was then killed and Hurrell hit in the hip, which he likened to being struck by a cricket ball.

For a time he continued in this fight for a location dubbed 'Butcher's Hill'. On being stretchered out, he was greeted by his younger brother Les, also a captain in the 2/31st. They said goodbye, not knowing that Les would be killed within weeks while reconnoitring the Kumusi River. According to Lloyd, the battalion commander, Lieutenant-Colonel Jim Miller (MID), told him that he intended to recommend Les for a decoration, but Miller died of scrub typhus before he could write it. Both brothers were living in New Guinea at the war's outbreak, Lloyd as a cadet patrol officer, Les an assistant agriculturalist, and were experts in jungle craft. Private Ernest 'Snow' Redgrave (DCM), a Queensland labourer, was credited with silencing two enemy posts with his Tommy gun on 10 November, taking over his section on 11 November and using a Bren to enable his platoon to advance. He also inflicted many casualties, including four dead, using his TSMG that afternoon. His feats barely figure in the records. Redgrave subsequently contracted scrub typhus and malaria and was discharged medically unfit in 1944.

In the fighting at Oivi–Gorari, the 2/1st Battalion was furthest east, holding ground against Japanese attacking from east and west. Lieutenant McCloy was again outstanding at Gorari. Patrolling with his platoon on 10 November, he came upon Japanese defences later discovered to have been held by 300 men. McCloy's 16-strong platoon sustained 11 casualties, but two members were decorated for bravery and the attack reportedly gained useful information. Corporal Roy Stoddart (DCM) led a section that surprised the enemy, killing 18 and taking their objective. A Japanese counterattack forced the section back, and Stoddart, though wounded in head, shoulder and foot and with his Tommy gun jammed, fought on with a rifle. He brought down another three Japanese and was the last in his section to withdraw. All eight members of a section under Corporal John Shearwin (MM) were wounded, and though hit himself, he covered the escape.

McCloy won more plaudits ten days later. His platoon, leading the advance, was pushing back the enemy when a Japanese stood beside the track and shot down the two leading scouts, who had not

Kokoda: Fighting retreat, fighting return (August–November 1942)

These four 2/31st Battalion men, pictured on the Kokoda Track in October 1942, had not shaved for a month. The soldier holding the TSMG is Private 'Snowy' Redgrave.
AWM 027058

spotted him. McCloy did, though, and from over 100 metres, killed the Japanese with three rifle shots, despite being under fire himself.

A Japanese counterattack westward along the track on 11 November brought hand-to-hand fighting. Firing from behind a tree, Corporal Harrowby St George-Ryder brought down three Japanese with a Tommy gun. He was changing his magazine when a sword-wielding Japanese attacked him. St George-Ryder's helmet was knocked off and he received a severe head wound, but he grappled with his assailant, kneeing and throwing him to the ground where another Australian killed the swordsman. St George-Ryder was later commissioned but died of injuries on Bougainville in 1945.

Despite desperate Japanese opposition, on 11 November, the 16th and 25th brigades completed their encirclement of Oivi–Gorari, where they killed some 600 Japanese. The Australians then marched towards the Kumusi River, where bombing had destroyed the wire-rope suspension bridge at Wairopi. General Tomitarō Horii and many other Japanese drowned there. By 16 November, the Australians had bridged the crossing. The momentous Kokoda campaign was over.

CHAPTER 14

EL ALAMEIN: THE DECISIVE BATTLE (OCTOBER–NOVEMBER 1942)

At 9.40 pm on 23 October 1942, a barrage from 880 guns heralded the 8th Army's decisive attack on Rommel's defences at El Alamein. That barrage is the most famous part of the battle, and artillery was vital to the Allied victory, but there was also much desperate infantry combat. A British general would by the battle's end describe the 9th Australian Division's fighting at El Alamein as 'homeric', evoking the contests of heroes in Homer's *Iliad*. There were indeed numerous Australian acts of bravery at El Alamein, not least because Australians did an inordinate amount of the fighting. While Australians comprised just 10 per cent of the Allied forces at Alamein, they sustained 20 per cent of the casualties.

'Operation Lightfoot', the codename for the great battle, referred to the need to negotiate minefields. Engineers were crucial on the first night. Typifying their bravery was Sapper Tom Broadhurst (MM) of 2/3rd Field Company. He was often in trouble with authority, especially for going AWL, but his citation said his courage had 'long been outstanding'. On this night he was assigned to a 2/17th Battalion company to deal with anti-personnel mines, including the dreaded 'S' mines which, once activated, leapt from the ground before exploding at groin height. Though under fire, he continuously moved across the company's front, disarming anti-personnel mines and booby traps, and warning the infantry of dangers. Later in the battle he acted as a runner, taking messages between his engineer company and the infantry, and guided two Matilda 'Scorpion' flail tanks through the minefield. Though wounded, he remained on duty.

Exemplifying the bravery of sapper officers was the 2/13th Field Company's Lieutenant Arthur Stevenson (MC). The former civil engineer was attached to the 2/15th Battalion to clear minefields and generally assist. He reconnoitred extensive anti-tank and anti-personnel minefields, and when word came that a forward company urgently needed ammunition, he made a minefield gap and drove the ammunition to the troops. Later that first night he helped capture a dug-in Panzer and its crew, then demolished the tank. Thanks largely to Stevenson, the battalion lost not one vehicle to mines at Alamein.

The Australians were on the right of the entire British line, and advancing on their right was the 2/24th Battalion. It made good progress, but the two leading company commanders were hit. Lieutenant Tony Greatorex (MC) took over one company. It was the 37-year-old farmer's first battle, but he confidently organised the troops on their first objective. A few days later, Greatorex was among many hit when an enemy machine gun opened fire from the flank. Greatorex personally led a section attack on the post, which was found to be a derelict tank. The Australians wiped out its crew. Greatorex was later wounded a second time, and ended the war a captain. He moved to the Northern Territory, entered politics and received an OBE for services to the territory.

On the night of 23 October, the 24th Brigade launched diversionary raids to the right of the main advance. The accompanying sappers included Lance-Corporal Francis Bingham (MM) of the 2/3rd Field Company. He used a Bangalore torpedo, a long hose full of explosives, to blow a hole in the enemy wire before rushing forward to widen the gap with wire cutters. Bingham then assisted the infantry in hand-to-hand fighting. A crack shot, he was credited with inflicting casualties and helping to destroy an anti-tank gun. When the platoon commander, Lieutenant Lin Thomas (MC), was wounded, 'Bing' lifted him onto his shoulder and carried him out with the help of Thomas's runner. Bingham briefly put Thomas down to shoot a German machine gunner with his pistol. When they passed three Germans hiding in a trench, Bingham captured them at pistol point and made them carry Thomas. Bingham, a 28-year-old from Gormanston, Tasmania, was a fine sportsman who won civil and Army shooting competitions. On 3 August 1945 in Borneo, Warrant-Officer Bingham died from an accidental self-inflicted wound.

The 2/15th and 2/17th battalions led the initial 20th Brigade advance. The 2/17th suffered many casualties from artillery and machine guns. Corporal 'Toby' Harris (DCM) energetically led his four-man section in knocking out one troublesome machine-gun post and killing its occupants. Though wounded in the thigh and shoulder, he refused to leave for treatment. The following night he led another successful attack and was wounded again by aerial bombing. He was hit again in New Guinea in 1943, and at his discharge from the Army in June 1944, the 34-year-old pastoral worker was carrying scars from a gunshot wound to the face and shrapnel wounds on the left shoulder, thigh and forearm.

Two companies of the 2/13th Battalion had to advance across a front more than two kilometres wide. When enemy minefields proved to be six times deeper than anticipated, gaps could not be opened in time for the supporting tanks, so the infantry went in alone. Determined Germans opposed them. A second pair of companies passed through at 3 am and encountered especially fierce resistance. One company commander, Captain Ross Sanderson, stepped forward to meet some surrendering Germans, only to be shot dead. Lieutenant Edward Norrie, the 22-year-old son of a distinguished medical officer, had already been seriously wounded, but took command and led the men on. When he too was killed, Lieutenant Charles O'Connor ignored his own wounds and took up the baton, calling for volunteers to attack a nearby post. He led 12 men in the attack, which overcame the post in hand-to-hand fighting but saw O'Connor wounded again, this time mortally. The company now had only one officer remaining, Lieutenant Fred Treweeke, who would be killed four days later. On the battalion's left flank, Sergeant Roy Easter (DCM) was commanding a platoon.

Following orders, he attached them to the Gordon Highlanders in an advance of more than 700 metres, personally destroying two German machine-gun crews.

Despite their exertions on the first night at Alamein, Allied infantrymen were unable to clear corridors in the minefields and enemy defences through which the British armour could sortie. The Germans had been surprised, not least because Rommel was in Germany for medical treatment, but by the time the northern objectives had been taken, late on 24 October, the Axis had formed a new defensive line. So began what General Bernard Montgomery called the battle's 'crumbling' phase, in which Axis forces, especially tanks, were whittled away by Allied infantry attacks and their own counterattacks.

On the night of 24 October, the 2/13th needed to complete its objectives for the previous night. Sergeant Easter proved his worth again. Tall and laconic, with a reputation as an outstanding patroller, he led a patrol to gather intelligence on enemy dispositions. When he discovered a group of unidentified troops between his patrol and the battalion lines, he challenged them, discovered they were enemy, and attacked. His patrol inflicted eight casualties for no loss and brought information that persuaded the commanding officer to attack without artillery support. Their surprise attack was a complete success.

When the 2/17th Battalion moved forward that night, their vehicles came under flanking fire. A truck carrying the 2/17th's machine-gun platoon went up in flames, but Sergeant John Cortis (DCM) extracted a Vickers gun and brought his subsection into action so effectively that it silenced several enemy Spandaus in the course of firing 20 000 rounds that night. Cortis received a severe thigh wound several days later but returned to action as an infantry officer in the Pacific.

The following day, 25 October, saw strong Axis counterattacks, shelling and sniping inflict heavy casualties. The 2/17th alone suffered 85 killed and wounded on what the battalion dubbed 'Black Sunday'.

About 40 Italian tanks attacked across the 20th Brigade front, but Australian anti-tank guns halted them. The 2/13th Battalion's two-pounder guns accounted for at least seven. Sergeant Allen Bentley (DCM) commanded the 2/13th's anti-tank platoon, which had lost its officer and other men. Helping to man a gun, Bentley waited until the leading tank was close (40 or 200 yards according to different sources) before opening fire and destroying it with his first shot. The other anti-tank guns then fired too, stopping every tank in the first wave. Bentley had qualified at an anti-tank course just three months earlier. His gun accounted for five or six tanks before he was wounded in the chest and head. He was only evacuated when he collapsed. Like Bentley, earlier casualties to this platoon forced Private John Taylor (MM) to an unusually senior role, and as the tanks approached, he commanded a gun crew. They knocked out two tanks. Though under fire, Taylor then took sticky grenades and went to destroy the abandoned tanks. The following day he and another man crawled out to two enemy tanks disabled on a minefield, destroying them while pinned in No Man's Land for five hours. Lieutenant Fred Wallder (MC) commanded a troop of 2/3rd Anti-Tank Regiment 6-pounders that accounted for nine tanks in the 25 October attack. His success was credited largely to his siting of the guns, a skill he also used to great effect later in the battle. Wallder, a Western Australian, had risen from the ranks. Manning these guns was dangerous, and the enemy destroyed 36 of the regiment's guns during the battle. More than 100 of its gunners were killed or wounded.

A platoon commander later wrote a tribute to the Australian FOO attached to the 2/17th and located just 40 metres away on this Black Sunday. Enemy shells fell on the area all day, reported this infantry officer, killing and wounding men, destroying vehicles and even entering the trenches. Nevertheless, the artillery officer, Lieutenant Tim Rodriguez (MC), stood in the open behind his Bren carrier, undeterred by shells bursting around him as he observed enemy fire and directed the friendly artillery's response. At one point, shrapnel penetrated his shirt, damaged his wallet and binoculars and struck the carrier. Rodriguez lived to enjoy a successful Army career, rising to lieutenant-colonel.

Trig 29: Seizing the high ground

On the night of 25/26 October, the 9th Division launched a highly significant attack. The 26th Brigade was tasked with capturing Trig 29, a spur permitting superb observation over the surrounding ground. After two companies of the 2/48th captured an intermediate objective, four Bren gun carriers drove through at 24 kilometres per hour, carrying a third company and depositing them on Trig 29 one minute after the supporting artillery concentration lifted. The contest for the well-defended spur involved some of the 2/48th's bloodiest hand-to-hand fighting. Corporal Robert Kennedy (DCM) threw a grenade that killed two Germans in a strongpost holding up his section's advance. He later used the bayonet to drive off Germans attacking a machine gunner who was out of ammunition. Even when wounded, Kennedy continued to organise the defence of the newly won ground.

Corporal Kingsley 'King' Albrecht (DCM) was leading another section when his platoon was halted by heavy machine-gun and cannon fire, apparently emanating from a strongpost. Albrecht charged with his rifle and bayonet, only to discover the 'post' to be a dug-in Panzer III. Rather than seek cover, he persevered and used a No. 73 anti-tank against the Panzer. This rendered the crew unconscious before they were killed with hand grenades. Albrecht sustained a head wound from shell fragments but continued to fight though covered with blood. Kennedy and Albrecht were both labourers from rural South Australia.

The supporting company following the carriers ran into fire as they approached the ridge. Lieutenant Colin Taggart and four others in his platoon were killed attacking a series of posts here, and soon only seven members remained unhurt. Two of them, 40-year-old Private Percy Gratwick (VC) and section commander Corporal Bart Lindsey, summoned the courage to stand and charge the posts. Gratwick, in the lead, destroyed one post with a grenade, bayoneted a submachine gunner firing at him, and ran into another post and killed an entire mortar crew before being shot down.

Lindsey would lose an eye in the fighting that night or the next day. Gratwick's action unnerved the Germans in the area, and his company commander, Captain Bob Shillaker (MC), grabbed the opportunity to secure vital ground west of Trig 29. Shillaker, just 23, had also been outstanding at Tel el Eisa in July. By daylight, the 2/48th's weary fighters were established in shallow trenches on Trig 29 and had laid 2000 mines.

That night, the 2/24th advanced on the right of the 2/48th. Most of its companies were already down to about half-strength, and their demanding task was to advance 2700 metres past enemy posts on a switch line, or second line of defences. Contrary to expectations, most of the defenders were German. The leading companies had almost reached the first objective when they ran into heavy enemy fire and some of the strongest defensive positions the Australians encountered at Alamein. Sergeant George Berry (DCM), commanding a platoon, subdued two enemy posts by himself before his platoon followed him through intense fire. Once the company reached its objective a cunningly sited enemy post proved an obstacle. A three-platoon assault was planned and Berry was first into the post, where in the words of his citation 'he carried out terrible execution with the bayonet' until a gunshot broke his arm. The 23-year-old's frontline career was over.

As mentioned, Lieutenant Greatorex performed well here until wounded. Then Sergeant-Major Fred Cameron (MC), who had been badly wounded in the face and hand in July, took over the company, which had lost all its officers and many NCOs. The company had overshot its objective and reached the edge of a formidable German defensive location that the Australians called 'Thompson's Post'. Acting Corporal Jimmy Anderson (DCM) distinguished himself when machine-gun fire from just 50 metres halted his platoon. Calling out 'I'll get them', Anderson began firing his TSMG from the hip and charging. The advance was in bright moonlight and two guns were firing at him, but he reached the post and killed all four gunners. Cameron withdrew his company, now just 14 strong, as the 2/24th fell back south-east of Trig 29. By the end of 26 October, it had captured 169 prisoners, two 88mm guns and many other weapons, at a cost of 114 casualties.

During daylight on 26 October, Rommel, who had returned to the front the previous evening, sent in his first attempt to recapture Trig 29. It failed, as did the 25 or so attacks that followed in subsequent days. Most were broken up by the tremendous artillery support available to the feature's defenders. Trig 29 became the most shelled location on the Alamein battlefield. A FOO there was the 2/7th Field Regiment's Lieutenant Bob Menzies (MC). On the battle's first morning, Captain Bill Ligertwood (MC), who was decorated for bravery in the earlier Alamein fighting, was mortally wounded when an armour-piercing round penetrated his Bren carrier on the forward slopes of Trig 33. Menzies was sent forward to replace him, and directed fire from that dangerously exposed position for the following 48 hours. Now on Trig 29, he established an observation post, again in an area offering little cover. For 48 hours he directed fire that dispersed many Axis counterattacks, and though relieved for one night, he returned on 28 October. From that dangerous but vital ground he could see up to 4500 metres in all directions. The affable charm of this young Western Australian endeared him to all in the regiment. From 28 October, the 2/17th Battalion took over the defence of Trig 29.

'Attack North'

Montgomery ordered Morshead to 'Attack North' after the fall of Trig 29, and on the night of 28/29 October, the understrength 2/13th Battalion occupied the mine-laden and booby-trapped 'Fig Orchard'. The 2/15th reached its objective too. Corporal Vincent 'Bill' Anderson (DCM) and his formidable section were prominent. This sub-unit had reportedly captured an 88mm gun and its crew in Operation Bulimba. On 23 October, Anderson led his men in overcoming an enemy post that was pouring enfilading fire on his battalion. His section had dug in on the left when two half-tracks towing 50mm anti-tank guns approached. He ordered his men to hold their fire until the vehicles were close, and then they set one alight. Anderson and his men captured the two crews – some 22 men – guns and the remaining half-track.

    The third battalion that attacked that night was the 2/23rd, tasked to drive between the ground just won by the 2/13th and 2/15th and to secure a foothold on the main road. Most of the battalion were to advance in Bren carriers, but unusually, others were to ride on British tanks. The plan went wrong from the outset, with seven tanks knocked out on 'friendly' mines. Enemy anti-tank guns inflicted more damage from close range and the infantry and tanks lost communications. Some 26 tanks were destroyed and the 2/23rd suffered over 200 casualties. Amazingly, though, small groups pushed on, and by the next evening, the 2/23rd had advanced 1000 metres. Company Sergeant-Major Ken Joyce (DCM), whose company was advancing on the left flank, was prominent here. He was behind the turret of one of the foremost tanks when it exploded, throwing him into the air. Though dazed, he clung to his Bren. All the company officers were soon hit by machine-gun and mortar fire, and Joyce took over. He led a successful attack on a gun position, then advanced some 300 metres and took a series of German trenches. He counted 75 Australians with whom to push on to the main objective, a ridge some 500 metres ahead, from which two machine-gun posts were constantly shooting at them. He arranged for Vickers machine guns to neutralise the enemy Spandaus. His force was just 100 metres from one post when the moon emerged from behind clouds and they came under fire again. A nearby soldier was felled and three rounds hit Joyce's haversack. When the moon clouded over again, Joyce approached the pit from the side and killed its occupants with grenades. The other pit was subdued, and once the Australians reached the top of the ridge, the defenders surrendered. Joyce sent 40 prisoners back, while his men, now numbering fewer than 40, dug in and held their ground. Joyce, a labourer from Korumburra (also George Berry's hometown), finished the war a lieutenant.

Joyce and the other Australians who advanced that night intensified Rommel's anxiety about his northern flank, leading him to shift his elite 90th Light Division to the Australian front. Rommel's commitment of ever more German forces to the north enabled Montgomery to plan a powerful armoured thrust, codenamed 'Supercharge', further south. It was set down for the night of 1/2 November but depended on the Australians maintaining the pressure on the Germans. On 29 and 30 October, Rommel's forces attempted to drive the 20th Brigade from Trig 29 and their newly won ground but failed.

On 29 October, a signals truck blew up on a minefield. Those aboard included Signalman Tom McAllister (DCM), who was severely wounded. From the beginning of the battle, the signallers had done vital work. On the first night, McAllister was in a 9th Division Signals team laying a line to a battalion headquarters when heavy shell fire wounded the NCO in charge. McAllister immediately took command, ensuring that line and others were completed. In subsequent days, until he was wounded, McAllister painstakingly repaired and maintained these vital means of communication lines cut repeatedly by traffic and enemy shelling.

Morshead's plan

On the night of 30/31 October, Morshead set in motion a plan to maintain the pressure on the Germans by cutting off many of those on the coast. In Phase One, the 2/32nd Battalion was to march north-east to the railway and road, creating a base for Phase Two at Barrel Hill. From there, the 2/24th and 2/48th battalions would advance east along the main road, clearing defences and attacking the German frontline from behind. In Phase Three, the 2/24th and 2/48th would advance south and north respectively. Finally, the 2/3rd Pioneer Battalion would march north from Barrel Hill to the coast, cutting off all German troops to the east.

This plan made tremendous demands on the Australian units

assigned to fulfil it. The greatest challenges were to the 2/3rd Pioneers, an unblooded and incomplete unit assigned no support weapons, and the 2/24th and 2/48th battalions, each of which was below half-strength.

Phase One went well, with the 2/32nd reaching the railway and occupying the Blockhouse, a railway gangers' hut that the Germans were using as a hospital. As the 2/32nd advanced, two machine-gun posts opened fire on one leading company from the right. Sergeant Duncan MacDonald (DCM) organised a party of four to attack these posts. Two men fell wounded as they got close. One dropped a Bren, which MacDonald picked up and used to continue the attack with Private Alex Davidson (MM). MacDonald fired on both posts while advancing, and then he and Davidson each charged a post. MacDonald killed all four occupants of one, while Davidson captured the other, bayonetting one man and taking six Germans prisoner. Davidson turned the captured machine gun on groups of enemy troops visible by the light of flares. Neither MacDonald nor Davidson is mentioned in the official history and only their official citations are in the battalion history. MacDonald had served with the 2/9th Battalion in Tobruk in 1941, where he sustained a serious penetrating gunshot wound in the abdomen and penis. He was hospitalised for six months. In June 1943, he was discharged from the Army, medically unfit. Davidson's subsequent record was also unusual. He was often in trouble for going AWL and for disobedience before Alamein, and once he was injured while riding atop a train! He repeatedly went AWL in Australia in early 1943 and was sentenced to three weeks' detention. Three times he returned from AWL with injuries. In October he deserted. He was court-martialled in January 1945, having been absent from his unit from October 1943 to December 1944. He was sentenced to two years' detention but escaped in March 1945. He was apprehended while stealing a bicycle in February 1946 and discharged in March 1946 after being found guilty in another court martial.

While the 2/32nd advanced, Australian engineers blew a gap in the railway embankment, so supporting vehicles and weapons could cross safely. German forces came from the west and inflicted casualties, but the gap was held open. The Australians captured both Barrel Hill, or B11, overlooking the road and the coast, and the Blockhouse. This building became the RAP for the 2/32nd Battalion, under the RMO, Captain Bill Campbell (MC). There was already much medical equipment in the building's six rooms, and he allowed the German occupants – three medical officers and nine orderlies – to stay. Some of them had to be prevented from escaping. One also tried to use a telephone, but Campbell disconnected it. The Blockhouse became an international medical post, and the German doctors worked skilfully not only on their own wounded but also on numerous Australians. Campbell was in charge, and constantly busy with a flood of casualties: he personally attended to every case. A large Red Cross flag flew over the building and Rommel scrupulously ordered that the 'Hut', as the Germans called it, not be targeted. Nevertheless, the building was in the middle of furious bombardment and fighting for two days, and one shell penetrated the roof. Some patients had to be dug out. For a day it was too dangerous for ambulances to approach the building.

Chaplain Eric Seatree (MC) of the 2/3rd Pioneer Battalion was working at his battalion's RAP, located in a hole in the railway embankment. He went out amidst heavy artillery and mortar fire, scouring an area 200 metres south of the railway for casualties. He personally brought in a casualty who was in a state of collapse. When an ambulance driver collapsed near his ambulance later on 31 October, Seatree went to his aid and helped bring him in. After shells were seen exploding among Australians 200 metres away, Seatree took a stretcher and helped carry a wounded infantryman. Another conspicuously brave chaplain was Edgar 'Jimmy' James (MC). Though recently arrived at the 2/15th Battalion, he threw himself into his task, often visiting the forward troops. His headquarters were at the RAP, where his calm attention to casualties had a cheering influence. He continually searched for wounded and buried the dead, despite the dangers of enemy shelling, mines and booby traps. He also helped stretcher-bearers bring in the wounded.

When on 25 October the RMO was killed under enemy shelling, James' cool and steady leadership inspired those around him. On 25 October, James took a truck by himself into No Man's Land and, in full view of the Germans, drove to a grave marked by a rifle stuck in the ground. He dug up four bodies and took them to the cemetery. He then went to a Bren carrier containing two corpses and left unmolested because it was in a minefield. Undeterred by a mine caught in the tracks, he carried the bodies out.

Fighting for every inch of ground

After the 2/32nd completed Phase One of the 30/31 October attacks, Phase Two began late. The 2/24th and 2/48th start-line was under fire and they set off 15 minutes behind the artillery barrage, thus losing its benefits in their exceptionally demanding eastwards advance. After making early progress, with 2/24th south of the railway and 2/48th on the northern axis, they had to fight for every inch of ground against dug-in artillery, machine guns and mortars. In small groups, Australians summoned the courage to rush and overcome successive posts with bayonets, grenades and submachine guns. Most famous was the 2/48th's Sergeant Bill Kibby, awarded a posthumous Victoria Cross for his actions earlier in the battle and that night, when he was killed in a lone attack. There were other exceptional efforts. In the 2/48th, Sergeant 'Snowy' Ranford (DCM) took over his platoon when the officer was wounded and led them in eliminating one tough position. They then came under intense fire from an 88mm gun and machine guns. Ranford organised and led his platoon against the source. They killed 14 men and captured the '88' and two machine guns, though Ranford was badly wounded. His platoon now comprised seven men, but he led them forward until, assaulting yet another position, he was hit again and evacuated with wounds to the head (depressed skull fracture), abdomen and leg. Ranford, one of his distinguished battalion's best soldiers, was killed in action in New Guinea in 1943. Apart from his Distinguished

Conduct Medal, he was twice Mentioned in Despatches. Other decorated 2/48th soldiers who died on this night included Sergeant Lindsay Goode, who had won the battalion's first decoration, a Military Medal, for laying signal wire under fire in Tobruk, and Corporal 'Spud' Hinson, hero of Tel el Eisa, dying as he charged forward among the enemy posts.

Meanwhile, the 2/24th's Sergeant Len Dingwall (DCM) led the platoon he had taken over when his platoon commander was wounded on the battle's first night. In the 25/26 October night attack, he personally led storming parties that took two enemy posts, killing the occupants. On 30/31 October, 'Ding' again led attacks on three successive strongposts and one 88mm gun post, all despite point-blank fire. He was eventually wounded but recovered to serve as a lieutenant with the 2/1st Battalion.

Following Dingwall's platoon, Lieutenant Eric McLeod courageously led his company, Bren in hand, against enemy anti-tank and machine guns firing at close range. When McLeod went down under this fire, Company Sergeant-Major Fred Cameron, who had earlier led this company near Thompson's Post, came forward to help. He was himself wounded, but on finding McLeod dead, took over the company again. He later pulled back the unit, now just eight strong, and the commanding officer ordered him out for treatment. Cameron received a Military Cross, unusual for a warrant-officer but entirely regular. In subsequent years, though, he was arrested several times by military police for wearing this 'officer's decoration'. Cameron later suffered much ill-health, especially from malaria, and although he went to officer training in 1944, he did not complete the course and never saw action again. His battalion history introduces this brave soldier as 'indomitable'. In April 1945, the 32-year-old prewar transport driver was discharged with 'Exhaustion state with anxiety features'. As mentioned, on 26 October, Corporal Jimmy Anderson had ably supported Cameron. Now, with Cameron's and another company delayed near the railway line, Anderson again leapt up and charged a post, silencing its occupants with his blazing Tommy gun. Anderson sustained a severe leg wound but crawled over to Cameron in time to return with him and the remnants of the company to a new defensive position. Anderson, a former tractor driver, would later, like Cameron, be discharged for ill-health.

Ultimately, both battalions had sustained too many casualties to continue. The 2/48th Battalion's rifle companies now comprised 41 men, some of them wounded. The 2/24th, halted several hundred metres short of its final objective, had a combined strength in its rifle companies of 74.

A report reached the 2/24th commanding officer, Lieutenant-Colonel Charles Weir (DSO), that a patrol had found Thompson's Post – a key objective of Phase Three – unoccupied. Dutifully, Weir took 16 men to investigate. One was killed almost immediately, and Weir's party withdrew hastily. Another man fell wounded as they departed, but stretcher-bearer Private John O'Brien (DCM) – the only bearer remaining in his company – turned back and brought him out under fire. Soon both battalions were withdrawing towards the Blockhouse. As they did so, disaster struck the 2/24th. Someone inadvertently set off trip wires that detonated two 1000-pound aerial bombs, killing 12 and wounding 16. Again, O'Brien showed his mettle, treating every casualty, including Weir, and assisting in their evacuation. That October night, the two battalions suffered over 350 casualties. Their stretcher-bearers, including O'Brien, ensured that no wounded man remained on the field. For O'Brien, Alamein was the height of a chequered career. He had lied about his age on enlistment in May 1941, when he was just 18. Thereafter, he was frequently in trouble for indiscipline – eight offences in the first year – and after El Alamein this continued. He was tried for desertion in January 1944, given a suspended sentence but later jailed for re-offending. One of the battalion's best boxers, O'Brien was discharged from the Army on 'compassionate grounds' in July 1944, aged 21.

Phases Two and Three of Morshead's plan had failed, but now the Pioneer Battalion needed to try Phase Four, advancing from the Blockhouse to the coast. They soon came under machine-gun fire, and Lance-Corporal Ted Mulley (MM) led a section in subduing a Spandau post. Two of the attackers were Hobart-born brothers,

Leonard and Allan Kerr. Allan, whose middle names were 'Douglas Haig', fell dead across the machine gun. Mulley was wounded in the right shoulder but, against the RMO's recommendation, soldiered on. The Pioneers reached their first objective, but as they neared their final objective, on the coast, their own artillery barrage halted them. Without communications to the artillery, they had to stop and consolidate, 1100 metres short.

Battle for the Saucer

Morshead's ambitious objectives for the night had not been achieved, but he had succeeded in distracting the Germans. Rommel believed that his forces east of the Blockhouse were cut off, and he became preoccupied with saving them. The Australians barring his way were mainly located between the Blockhouse and Barrel Hill, an area the Australians called 'the Saucer'. Rommel first used superior forces to clear the Pioneers between Barrel Hill and the coast. Ted Mulley was wounded a second time in mid-morning but again refused to leave his section. When his battalion fell back, he organised his section, including the other wounded. He was wounded a third time but carried on as the men set up in new positions. While moving between them he sustained a fourth wound. This time he had to be carried to the RAP and evacuation.

Most of the 2/3rd Pioneer Battalion retreated to the Saucer, but some brave individuals clung to the forward slopes of Barrel Hill. Around noon, they became spectators to a remarkable tank battle between Panzers advancing towards the hill and outgunned Valentine tanks that came forward to tackle them. Most of one 2/32nd company was forced to surrender. The British tanks suffered heavy casualties, but together with anti-tank gunners managed to repel the Panzers. Two further heavy German attacks that afternoon failed to penetrate the wall of artillery, anti-tank and infantry fire. British tank units had often disappointed the Australians, but the 2/48th Battalion historian described the efforts of the 40th Battalion,

Royal Tank Regiment, this day, including the sacrifice of 21 tanks, as 'magnificent'. Most anti-tank gunners in the Saucer were Rhodesians, but there were Australians too, including Gunner Albert Schwebel of the 2/3rd Anti-Tank Regiment. When a German tank knocked out his 6-pounder near Barrel Hill, Schwebel's crew were all killed or wounded. Schwebel was hit in the arms and legs but carried his two wounded crewmates through enemy fire and into the Blockhouse. He then returned to his damaged gun and, by salvaging parts from other unserviceable 6-pounders, was able to bring it into action again. Once more, enemy fire hit the gun and he received another wound, this time to the head. Undeterred, he took a Bren and joined the infantry defence. The following day he carried a wounded soldier 500 metres to the Blockhouse and was only stopped from returning to the battle when it was found that his wounds included a bullet through the head. Schwebel, a Sydney mechanic's assistant who appears to have lied about his age and was just 19, received no award.

The Australians held the Saucer throughout 31 October, but Rommel would try again to smash it. Morshead wisely relieved the exhausted and depleted 26th Brigade units in the Saucer with the fresher 24th Brigade. In the early morning of 1 November, the 2/32nd was joined by its sister battalions, the 2/28th and 2/43rd. Both had been involved in diversionary actions on the first night of the battle, but nothing significant since. Their greatest ordeal was imminent.

From 10 am on 1 November, the Saucer's defenders were under continuous artillery fire from east, north and west, while German infantry and tanks sought repeatedly to destroy the Australian forces there and on Barrel Hill. The Germans concentrated on the Rhodesian anti-tank guns and destroyed eight of them. No British tanks were available, but Lieutenant Wallder again performed wonders, somehow getting his troop across the railway and into positions in the Saucer, where it knocked out two tanks. Another Rhodesian troop arrived too. Most of the Allied anti-tank guns and gunners did not survive the day. Artillery fire dispersed most German infantry attacks, but at about 3.30 pm, German tanks and infantry forced the Australians off the forward slopes of Barrel Hill and captured part of the summit. How the retreating Australians of the 2/43rd Battalion responded would be crucial. First, two officers intervened. One was Captain Collin Newbery, from the neighbouring 2/28th Battalion, whose inspiring leadership is noted in the official history and who would rise to brigadier. The other was the commander of the retreating troops, Captain Ivan 'Bunny' Hare. This 34-year-old schoolteacher from St Peter's College, Adelaide, had received a Military Cross for fine leadership at Ruin Ridge in July and courage in rescuing a lost patroller in August. His company admired him and now, waving his pistol, he yelled at them to go back. An eyewitness noted the resolute determination on the faces of Hare's men. While leading one counterattacking group, Hare was killed by airburst artillery fire. One of Hare's platoons, located further north than any other 24th Brigade unit on the battlefield that day, was under Sergeant 'Alby' Joy (MM). Tanks fired directly at the platoon's bunkers from close range and it retreated. Joy reorganised his men and led them back, where they captured all but one post they had lost and held them until the Germans eventually abandoned all attempts on the position. Joy, a former labourer and just 5 feet 4 inches tall, would become an officer in 1944.

The 2/43rd Battalion alone suffered more than 100 casualties on 1 November and the 24th Brigade had sustained nearly 500 since 30 October – but their sacrifice greatly benefited the Allied cause. When the pressure on the Saucer finally eased at 2.30 am on 2 November, the decisive British attack, Operation Supercharge, had begun further south. It was the beginning of the end for Rommel: by 4 November he had ordered a general withdrawal. General Montgomery praised the Australians' 'magnificent work'. Immediately after the battle, a British corps commander visited Morshead to congratulate him on the 9th Division's prodigious efforts. Morshead's response was, 'Thank you, General. The boys were interested.'

CHAPTER 15

THE BEACHHEAD BATTLES: GONA, BUNA AND SANANANDA

Having saved Papua from Japanese conquest at Milne Bay and Kokoda, the Australians next had to evict their enemies from strong bases across an 18-kilometre front on the Papuan coast, at Gona, Buna and Sanananda. The area was flat, covered with jungle and swamp, and disease-ridden. Sickness would hit both sides hard. The determined and well-entrenched Japanese defenders of the bases numbered about 9000. Gona, Buna and Sanananda were effectively separate fronts.

Desolation at Gona

The 25th Brigade's advance on Gona initially progressed well, but its men were tired, sick and dependent on airdrops for supplies. They launched a full assault on 22 November 1942, when the 2/31st and 2/33rd battalions lost 65 men to the well-entrenched enemy, who ceded none of the 275-metre by 275-metre area they were holding. A 2/25th assault the following day made little headway, and the brigade had lost 20 per cent of its strength in five days. On 22 November, Signalman Neville 'Irish' Mulally (MM) of the 2/33rd mended five breaks in the line between his company and headquarters, all under fire. At one point, he even held the parted ends of a telephone cable together in his teeth to maintain the connection. On 24 November, when the rest of the battalion withdrew, he kept his telephone in a forward position with just ten other men. On 26 November, when the Japanese counterattacked, the line was cut eight times: each time, Mulally repaired it. He also left his post to do effective work with his TSMG. Between campaigns, Mulally was often in trouble with authority. He was found guilty of more than a dozen charges during his service, usually for going AWL. He was hospitalised in January 1943 for 'Contusion Right Eye and Alcoholism'. By 1945 he had been medically downgraded, and soon after being arrested while on leave for 'indecent language', he was discharged, 'there being no suitable vacancy in which his services could be employed'.

The 2/31st's Corporal Roland Duncan (MM) established a forward RAP at Gona on 23 November. A prewar woodcutter, 'Dunc' was hospitalised for lengthy periods in 1941 and 1942 with venereal disease. At Gona he created order amidst chaos, dressing wounds and arranging stretcher parties late into the night. The medical officer never needed to reapply any dressing made by Duncan. Stretcher-bearer Geoff Hamlyn-Harris marvelled at the calm and deftness of 'Dunc', his 'boss', who injected morphine to make the last hours of many casualties 'free of insufferable agony'. Duncan risked his life tending such men and treating those who could be saved. He ended the war a sergeant.

On 25 November, another attack at Gona foundered, despite help from the 180-strong 3rd Battalion and four field guns. Three days later, the 21st Brigade began arriving: first the 2/14th Battalion, refreshed but just 450 strong, soon followed by the 2/16th and 2/27th, at similar strength. Sixteen days earlier, General Blamey had addressed an assembly of other ranks and then officers of the brigade at Koitaki, near Port Moresby, and made thinly veiled accusations that they had run like rabbits during the Kokoda operations. This offended his audience, and probably spurred them on to reckless deeds at Gona. Nevertheless, in late November, not even the combined forces of the 21st and 25th brigades and the 39th Battalion could capture Gona. On 4 December, Vasey relieved the decimated 25th Brigade and allotted Gona to the 21st Brigade and 39th Battalion. The 25th

Signalman Neville 'Irish' Mulally in the foreground at Gona. He mended at least 13 breaks in telephone wire, once holding parted ends in his teeth to maintain communications. Often in trouble with the authorities, Mulally was eventually forced out of the Army.
AWM 013760

had suffered more than 200 battle casualties at Gona, while the 21st incurred 340 in five days. The 2/16th and 2/27th battalions were so depleted that they were formed into a composite battalion, which on 6 December joined the 400-strong 39th Battalion in another unsuccessful attack. The 39th lost 58 men in capturing 50 metres of ground. Thirty-year-old Corporal Reg Edgell (DCM), a 5-feet-6-inches-tall Moonee Ponds hairdresser, took advantage of the noise and distraction of the main attack to take his section through semi-darkness into the heart of the Japanese positions. Discovering that his section was alone, he wisely decided to pull out, leading his men towards an enemy post that was busy facing another attack. With his Owen submachine gun – an Australian invention just now being issued – and aided by a Bren gunner, Edgell killed about 12 Japanese before reaching safety.

Some 150–200 Japanese were still holding an area 275 by 200 metres at Gona, but a similar number were estimated to be on the Australian left flank near the Amboga River where just 45 men of the 2/16th opposed them. Since 21 November, Lieutenant Alan Haddy (MID), who had shown initiative and courage in Syria, and the men he called his 'children' had been watching and harassing the Japanese in the area. His smiling countenance and great physical strength, apparent as he usually went shirtless and carrying a Tommy gun, inspired his men, as did his willingness to be first in, as forward scout, and last out if they were attacked. He also used a 2-inch mortar to deadly effect against Japanese reinforcements landing nearby.

However, during a storm on the night of 6/7 December, an overwhelmingly large group of Japanese approached Haddy and 20 sick and exhausted volunteers located in a cluster of buildings known as 'Haddy's Village'. Haddy sent some men away to bring reinforcements. Fourteen, under Corporal Gordon Murphy (MM), arrived in time to hold off the attackers until fresh troops could be summoned.

Acting Corporal Bob Thompson (DCM) of the 2/16th had on 1 December rescued three wounded men in separate and dangerous trips. Now he led his section across open ground to grenade-throwing range. Though wounded, the 31-year-old Kalgoorlie trucker persisted until hit again. Only when four other casualties from his section had been evacuated did he, with wounds to his forearm, thigh and back, agree to follow. Thompson survived his wounds but fell dangerously ill with scrub typhus. Though evacuated to Australia, he died on 29 December. Thompson had often been in trouble for going AWL – even spending several weeks in detention barracks in April 1941 before fighting bravely in the Syria campaign. His deeds, which won him a Distinguished Conduct Medal, are not mentioned in the official or battalion histories.

On the morning of 7 December, the 2/14th's Lieutenant Bob Dougherty reached Haddy's Village with a 50-strong relief force. In fierce fighting, the Australians inflicted up to 90 casualties at the cost of just six wounded: Dougherty himself was said to have killed 14. A superb patroller, Dougherty's battalion history classed him with the 14th Battalion's World War I Victoria Cross winner, Albert Jacka, even though he received no award. Short but strong, the 23-year-old former iron foundry apprentice was killed on patrol four days later. After Dougherty's patrol relieved Haddy's men, the Japanese still outnumbered them and sought to encircle Dougherty's force on the beach. Acting Corporal Stan Weeks (MM) and Private Les Crilly (MM), section mates, stepped forward. Weeks had a Bren and TSMG, Crilly a TSMG, and together they attacked the Japanese in the flank. Each took turns to dash into the jungle, kill a few and dash out, covered by the other before moving on. This halted the enemy and allowed the patrol to withdraw to safer ground. Their citations credited them with killing 23 Japanese. Crilly was yet another often in trouble for going AWL, but he also exemplifies the health problems that struck Australians on the beachheads. He had 11 wartime hospital admissions for malaria and spent 175 days in medical facilities. He was also wounded in early 1944. Both he and Weeks were discharged as corporals in 1944.

Haddy's force had been saved but their leader was dead. Soon after sending for reinforcements, he had told his men to withdraw, and that he would leave last. Haddy's body and that of Private Syd

The 2/14th Battalion historian compared Lieutenant Bob Dougherty, seen here in characteristic pose at Gona, to the 14th Battalion's World War I Victoria Cross winner Albert Jacka. However, this outstanding leader and patroller, who was killed at Gona, received no award.
COURTESY OF JIM MCALLESTER

Stephens were found in his headquarters under a hut. Around them lay dead Japanese. His RMO, 'Blue' Steward, considered Haddy the embodiment of the laconic, strong, great-hearted Australian soldier. Once, as Haddy hurled a grenade, Steward overheard him call out words one can imagine him saying at the end: 'Mix that with your rice, you bastards!'

On 7 December, the remainder of the 2/14th Battalion was sent to support Lieutenant Dougherty. Their combined forces numbered only about 100 as they formed a defensive perimeter.

The 21st Brigade, now only 792 strong, was sent into a desperate attempt to seize Gona the following day. General Vasey promised 250 rounds of artillery support but warned that if this attack did not succeed he would go on to the defensive at Gona.

The attack began with 15 minutes of artillery and mortar bombardment, during which the 39th's Captain Joseph Gilmore (MC) took his men right up to the enemy positions. Two minutes before the bombardment ceased, Gilmore led them into the attack, which made a breach that enabled two following companies to break into Gona's defences. Gilmore, a Queensland farmer, ended the war a major with the 2/2nd Battalion. Lieutenant Hugh Dalby (MC) commanded one of Gilmore's platoons, which he personally led against the first post encountered. He killed a gunner manning a Woodpecker and seven other Japanese. Only then could his men, close behind him, join in the hand-to-hand fighting for the position, which concluded with 38 Japanese dead and four machine guns captured. Corporal Stan Ellis (DCM), of the same platoon, then pushed on, single-handedly wiping out four more posts. Private Rudolph Wilkinson (MM) found a location from which he could see and fire at the enemy's positions. He too was in full view of the defenders, standing in the open with his Bren mounted on a four-feet-high post.

While the 39th attacked Gona from one side and reached the village, the composite 2/16th–2/27th attacked across open ground east of Gona. Again, the cost was high, with three platoon commanders hit, but they gained ground. Captain Bill Atkinson was outstanding and received a Bar to the Military Cross he had won in Syria. By nightfall, the composite battalion was dug in within grenade-throwing distance of the Japanese, who were almost encircled. More than 100 Japanese were killed that night trying to reach the sea.

On the morning of 9 December, Australian patrols entered Gona Mission. The 39th commander, Lieutenant-Colonel Honner, sent a famous message: 'Gona's gone!' The Australians buried 638 Japanese. The stench of death and excrement was appalling. Many Japanese were still west of Gona Creek, however. With much still to do, the four Australian battalions at Gona had lost 530 killed and wounded, 41 per cent of the strength with which they started.

The 39th Battalion was advancing west in swamp on 10 or 11 December when it encountered Japanese defences on the seashore in Haddy's Village. Corporal Reg Edgell, the section commander who had briefly penetrated the enemy positions on 6 December, was hit twice in the right arm when an enemy machine gun opened up. Using his left hand to fire his Owen, he rushed the post, killing the three machine gunners. This enabled the rest of his company to advance. Edgell helped evacuate two casualties before seeking assistance himself. Due to his wounds and malaria, Edgell was discharged medically unfit in September 1943.

Lieutenant Ron Plater (MC), a 21-year-old regular soldier, proved the value of his Duntroon training. In Gona Mission the previous day, he had thrown grenades that killed six Japanese trying to escape in the head-high kunai grass, including an officer whose sword he captured. Now, west of Gona, he maintained the impetus of the attack down the main track, leaving a trail of dead Japanese who tried to stop him. When one post fired on the Australians from the right, Plater made a stealthy, lone attack in which he killed two officers and four other ranks, capturing their machine gun and four mortars. For four more hours he was everywhere, striking personally with his Owen or grenades or directing sections into position. Late in the day, while preparing an attack on a machine-gun post, the section leader was wounded beside him. Plater was bandaging the man when he himself was seriously wounded in the shoulder blade.

Undaunted, he personally led the section in a successful attack. Sadly, his wound and osteoarthritis meant that his fighting career was over almost as soon as it began: he was downgraded medically and became an instructor.

Plater's replacement proved as brilliant as he was. Lieutenant Phillip Gartner (MC) first led his own platoon in attacking Haddy's Village that day. It took four hours of fighting to reach the village, by which time his platoon comprised just 11 men. A fresh company relieved them, but Gartner stayed, taking over Plater's platoon and continuing the perilous advance down the main track. For five days he led this platoon, not just by directing the men but by personal example: making grenade attacks on the enemy, and for hours firing a 2-inch mortar and EY rifle (a rifle grenade discharger). Packing his ears to deaden the sound and oblivious to Japanese attempts to find him, this 6-foot-1-inch tall target fired bomb after bomb. He was also a fine shot but, on 16 December, while sniping at the enemy, he was finally hit, receiving a bullet wound to the left side. He bandaged the wound and led his men 40 metres into an attack credited with killing 35 enemy. Six hours after being hit he could no longer walk and was carried to help. Gartner later served with the 2/2nd Battalion, the 1st New Guinea Infantry Battalion and, in late 1945, the Indian Army. A university student on enlistment, Gartner retired a major.

The Japanese still numbered some 600 near Haddy's Village, including many fresh troops. Nevertheless, the 39th and 2/14th battalions hemmed them in from east, south and west. Corporal Stan Ellis was prominent again here. For three days he went into No Man's Land before daylight, dug a new hole and lay in it. From there he threw grenades towards a troublesome Woodpecker and sniped at Japanese before returning to his section. He was credited with 12–20 kills. Early on 18 December, he crawled to within 10 metres of the machine-gun post and killed its crew with grenades. The former grocer's assistant then led his platoon in the decisive assault at Haddy's Village early on 18 December. Lieutenant Hugh Dalby was again significant, dashing ahead and wiping out a seven-man

Woodpecker crew. Dalby had risen from a private with the 2/27th in the Middle East to lieutenant in the 39th. He ended the war a captain in the 2/14th. Ellis, 31, would suffer badly from malaria and be sent to a junior leader's course. He was then transferred to the 2/8th Battalion before being downgraded medically with 'incipient hypertension', ending the war a sergeant in a Works Company.

Bloody Buna

Buna, defended by about 2000 Japanese, demanded even more bloodshed than Gona. It was initially allocated to the 32nd US Division, but the inexperienced Americans struggled in the swampy terrain, and on 30 November, MacArthur replaced their commander with Lieutenant-General Robert L Eichelberger. The latter organised an attack by five American battalions on 5 December. Spearheading one attack were five Australian Bren carriers, brought forward amid many hardships by boat and barge. Their crews – four men per carrier – were Australians, four from the 2/7th and one from the 2/5th battalions. Their commander was Lieutenant Terence Fergusson, who had earlier served in the 6th Division Cavalry Regiment under his father, now Brigadier Maurice Fergusson, who had won the Military Cross and Bar in World War I. Young Fergusson recognised that using open-topped carriers as tanks went against current doctrine, and that leading carriers against entrenched defenders in difficult terrain was dangerous, but he and his men were keen to achieve a breakthrough and support their American allies.

After a preliminary bombardment, the carriers drove in at walking pace, so the American infantrymen could accompany them. Unfortunately, the carriers found themselves unsupported and on emerging into the open came under fire from strongposts in front and from snipers high in the trees. The advance commenced in line-ahead formation, with the carrier of Sergeant 'Jock' Taylor (DCM) leading. Taylor was 6 feet tall and born in Aberdeen, Scotland, one of twins. His birth date was officially 1907 but probably 1901.

The official historian singles him out as already having shown himself in North Africa and Greece to be 'one of the outstanding fighting men of the A.I.F.'. When Fergusson ordered the carriers to spread out, Taylor went to the right until he halted his carrier about 25 metres in front of a post that was firing on them. His crew replied with grenades and Bren-gun fire. Taylor ordered the crew to move to the rear of the post, but as it did so, a Japanese mortar bomb landed in or just behind the vehicle, killing one crewman. The carrier also became temporarily bogged in a communication trench. A Japanese emerged and attempted to grenade the carrier, but Taylor dismounted and shot him with his Bren. After silencing this post, Taylor ordered the carrier to attack another from behind. The mortar explosion had damaged the carrier but the crew managed to tackle a previously hidden intermediate post. As before, enemy fire could not penetrate the carrier's armour, but when Taylor rose to fire the Bren, a burst struck his left arm and he bled profusely. Accounts vary as to what he did next. Some say that he went to help Fergusson, that he threw more grenades, that he passed grenades to another man, while his citation and one eyewitness say that after losing and regaining consciousness he went to the rear for aid. His brave driver, Private Angus Cameron, and rear Bren gunner, Leslie Locke, carried on the fight until the motor stopped altogether and both were wounded. Locke covered Cameron's departure and then, suffering from a serious stomach wound, lay on the ground feigning death until nightfall. Within 30 minutes, all five carriers were knocked out. The Australian dead included Fergusson, shot while standing up to call to an adjacent carrier, and his second-in-command, Lieutenant Ian Walker, who marched from headquarters to risk his life searching for the dead, wounded and any abandoned weapons. Fergusson and Walker were each posthumously awarded an American Distinguished Service Cross.

By 14 December, the reinforced Americans had taken Buna village, but the main Japanese defences at Buna remained intact. General Blamey, as Allied Land Forces commander, had by then decided to employ Australian troops at Buna. He chose the

Sergeant Douglas 'Jock' Taylor (DCM). He was over 40 when he led an open-topped Bren carrier towards hidden enemy positions in an extraordinary action at Buna. Though badly wounded, he survived to fight on.
AWM 140011

18th Brigade, which had recently fought at Milne Bay. A squadron of the 2/6th Australian Armoured Regiment, armed with Stuart light tanks, accompanied them. On 18 December, the 2/9th Battalion and seven tanks attacked along the coast towards Cape Endaiadere.

Their main objective was a coconut plantation, but the attackers knew almost nothing about the defences. These were formidable and possibly contained more men than the 2/9th sent against them. There was a 10-minute supporting artillery barrage and the Australians went in alongside or behind the tanks, but a line of enemy pillboxes spat tremendous fire at the three proud companies who walked upright and apparently calmly towards them, returning fire. The defenders inflicted heavy casualties, but wherever the tanks and infantry reached them, there followed close-quarters fighting to the death. Lieutenant Bill MacIntosh (MC) and his platoon were outstanding on the far-right flank near the beach. MacIntosh had won a Military Medal as a sergeant at Giarabub in 1941 and was promoted after the Milne Bay battle. Now, with a tank in support, he went straight for an enemy post that he and the tank's commander, Corporal Evan Barnet (MID), had reconnoitred by crawling into No Man's Land the night before. Together they and their men blew up this strongpoint.

MacIntosh had not spotted another post, which fought back fiercely against a section under Corporal Reg Thomas (DCM). Thomas, a 38-year-old Townsville horse trainer, led the attack on this position, in which the defenders used a Bren and grenades taken from Fergusson's carriers after their ill-fated attack. A grenade burst near Thomas's face as he charged, but though knocked down, with blood streaming from his face, he persevered, killing two defenders with his Tommy gun. Spotting another Japanese firing the captured Bren from between logs in the post's wall, Thomas grabbed the muzzle and wrenched it through the opening before killing the gunner. Thomas only left the field two days later when MacIntosh ordered him out for treatment of his swollen face.

MacIntosh would himself be evacuated on 22 December after being seriously wounded in the knee and arm while urging his exhausted men forward. During the interval he had rescued one of his men under heavy fire, assisted by an exceptionally brave young reinforcement, Bren gunner Eric Cristenson (MID). MacIntosh, who also received a Commander-in-Chief's Card and was Mentioned in Despatches, ended the war a captain at 18th Brigade Headquarters.

After taking the first two posts, MacIntosh, Thomas and their men captured another three. The leading forces on the right reached Cape Endaiadere, but the company on the left, initially unsupported by tanks, lost more than half its men in advancing about 100 metres. When three tanks arrived, the battalion took 16 bunkers in 30 minutes. Warrant-Officer Jim Jesse (DCM) moved in with the tanks, indicating targets by firing flares at the bunkers. By day's end, 171 infantrymen – half the attacking force – and two tanks had been lost. Jesse, a Brisbane labourer, was an outstanding leader, as exemplified by his 'distinguished' result in a 1941 course for company sergeant-majors in the Middle East. His citation for the Distinguished Conduct Medal referred to him temporarily commanding a company at Buna, and predicted that given his 'remarkable leadership, judgment, coolness and courage', he would make 'a future senior officer'. He was promoted to lieutenant on 25 January 1943, but by December that year had left the Army, suffering from malaria and 'Anxiety State'.

The tank squadron, a 'vital factor' in the day's success, was commanded by Captain Norm 'Boof' Whitehead (MC). The official history calls him 'a massive fourteen and a half stone product of the land, broad shouldered and confident'. The 33-year-old made excellent preparations for the unit's involvement in the Australian Armoured Division's baptism of fire. Whitehead originally intended to use his Stuart tank, 'Captain Kidd', as a command tank for controlling the battle at a distance, but poor communications and the close country made him enter the fighting. Spotting a sniper in a tree, his crew destroyed first the tree and then the sniper. His tank went to the left flank to help the hard-pressed infantry there. Whitehead destroyed a strongpost before a Japanese soldier jumped onto the Stuart and pushed his rifle through the glass vision slit that Whitehead was using to direct his crew. The Japanese fired the rifle, wounding Whitehead in the eye and arm. Australian infantrymen shot dead the assailant, but Japanese tracer rounds from a nearby machine gun also hit the vision slit, before Whitehead's driver followed prior orders to take the wounded officer to assistance. His tank returned to battle that day and Whitehead rejoined the unit six months later. His Military Cross was the first awarded to the Australian Armoured Corps. Another should probably have gone to Lieutenant Grant Curtiss, who took over the tank detachment after Whitehead was wounded. His own tank had become stuck on a stump and he narrowly escaped with his life after Japanese lit a fire under it, but in the afternoon, in another Stuart, he led the three tanks that clinched the fighting on the left. The official historian described Curtiss as short and overweight but determined not to let others down.

The Australians broke through the main Japanese defences and by the end of 22 December held a strip of land leading to Simemi Creek. The next phase of operations involved the 2/10th Battalion and tanks capturing an airstrip, 'Old Strip'. Christmas Eve 1942 was the 2/10th's hardest day of fighting. Its men followed close behind the tanks through kunai grass, again unable to see the enemy's bunkers. Within 30 minutes all four tanks were knocked out – Barnet sustained a wound which cost him an arm – leaving the infantry to advance up the strip alone. When they halted, pinned down in the late afternoon, they had suffered 112 casualties. Corporal Bill McAuliffe (MM) sustained a head wound from a mortar bomb splinter but remained on duty, and when two decimated platoons fell back in the late afternoon, he took control and organised them into one force. They repelled a Japanese counterattack and McAuliffe, despite his painful wound, led two attacks and organised the evacuation of casualties. A 32-year-old unemployed labourer from Berri, McAuliffe was a mate of Tom Derrick. As an acting sergeant, the calm and inspiring McAuliffe would be severely wounded in the right arm at Sanananda on 17 January 1943. He was discharged medically unfit in February 1944, carrying scars on his forehead and right forearm.

The 2/10th tried again to take the Old Strip on 26 December. In the centre, an Aboriginal soldier, Private Tim Hughes (MM), enhanced his reputation for bravery. With his platoon pinned down, he took the initiative, climbing onto higher ground, and used grenades and a Tommy gun to kill enemy troops and cover his comrades. His battalion history called Hughes 'a true native of Australia, a soldier, and a gentleman admired by all'. On enlistment, Hughes was an unemployed labourer. He would be wounded in the arm in January 1943, suffer from various ailments, including bouts of venereal disease and malaria, get into trouble several times for indiscipline and be downgraded medically in early 1944. After the war he overcame adversity to become a successful farmer and land rights activist.

Acting Sergeant Frank Duffy (MM) had effectively been commanding the 2/10th's Mortar Platoon since their officer was wounded early in the Buna fighting. The Broken Hill labourer was often in trouble with authority, losing his rank several times, but now proved a superb battlefield leader. His mortars were sited on both sides of the airstrip, which 'Duff' repeatedly crossed under fire. He also exposed himself to enemy fire to obtain observations and give targets, even from No Man's Land. Despite sickness and feet crippled by long immersion in mud, he saw the campaign through. His cavalier attitude to discipline continued, but malaria and concussion led to his discharge in February 1944.

Late on 27 December, a Japanese counterattack evicted two Australian platoons from newly won positions. Lieutenant Murray Brown (MC) led a battalion reserve of about 25 men into the danger area. Waving a bayonet in the semi-darkness, Brown figured prominently in the ferocious hand-to-hand fighting, and though twice wounded, remained until every Japanese had been killed. Since the death of the company commander three days earlier, Brown had led his company through heavy fighting and a 650-metre advance. He ended the war a captain and battalion adjutant.

On 29 December, the 170 men now comprising the 2/10th Battalion were ordered, helped by the 2/9th and four tanks, to seize the ground between Giropa Point and the Simemi Creek mouth. The official historian singles out Sergeant George Spencer (DCM), a 33-year-old labourer from Maggea, for praise as 'a soldier of unwearied courage'. Tall, well built and something of a father-figure to his men, Spencer 'was always found in the most dangerous position in his platoon'. At Milne Bay he had tried to attach sticky grenades to enemy tanks, at Buna taken over his platoon when the commander was wounded, and on 29 December braved deadly fire, crossed open ground and then set up and fired a 2-inch mortar so effectively that enemy fire diminished and the wounded could be rescued. Even he could not capture that day's objective, however.

At 8 am on New Year's Day, the newly arrived 2/12th Battalion, flanked by the 2/10th, two American battalions and six tanks, spearheaded an advance on the Giropa Point/Simemi Creek area. One man per section carried a demolition charge comprising one kilo of ammonal, a grenade and an instantaneous fuse. Mortar bombs fell among the advancing Australians and tree snipers picked off five, but soon artillery, mortars and machine guns supported the attackers. The tanks drove across the open to the enemy defences among the palm trees. The Stuarts' fire blasted loopholes and doors so that the Australian infantry could rush from behind the tanks and finish off the bunkers by hurling in their ammonal charges. Nevertheless, two company commanders were killed and numerous other officers wounded. On the right flank, 22-year-old Corporal Alf Dyne (MM) initially commanded a ten-man section. By day's end he was the only member still standing. In the meantime, their platoon commander was wounded. For the first of two occasions, Dyne took over and led them to a flanking position. On 1 January 1943, the Australians reached Giropa Point and the adjacent coast, overcoming enemy strongposts, tangled vines and oozing swamps. Wherever the tanks could not negotiate the ground, infantry fought on alone. Even the battalion's Headquarters company was thrown into the fight, and Lieutenant Bill Bowerman (MC) led dismounted transport drivers in five successive attacks. He charged 30 metres over open ground to throw an ammonal bomb into one bunker. By nightfall the Japanese had been swept from all objectives except a pocket at the Simemi Creek mouth. One of the scattered groups seeking to escape approached the battalion medical post under

Captain Victor Sampson (MC). Sampson, his stretcher-bearers and RAP personnel were armed for such an eventuality and, with the help of nearby American troops, killed their attackers. Sampson received a gunshot to the neck. The Queensland doctor won universal praise for courageously placing his aid post close to the front so that the wounded could receive treatment soon after they were hit.

Thirty-two-year-old Cairns truck driver Private Enever Hudson (MM) had a mixed disciplinary record and had been plagued with illness throughout his service, hospitalised consecutively with laryngitis, mumps and influenza. On 2 January he took over after his section commander was killed. On leading his men close to a post that was delaying the advance, Hudson rushed forward, throwing grenades inside and enabling his men to capture the position, which was found to contain 25 dead Japanese.

Sergeant Arch Kimberley (MM) had won his men's admiration on the hard march to Buna, reportedly carrying twice as much as any other man, and helping others with their gear and ammunition. On 2 January, when an enemy strongpost halted the advance, Kimberley located it. Rushing forward, he hurled a blast grenade inside, then occupied and held the post until help arrived. He was credited with single-handedly killing 14 Japanese. He appeared full of energy while all around him were exhausted. An arm wound sustained at Sanananda while helping a casualty to safety ended his frontline service.

By the end of 2 January, the Japanese had effectively been cleared from the Giropa Point/Simemi Creek area. In the previous 16 days, the 18th Brigade had lost well over 800 men, some 45 per cent of its original strength. That same day, American troops seized Buna Mission and linked up with the Australians.

Sanananda: End of the road

Fighting began at Sanananda in mid-November, when the 16th Brigade moved along the main Soputa–Sanananda track, leading into the heart of the Japanese defences.

The Australians progressed well until 20 November, when mountain guns fired on them. Lieutenant-Colonel Cullen sent Captain Bruce Catterns, already prominent in the Kokoda campaign, on an outflanking move to the left. Captain Colin Prior (MID) led an advance on the right. Soon Japanese automatics and rifles opened up on Prior's men from 20–30 metres, inflicting heavy casualties and pinning down the company. Alongside Prior was his company quartermaster-sergeant, Staff-Sergeant Stan Miller (DCM). He usually dealt with rations, but on hearing that a soldier lay immobilised, Miller rescued him. Later, an NCO lay in the open with a severe stomach wound. His cries of agony were demoralising. Miller went out to treat him, and although this seemed suicidal, reached him and administered morphia. He and a brave stretcher-bearer, Corporal Bill Kemsley (MID), later dragged a stretcher to the NCO and brought him out under fire. The man died, but Miller brought in another casualty that afternoon. As Miller's citation said, his conduct was 'an inspiration to all'.

By 6 pm, Catterns' 90-strong force was stealthily approaching the main enemy base from the rear. Their forward scout was Corporal Ralph 'Bees Knees' Albanese (MM). He took a leading role when, just 50 metres from the Japanese positions, the Australians were spotted. The attackers broke the silence with a deafening burst of gunfire. Then they charged, hurdling trenches and vine fences, and entering the heart of a base for hundreds of men. Some Japanese manned guns and shot down attackers, but soon they in turn were killed, or ran, some screaming. Approximately 80 Japanese died, but so did many Australians, including five of the 2/1st's best officers. The surviving Australians dug in to face the inevitable counterattack. The wounded were laid around a huge tree, the protruding roots acting like protective walls.

After dawn broke, the Japanese attacked Catterns' men from three sides. Corporal Jack Ledden (MM), a 31-year-old wharf labourer, was a member of the Anti-Aircraft Platoon but had attached himself to Catterns' group the day before. He had moved with the foremost troops, and during the attack used a Tommy gun and grenades effectively. Now he defended with skill and courage, initially on the western flank – until Japanese fire put his TSMG out of action – and then on the eastern flank, to which he crawled across bullet-swept ground until he reached a Bren in a dead comrade's position. He relocated and recommenced firing, all the while urging on his compatriots. He killed at least eight enemy. In the Middle East, Ledden had spent ten days in detention barracks for 'offering violence' to an officer. By 1945 he was in a Docks Operating Company and suffering anxiety and nightmares, which sometimes found him waking with a knife or other weapon in hand.

Albanese was again outstanding, crawling from position to position, wherever the danger was greatest. He repeatedly stood up to deliver aimed fire at advancing Japanese or to direct fire. Albanese was wounded eight days later but returned to the 2/1st and ended the war a sergeant, with an outstanding record as a patroller.

Private Eric Soltan (MM) was among the wounded around the big tree. A bullet fractured his leg the night before, and although it was bandaged, there were no splints to hold the break in place. Heavy Japanese fire killed some of those around him. Soltan dragged himself ten metres towards the enemy and from this exposed position passed messages and ammunition along the line as well as vital information about enemy movement. He encouraged his comrades too, even though he was wounded twice more, in the other leg and body. Soltan had caught his company commander's attention the previous month when the fit, independent and exceptionally able Bren gunner had asked at Menari if he could go ahead of the battalion on his own: having sprained his ankle, he was afraid of falling behind when action commenced. Soltan's wounds necessitated the amputation of his left leg.

On the circle's opposite side, Private Arnold Varnum (MM) was by 10 am the only unwounded Australian along a 30-metre stretch of the perimeter. A Woodpecker was just 15 metres distant. Though eventually wounded in the shoulder, the former unemployed labourer remained at his post, keeping his Bren in action for 10 hours, until dark.

Nightfall brought rain and a spectacular thunderstorm. After consultation with Cullen, Catterns began withdrawing. Lieutenant McCloy, an inspiring leader at Oivi–Gorari, took a party of volunteer stretcher-bearers into the deadly salient. Bullets were still flying and three men were hit, but the wounded were rescued.

Of Catterns' 91 men who entered this battle on the Sanananda Track, all but 24 were killed or wounded. The Japanese abandoned their defensive position here, another further north and one of their hated mountain guns.

The 16th Brigade contributed substantially to the march on Sanananda, but by the time its relief began, from 6 December, 605 officers and men had been killed or wounded in the campaign, and nearly 1000 evacuated ill. This represented 85 per cent of the strength with which the brigade had set out in October. American troops arrived and although they made little progress, they did establish a position called 'Huggins' road-block' (often shortened to Huggins') on 30 November, on the track behind the Japanese front.

Two CMF battalions, the 49th and 55th/53rd, were brought up and on 7 December they attacked with the aim of clearing ground south of Huggins'. Going into their first action, the Queenslanders of the 49th were in many cases young, poorly equipped and undertrained, and their morale was doubtful. So was that of the 55th/53rd, a composite of men from the untried 55th and the derided and disbanded 53rd. Ominously, Japanese fire felled some 49th Battalion men as they waited for the three-minute supporting barrage to lift. When they advanced into the 'bush', casualties rose alarmingly. Captain Russell Forster (MC) destroyed one machine-gun post with grenades. He was attacking another post when a gunshot shattered his jaw. He had also been wounded at Tobruk with the 2/9th Battalion, and this wound ended his frontline service. Lack of effective communications meant the first two waves became separated, but the men advanced bravely. One company lost its first commander wounded, the next killed. Ultimately, Corporal Clive Blair (DCM) gathered as many of the company as he could (perhaps a platoon-strong) and resumed the advance. When his men became pinned down he led an outflanking move that silenced the enemy position. Though wounded while attacking another post, he carried on as long as possible. Blair had turned 20 just nine days earlier. The efforts of Blair and those around him gained several hundred metres, but brigade headquarters ordered a withdrawal. Fourteen of the 49th Battalion's 24 officers were casualties among 250 for the battalion, which Tobruk veteran Captain Bill Noyes now organised. Lieutenant Douglas Wylie was wounded in the head and lost his spectacles early in the action. He and two others became separated from the unit's main body. Within minutes, one of the two was killed by a sniper, but the other man, Lance-Corporal Edward Butler (MM), took care of his platoon commander. Without a compass, he guided Wylie through enemy defences for 10 days until they reached their own lines.

Despite the failure of the 49th attack, the 55th/53rd was sent in, its main assault going straight down the road. It suffered 130 casualties and gained about 100 metres.

During a 12-day pause, the fresh 36th Battalion (militia) and the 2/7th Cavalry Regiment (dismounted and little over half the strength of a battalion) were brought forward. On 19 December, the cavalrymen launched an attack down the track from Huggins' road-block towards the coast. The 30th Brigade, now including the 36th Battalion, was to clear the track behind them. The leading cavalry squadron advanced more than 400 metres without opposition and then chased several Japanese they saw running, but in doing so found themselves inside the main Japanese position. The commander and all his troop leaders were killed or mortally wounded. Trooper Peter Hooke (MM) was twice wounded going to his troop leader's aid. He received a third wound while bearing a message to headquarters. He soldiered on for another five days before being evacuated. The troop furthest forward now came under Sergeant Lionel Oxlade

(MM) who, though still under heavy machine-gun fire, gathered the survivors in a shallow trench and formed a perimeter. He personally helped several casualties reach this position, from which he directed a vigorous defence before returning them to the unit's main body that night. The regiment's chaplain wrote that Hooke and Oxlade seemed to be everywhere, their courage contagious. Oxlade even scoured Japanese supply dumps for wounded comrades.

As the rest of the regiment sought to advance from Huggins', the Japanese pressed in on them and inflicted many casualties. The commanding officer, Lieutenant-Colonel Edgar Logan, was mortally wounded, but not before he sent 23-year-old Captain Jack James (MID) on a left flanking movement. James' men became embroiled in intense fighting. Corporal Oswin 'Sandy' Sanderson (MID) used an Owen, grenades and a rifle and bayonet to kill three Japanese manning a machine gun hidden just metres from James' squadron. Sanderson, a Sydney labourer, lost his life in this lifesaving act. James and his hard-pressed men established a perimeter about 400 metres from Huggins'. This perimeter came to be called 'James' perimeter' or, more often, James'. James was later a company commander with the 2/31st Battalion at Balikpapan. In 1956, at age 36, he was appointed a brigadier commanding the 1st Armoured Brigade.

An Australian advance on the right was less successful. Noteworthy among the casualties was Corporal Ned Connell (MID) who on being hit called to his mates to stay clear and stay alive. When they kept coming in the hope of saving him, Connell intentionally raised himself from the ground so that he would be killed.

At night on 20 December, James sent three men to find the Huggins' road-block and report on its situation. Corporal Ham Morton (MM) and Troopers George Chesworth and Frank Hancox went cautiously through enemy-held territory, but when close to Huggins' they stumbled across enemy positions and a grenade exploded in the mud at their feet. They charged forward, firing their Owens. Chesworth and Hancox died under enemy fire. Morton was hit in the arm but kept running, encouraged by the last calls of his dying mates. After throwing a grenade, he was hit again, in the shoulder, but on calling out, 'Huggins', are you there? Ham Morton here!', friendly voices replied, and he was pulled to safety. It emerged that his last attack had been on an American position and that American fire had wounded him the second time. His shoulder wound was life-threatening but he survived, thanks to men holding a pressure point in his neck all night. Though preoccupied with the loss of his men, Morton delivered his message. The jackeroo, who was 6 feet 2½ inches tall, said he had killed five Japanese. Morton would be discharged medically unfit in 1944 and lose his life in an aircraft accident in 1953, aged just 35.

Captain Henry Cobb, who led the cavalry advance on the right on the 19th, tried to take a troop to James' on 20 December. Resistance was so strong that eventually he sent his surviving men back and made a lone stand. When his body was found about a month later, his haversack lay buried beneath his head, apparently a last act to prevent the papers in it from falling into Japanese hands. A dead Japanese lay beside him.

As mentioned, the 30th Brigade had to attack on 19 and 21 December. The 49th and 36th battalions reached Huggins' but all three of the brigade's battalions sustained severe losses. Their brigade commander, Selwyn Porter, was scathing of their efforts. He said that any success achieved by the 36th and 55th/53rd battalions in this period was 'due to a percentage of personnel who are brave in the extreme'. Yet not a single individual in the 36th appears to have been awarded a medal for bravery at Sanananda.

On 23 December, Lieutenant Sam Hordern (MID) led a strong 7th Division Cavalry party well right of the track from Huggins' and reached James' without loss. On Christmas Eve, most of the regiment followed, copying this nerve-racking but successful move. In six days they had captured 400 metres of ground but lost 40 dead and as many wounded. This toll rose on 29–30 December as the regiment launched two unsuccessful attacks – one under Hordern – against a strong Japanese post threatening its supply line.

The Australian commanders, Generals Herring and Vasey, agreed that capturing Sanananda required fresh troops and tanks.

The Japanese advanced towards the four Australian field guns on 28–29 December, destroying one. That night, Corporal Lionel Burgess (MM) brought credit to the much-maligned 55th/53rd Battalion. This 36-year-old member of the Ordnance Corps was attached to the battalion as a bootmaker, his civilian occupation. Casualties due to battle and malaria necessitated everyone taking a turn in the trenches, and on 28 December, Burgess took over when his section leader was evacuated. Shortly afterwards the section was attacked, a nearby mortar observation party was killed and several men on the flank withdrew. Burgess, however, stood fast, killed at least three Japanese and enabled the position to be held until reinforcements arrived. He set a great example in other roles, including cooking 'excellent meals' for a company. He was often hospitalised with malaria in subsequent years and only received his Military Medal belatedly in April 1944. As a result of a March 1945 court martial for 'stealing public property', he was reduced to the ranks and fined a hefty 20 pounds.

With Buna cleared, the 18th Brigade moved to Soputa from 7 to 9 January 1943, preparatory to advancing on Sanananda. It included about 1000 recent reinforcements, keen but inexperienced. The brigade was ordered to clear the formidable Japanese defences at the junction of the Sanananda Track and the Cape Killerton Track, about one kilometre south of Huggins'. Assisting them would be the 2/7th Cavalry, which had been relieved at James' by American troops now tasked with blocking the escape of any Japanese down either track.

On 12 January, the 2/9th and 2/12th battalions attacked along the track, supported by twenty 25-pounders and three Stuart tanks. The two leading companies of the 2/9th were now under lieutenants. Lieutenant George Jackson's company was consolidating on its objective when a head shot killed him. Since being commissioned a lieutenant after the Milne Bay fighting, Jackson (MID) had been an intelligence officer and adjutant before taking over a company in December. In a 1943 recording, several 2/9th men spoke of his apparently fearless leadership in defence and attack. One told of shrapnel slicing Jackson's thumb at Buna and his decision to stay on duty, despite it swelling enormously and medical warnings that it would be permanently stiff unless he received proper treatment. Now, as Jackson lay lifeless near the Sanananda Track, his second-in-command, Lieutenant Ron McInnes (MC) took over the company. McInnes was a reinforcement to this proud battalion but won credit with all ranks on this and subsequent days. Lieutenant Paul Lloyd, commanding the other leading 2/9th company, was also killed, and Warrant-Officer Jesse took over and linked up with McInnes' company on the objective. The battalion sustained more than 30 casualties, but the 2/12th and three tanks, on its left, fared worse. The soft ground on either side of the raised road confined the tanks to this narrow jungle defile. The crews were told to expect no enemy anti-tank guns, but when the first tank under Lieutenant Des Heap had driven just 55 metres, a concealed 37mm anti-tank gun opened fire. Struck four times, the tank drove off the road to the left and the second tank came forward. It too was hit, with one round penetrating the driver's visor and wounding four of the crew. Its commander, Corporal Geoff Boughton, was mortally wounded, the gunner so badly hit that he could not operate the guns. The tank and its crew seemed doomed. The driver, 32-year-old Lance-Corporal Ray Lynn (MM), remained calm in this crisis. The Glen Innes farmer had received a penetrating gunshot wound to the right jaw and neck and was forced to look through a shell hole in the tank to manoeuvre, but although it seemed impossible, he turned the tank around and drove it out of the fight. Sergeant Ken MacGregor now brought the third tank past Heap's and Boughton's, but it suffered a still worse fate: Japanese troops thrust a mine attached to a pole under a track, which was broken in the explosion. A tank-hunting team then threw a Molotov cocktail onto the tank, which burned out. All five crewmen perished. Thus all three Stuarts supporting the 2/12th's advance were out of action within 45 minutes. That day, the 2/12th sustained nearly 100 casualties and made little progress. Nevertheless, the Japanese were retreating from the track junction, which Australians occupied on 14 January. The 18th Brigade now advanced along the Cape Killerton Track and then eastward through swamps and along the seashore. Storms and heavy rain contributed to an apocalyptic atmosphere. In several crucial actions, Captain Frank Cook (DSO), who had led a remarkable bayonet charge in Tobruk, commanded a depleted company of the 2/10th Battalion attached to the 2/12th. Sometimes they trudged through waist-deep mud and water, and early on 19 January, Cook led a successful charge against a stubborn Japanese position approachable only across a 15-metre-wide tongue of land surrounded by deep water. One of Cook's men, Corporal Arthur Weston (MM), commanded a platoon in an encircling manoeuvre, which involved silencing four pillboxes. He personally grenaded several positions and contributed hugely to his company overcoming a complex of bunkers and huts. Private Murray Saint (MM) of the 2/10th was in a forward section, which became pinned down and was ordered to withdraw. Saint was in his first action here but fired his Bren from the hip to cover his mates. Doing so involved occupying a position exposed to enemy fire. He was hit four times, one bullet gashing him over the eye, but by the time another bullet disabled his Bren, his section had fallen back. Saint, a 20-year-old South Australian butter factory worker, was discharged medically unfit later in 1943.

On the beach near Sanananda Point on 21 January, Private Dick Allen (DCM) remained in an exposed location for over an hour, protecting a nearby platoon with his Bren. An enemy machine gun tore his haversack and equipment to shreds, but he in turn killed at least three Japanese as they tried to bring another Nambu into action.

Barges brought out about 1200 Japanese casualties in January, but by the time the last determined resistance ended, on 22 January, at least 1600 Japanese had died at Sanananda, the Australians sustained more than 1400 casualties (excluding sickness) in the fighting.

INTERLUDE 3
THE TYPICAL HERO?

The typical infantry battalion, from which most of the heroes in this book came, was a cross-section of Australian society. As in the battalions, the occupational backgrounds of the heroes were very diverse: they ranged from the unemployed to affluent graziers, from hairdressers to woodcutters. Men from the professions were probably underrepresented – fewer than 20 doctors, barely ten schoolteachers and a handful of solicitors. That probably reflects the fact that the most common feature of the heroes in this book was their youth. So many were in their twenties that, as mentioned in the introduction, unless stated otherwise, readers should assume any individual was in that decade of his life. There were several remarkable teenagers: Ken Hickey in Timor, John O'Brien at Alamein, Ron Dridan at Kokoda, Frank McLennan and Ken Ward on Bougainville, and possibly Albert Schwebel at Alamein. Among the oldest heroes, William Symington was 45 at Bardia. Gratwick was 40 when he won the Victoria Cross, Kelliher 38 when he won his; at the other end, Partridge was just 20. Tom Shannon was 41, Walter Scott Orr 44 and Richard Howes 41 in Syria. Lieutenant-Colonel Charles Assheton was 40 when killed in Singapore, Carson 49 on the Kokoda Track, Joseph North 40 and Colin McKinley 45 during their heroics on Borneo. Stretcher-bearer Sergeant Gordon Ayre was 41 at Wau-Salamaua, as was Jack Leonard when killed near Lae. Hector Mackay was said to be over 60 (though officially 36) in Syria. About one in eight of the men whose deeds were discussed in the book were in their 30s at the time. Most of the heroes were single on enlistment. In an army where 5 feet 6 inches and later 5 feet was the minimum height requirement, some 20 men were recorded as 6 feet tall or over (O'Regan and Kent being the tallest), but there were another 16 who were recorded as 5 feet 6 inches or lower (Luff and Deal being the shortest).

The classic image of men from rural Australia making fine soldiers has support here. Over 90 of the 700 mentioned in the text had a rural background, including 15 farm workers or farm hands, and at least 30 farmers. It seems unlikely that there was a marked overrepresentation of any particular type of locality or occupation. The single most common occupation given was 'labourer', applying to at least 50 men, and a term that soldiers might use to cover their status as unemployed or in a reserved occupation that could exclude them from enlistment. Sixteen regular soldiers feature among the medal winners – including Swanson, Power, Plater and Coleman – and they were an outstanding group.

These full-time soldiers were quite different from the citizen soldiers who had signed up for the war only, and who in many cases baulked at military discipline. An archetype of Australian soldiers is the man undisciplined behind the lines but a great fighting man. That trope has some validity, as readers will notice that many soldiers whose brave deeds are described here also got into trouble with the military authorities. They number about 50, and at the extreme involve men like Harold Bloffwitch and Allan Smith, both of whom were court-martialled three times and spent time in military prison but who stepped forward in desperate situations and provided leadership. That ability to lead in a crisis typified many of the heroes. At the other end of the misbehaving spectrum were young men who had signed up for adventure and took opportunities to absent themselves from barracks for a look-see. The vast majority – over 90 per cent – of the medal-winning heroes were remarkably self-disciplined given the danger, boredom and regimentation of their army lives.

It is noteworthy that most of the heroes survived the war. Just over 100 men named in this book did not: they were killed in action or died of wounds, sometimes in performing their noteworthy deeds, more often in the days or years afterwards. The number who carried physical wounds was high too. Among the innumerable wounded soldiers referred to, over 220 men named in the text were wounded at least once, about 10 per cent of them more than once. At least four (Phillips, Mulley, Soltan and Beale) were wounded three times. Six men (Smithers, Wankey, Soltan, Parnell, Stanley Smith and Groux) had limbs amputated. They were not the only ones whose wounds ended their frontline careers: some 16 others are named in the text. The number with recorded postwar psychological problems was not remarkably large. At least 11 were diagnosed with 'anxiety state', 'anxiety neurosis' or something else denoting psychological trauma. Three suffered 'shock' but remained on duty. At least ten – but probably quite a few more – were discharged medically unfit.

To the degree that it is possible to talk meaningfully of a 'typical' hero, he was a young Australian of the Depression era. He had initiative, determination, skill and, above all, was prepared to risk his life.

CHAPTER 16

WAU–SALAMAUA: HEROISM IN THE HILLS

Within days of the Papuan fighting ending at Sanananda, a fierce battle occurred at Wau, in the Mandated Territory of New Guinea. Wau figured prominently in both Allied and Japanese strategic planning in early 1943 because its airstrip could support future offensives for either. Blamey considered Wau a potential springboard for attacks towards the major Japanese bases at Lae and Salamaua. On 7 January, when the Japanese reinforced Lae with 4000 troops, Blamey decided to send the 17th Brigade to Wau, where its commander, Brigadier Moten, took over Kanga Force, the Australian commandos and locally raised militia operating there.

Bad weather and a shortage of transport aircraft meant that the leading battalion, the 2/6th, was not at Wau in force till 19 January. Its companies then deployed along the Buisaval and Black Cat tracks, obvious routes by which the Japanese might attack from their forward base at Mubo. On 21 January a patrol spotted enemy troops moving along the Black Cat Track, and soon it was apparent that more Japanese were cutting their way along a disused track, now dubbed the 'Jap Track'. Moten, thinking the enemy forces merely a strong patrol, decided to attack along the Black Cat and Jap Tracks and sent out 2/6th companies on 26 January. The following day, the main body of the 2/5th Battalion arrived at Wau. However, early on 28 January, the main Japanese body, estimated at 350, struck unexpectedly at Wandumi, just a few kilometres and hours from Wau. They ran into a 60-strong 2/6th company and about 20 commandos of the 2/5th

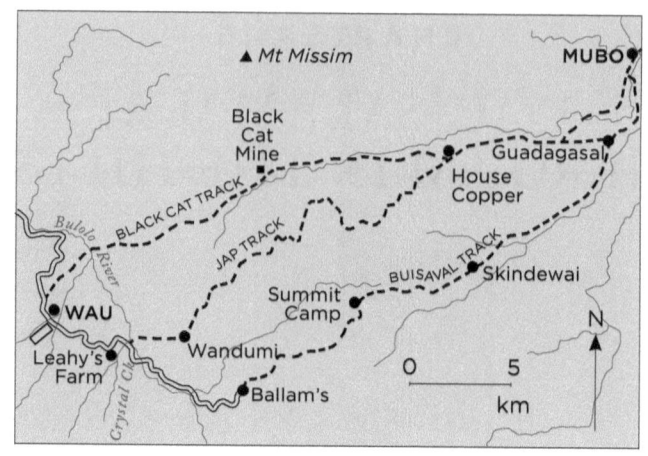

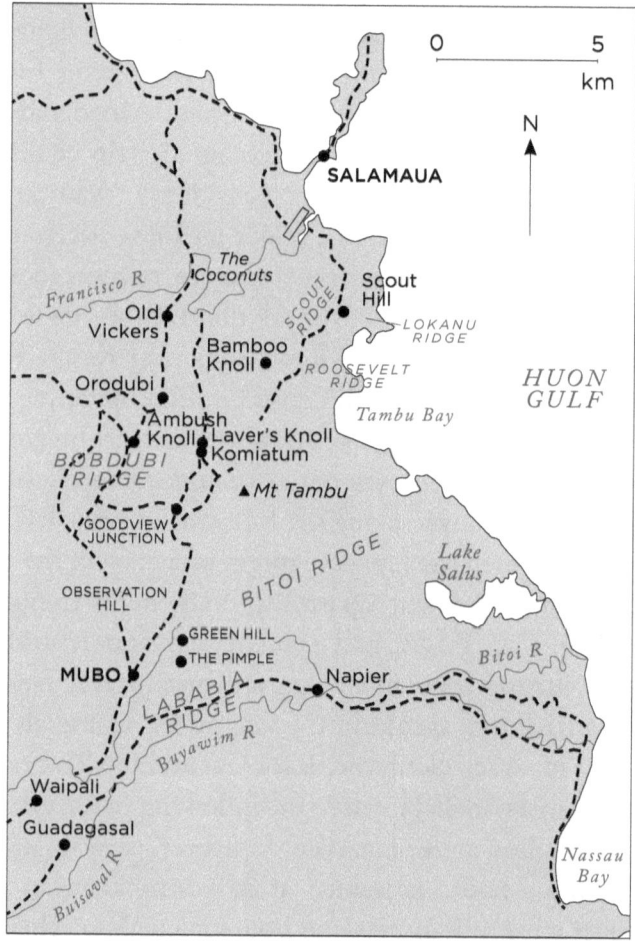

Wau and Salamaua

Independent Company, all under Captain Bill Sherlock (MID). Sherlock, a 34-year-old grazier from Victoria, positioned his men on a ridge overlooking Wandumi village and held off the Japanese for most of the day. This was crucial for Wau's protection, as only four of 30 aircraft expected from Moresby that day made it to Wau before bad weather set in. There was little cover on and around the ridge, and hard ground made digging difficult, so most of the defenders lay flat looking through the kunai grass over the crest. At 3.10 pm, Sherlock signalled to Kanga Force: 'Things very hot. Any help may be too late.' His strongest platoon, holding a key knoll, had after a hard fight been forced off the position. Sherlock added to this signal: 'Am counter-attacking now.' Gathering some 20 men, including the remnant of the overrun platoon, a few commandos and a section of just-arrived 2/5th Battalion reinforcements, Sherlock grabbed a rifle, its bayonet fixed. The others followed him in delivering a bayonet charge that forced the Japanese off the knoll. Sherlock bayoneted four Japanese. The enemy pressure continued, though, and many Japanese streamed past the ridge towards Wau. More reinforcements reached Sherlock and command passed to a higher officer, but pressure forced them all to withdraw. Sherlock's original force now numbered just 18. The next morning, as Sherlock led men at a crossing of the rain-swollen Bulolo River, he was killed, shouting epithets at the Japanese as he died. Sherlock's courage, tenacity and tactical skill saved Wau, but rather than the posthumous Victoria Cross that was his due, Moten recommended him for only a Mention in Despatches. Others had ably assisted Sherlock. Lieutenant Ted St John (MC) held the knoll for crucial hours despite a lack of cover. He and his platoon sergeant, Jamieson Gray (MM), went out under heavy fire and rescued a wounded Bren gunner. St John, a 33-year-old salesman who had risen from the ranks, was seriously wounded in the thigh the following day. Gray, a 33-year-old stock and commission agent, had only joined the battalion a few weeks earlier, having previously been in base units. He took a leading role in Sherlock's bayonet charge. He received a gunshot wound to the right chest that day and never saw combat again.

Battle for Wau airstrip

By dawn on 29 January, enemy mortar and small arms fire was falling on the south-east of the airstrip, but the weather cleared that morning and transport aircraft began landing. During the day, 60 aircraft disembarked more than 800 Australians, including the 2/7th Battalion and the remainder of the 2/5th. On leaving the aircraft on 29 January, Major Keith Walker (DSO) of the 2/7th had his hat shot off, and one of his men was wounded so quickly that he returned to the aircraft that brought him. Walker then led his company to a position called Leahy's Farm, killing some 15 Japanese and thereby preventing a serious Japanese thrust on Wau that day. Walker's men took the initial brunt of the major Japanese attack on 30 January, and although most were forced back from their diggings, Walker led them in regaining those positions. In the afternoon, 300-400 Japanese appeared again on the road near Leahy's Farm, apparently unaware of the presence of Walker's men until they were just 60 metres off. His company, now numbering only 60, received welcome fire support from two newly arrived 25-pounder guns. Together with six Beaufighters that flew overhead, they killed an estimated 150 Japanese. Walker, a Mildura car salesman who was only 5 feet 6 inches tall, was Mentioned in Despatches in the Middle East. His campaign ended on 4 February after he was wounded by a booby trap. His younger brother Ian had been killed with the 2/7th carriers at Buna. Keith, known to his men as 'Luger Joe', was court-martialled in November 1944, pleading guilty to creating a disturbance in the 2/7th lines by firing a rifle, boarding an RAAF aircraft without permission and making an unauthorised descent from an aircraft by parachute without the pilot's consent. He was fined 20 pounds and lost seniority. In May 1945 he was discharged so he could join the British Army in India.

The Japanese lost about 1200 men in the battle for Wau and by 5 February the survivors were making a fighting withdrawal towards Mubo. Stocky and energetic Captain 'Jo' Gullett (MC) of the 2/6th led his understrength company in three separate attacks between 4 and 8 February. On 8 February, when at least 100 enemy flanked his company, he and another officer covered the withdrawal. Gullett helped carry out a severely wounded man and was credited with personally killing at least eight Japanese with rifle fire and three with grenades. Gullett had enlisted as a private and, as a sergeant, commanded a platoon at Bardia, where he was wounded. By war's end he was a major, had received wounds from the Italians, Germans and Japanese and had served with the British Army in Normandy. His influence in these operations is apparent in that his company, a conglomerate of several units, was known as 'Gullett Company', and a new track was dubbed 'Gullett's Track'. He was an inspiring war leader and an inspired war writer: his memoir, *Not as a Duty Only*, is one of the finest by an Australian soldier.

Sergeant Neville 'Blue' Gibbons (MM), of Gullett's company, had joined the AIF at 19 in 1939 and served in medical units until he transferred to the 2/6th in August 1941. At his own request he was demoted from sergeant to private, but by January 1943 had regained his stripes. On 4 February, fighting his first campaign, he took over his platoon after the commander was killed. Gibbons proved an outstanding patroller. On the night of 7/8 February he made two solo patrols, each lasting several hours, behind enemy lines. The following day he led a successful platoon attack. Gibbons was commissioned in the field on 12 March 1943. Gullett liked him as someone who walked fast and was intelligent, like him. A fellow member of the battalion described Gibbons leaving on a six-day two-man reconnaissance patrol several months later as 'the gamest man in the battalion'. Gibbons was ambushed and killed on this patrol.

Crystal Creek slaughterhouse

On 7 February, 21-year-old Lieutenant Eddie Reeve (MC) of the 2/5th led his understrength platoon in capturing the eastern end of a strongly defended ridge overlooking Crystal Creek, several kilometres south-east of Wau. The platoon negotiated dense jungle and a steep slope, then surprised the Japanese in a bayonet charge, killing many and capturing a Woodpecker, which they turned on its owners. Reeve was cocky, and on enlisting in 1939 at 18 put his age up two years, despite his youthful appearance and small stature. He was a lance-corporal at Bardia, where he was wounded. He was promoted to acting sergeant while recovering but was soon reverted to private for misbehaviour. He became a lieutenant in January 1943. He led another brilliant attack to seize a knoll at Mount Tambu in July but was wounded in the groin. In December 1944 he was court-martialled and reprimanded in New Guinea for disobeying his commanding officer's order to help construct an officers' mess. Nevertheless, in March 1945, Reeve was promoted to captain in the 2nd New Guinea Infantry Battalion and was Mentioned in Despatches in 1946.

On 8 February at Crystal Creek, the 2/5th's Lieutenant Lin Cameron (MC) took the lead in attacking the western end of the same ridge. Using an encircling movement, he achieved complete surprise as he and a Bren gunner emerged from a steep jungle-clad hillside. The two accounted for a dozen Japanese before the rest of the platoon arrived. The official history says Cameron used a submachine gun; his citation credited him with shooting dead ten Japanese with his rifle. Either way, his charge took the western end of the ridge, which was soon completely in Australian hands. In March, Cameron, a civil service clerk from Warracknabeal, was made a captain and company commander. Tall and demanding, he showed no emotion in battle but afterwards was deeply affected by losses among his men. He won a Bar to his Military Cross in January 1945 for leading the capture of another ridge, at Perembil, then holding it against counterattacks.

On 7–8 February, Private Les 'Bull' Allen (MM), a 2/5th stretcher-bearer, carried three casualties to safety. On the first occasion, he crossed bullet-swept ground to a wounded man, hoisted him over his shoulder and carried him 200 metres. A machine-gun bullet struck Allen's haversack.

On 9 February, the 2/5th Battalion killed another 150 Japanese in the Crystal Creek area, now dubbed the 'Slaughterhouse'. The

Japanese retreated, and in subsequent weeks a stalemate developed in front of their base at Mubo. Lacking the supplies and manpower to attack Mubo, by March the Australians were patrolling forward to it.

Allied plans included recapturing Salamaua and Lae. General MacArthur still depended in 1943 on Australian troops as his main fighting force. Blamey intended to use Salamaua as a magnet to draw Japanese forces away from the bigger prize of Lae. The 3rd Australian Division, a militia force, took over from Kanga Force at Wau. The 17th Brigade remained the main strike force in the area, supplemented by the 2/3rd Independent Company and a growing number of militia units. In late April, the 2/7th Battalion was in contact with the Japanese near Mubo, the 2/3rd Independent Company harassing the enemy supply line nearer the coast and the 24th Battalion in the upper Markham Valley guarding a route between Wau and Lae. Conditions in these campaigns were as challenging and disheartening as those in the Kokoda campaign: claustrophobically dense vegetation, well suited to ambush from enemies seldom seen but often present around the all-important tracks. The men were eternally wet, their rotting clothes and boots constantly worn. By the end, few had underclothes or socks, though ironically water was often scarce on the crucial hilltops. The ground was rarely flat and the campaign was called 'The Battle of the Ridges'.

On 9 May Japanese forces surrounded a 2/7th Battalion company forward of Lababia Ridge, but the Australians held off eight attacks until relieved on 11 May. Even the cooks volunteered to join the relief force. There was jubilation throughout the battalion when the relief was effected. The defenders were still full of spirit and determination. Much credit fell to their company commander, Captain Vin Tatterson (MC), a butcher from Newry, Victoria, who had risen through the ranks. Though wounded at Wau in January and in this Lababia action, 'Vin Tatt' remained on duty. His luck ran out on 4 August 1943 when he was shot dead by a sniper while leading an attack at the Old Vickers Position. At Lababia, grenades did much of the killing, but so did automatic weapons, including the Bren of

Private Len Waters (MM). On 9 May, three enemy LMGs poured intense fire on Waters and his weapon pit. The Nambus shot away one bipod leg that afternoon and the foresight that evening. Nevertheless, Waters kept returning fire. The following morning, the Bren's flash eliminator was damaged, and Waters was wounded in the arm. He repaired the gun but could not keep shooting, instead supporting his No. 2 who took over. Eventually, his section commander ordered Waters back to the company aid post, where the RMO, Captain Bruce Peterson (MC) had become trapped with some of his bearers, and treated Waters and others. Sergeant Bill Russell (MM) exemplified the quality of Peterson's team when on 24 April, just 20 metres from an enemy machine gun, and working by the light of a cigarette, he successfully stitched a casualty's sucking chest wound.

Bravery behind the lines

From May 1942 to May 1943, Sergeant Ben Hall (DCM) was a member of one of several Australian intelligence units operating behind Japanese lines. He worked first on New Britain and then at Saidor, reporting on Japanese small craft and barge traffic. This was dangerous work, but when offered relief, Hall volunteered to stay. The Japanese established a base at Saidor in March 1943 and one of Hall's fellow coastwatchers was betrayed and killed, another wounded. While the main party in the area withdrew, he remained for six weeks, transmitting vital information, even though Japanese patrols passed within metres of his observation post. He left only when ordered. This 30-year-old planter from Madang was later commissioned.

At Cissembob north-west of Salamaua, the 24th Battalion's Lieutenant Leslie Looker (MC) was commanding 25 men, some of them commandos, when two Japanese companies attacked early on 19 May. The Australians inflicted about 50 casualties, half from a Vickers gun. Two men helping Looker to find targets for the Vickers were suddenly hit when a Japanese machine gun opened fire just 25 metres away. Looker knocked out the gun with grenades and then helped the wounded. He proved superb at patrolling behind enemy lines.

The PIB also did remarkable work behind the front. In December 1942, it was ordered to prevent Japanese forces from escaping north from the Kokoda and beachhead fighting. Sergeant Nicholas Farr (MM) and a four-man patrol intercepted about 40 Japanese trying to cross the Kumusi River on 23 January. After the Japanese scattered, all were hunted down. Farr was personally credited with killing 11. Farr, a 'native' soldier, was aged 30 and a local overseer. Only on returning to his home in Port Moresby in August 1943 did he discover that the Army had taken it and its contents in 1942. He served out the war with ANGAU.

About 40 PIB members were at Ambasi Mission, where the arrival of two Brens in early January 1943 was greeted as a 'godsend'. Sergeant John Ehava (DCM) was a highly effective leader, and his call 'Come on PIB' became the unit's war cry. On 8 February 1943, he led a nine-strong patrol that engaged a group of Japanese attempting to cross the Kumusi at its mouth. When Ehava noticed a second party of about 50 Japanese approaching from the left, he went alone with a Bren and set up in a hidden position. Only when the Japanese were less than 40 metres away did he fire. He was credited with killing 30. On 21 February, John's brother, Lance-Corporal Gabriel Ehava (MM), detached himself from a six-man patrol to make a lone reconnaissance. On hearing firing he ran towards the source and discovered that the patrol was under attack. Ehava came in firing his 'automatic,' killing four Japanese and then leading the patrol in pursuit. Gabriel Ehava later set up an ingenious means of ambush: he left a canoe on the Japanese side of the Opi River. Unbeknown to the Japanese who used it, the canoe was attached to a wire and pegs, which prevented the canoe from getting more than halfway across the creek. When the canoe stopped, Gabriel and his watching men shot those aboard. Sergeant Kari (MM) was credited with personally killing 31 Japanese in an ambush at Sabari. Like the Ehava brothers, he came from Moviavi, which claimed to be Papua's most decorated village.

Lababia and Nassau Bay

The 2/6th Battalion relieved the 2/7th and by 9 June found a route from Lababia Ridge to Nassau Bay, an area Blamey wanted as a base for future amphibious operations, supplying Australians at Mubo and enabling American forces to enter the campaign.

On 20 June, shortly before the Nassau Bay landing, Japanese forces attacked the 2/6th's forward company, again at Lababia Ridge. The 80 Australians were reinforced by another 70 men the following day but now faced a full-scale attack. Commanded by Major Bill Dexter (DSO) and benefiting from his foresight in clearing much of the surrounding scrub, the defenders held on until 23 June, when the Japanese attacks ended. The Australians lost 11 killed and 12 wounded, the Japanese 41 killed and 131 wounded from an imposing force comprising some 1500 men. The Australians knew they were facing heavy odds, not least because the attackers let out a shout that one eyewitness likened to the loudest roar from a football crowd. Acting Corporal Allan Smith (DCM), standing just 5 feet 4 inches tall, commanded the section that first encountered the Japanese attackers. They delayed the Japanese advance, then withdrew under covering fire from Private Arnold Watt (MM), who also killed six with grenades and re-set booby traps. The next day Smith led a patrol looking for the enemy. On encountering a 25-strong Japanese group, Smith's rifle was shot from his hands, but only after he hit five Japanese. Using a wounded comrade's rifle, he kept firing until able to pick up the casualty and carry him to help. Later, when Smith's post came under bayonet attack, he led a counter-charge, which annihilated the assault party. Smith, a Melbourne labourer, was constantly in trouble for going AWL and for desertion from late 1942. He was court-martialled three times and reprimanded, fined and even imprisoned. He later served at Balikpapan with the 2/9th Battalion.

Private Robert Ryan (DCM) was one of just three men in his section not killed in the main Japanese assault of 21 June. He took command and coolly used his Bren to rebuff the attackers. He did the

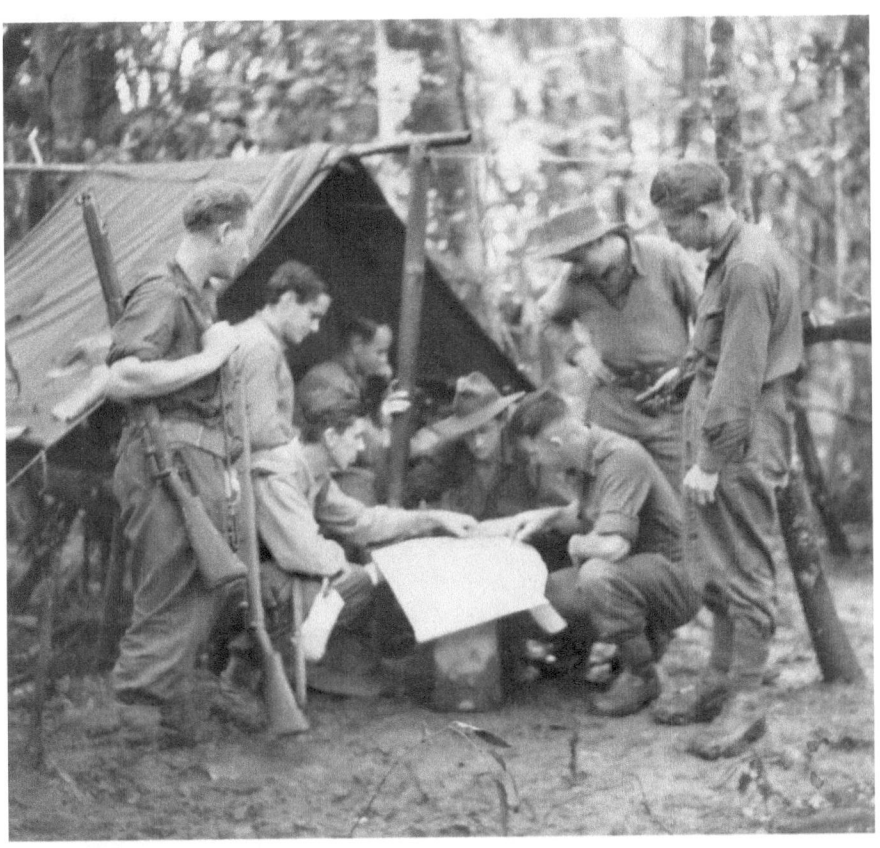

Lance-Sergeant John 'Smoky' Hedderman, fifth from the left in a hat, was an outstanding patroller who was credited with rescuing casualties under fire, taking forward a telephone at great risk, and silencing enemy weapons with crack shots from an EY rifle.
AWM 055635

same the following day and then, when almost out of ammunition, ran from pit to pit holding off the enemy with grenades.

All three platoon commanders at Lababia were decorated. Lance-Sergeant John 'Smoky' Hedderman (MM), a tall Melbourne labourer and outstanding patroller, commanded the foremost platoon throughout. He helped carry out two casualties under fire, crawled forward with a telephone close enough to the enemy lines to call in mortar fire and used an EY rifle to silence a mortar and a machine gun. Lieutenant Laurie Roach (MC) was a militia lieutenant before joining the 2/6th as a reinforcement. In combat units, reinforcement officers were often resented for preventing the promotion of battle-tried NCOs. The Lababia action was Roach's first, and he was credited with gallant leadership but also with personally stalking and shooting three snipers and leading a local counterattack that frustrated an enemy assault. Lieutenant Ted Exton (MC) came from the militia too, fighting his first action. When his mortarman was killed, Exton ran forward and fired the 2-inch mortar himself. He was also a crack shot: his platoon sergeant broke off one telephone report to Dexter to say 'there's a Nip getting up a tree about 100 yards away – Exton's going to have a shot – he's got him and he's bouncing'.

Hedderman's runner, Private Greig Smith (MM), also exercised leadership. He carried ammunition to the forward weapon pits and at critical times jumped into those pits and fought. He assisted two wounded men to safety, shooting two Japanese en route. Smith inspired young reinforcements by nonchalantly standing above their weapon pits and offering them hot drinks. The men's amazement and admiration were boosted when a bullet struck one of Smith's submachine-gun magazines, drawing only a comment that it would make a good souvenir. Smith, a fine patroller, was a section leader by March 1945, when he was killed leading a dangerous advance.

An American force landed at Nassau Bay on 30 June, helped ashore by a covering force from the 2/6th Battalion. After a few skirmishes, the 2/6th cleared the path for the inexperienced and cautious Americans to Napier. By 4 July they were at Bitoi Ridge. Corporal Tapioli (MM) of the 1st PIB assisted the American

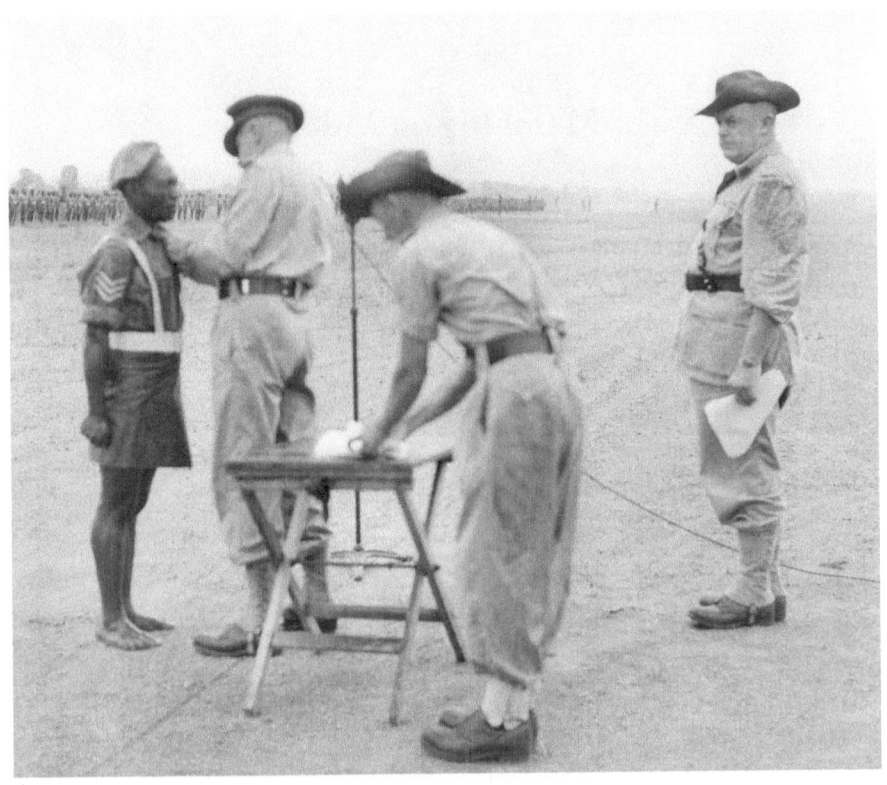

Sergeant Tapioli receiving a Military Medal at Rabaul in 1946. Tapioli escaped from Japanese imprisonment to be an extraordinary soldier in the Australian Army. He showed bravery not only on the battlefield but in speaking up for the rights of his fellow 'native' troops.
AWM 099827

advance and won their admiration. Once he killed seven Japanese single-handedly; another time he made a lone attack on a pillbox and killed three machine gunners; a third time he killed enemy lookouts on the wide, fast-flowing Masaweng River. This bayonet expert later showed courage of a different kind, leading a protest in February 1945 against New Guinea Infantry Battalion troops being required to wear stripes on their lap-laps rather than their sleeves.

Marching on Mubo

On 30 June, an untried and inadequately trained Australian unit, the recently arrived 58th/59th Battalion, attacked Bobdubi Ridge on the way to Salamaua. It failed to capture its objectives, Old Vickers Position and Orodubi, largely because of inexperience at all levels and competent opposition. AIF units severely criticised the battalion in succeeding weeks, but with experience its troops and leaders improved markedly.

On 7 July, the 2/6th attacked Observation Hill near Mubo while the Americans advanced towards them from Bitoi Ridge. Private Ron Moss (DCM) had only joined the battalion on 15 February as a 19-year-old. A good shot, he provided excellent covering fire when the attack went in. The enemy launched a counterattack, but Moss recognised the threat, ran forward and, by shooting dead four Japanese, dispersed the assault. By then all the NCOs had become casualties in his platoon, which withdrew, Moss covering the withdrawal. Moss enjoyed patrolling solo and picking off individual Japanese. He was credited with pinning down enemy forces for two hours while other Australians launched a successful flank attack on 11 July. This natural soldier was a sergeant by war's end, when he joined the British Commonwealth Occupation Force in Japan.

The 7 July assault succeeded, and continued pressure from Australian and American troops and artillery led the Japanese to abandon Mubo by 13 July. A contributor to this success was the 2/3rd Independent Company (notionally 295-strong), under Major

George Warfe (MC). This commando unit attracted men of daring, and Warfe's flamboyance and cool courage were appropriate for its leader. He directed its superb reconnaissance and ambush work and added four Vickers machine guns to its arsenal to provide tremendous firepower in tasks like flank protection. In early July its assignment was to attack Japanese escaping from Mubo into the Komiatum–Goodview Junction area and to prevent reinforcement of Mubo. Warfe took a leading role in cutting the Komiatum Track against much resistance and then marching his unit overnight to a successful attack on Ambush Knoll. Corporal Keith McEvoy (DCM), a Western Australian truck driver, led five men in the central assault on Ambush Knoll. He hoped that a half-hour preliminary bombardment would have killed the defenders, but instead the Japanese threw Australian grenades (deadlier than the Japanese ones) at the attackers from behind a bamboo barricade. One grenade wounded all but one of his companions, and as McEvoy crossed the bamboo barricade with his shirt ripped by a machine-gun bullet and bullet grazes across his ribs, he thought about going back. However, urged on by the one man still with him, Private Ron Collins, he persevered. Now under attack from close range, the Japanese in the forward trench fell back, enabling other Australians to advance and bring heavy fire to bear. Bren gunner Private Claude Wellings (MM) stood up and, firing from the hip, silenced a pillbox. The following morning, the Japanese abandoned the knoll. In subsequent days they counterattacked, targeting Wellings' weapon pit. The parapet was shot away, exposing him again to enemy fire. He stayed where he was, though, until severely wounded in the right knee on 22 July. This ended the timber cutter's frontline career. McEvoy was wounded too, but recovered and rejoined the company.

The Japanese defences in front of Salamaua now ran in an arc from Bobdubi Ridge to Orodubi, Goodview Junction, Mount Tambu and Roosevelt Ridge. The dominant feature was Mount Tambu, where on 16 July, Captain 'Mick' Walters (MC) led his understrength 2/5th Battalion company in a surprise attack that seized two slight knolls at the southern end. Lieutenant Reeve led the capture of one knoll, Sergeant Bill Tiller (DCM) the other. Tiller, a 36-year-old farmer, moved alone ahead of his platoon and used his rifle to eliminate a Japanese machine-gun crew. The Japanese positions could accommodate 100 men, but only 30 were there. All of these were either killed or ran, abandoning their well-built defences to the Australians who lacked the tools or time to dig their own pits before the inevitable Japanese counterattacks. That night, Japanese infantry, supported by mortar and mountain-gun fire, tried to recapture the lost ground, crawling through thick undergrowth and launching eight screaming charges. Walters, a veteran of the Middle East and Wau, described the small arms fire here as the thickest he had seen. His resolution steadied his men. Tiller also moved from post to post encouraging the men and tending casualties. By morning, Walters' riflemen were down to five rounds each, each Bren gunner to two magazines. Lin Cameron sent two platoons, supplies and a mortar to reinforce Walters' men.

More attacks, at midday on 17 July, were halted, largely by the mortar. Private Fred McCormack (MM), aged 38, shot eight Japanese assembling for one assault. Reeve's platoon was attacked again at dusk, but though outnumbered 10 to 1, held on, hurling epithets as well as bullets across the now clear ground in front of them. The Australians had by then repelled 24 attacks and inflicted hundreds of casualties.

On 18 July, Walters' men advanced another 75 metres. They had artillery and mortar support, but also crucial was Lance-Corporal Jimmy 'Lofty' Jackson (DCM), who used three grenades to destroy a machine gun and then a Tommy gun to kill three occupants of a pillbox.

That night, a severe earth tremor was followed by torrential rain, under cover of which the Japanese sought to encircle and destroy the Australian companies. The rear platoon under Lieutenant Cyril Miles (MC) took the brunt of the unexpected attack early on 19 July. His Bren gunner knocked out the attackers' machine gun with an educated guess as to where its fire was coming from in the pitch dark, and enemy corpses piled up as the raiders tried unsuccessfully to recapture it. Screaming Japanese called 'Cyril, Cyril', the disturbing effect of which would forever stay with Miles. He was wounded in the arm, his batman and six others killed. Nevertheless, the survivors held on. By daylight the Japanese had fallen back, leaving 21 dead.

That afternoon, Japanese from Mount Tambu attacked Walters' company. Most of the foremost section was out bringing up supplies and ammunition, and Private Percy Friend (MM), with a TSMG, and Bren gunner Jack Prigg held up the attackers for 20 minutes. Friend directed fire and reloaded the Bren until the rest of the section arrived. When the section leader was wounded, he assumed command, and was credited with at least 20 enemy casualties. Tiller was again prominent, advancing and throwing grenades to such effect that the enemy fell back. Jackson inflicted some 30 casualties that day too. By mid-afternoon, Walters' men knew that they had the Japanese beaten, and yelled mock versions of the enemy's war cries back at them. The Australians sustained 39 casualties but estimated that they had inflicted at least 350 since 16 July. Walters, a Tasmanian bank officer, had been wounded in the thigh at Wau and in the shoulder on 19 July but remained on duty. He would sustain abdominal injuries in an explosives demonstration in April 1944. By war's end he was with the British Army in India.

The most formidable part of Mount Tambu, including the peak (called Tambu Knoll), remained in Japanese hands. Its elaborate defences included interconnected weapon pits protected by up to four layers of logs, tunnels and underground bunkers, as well as the natural protection of a ravine and steep walls. Lin Cameron was ordered to take this position by a frontal assault. He had just under 60 men, the Japanese defenders up to 400. Even with artillery support, the attack was doomed. Cameron was soon wounded and handed command to Lieutenant Howard Martin. Martin put Corporal John Smith in charge of his platoon. Smith had won a Military Medal in Syria, but on 24 July 1943 was to surpass that feat. His 11-man platoon obeyed his call to 'Follow me' and advanced up Mount Tambu, bayonets fixed. Men fell around him but Smith and three others made it through lines of defences. Then grenades landed among them. Though wounded, Smith kept going, reaching the peak and calling back: 'Come on, boys!' When Martin ordered a withdrawal, Smith had to be dragged out semi-conscious. Cameron heard from his RMO that Smith sustained 40 wounds. These proved fatal on 26 July. Cameron requested awards for his men in this action but was told that the brigadier was unsympathetic considering the attack's failure. Smith, six-feet tall and weighing 14 stone, was described in glowing terms in the Melbourne press, quoting a fellow soldier who called him 'the greatest soldier in the A.I.F.'. Although his father wrote to Prime Minister Curtin, Smith received no official recognition for his deeds on Mount Tambu.

Another casualty on 24 July was Bill Tiller, killed while acting as forward scout on an unsuccessful attempt by Walters' company to block the track between Mount Tambu and Komiatum. On 30 July, American troops attacked Tambu Knoll. They had strong artillery support, but their frontal assault was also halted. Corporal Les 'Bull' Allen, who had won a Military Medal at Crystal Creek and carried out wounded in the Australian fighting for Tambu Knoll, was prominent again. Responding to calls for 'Bull', he braved enemy fire, which repeatedly creased his uniform, to carry 12 American casualties to safety. The United States government rewarded his superlative courage, encapsulated in a magnificent photo, with the award of a Silver Star. Allen's nickname came from his aggressive attitude in Australian Rules football and suited this man of great strength and a booming voice. He had a fine sense of humour, but a childhood in which he had suffered domestic violence before being abandoned and raised in an orphanage probably contributed to his lack of respect for military authority. He had worked bravely in Libya but was subsequently hospitalised with 'anxiety neurosis'. He won praise for attending casualties all night under shellfire in Syria. Allen never showed fear during combat, but after returning to Australia in September 1943 began behaving erratically. He was demoted for striking an officer in February 1944, before being diagnosed with 'constitutional temperamental instability and anxiety state' and medically discharged in September. For six months he lost the power of speech. He was recovering on a farm in February 1945 when news came of his Silver Star. The life of Australia's most famous World War II stretcher-bearer continued to improve thereafter: he married in 1949, had four children, and became a popular figure demonstrating historical mining methods at Sovereign Hill.

The Old Vickers Position

While fighting swirled around and on Mount Tambu, Australians were tackling a similar obstacle further north, at the Old Vickers Position. A famous photo shows a wounded Australian being helped across a nearby creek. The wounded man, Private Wal Johnson, had suffered grenade wounds to the face and arm while patrolling. Helping him was Sergeant Gordon Ayre (MM) who, like Johnson, was in the 58th/59th Battalion. In commanding the battalion's stretcher-bearers, Ayre, a 41-year-old carpenter from Shepparton, demonstrated courage and organisational skill in circumstances that really strained his unit.

The 58th/59th continued to be criticised, but on 28 July they changed many minds. Supported for the first time by substantial artillery fire, the battalion advanced through smoke on to the Old Vickers Position that had become its nemesis after four unsuccessful attacks. In scenes immortalised in a magnificent Ivor Hele painting, the 58th/59th forced the Japanese to abandon the position with its 57 covered weapon pits, four bunkers and mountain gun. Lieutenant Lawrence 'Butch' Proby (MC) led the advance to the crest along a narrow ridge. The Japanese were emerging from their dugouts after the bombardment, and soon Australians and Japanese were duelling with grenades. Proby personally killed the mountain gun crew before being wounded by grenade splinters and then, after being bandaged, insisted on returning to the fight trailing yards of bandage. Proby won a Bar to his Military Cross on Bougainville. The 58th/59th company that took Old Vickers was just 31-strong when a 2/7th Battalion company relieved it the following day.

Determined to regain Old Vickers, the Japanese attacked this company at dawn on 2 August. Corporal Allan Naismith (DCM) was the only NCO in his platoon, which he commanded and which held the right forward sector. It comprised just 12 men, split into three reliefs of four. A Bren gun pit was sited slightly in front of the other weapon pits. The enemy was just 15 metres away but could only approach Naismith's position up a slope. Private Don Finn (MM) was a Bren gunner on one relief, and whenever he heard Japanese bayonets being fixed, he threw grenades down the slope, called out, 'It's on again, boys', and opened fire. The Japanese launched 12 attacks over four days – and especially nights – but Naismith and his men repulsed them. The Australians kept score of grenades thrown by sticking the pull rings into the side of their pits. Naismith crawled forward after each attack and gathered grenades from enemy dead. His unit thus gained an extra 200 Japanese grenades. These included grenades from five Japanese he surprised and killed as they were priming them. Naismith was fascinated by explosives, setting booby traps that caused many Japanese casualties near Observation Hill, and including devices designed to explode only when walked into from the enemy side of the wire. One Japanese night attack came to hand-to-hand fighting over the weapon pits. Naismith was wounded in the right shoulder. Before he left for treatment, yet another of his skills came to the fore when this former ambulance sergeant used his left hand to stitch a fellow casualty's wound. Naismith's and three other platoons held off the Japanese attacks on Old Vickers. The Ballarat labourer would be discharged medically unfit in September 1944.

By August 1943, elements of all three Japanese divisions in New Guinea had been attracted to the 'Salamaua magnet'. Nevertheless, they could not prevent the Australians and Americans from taking ridge after ridge in early August. The Japanese still held Mount Tambu, but the Australians found a way to bypass it and isolate its defenders. The key was Komiatum Ridge, from which supplies to Mount Tambu could be blocked, so the 2/6th Battalion's Captain Harold Laver (MC) was ordered to occupy it. By 7 August a patrol under 'Smoky' Hedderman had found a path to Komiatum through dense jungle. Following a long approach march, Laver led a two-company surprise attack on 16 August that seized the ridge and cut the Japanese supply line to Mount Tambu. With artillery and Vickers machine-gun support, Laver's men held off the inevitable repeated Japanese counterattacks, one of which came within a few metres of the defences. Blamey's deputy, General Frank Berryman, called Laver's attack the 'best bit of tactical surprise' of the whole campaign. Laver was able, experienced and could be a forbidding superior. He ended the war a major, second-in-command of the 2/7th.

On 19 August, the Japanese retreated from Mount Tambu, Goodview Junction and Orodubi to the last high ground before Salamaua. That month, Lieutenant John Bethune (MC) and his 34-strong company held off a Japanese company over two days on Arnold's Crest before withdrawing, and although brigade headquarters initially considered this a sign of the 58th/59th's 'unreliability', eventually they recognised that Bethune had done well. On 22 August, two 42nd Battalion platoons occupied Bamboo Knoll, from which they could see the Salamaua peninsula. Japanese forces encircled and sought to recapture it. Captain Rod Cole (MC) led the defence, moving among and encouraging his men. Japanese tree snipers inflicted casualties, including one section leader killed. Lance-Corporal Frank 'Shorty' Deal, who stood 5 feet 3 inches tall, joined Cole in hunting them down beyond the perimeter. Demoralised, the Japanese eventually dispersed. Cole, a 33-year-old Queensland bank manager, was later wounded, but by 1945 was a major. Deal, a sugar worker, was badly wounded in the face and leg on Bougainville.

Last ridges before Salamaua

On 21 August, the militia 29th Brigade began relieving the 17th Brigade, which had been fighting since January. Allied forces now confronted the last line of Japanese defences, including Scout Ridge, Charlie Hill, Lewis Knoll, Rough Hill and Arnold's Crest.

The 15th Brigade concentrated north of the Francisco River, the 29th south of it. The 15th Battalion was ordered to advance along the coastal flank and seize Scout Hill in a surprise attack. Fresh Japanese reinforcements, formidable and alert marines, defended the area. The attackers became pinned down before they reached Scout Hill and, without artillery support, suffered heavy casualties. Stretcher-bearer Ervine Sallaway (MM) ignored shrapnel wounds to his thigh to treat and evacuate 15 men. When evacuated himself, the tall Queensland shearer was totally exhausted.

With a stalemate at Scout Ridge, the 15th moved on Lokanu Ridge, from which the enemy could threaten their flank. A platoon under Lieutenant Leslie Byrne (MC) was ordered to seize the ridge's eastern end. An artilleryman by training, Byrne had no infantry experience, but now led a four-man reconnaissance patrol, including himself, Private Frank Kane and two 2/6th Battalion men, Arthur Dehne and Allan Rose, who had stayed behind to 'foster in' the inexperienced 15th. Rose and Dehne were leading when enemy machine guns opened fire. With grenades and Owens they killed three Japanese in a pillbox. During a friendly artillery barrage, Byrne led a dash to seize the eastern end of the ridge and found the defences abandoned. On 5–6 September, the Japanese tried with increasing determination to shift Byrnes' platoon. Australian booby traps claimed some attackers, but a key figure was Bren gunner Herb Troughton (MM), a tall 20-year-old with a stutter, who halted a bayonet charge, the seventh attack, on 6 September. A Japanese grenade blast temporarily blinded Troughton, but his mates covered him until he recovered. He was often in trouble with authorities and was court-martialled in 1945 for being AWL for over a month. In this firefight he was credited with killing 17 Japanese. On 9 September, the 15th Battalion took Lokanu Ridge and Scout Ridge unopposed.

On 26 August, the 47th Battalion advanced towards Kunai Spur. Lieutenant Len Barnett (MC) soon became a byword for bravery in the battalion. During an attack on Japanese pillboxes on 28 August, he grabbed an LMG from the hands of a Japanese and threw it over a cliff. Unable to reload his own weapon in time and finding that his last grenade had a faulty pin, he jumped into a trench with another Japanese whom he clubbed to death. He then grabbed at the rifle of a third enemy, who fired and wounded Barnett in the hand. Still, Barnett managed to bash this man to death. Enemy crossfire was such that Barnett had to pull his platoon out, during which the 36-year-old engine driver was wounded in the other hand. After a supporting bombardment, the 47th took the spur in bloody fighting.

Lieutenant Ron Garland (MC) of the 2/3rd Independent Company led a daring raid into the heart of the enemy's defences on 3 September, killing eight before withdrawing. Garland had been a leader in many actions since June, including the attack on Ambush Knoll and the defence of the same position for 56 continuous hours in July. He added a Bar to his Military Cross in 1945 as a company commander in the 2nd New Guinea Infantry Battalion.

On 9 September, the 42nd Battalion captured Charlie Hill. Two days later it occupied Salamaua itself. An enemy rearguard engaged the 47th and a company of the 2/7th. The latter became pinned down and virtually encircled on a knoll, sustaining 12 casualties. The company was extricated largely because of Lance-Corporal Tom Frawley (MM), a signaller who recognised the danger and volunteered to take a line out to the company. The young cheesemaker encountered intense fire, which twice cut the line behind him, forcing him to go back and repair it. After crawling for an hour he got the line through and the company was reinforced. Frawley was often in disciplinary trouble and had been reverted to private by the time he left the Army to return to farm work in 1944.

From April to September 1943, in the advance on Salamaua, the Australians suffered over 1100 casualties, including at least 349 killed. They succeeded brilliantly in their role of acting as a magnet to draw Japanese troops from Lae.

CHAPTER 17

BY AIR, SEA AND LAND: LAE AND THE HUON PENINSULA

Capturing Lae involved unusual and demanding operations. The 9th Division made an amphibious landing east of Lae, while the 7th Division travelled by air to Nadzab and advanced down the Markham Valley towards it. The 9th Division landings on 4 September 1943 were unopposed except from the air. Then began a march towards Lae, through jungle and oppressive heat. Corporal Allan Jones described marching on a front one-man wide, and traversing 'creek beds, rocky outcrops and very rough ground'. The first major clash occurred on 5 September near Singaua Plantation. Sergeant Don Lawrie (DCM) of the 2/23rd Battalion took a lightly equipped platoon some 4000 metres west of the leading troops to establish a listening post at the Bunga River mouth. As these men rested in the dark, a group of 127 Japanese, big and well-armed naval troops, passed them, clearly heading east towards the Australian main party. Lawrie's radio was not working but Corporal Dave Fairlie (MM) and Lance-Corporal Alan Schram (MM) volunteered to try to beat the Japanese to the Australian lines and warn the 2/23rd of the Japanese approach. After discarding weapons and equipment, the pair waded in the sea – up to neck deep – for part of the journey, Fairlie managing despite being unable to swim. They arrived at the 2/23rd at 4.30 am, 15 crucial minutes before the Japanese did. The attackers were repulsed before they could dig in. In the early afternoon, about 60 retreating Japanese came across

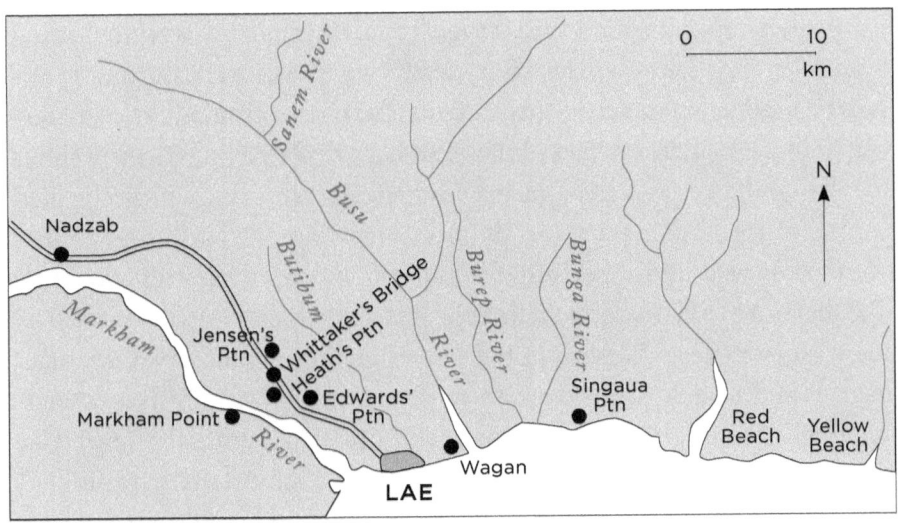

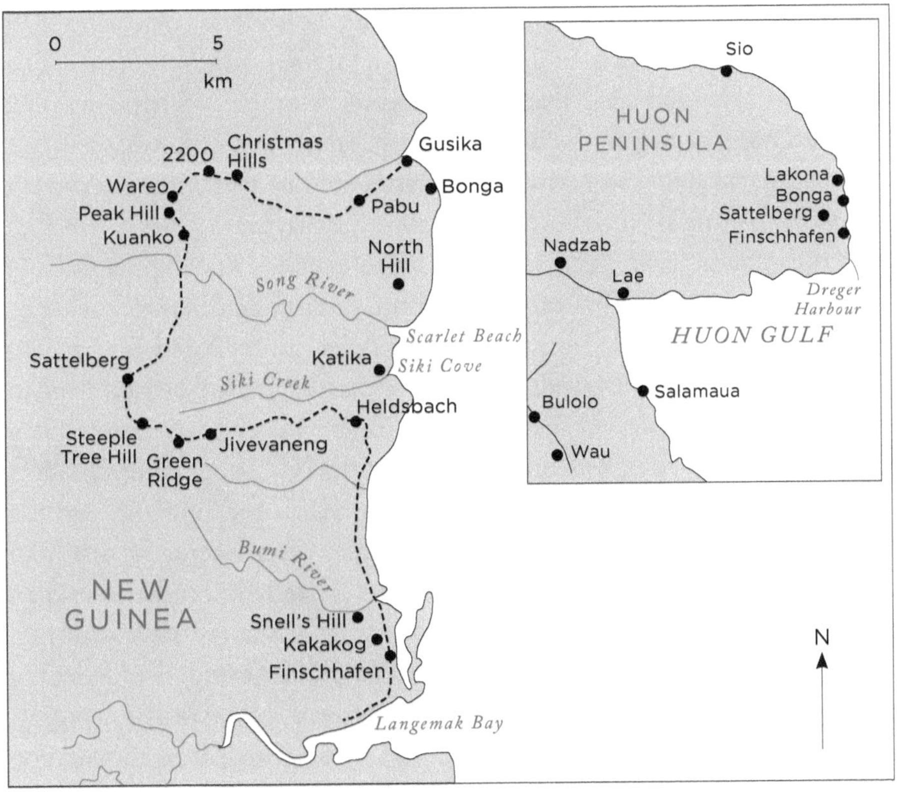

Lae and the Huon Peninsula

Lawrie's platoon, which had 'stood-to' all night and was sheltering behind trees. The platoon shot dead two Japanese scouts but was nearly fooled when an enemy called, 'Stop shooting, we're Aussies'. Six or more Japanese attacks followed, heralded by a bugle. Sometimes the Australians' position appeared hopeless, but Lawrie took the lead in maintaining contact with his men, ensuring ammunition supplies were preserved and especially fending off attacks with grenades, rifle and bayonet. Six platoon members testified to seeing Lawrie kill at least ten Japanese. Lawrie noted later that the Japanese would, after each failed attack, head back to their starting position, like bowlers playing cricket. His platoon lost four killed. Eventually, after two exhausting days, the platoon made its way back to the battalion. A former stockman and regular soldier, 25-year-old Lawrie was 6 feet 2 or 3 inches tall, spoke with a deep and confident voice, and had twice been Mentioned in Despatches while serving with the 2/5th Battalion. He had also been wounded at Alamein. Within a week of the Singaua action he was commissioned, but this was his last campaign. In late 1944, this exceptional soldier was diagnosed with 'Anxiety Neurosis' and discharged from the Army.

Lieutenant Jack Atkinson (MC) also excelled at Singaua. While attempting an encircling movement on 6 September, heavy machine-gun fire forced his platoon to ground. Atkinson crawled forward to a man with a thigh wound, got him on his back and carried him to safety. On returning to his men, Atkinson was preparing to lead a bayonet charge when he heard that one of his NCOs, Sergeant Robert Innocent, lay wounded near the Japanese. Atkinson now ordered his men to concentrate their fire and grenades on the enemy machine gun. The unfortunate gunner died when a grenade landed between his legs, enabling Atkinson and his platoon to advance. Atkinson then crawled to Innocent, who had a serious shoulder wound. Thinking his wounds mortal, Innocent refused to be moved, but Atkinson piggy-backed him out. There were no bearers at company headquarters, so Atkinson went on to battalion headquarters, where there was so much blood on him that it was wrongly assumed that he too had

Sergeant Don Lawrie (DCM) autographs a Japanese flag for fellow troops of the 2/23rd Battalion. Near Lae in September 1943, the tall 25-year-old led his platoon against a much larger Japanese attacking force, personally killing at least ten Japanese.
AWM 061700

been wounded. However, the physical effort of two evacuations had reignited an ankle wound Atkinson had sustained at Alamein. The medical officer ordered his evacuation, but Atkinson refused to leave, instead soldiering on after receiving a morphia injection. The 23-year-old Queensland dairy farmer only left when his brigadier ordered him out. Atkinson's boot had to be cut from his swollen foot. Thus ended his frontline career, which included a Commander-in-Chief's Commendation Card in the Middle East, together with wounds at Tobruk and Alamein. When the Timboon community congratulated Atkinson in the local hall in October 1944, he stated that the honour really belonged to his platoon of 30, all of whom deserved the medal.

Across the Busu

Heavy rain slowed the 9th Division advance, while stifling heat and lack of rations also affected the men. Late on 8 September, the forward units reached the swollen and deep Busu River. They struggled to find a viable crossing place, but eventually the 2/28th Battalion waded to a sheltered island and then moved to the far bank in four extended lines. This daring and inspiring manoeuvre was nightmarish for the participants: 30 were dragged off their feet and 13 drowned. The Japanese expected the Australians to cross closer to the river mouth, and by the time they turned their attention to the 2/28th, most of the Australians had crossed and reached cover. Enemy machine-gun fire killed a young reinforcement who raised his head above the long grass. Corporal Neville May (DCM), who had held his section together in the crossing, went forward alone and found the Japanese machine-gun post about 150 metres from the riverbank. May eliminated the post's defenders with grenades and his Owen. This Western Australian goldminer had been Mentioned in Despatches and received a Commander-in-Chief's Commendation Card for his efforts at Alamein.

The official history praises the cold courage of the Australians who walked into the raging Busu, asserting that Australian soldiers in the Pacific generally found the prospect of facing 'an angry Nature' even worse than that of 'an aroused enemy'.

On 10 September, Japanese machine-gun and mortar fire hit the 2/28th's bridgehead, based on the riverbank, which was fringed with high kunai. When Japanese grenades began falling among one platoon, Sergeant Alex 'Sandy' MacGregor (MID) moved alone to the beach and, partially hidden by overhanging foliage, directed his platoon's fire to eliminate six Japanese taking cover in a depression hidden from the other Australians. A Japanese machine gun further down the beach mortally wounded 36-year-old MacGregor, who refused to move to safety or to allow attempts to rescue him.

The platoon's commander, Lieutenant John Brooks (MC), was at company headquarters during this fight, and on returning and finding MacGregor dead and others wounded, showed a new side of his personality. In training he had never raised his voice to the men, but now, on obtaining permission to lead an attack, ordered them to fix bayonets. This 39-year-old farmhand from Mount Barker, WA, had been identified as an outstanding potential leader during an officer training course in 1941. As a lieutenant he had been wounded at Alamein and placed on the 'dangerously ill' list on account of gunshot wounds to the face, thigh, forearm and abdomen. Now at the Busu, the Japanese were holding clumps of kunai-covered high ground in a swamp, while the outnumbered Australians advanced in water that was in places chest-deep. Nevertheless, the Australians' superior firepower and Brooks' encouragement and seeming omnipresence pushed them forward. Ultimately, 63 Japanese lay dead, their islands overrun, and at least five of their machine guns captured. The Australians sustained some 20 casualties, including Private Jack Leonard. The 41-year-old Kalgoorlie prospector, the unit's champion axeman, was found shot through the head but closely encircled by dead Japanese.

The advance resumed and on 13 September, the 2/28th's lead platoon encountered Japanese entrenched at a track junction on the coast. Acting Platoon Sergeant Andy Torrent (MM) was fired on when he and another man went on a reconnaissance. They retired unharmed, and a firefight followed as the platoon moved forward cautiously. Torrent and the platoon commander, Lieutenant Eric Connor, led, with Torrent personally grenading six Japanese in their weapon pits. Connor was killed, reportedly by a grenade he had thrown that the Japanese threw back at him. Torrent, a 39-year-old station overseer from Busselton, took command, leading the platoon in killing another 12 Japanese before the defenders fled.

As Torrent led his platoon in action the following month, an observer likened him to the great conductor Toscanini for the way he directed his Bren and Owen gunners and his riflemen. The day before his medal-winning action, Torrent had killed a Japanese machine-gun crew with a rifle grenade: the Australians found the four-man crew spreadeagled around the gun. Torrent would contract scrub typhus later in the campaign, narrowly survive, and finish the war medically downgraded and bitter about having to work at a POW camp in Western Australia.

The 2/4th Independent Company was tasked with crossing the Busu higher up. One section was sent across a kunda bridge, but Japanese defenders watched a number of commandos cross then opened fire. The bridge was severed, some Australians thrown into the water and three killed. Seven had made it across but were now marooned. Private Brian Jaggar (MM) took the initiative, personally 'cleaning out' two Nambu nests and a mortar post, killing two and driving off the remaining Japanese. At night the Australians destroyed the LMGs and mortar, then tried to swim the river. Two were drowned but Jaggar, a fine swimmer, dragged a seriously wounded man to safety.

On 4 September 1943, the 24th Battalion of the 5th Division was sent to attack strongly held Japanese defences at Markham Point, in order to threaten Lae. This poorly planned and supported operation cost 12 Australian lives. The battalion arrived in the battle area only the day before the attack, and Lieutenant Fred Childs (MC) had barely met his new platoon. As he led them in his first action, heavy machine-gun fire forced the platoon to ground and wounded him in both legs. He lay on his own just 15 metres from

Japanese positions. After dark he crawled away and found four men. Afraid of making too much noise if they moved, they waited until dawn before trying to escape through swampy ground. Japanese heard them and followed. One tried to strangle Childs, who shot him with his pistol, but other Japanese killed two of his men. The surviving three, all badly wounded, lay hidden for a day before Childs and James Walker (MM) moved off, reluctantly leaving a severely wounded comrade. After four days of surviving on rainwater and with badly flyblown wounds, they reached their own lines. Childs' wounds, especially to his right foot, led to him being classed unfit for further frontline service.

By air to Nadzab

While Childs struggled back to safety, 7th Division troops were marching on Lae from Nadzab. Australian engineers had prepared an airstrip in the Nadzab area, which was secured by American paratroops and Australian artillerymen who landed with their 25-pounders on 5 September. More than 40 aircraft transported Australian troops to the airfield the following day, and by 9 September the 2/25th Battalion was leading the 65-kilometre advance on Lae. That battalion sustained its first casualty of the campaign the following day when a patrol leader, Lance-Corporal Jack Littler, was wounded on encountering a Japanese patrol. Acting Corporal Harold Brockhurst (MM) led out five men to rescue Littler. One report called the area 'a lead-filled zone', but Brockhurst's group reached and attended Littler. Nine Japanese were firing at them from the rear, another group from in front. Brockhurst took charge of the defence, moving around his men, directing their fire and personally shooting two Japanese before finding a route back, enabling all his men and Littler to return safely. Brockhurst, a Queensland stockman, ended the war a sergeant and veteran of all the 2/25th's campaigns.

On 13 September, firmly entrenched Japanese halted the 2/25th advance at Whittaker's Bridge. Japanese marines on a ridge killed five Australians and wounded three in one platoon, including section leader Corporal Billy Richards (MM). Though hit in the stomach, back and arm and lying in an exposed position, Richards continued giving orders to his men, including instructions not to rescue him. However, one of them, 38-year-old Private Richard Kelliher (VC), decided he would leave his cover and bring Richards in. He silenced the enemy post first, using grenades and a Bren. Then, still under fire, he rescued Richards and helped recover two other men wounded while trying to save Richards. Thirty-year-old master pastrycook Richards would be reverted to the ranks for going AWL in April 1944, and then be medically downgraded because of his wounds.

Nearing Lae

By 14 September, the Japanese were clearly retreating from Lae. Japanese resistance was crumbling but there was some hard fighting. That day, the 2/32nd Battalion was advancing along the coastal track near Wagan when first drawn into action. A platoon sent into a frontal attack lost its commander just metres from the start-line, and Sergeant Harry Bell (MM) took over. When heavy machine-gun fire delayed the advance and inflicted casualties, Bell found open ground where he could see the Woodpecker. Methodically and coolly he shot the crew, and his platoon followed up to destroy the enemy position. Bell had won a Distinguished Conduct Medal at Alamein, where over successive days he led his section in silencing an enemy machine gun and anti-tank gun, holding on against an enemy tank attack, and leading a successful raid. He had twice saved his platoon commander, who when wounded on the raid had told Bell to leave him behind. '15 Platoon has never left one of its men', Bell replied while tending the officer's wounds, 'and they will not start now'. This natural leader, a former grocery salesman, was idolised by his men and would have loved to become an officer, to the point where he once told a comrade that he would have preferred a commission to his decorations. However, Bell suffered severely from malaria and was discharged from the Army in October 1944. By the end of 14 September, the 2/32nd had killed 70 Japanese and lost 10 men.

The following day saw the 9th Division approaching Lae against negligible opposition, but the 7th Division faced stiff resistance from enemy rearguards at Edwards' Plantation. The 2/31st and 2/33rd battalions launched a combined attack. Captain Doug Cullen (MC) of the 2/33rd had the previous day led a bayonet charge that drove back a Japanese force. On 15 September he moved among his men, directing them during the action, and at a crucial point mounted a Bren gun on the shoulder of one his men – the bipod being unusable in the very thick undergrowth – and by expending three magazines personally knocked out a machine gun. The last Japanese burst wounded Cullen severely in the shoulder. This, his second wound, ended his frontline career. Cullen, a 24-year-old regular soldier, had enlisted as William Copp, fought superbly in Syria, and was Mentioned in Despatches in Papua. Corporal Dave Green (MM) of the 2/33rd was also outstanding on 15 September. His citation described him eliminating a machine gun; other accounts show that he did more, including grenading and submachine-gunning a line of enemy weapon pits and saving his company commander from a charging Japanese. This brave and energetic Sydney milk carter was mortally wounded three weeks later.

As the 2/31st Battalion manoeuvred behind the Japanese defences, thus trapping the rearguard at Edwards' Plantation, Acting Corporal Ronnie Groundwater (MM) led his section through deep jungle and, on finding the enemy's flank, called out, 'Right boys, into them!' His section killed 14 in the close-quarters fighting that followed. A bullet struck Groundwater's arm, fracturing his humerus and ending the lorry driver's military service at age 26. Stretcher-bearer Private Laurie Clark (MID) tended to and rescued Groundwater and three other men. Private Lisle Rowe was severely wounded in the throat and arm early in the firefight and lay in the open. Enemy fire forced back several men who tried to approach him. Stretcher-bearer Alfred Scott (DCM) arrived, threw off all his gear except his medical haversack, and rushed into the clearing under fire. He reached Rowe and was wrapping a dressing around his throat when another bullet struck the casualty in the foot. Holding the dressing to Rowe's throat, Scott carried him through intense fire to cover. Leaving other bearers to carry Rowe, Scott then returned to the clearing and rescued two more casualties. Rowe died later that day. Scott had often been in trouble, especially for going AWL, and faced court martials on three occasions. He was found not guilty on the third occasion. He was discharged medically unfit from the Army in March 1944, after a diagnosis of 'psychopathic personality'. On discharge, this labourer from Fitzroy was just 28.

The fighting at Edwards' cost the Australians 57 casualties, including 15 fatalities, but more than 100 Japanese were killed and the road into Lae now lay open. The 2/25th Battalion entered the ruined town that 15 September morning, but 'friendly' artillery and aerial bombardment forced them out. In the afternoon, Australians of the 7th and 9th divisions met in the town and raised an Australian flag. The Japanese lost at least 1500 men killed around Lae, but more than 8000 escaped to continue fighting.

Capture Finschhafen!

The capture of Lae ahead of schedule allowed MacArthur and Blamey to press ahead with the capture of Finschhafen, further east on the coast of the Huon Peninsula from Lae. Finschhafen was potentially a major air and naval base for future operations in the Solomons, New Britain and Bougainville. The 20th Brigade made the landing at Scarlet Beach, about 10 kilometres north of Finschhafen. In the meantime, the 22nd Battalion marched overland towards Finschhafen from the south. Enemy resistance was expected to be light, but Allied intelligence underestimated Japanese strength. The Australians went ashore at Scarlet Beach in American vessels on 22 September. Several craft missed their beaches and there was intermingling of troops. Stretcher-bearer Lloyd Thomas (MM) of the 2/15th Battalion was travelling in one landing craft that collided with another. Enemy mortar fire heaped more misery on the occupants, ten of whom were killed or wounded. Thomas aided the wounded and, just as he finished his dressings, discovered that the craft was pulling away from the beach. He jumped into the water fully laden and swam ashore.

Despite the confusion, the Australians soon overcame Japanese resistance on the beach. They encountered more serious opposition near Katika village. Lieutenant Howard Pope (MC) and his platoon of the 2/13th had knocked out two Japanese machine guns on the beach when they were ordered to attack the Katika defences from the north-west. Pope received a painful wound above the left eye from a mortar bomb fragment but carried on until, with 11 of his men hit, he was ordered to withdraw his platoon. Here, despite enemy fire, 33-year-old Private Bob Dutton (MID) evacuated three casualties on his back. That afternoon the Japanese abandoned their strong defences. Later in the campaign, Pope, a 23-year-old law student, was severely wounded in the abdomen. His military career continued after the war, and he served as a major with 3RAR in Malaya.

The following day, 23 September, the 20th Brigade advanced down the coast towards Finschhafen. The lead battalion, the 2/15th, reached the Bumi River and found Japanese entrenched on the opposite bank near the river mouth. Corporal Reece Tart led the foremost section to the riverbank but was shot dead while examining a crossing. Corporal Harry Cousens (MM), in the following section, in full view of enemy machine gunners risked his life to save Tart but was himself wounded. Private Lloyd Thomas, who had saved lives on Scarlet Beach, then rescued Cousens and another casualty. Six days later, while dressing a soldier's wound, Thomas, a 6-foot-2-inches-tall Queenslander, was himself wounded and evacuated.

By 23 September, the 2/12th Field Regiment's 25-pounder guns were bombarding Kakakog spur, key to Finschhafen's defences. Japanese aircraft attacked the guns, missing them but inflicting over 50 casualties. The dead included Captain 'Joe' Nelligan, who had won a Military Cross at Alamein, where he had been a FOO at Miteiriya Ridge (controlling three regiments at one point), Bulimba and the October battle.

On 24 September, the 2/15th Battalion established a foothold across the Bumi River. Two companies were sent to take a commanding position, later called Snell's Hill after Captain Len Snell. Just reaching the elite Japanese marines holding this hill was a challenge, for after leaving the start-line, the Australians tumbled downhill through vines, bamboo and timber, and then some 400 metres from the start encountered a steep slope which they had to scale. They maintained their formation on a 150-metre-wide front and then saw Japanese grenades rolling towards them. One that landed just 30 centimetres from the foremost man blew him downhill but did not prevent him from getting up and resuming the lead. This man, Corporal Robert Norris (MM), led the capture of a key Japanese post. Most of the marines' fire went over the Australians' heads. Snell sent Sergeant Fred Fink (MM) around the right flank with a section that drew much enemy fire. Though wounded in the back, Fink continued to lead the attack. He and his men killed 30 Japanese. Fink received a Bar to the Military Medal he had won at Alamein. This Yandina farm labourer was a superb patroller, whose cool courage and judgment drew frequent comment. He ended the war a lieutenant.

On the left flank of the assault on Snell's Hill, Lance-Sergeant Clem Guilfoyle (MM) advanced on a well-sited Japanese machine-gun post, fire from which cut an inverted tunnel down through the jungle. He carefully avoided this tunnel until he was just two metres from the gun at its apex. There he had to enter the field of fire to shoot the gunner with his Owen. Both he and the marine fired simultaneously: the Japanese fire hit Guilfoyle in the chest, while his hit the Japanese in the forehead. Guilfoyle remained where he was, in the open, calling instructions and encouraging his men. He would be evacuated, recover and end the war a captain. On the left, Lieutenant Lex Starmer (MC) led his platoon, though already tired on reaching the hilltop, in a 50-metre charge through relatively open kunai grass. One of two 13mm Japanese machine guns caught fire when struck by Australian gunfire. Starmer's men killed at least 20 Japanese. Another 40–50 Japanese ran. By the time the Australians had cleared the hill, they had inflicted about

100 casualties and sustained 10. The 2/13th Battalion expanded the bridgehead.

The advance on Finschhafen was proceeding well, but supplying the troops required prodigious efforts from most infantrymen not involved in fighting. For example, on 24 September, a group of 60 men from 2/17th Battalion carried supplies 5500 metres across steep terrain to resupply the forward 2/15th Battalion companies, before returning in darkness, guided only by signal wire they held as they stumbled and slid.

The epic defence of Jivevaneng

While the 20th Brigade was stretching south towards Finschhafen, on its flank Japanese strength and aggression were growing. The 2/17th Battalion, responsible for guarding the beachhead and flank, saw evidence of a Japanese build-up when it sent a company to occupy Sattelberg, a mission station over 1000 metres above sea level and a few kilometres inland from Scarlet Beach. Enemy resistance proved far too strong here, and on 25 September, the company dug in further east on the track from Sattelberg, at Jivevaneng. The company commander, Lieutenant Hugh Main (MC), chose this location for its cleared field of fire on the junction of the Sattelberg Road and Tareko Track. Main, a Queensland jackeroo, had served with Scots College cadets and the militia, was 6 feet 1½ inches tall and had enlisted as a private. When wounded in the shoulder in Tobruk he was a sergeant. At Jivevaneng, Japanese patrols repeatedly cut his company's communications, forcing him to depend on his own initiative. Over five days, Main and his men beat off six separate attacks and killed 30 Japanese for the loss of three wounded. The 20th Brigade commander, Brigadier Victor Windeyer, later called Main's Jivevaneng defence 'one of the finest company stories I have known'.

While attacking Main's force at Jivevaneng, the Japanese also attacked a 2/17th company near Katika. A captured order showed that this was part of a Japanese attempt to cut through to the coast.

Windeyer called for reinforcements and MacArthur grudgingly provided sufficient craft to send the 2/43rd Battalion. On arrival, on 30 September, the 2/43rd was sent to positions formerly held by the 2/17th Battalion, which was thereby freed to join the attack on Finschhafen. One 2/43rd company relieved Main's at Jivevaneng.

Captain Eric Grant (MC), a regular soldier before enlistment, led the defence of Jivevaneng from 30 September to 4 October. Grant and his company, supported by Australian artillery, repelled eight enemy attacks. The Japanese left 70 dead on abandoning the siege. However, they too inflicted heavy casualties on the 2/43rd men sent into attacks to relieve Grant's beleaguered company. After the siege, Grant returned to his old position to retrieve equipment they had buried earlier, and on the way saw the bodies of comrades who had died trying to reach him and his men. He was saddened by the loss of good soldiers in forlorn attacks against dug-in Japanese machine guns. Some survivors of those relief attempts were rewarded.

Lieutenant Gordon Combe (MC) commanded a company attack on 3 October. He was ordered to use the same track that a failed relief attempt had taken the previous day, so there was no element of surprise. Firing his Owen as he advanced, Combe personally led the assault across open ground against enemy machine-gun and mortar fire. Though wounded in the chest he continued to move among the foremost troops right across the front, and when retreat became unavoidable, he was last to leave. Combe ended the war a captain, adjutant of the battalion.

One of Combe's men was Private Ray Ronan (MM). His platoon became pinned down, but he crawled to a position from where he could see the enemy. Though constantly under fire, Ronan quickly shot six Japanese. Later he covered another platoon's withdrawal. Private Bert Garwood (MM), a 35-year-old Tasmanian stretcher-bearer, saved men over three days at Jivevaneng. On 1 October he crawled forward under fire and rescued four casualties. The following day, just 10 metres from an enemy machine-gun post, he bound the wounds of an NCO, then evacuated him under fire. On 3 October he tended and encouraged numerous casualties of Combe's company.

Grant's company withdrew from Jivevaneng on 4 October, but that day, the Japanese abandoned their roadblock, enabling the Australians to occupy Jivevaneng village.

Attack on Kakakog

Meanwhile, the 2/13th Battalion, with air and artillery support, attacked the main Japanese defences at Kakakog. As the battalion formed up to advance, one platoon discovered previously undetected defences on the left flank. From there the Japanese could enfilade and decimate the nearby Australian company. The company commander, Captain Paul Deschamps (MC), recognised the danger and directed two platoons along Ilebbe Creek towards these defences. Most of these men became trapped when the enemy spotted them and poured small arms and mortar fire down. Japanese snipers fired from treetops. Sergeant Geoff Crawford (DCM) took command of the men in the creek and ordered the able-bodied to follow him. While a third platoon fired mortar bombs at the Japanese, Crawford used a pre-arranged signal – the throwing of a grenade – to indicate a charge. He called out orders and advice while his men immediately found themselves in ferocious action. Private Fred Rolfe (DCM) stood on the creek bank in full view of the enemy and, firing his Bren from the hip, silenced a Japanese post. Enemy machine guns inflicted many casualties on those around him and delayed the advance, but Rolfe pressed forward alone towards the nearest machine-gun post. He killed the crew from close range. While shooting up a third post, he was severely wounded in the chest. Crawford also killed many, and was wounded severely in the head while trading fire with numerous Japanese. He continued leading until the position was taken. As the official historian observes, Crawford exemplified the way that 'when a situation seemed desperate the Australian Army appeared to have the knack of producing a leader of the necessary character'. In the end, the Japanese fled, leaving some 50 dead, many more than the Australians lost. Crawford, a share farmer, later served in the New South Wales parliament.

Forced to defend

By 2 October, the 20th Brigade had occupied Kakakog and Finschhafen, just 11 days after the landing and despite hard fighting, difficult terrain and meagre supplies. They were about to face an even greater challenge. The main body of a Japanese division was heading for the Finschhafen area, where more than 5000 Japanese soldiers remained. There was disagreement and uncertainty at Allied headquarters about Japanese strength and intentions, and therefore about the urgency of using the limited available shipping to send reinforcements. Ultimately, the 24th Brigade was sent to reinforce Finschhafen. General Wootten, now commanding the 9th Division, was ordered to advance around the coast to Sio, on the north of the Huon Peninsula. A vital preliminary to this would be capturing the Sattelberg heights and the Japanese supply line running to them along the Wareo–Gusika ridge.

Before the Australians could advance, they had to defend. News reached Wootten that the Japanese would attack towards Scarlet Beach on 16 October. They did come, but their assaults on Jivevaneng and an attempted seaborne landing at the northern end of Scarlet Beach were repulsed.

A bigger Japanese assault, on 17 October, captured high ground at Katika. The 2/28th Battalion halted this attack and sought to recapture Katika. In days of thrust and counter-thrust, the 2/28th learnt first-hand about Japanese attack in the jungle: bugle blasts, shouts, massed attacks and enemies appearing in unexpected locations. Lieutenant Claude Wedgwood (MC) played a key role in blunting the Japanese attack by positioning his platoon on the main enemy axis of advance. His men suffered 11 casualties but killed 33 Japanese. When his commanding officer ordered him to withdraw, Wedgwood asked permission to stay, as his men were dominating the position. He got his way, but later that day, the entire battalion had to retreat from Katika. When the following day the 2/28th pushed forward, Lance-Corporal Bert Nankiville (DCM) led his section of Wedgwood's depleted platoon in seizing and defending high ground. On 20 October, his section made an unsuccessful attempt to retake Katika, and one of the four wounds this Kalgoorlie labourer sustained necessitated the removal of his right eye. Nankiville had previously been in the news for rescuing a comrade who had been slashed and knocked down by a Japanese. Nankiville had killed the Japanese a split second before he could deliver the coup de grâce. Twenty-five-year-old Nankiville would be discharged from the Army within six months, officially on 'account of age'! In early 1944, a Perth newspaper reported on Wedgwood and Nankiville catching up. They recalled expecting to encounter 'a few Japs' on 20 October and instead running into 200–300. Nankiville died in 1977, aged 59, for 'service related' reasons.

Among those treating his company's wounded was Private Frank Waterman (MM), who on 18 October set up an emergency RAP, and tended wounded for four hours before collapsing from exhaustion. On being revived, he insisted on continuing. On 20 October, this 30-year-old skipman was wounded painfully in the arm while evacuating casualties. Again he continued, only leaving when wounded again in the back and hand. His wounds necessitated his discharge from the Army.

On 22 October, the Japanese launched a determined thrust down the main track. The brunt fell on a platoon under Lieutenant Peter Rooke (MC). Lance-Corporal 'Tinny' Broun (MM) manned a Bren in an exposed but vital position – something he did for several days – and the Japanese fell back, leaving nearly 50 dead.

The relatively fresh 2/32nd drove off the last Japanese attacks on 25 October. The Japanese attempts to regain the beachhead cost the 9th Division 228 casualties, including 49 killed, to 1500 Japanese losses. During the fight for Scarlet Beach, the 26th Brigade and the 1st Australian Tank Battalion arrived at nearby Langemak Bay. Their arrival ensured that the Australians would soon be attacking again.

CHAPTER 18

TO SATTELBERG AND SHAGGY RIDGE

While the 9th Division was fighting around Finschhafen, the 7th Division moved inland, up the Markham River Valley and into the Ramu Valley. Flanked by high mountain ranges, this was the largest area of open and flat terrain in New Guinea and well suited to airstrips.

MacArthur ordered Blamey to establish airfields at Kaiapit and Dumpu. The 191 commandos of the 2/6th Independent Company were flown to a makeshift airfield, from which they marched the 24 kilometres to Kaiapit on 19 September. They were armed to the teeth, with 18 Brens and 90 Owens. Commanding them was hard-driving 24-year-old Captain Gordon King (DSO), who was hit in the leg by Japanese machine-gun fire soon after the company reached the Kaiapit area. Once a mortar had silenced the enemy machine gun, the commandos stormed the village, benefiting from King's hard training in fire and movement and from expert use of grenades to pin down the Japanese. The defenders eventually ran, leaving 30 dead.

Before dawn the following day, a Japanese column, perhaps 500-strong, approached Kaiapit from the north-west. The nearest Australian platoon opened fire and pinned them down. Though short of ammunition, King decided to seize the initiative and attack the confused enemy force as well as the dominating Mission Hill. The Japanese were demoralised and routed, losing 200 or more killed, as well as 19 machine guns. The Australians lost 14 killed

Markham and Ramu valleys

and 23 wounded. The 7th Division commander, General Vasey, expressed amazement at the carnage wrought by these extraordinary commandos, and guilt at the way they had been left so outnumbered. He recommended awards for outstanding survivors. Corporal Syd Graham (MM), a wool sorter from Broken Hill, was wounded in the face but wiped out a strongpoint with grenades and an Owen and was credited with one-third of the unit's kills. Though sent to the RAP for treatment, Graham returned to his section the next morning when the fighting recommenced. This inspiring fighter was prominent in driving the Japanese out of Kaiapit No. 2 village, even though he was wounded again in the chest and hands.

Lieutenant Bob Balderstone (MC) led an advance on 20 September and, while he sheltered behind a coconut palm as his men replenished their ammunition and assembled for the next stage of the attack, an enemy bullet nicked the top of his arm. Incensed, he led a charge on an enemy post boasting three machine guns. He reportedly advanced alone across 70 metres of open ground before grenading the post. Balderstone had joined the unit with two other officers, Lieutenants Bert Westendorf and Reg Hallion, both of whom died leading their men in action at Kaiapit. Hallion was killed leading a third bayonet charge on a machine-gun post below Mission Hill. Though wounded in the hand, Corporal John 'Butch' Wilson (MM) took over Hallion's section and continued the advance. He ordered his men to pick up Japanese rifles if out of ammunition. A newspaper described the tall, laconic Wilson, twice Mentioned in Despatches, as one of the war's outstanding South Australian servicemen. Captain King received deserved credit for his leadership at Kaiapit, but also took with him sadness about the cost. The unit's policy was not to take prisoners, but King had indicated that one or two would be useful. Consequently, a medical orderly, Private Bert Harris, after attending to the Australian casualties, went to treat a wounded Japanese. However, as he bent over to help the casualty, the Japanese detonated a grenade, killing himself and mortally wounding Harris. As Harris lay dying, he told King that he blamed him.

Victory at Kaiapit enabled the 7th Division to advance rapidly up the valleys. By 4 October its men had reached Dumpu, thus securing the Markham and Ramu valleys as sites for American air bases at Nadzab, Gusap, Kaiapit and Dumpu. The Japanese commander in the area decided to concentrate his forces in formidable defensive positions on the Kankiryo Saddle in the Finisterres.

The road to Sattelberg

After the defeat of the Japanese counterattack against Scarlet Beach, the 9th Division returned to the offensive. Wootten was determined to carry out his postponed plans for the 9th Division to capture Sattelberg and Wareo (see p. 271 map). He decided to employ the relatively fresh 26th Brigade and nine tanks to capture Sattelberg, after which the 24th Brigade would take Wareo. First the Japanese roadblock east of Jivevaneng had to be cleared. The 20th Brigade did this in intense fighting that ended on 6 November. A 2/15th Battalion company seized a key Japanese position west of Kumawa in 30 minutes of bitter struggle on 13 October. Sergeant Alick Else won a Bar to the Military Medal he earned at Alamein. Private Bill 'Dadda' Woods (DCM) was commanding the leading section in Else's platoon when it charged an enemy machine gun from some 30 metres. Two of his eight men were killed and four wounded, but he kept going, overcoming the first post and then engaging a Woodpecker just 20 metres away. This distraction enabled Else's other sections to knock out the remaining posts. During this action, the 32-year-old Nambour stockman used 12 grenades and some 15 Owen magazines. His preferred weapon was a rifle! His commanding officer unsuccessfully recommended Woods for a Victoria Cross. Woods was killed in action in Korea, aged 40. Fifteen of the 26 men in Else's platoon were hit in this action, but the Japanese fled, leaving 39 dead.

The 2/13th lost the services of one of its best NCOs in this period, Sergeant Reg McKellar (Bar to MM). McKellar had a Military Medal from Tobruk, where feats such as the single-handed capture of a German truck with five prisoners won him a great reputation. In New Guinea he added to that fame: in late September he despatched two snipers who fired on a reconnaissance patrol he was leading, and though wounded in the arm and leg, continued until he located the patrol objective. He and another man patrolled perilously close to a strong enemy party on 20 October; and then at Sattelberg, on 30 October, he was badly wounded as he crawled towards heavy fire directed at his patrol from thick bamboo. Lance-Sergeant 'Snowy'

Dawes (DCM) of the 2/17th was a section commander in the last stages of the Jivevaneng fighting. On 3 November, the two leading 2/17th platoons came under heavy fire from Japanese concealed in dense bamboo. Dawes' platoon commander was mortally wounded, four members of his section hit. Though just 15 metres from the enemy, Dawes evacuated all the casualties to cover and arranged their evacuation. Soon afterwards, some 25 Japanese counterattacked his section. Dawes ordered his men to wait for his word to fire, which came when they were just 10 metres away. The Japanese were repulsed. Dawes then went forward to a position later found to be just 6 metres from the enemy and, under flooding rain and enemy sniping, remained there for 36 hours. While there he threw some 60 grenades and kept his men on the alert until 5 November, when the Japanese evacuated the position. Dawes suffered ill-health for much of his service. He was wounded at Alamein, and in May 1944 was evacuated with 'Anxiety neurosis with depression'. The 30-year-old Queanbeyan bread carter was discharged medically unfit four months later.

The Japanese evacuation of Jivevaneng enabled the long-blocked Sattelberg Road to be re-opened. The 2/48th Battalion advanced along that road towards Sattelberg, capturing Green Ridge on 16 November. The offensive opened officially the following day, with artillery, machine-gun and especially tank support. The determined Japanese were dug in on the precipitous terrain all the way to Sattelberg. In an all-day fight for Coconut Ridge on 17 November, Corporal Reg Leary (MM) led one of the foremost sections against positions concealed in dense bamboo beside the road and running along a razorback track. Early on, he sustained shrapnel wounds to the head, and enemy fire smashed his rifle. Rather than retreat, he crawled forward alone, ahead of the leading tank and just 'a few feet' from the enemy. From this perilous position he relayed information about the Japanese dispositions to the tanks, which destroyed two pillboxes and enabled the infantry advance to resume. The 25-year-old Kalgoorlie labourer was just 5 feet 6 inches tall and had already been Mentioned in Despatches and received a Commendation Card for gallantry at Alamein.

Lieutenant Hortle Morphett (MC) commanded Leary's company and had trained it for these operations. Even after the two lead tanks were out of action and with his company 61 under strength, he continued the attack. Educated at Geelong College and Oxford University, Morphett was a natural leader: in Tobruk, 'Diver' Derrick described him as 'the best officer and man in the battalion'.

On 19 November, the Australians could not outflank the Japanese machine guns and the terrain temporarily halted the tanks. Australian engineers tried igniting two four-gallon drums containing petrol and dieseline in the hope of spraying liquid over the defenders. This 'fougasse' burned out almost immediately, but the infantry commander on the scene, Lieutenant Jim Barry (MC), decided to exploit surprise among the enemy and charge up the hill towards them. They went in shoulder to shoulder, firing automatic weapons from the hip or throwing grenades, and shouting the divisional war cry, 'Ho, Ho, Ho'. It took 20 minutes of fighting to shift the last defenders of 'Fougasse Corner'. A resolute Japanese counterattack at last light was repulsed. On 22 November, the 2/48th reached the lower slopes of Sattelberg, some 600 metres from the heights. The tanks had been very effective, but a landslide prohibited their further use. On 24 November, a platoon under Sergeant Tom Derrick (VC) found a way up the steep slopes and evicted the enemy from apparently impregnable positions. Derrick, who personally led the attack with great skill and courage, added a Victoria Cross to the Distinguished Conduct Medal he had won at Alamein. He gave enormous credit in his diary and in interviews to the handful of men who supported him in the attack – Don Spencer, Stan Davies, Charlie Barratt, 'Slogger' Sutherland, Ron Logue, 'Swanny' Washbrook, 'Shorty' Edmunds and Wally Everett – but none of them received medals for this extraordinary feat, which has become famous as a 'one-man show'. Private Wally Everett, whose section Derrick praised as 'magnificently commanded' in the assault, was Mentioned in Despatches. On 25 November, Sattelberg was found abandoned, and Derrick raised an Australian flag there.

Pabu: Australian island in a Japanese sea

During the advance on Sattelberg, 24th Brigade troops further north had a remarkable success. The brigade's immediate role was to cut the track from Gusika, on the coast, to Wareo. Consequently, on 19 November, part of the 2/32nd Battalion was sent to occupy a high feature on the Gusika–Wareo ridge. The Australians called it 'Pabu', after a 'native' boy who was assisting Major Bill Mollard (DSO), the 2/32nd's acting commanding officer. Helped by two locals, the Australians moved undetected by the many Japanese between the Song River and Pabu, which two companies occupied without loss. They used tracer rounds to set fire to the surrounding kunai grass, thus giving them a good field of fire when the inevitable Japanese counterattacks began. While it burned, a 'native' carrier party brought ammunition and much-needed water. Some likened the surrounding open spaces to the familiar North African desert, while Pabu was also likened to an Australian island in a Japanese sea. The Japanese surrounded, shelled and stormed Pabu but could not recapture it. Its occupation severed the main Japanese supply route to Sattelberg and Wareo, and its week-long defence was extraordinary.

Lieutenant Merv Keley (MC) commanded one company. He conducted two hair-raising patrols – one requiring an overnight stay – that ascertained the considerable strength of the nearby Japanese. On Pabu, the Australians were dug in under head cover, but enemy shelling was dangerous, especially for those leaving cover to help casualties. One shell killed a company commander and two stretcher-bearers who came to his aid, including Tom Langford, who was prominent at Alamein. Sergeant Pasquale Robino (DCM), an attached 2/3rd Field Ambulance man in charge of the stretcher-bearers, ensured that no wounded men remained unattended. On 26 November, when the Japanese bombarded Pabu with two mountain guns and mortars, he personally dressed and carried at least five casualties to the dressing station. One casualty lay in full view of the enemy, and while the men in slit trenches around him warned him to take cover, Robino splinted a compound fracture of the leg. The cane worker then carried the patient to cover, while shells and mortar bombs hit the trees above and landed around him. He volunteered to remain on Pabu when the 2/43rd relieved the 2/32nd on 28–29 November.

While Robino was saving lives on 26 November, Japanese infantry sought to infiltrate Pabu under cover of artillery fire. Keley's entrenched men repulsed them in 150 minutes of fighting, some of it hand-to-hand. Keley was wounded in the knee.

Private John Saaby (MM) manned an observation post on a small ledge on 26 November. The bombardment smashed a large tree there, while Saaby received a bullet wound to the head. Unperturbed, he remained in the post and, taking grenades that were handed up, dropped them among Japanese sheltering under the ledge. Throughout the attack, the 36-year-old could barely move because of enemy sniper fire. Sergeant Sims Reeves (DCM), who had held a defensive position for 36 hours at Katika during the Japanese counterattack, commanded the platoon sector that took the brunt of the 26 November attack. Unemployed on enlistment at age 20 in Sydney in 1940, he had for a time been reported missing and believed captured at Alamein.

On 22 November, the Japanese sought to dislodge the Australians located around the mouth of the Song River, but the well-supported Australian infantry pushed them back. In one extraordinary incident, Private Arthur Grayson (DCM), who was firing from a weapon pit with two others, intentionally placed his foot on an enemy mortar bomb that landed among them. Though gravely wounded, Grayson, whose real name was Gray, thereby enabled the other two to fight on.

On the tracks to Wareo

The 24th Brigade's objective now was Gusika and the track to Wareo, which the 26th Brigade was to capture. The 2/28th, with three tanks, occupied Gusika without loss. Its patrols then advanced west and joined the Pabu garrison. This enabled the 2/43rd to progress along the Wareo track. Only 400 metres west of Pabu, the lead section engaged Japanese who had just jumped into weapon pits near the track. The Australian section leader was killed, but the Bren gunner, Private Ben Bamess (DCM), led the section forward. When two enemy machine guns delayed the Australians, Bamess advanced alone and destroyed both. Sergeant Ron Bonner (MM) eliminated two more, then led a platoon assault.

Meanwhile, the 2/23rd marched from Sattelberg, crossed the Song River and began the push towards Wareo. From Sattelberg to Wareo was about 5500 metres in a straight line, but four times that via the steep winding tracks. The Japanese rearguard counterattacked the 2/23rd at Kuanko, but on 6 December, the 2/24th outflanked this position by occupying Peak Hill. The 2/24th fought alongside and acted as porters to the 2/23rd, which occupied Wareo village's abandoned ruins on 8 December. The officer whose company raised the Australian flag at Wareo was 24-year-old Lieutenant Neil Gilmour (MC), and it was a fitting conclusion to a month in which he was outstanding. As a platoon commander he had led an eight-man patrol behind enemy lines to reconnoitre the Sattelberg Road. They stayed overnight near Japanese troops, nine of whom halted and prepared breakfast no more than 20 metres from Gilmour and another man. One came within 5 metres to collect bamboo. Another Australian accidentally discharged his Owen into the ground, but the Japanese merely stopped talking for a few moments before resuming. Gilmour later led his platoon in capturing Steeple Tree Hill, a typically well-defended precipitous slope. During that attack, fire from a well-sited outpost pinned down Gilmour's and Lieutenant Barrand's platoon. Sergeant Percy de Forest (MID) charged the position single-handed. He fell wounded but rose again to charge, only to be hit a second time and then, a few metres from the Japanese machine gun, a third time. When his comrades reached him, de Forest had sustained eight wounds, which together proved fatal. Barrand unsuccessfully recommended de Forest, an Orbost grocer's assistant, for a Victoria Cross. By the time de Forest died at the RAP, Gilmour's platoon had captured the outpost, after which Gilmour took two sections to an ambush position where they killed the retreating survivors. A week later, Gilmour took over his company when the commander fell ill. He led them into Kuanko, but when the Japanese sought to recapture it on 2 December, the situation looked grim. The 2/23rd commanding officer selected Gilmour's company to push them back in a night attack, a risky venture in the jungle and the battalion's first. Wearing a scarf around his head like a buccaneer, Gilmour personally led an inspiring charge. It was halted, largely because of Japanese gelignite bombs thrown down a slope, but gave the 2/23rd precious time to reorganise its defences. On 10 December, exhausted infantrymen of the two advancing brigades met.

The 24th Brigade had its trials reaching this rendezvous. On 6 December, as the depleted 2/32nd attacked Christmas Hills, Corporal Alan Scott (MM) took over his platoon when the commander was killed. In close-range fighting, Scott killed two Japanese but suffered shock when enemy fire from a flank sent a burst of bullets through his hat. Nevertheless, he continued to command his platoon, which acted as rearguard while the rest of the company fell back. With courage and skill, Scott led the platoon, including all wounded, back to the company perimeter, where he collapsed. On recovering consciousness, he refused to be evacuated, only to be knocked unconscious again by a mortar blast. Scott, who had already fought well at Katika and Pabu, was evacuated on a stretcher.

Even after the brigade link-up, Japanese resistance around Wareo continued until mid-December. On 12 December, the 2/24th attacked a rearguard at the important 2200 Feature, where the lead company faced a 2-metre-high sheer bank, then Japanese defenders dug in behind large trees. The first seven who climbed this bank were killed or wounded, except for Private Les Legg (DCM), who stayed on top with his Bren, firing every magazine tossed up to him. The timber cutter from Emerald destroyed an enemy machine-gun post. Another platoon got around the flank and, as they came over a rise, Legg saw and joined them. Led by Legg firing from the hip, the Australians drove the Japanese off with 27 dead.

Militiamen take the lead

The 4th Brigade – comprising the 22nd, 29th/46th and 37th/52nd battalions – now took up the advance along the coast north of Gusika. Relatively fresh Japanese stood in their way, determined to enable comrades from the Wareo area to escape. They were short of food and ammunition, though, while the Australians now had much artillery support and tanks alongside. The relatively inexperienced militia battalions still faced hard fighting against enemies firing from hidden jungle positions.

On 6 December, Acting Corporal Roy Deslandes' section of the 29th/46th Battalion became isolated close to an enemy machine gun. He ignored four wounds to attack the gun and was pulling the pin from a grenade when a fifth wound felled him. The blast of the grenade killed this young paint machinist. The rest of his section were also killed or wounded. Like many in original militia battalions, Deslandes had in 1942 converted to AIF status. Two days later, with the vanguard pinned down by a hidden machine gun in rock-strewn terrain and snipers firing from high ground above, Corporal 'Scotty' McNee (MM) stalked and grenaded the machine-gun post, killing two and capturing the gun. His company then confronted a 6-metre-wide chasm. A Japanese 75mm artillery piece suddenly fired on them from just 70 metres across this gap, killing three. Lance-Corporal John Hamilton (MM) noticed what appeared to be an observation post directing the gun. Disregarding his own safety, he stood up and fired. His citation states that he killed three of the gun crew, while the official history says that he destroyed the observation post before spraying the gun site. Either way, the gunfire ceased. The next day, the Australians crossed and found the 75mm gun spiked and abandoned alongside two dead Japanese and six graves.

Advancing along an inland route, the 37th/52nd Battalion found the only way forward on 8 December was along a single razor-back spur negotiable by just one platoon at a time. On nearing the top of this arduous climb, the lead platoon encountered the main Japanese force. The platoon commander was killed and other men wounded, and the Japanese counterattacked. Corporal Ron 'Kanga' Drew (DCM) came forward and took a Bren from the wounded gunner. Climbing to an exposed position on top of the ridge and shouting 'Little yellow bastards', the Melbourne labourer fired from the hip into the Japanese attackers, killing four and breaking up the assault. The platoon lost another 10 killed the following day. On 13 December, Japanese attacked the leading company for four hours. Within seconds Private 'Charlie' Cameron (MM) was the sole unwounded man in his section, but he held to his Bren gun position through the night, defying repeated attempts to dislodge him. Cameron was soon evacuated ill, and the 31-year-old station hand died of scrub typhus on 7 January 1944, unaware of his bravery award.

The 22nd Battalion played its part in the advance. Its men were affected by the death of Lance-Sergeant Nev Kennedy, who on 12 December lay wounded in a position out of reach of his section. He directed the fire of others in his platoon, even though each call brought more enemy fire at him and more wounds. In a decisive action at Lakona on 16–17 December, Captain Aubrey Baldwin (MC) coordinated his platoons and accompanied tanks to deadly effect: 43 enemy were killed and four machine guns captured. Baldwin, a regular soldier from Darwin, later rose to lieutenant-colonel and served in the Malayan Emergency.

When the 4th Brigade reached the high ground at Fortification Point on 20 December, its campaigning ended for the moment. The following day, the 20th Brigade took over the pursuit. It reached Sio on 15 January 1944, and the 8th Brigade took up the advance, assisted enormously by the 1st Papuan Battalion. Corporal William Matpi (DCM), a deadly patroller, fought what his battalion history calls a 'one man war', killing Japanese with bayonets, knives, rocks, and especially an Owen gun. He and Sergeant Bengari once killed 44 Japanese, some with rifle butts. On other occasions, Matpi, who hailed from Manus Island and was just 5 feet 4 inches tall, narrowly survived a booby trap explosion, was creased on the forehead by a bullet, and exchanged fire with Japanese as he swung above them

Corporal William Matpi of the 1st Papuan Infantry Battalion earned a Distinguished Conduct Medal in New Guinea in 1944. This deadly fighter killed over 100 Japanese.
AWM 070751

on a rope. He was told off more than once for going ahead alone, but was awarded a medal in 1946: his official count of enemy dead was 110.

Shaggy Ridge and beyond

From Dumpu, the 7th Division advanced towards the enemy's coastal base at Bogadjim. To reach the coast, the Australians needed first to overcome formidable natural and man-made defences at Shaggy Ridge, a 6-kilometre long, 1700-metre-high razorback spur that dominated the approaches to Dumpu along the Faria River. Beyond that lay another daunting obstacle, the 1250-metre-high Kankiryo Saddle.

The 21st Brigade led the advance, flanked by the 25th Brigade on the right and two dismounted cavalry squadrons on the left. The terrain was mountainous and generally clad in dense jungle. On 11 October, it was discovered that Japanese troops had occupied a hill behind the leading battalion, the 2/27th, and cut the Australian supply line. The brigade responded rapidly, ordering the 2/14th to recapture the hill before the Japanese could reinforce its garrison, and bringing artillery, mortars and Vickers guns into position to support them. The platoon allotted to capture the hill, under Lieutenant 'Nol' Pallier (MID), had a formidable task. Their base, King's Hill, was nearly a kilometre from the Japanese position, which was connected to theirs by a knife-edged ridge. From a 'pimple' or bump about halfway along, the slope went upwards to the Japanese hill, with no covering vegetation and a drop on the right-hand side so steep that a slip would mean death in a stream hundreds of feet down. The platoon was under no illusions – even if they took the objective, they would suffer casualties. Thanks to the supporting fire, the Australians reached the intermediate pimple without loss. There they left three men behind with a mortar and Bren and continued. To their amazement, the Japanese did not shoot at them. Only when the covering fire ceased, with the Australians just 20 metres from the

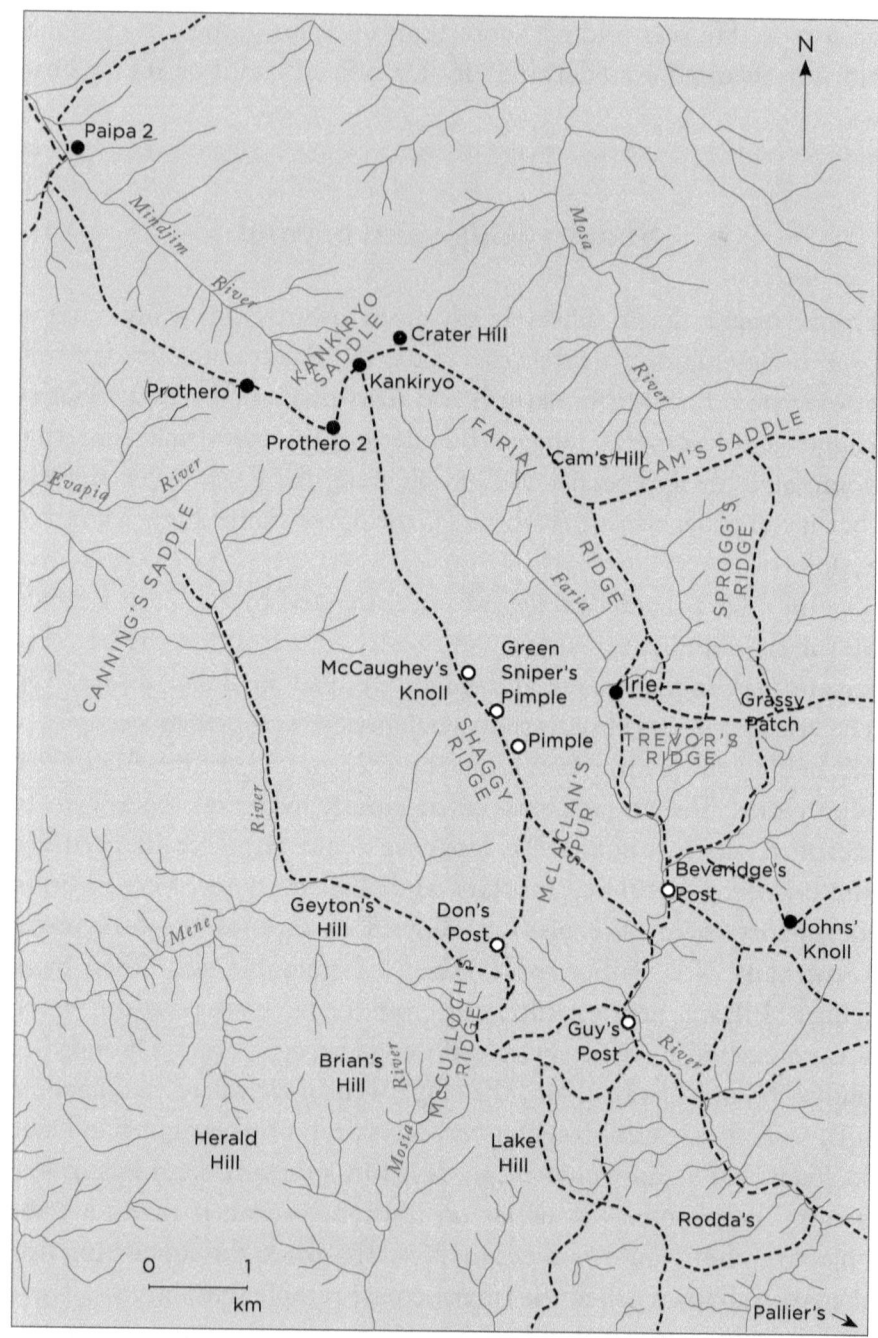

Shaggy Ridge area

summit, did the Japanese open fire. The defenders numbered about 60, so the fire was heavy. Two of the three Australians at the pimple were killed after offering valuable support. The Japanese rolled numerous grenades on the Australians some 6 metres below. Most of the grenades kept rolling, many helped on their way by the attackers. After throwing their own grenades, the Australians scrambled up the last metres towards their tormentors.

The Japanese concentrated their fire on a section on the right under Corporal Ted 'Heigh-Ho' Silver (MM), a tall, tough 31-year-old timber worker, described in the 2/14th's history as one of the most able and courageous leaders of this much-decorated unit. With them was the platoon sergeant, Lindsay 'Teddy' Bear (DCM). After charging up the near perpendicular slope, Bear fired his rifle into the defenders. As he and Silver came over the ledge they saw a Japanese in a foxhole. All three sought to fire, only to find their magazines empty. As he heaved himself up, Bear used his bayonet to kill the Japanese. He then moved to the second pit and crushed the occupant with his rifle butt. The two Australians reloaded and with Silver's section ran along the successive pits, killing their defenders. Bear's citation says that he bayoneted two and caused the death of at least ten more by 'driving them over a sheer precipice'. This was despite being wounded in the back by one of the rolled grenades. Indeed, he should not even have been in this action as he had not fully recovered from severe wounds sustained in the Kokoda campaign, where he won the Military Medal as a corporal at Isurava. While commanding a platoon there, he reportedly killed at least 15 Japanese with his Bren before handing it to Bruce Kingsbury. He escaped from hospital to join the 2/14th for this campaign. A fine competitive cyclist, this big, jovial and boyish soldier, one of Australia's best in World War II, was sent to officer training in 1944. He duxed the course taken by Tom Derrick and Reg Saunders and, like them, had the unusual honour of being allowed to return to his original unit as an officer.

On the left, Corporal 'Bluey' Whitechurch (MM) came in firing his Owen from the hip. One of his men gave a shrill hair-

Sergeant Lindsay 'Teddy' Bear, DCM, MM, pictured at left on the eve of a parade in Melbourne in April 1944, was one of Australia's finest fighting soldiers of the war. His pictured mate, Les Crilly, MM, won great credit at Buna.
AWM 065542

raising yell that shocked even his comrades, and Whitechurch believed this contributed to some Japanese fleeing their positions in panic and plunging to their deaths. The official historian lauds this platoon that, for the loss of three dead and five wounded, killed 30 Japanese and captured an apparently impregnable position, which became known as 'Pallier's Hill'. Lieutenant Pallier was among the wounded, struck in the knee by grenade fragments and in the groin by a bullet. Bear, too, was hit by a machine-gun bullet in the knee. Despite the cost, Pallier's platoon restored the 2/27th's supply line for imminent hard fighting.

Johns' Knoll

That fighting began the following day, on 12 October. The 2/27th held features they called 'Johns' Knoll' and 'Trevor's Ridge'. The Japanese attacked with about 500 men supported by five Woodpeckers, mortars, Nambus, grenade-throwers and two mountain guns, which had already inflicted casualties on the Australians. This force's main attention initially fell on Johns' Knoll and its small 19-strong garrison under Lieutenant Bob Johns (MID). A platoon joined them after the first attack, during which the enemy got astride the battalion supply lines, and Johns' Knoll was fired on from three sides during subsequent attacks. The Japanese came on in screaming waves hoping to use the bayonet, but although they got within 6 metres of Johns' platoon, the Australians repulsed every attack. Accurate supporting mortar fire helped. No more than six men could hold the kunai-covered crest at a time, so the rest were on lower slopes.

Corporal Paddy Carey (MID) was on the knoll's crest all day. Several times Japanese came within metres, but with his Owen and grenades, he forced them back down the steep slope. Private Ray Fisher (MID) was prominent, even after an explosion slashed his clothing, smashed his rifle and destroyed his entrenching tool. Though shocked, he would not leave his post when Johns told him to attend the RAP for treatment. Instead, he carried ammunition to the forward troops under fire all afternoon. Private Ron Barnes, Johns' batman, dashed across open ground to obtain a dead gunner's Bren, which he used all day, and took further perilous trips for ammunition and water. He was recommended, unsuccessfully, for a Military Medal.

Lieutenant-Colonel Bishop of the 2/27th was given permission to withdraw and Johns told him the situation was critical, but Bishop wisely sent in a counterattack from two flanks. On the left flank, Lieutenant Rex Trenerry (MC) and his platoon, under the cover of heavy rain, came upon half a dozen groups of Japanese attacking Johns' Knoll. The Australians threw approximately 16 grenades among these Japanese, killing many. The survivors quickly dispersed, running into the fire of Trenerry's two sections, whose gunfire killed 24. On the left, Lieutenant Bob Paine (MID) led a similarly successful counterattack, killing at least 16. Paine was killed in action the following day by a rebounding 'friendly' grenade. Paine's and Trenerry's counterattacks gave Johns' men precious relief, but the decisive action on 12 October came when a company under Captain Seymour Toms, which had been out of touch with headquarters, launched a surprise attack on the Japanese rear north-east of Johns' Knoll: it knocked out all the Woodpeckers.

When much-needed supplies arrived at the battalion that night, each man had on average just five rounds remaining. For 35 casualties, including seven dead, the 2/27th had killed about 200 Japanese. Bob Johns, the 2/27th's youngest officer, had led like a veteran. He had won a Military Medal as a sergeant in Syria for a lone reconnaissance on a captured motorbike to determine whether Sidon was occupied. Awards for the fight at Johns' Knoll were miserly.

While most of the 2/27th rested, Bishop ordered Lieutenant Bob Clampett's company to patrol Shaggy Ridge, so-called after Clampett's nickname. Patrols found that the Japanese had occupied the vital points of high ground, which could be neither outflanked nor easily rushed. In November, the 25th Brigade relieved the 21st, while the Japanese reinforced their Finisterres defences. At the same time, malaria was taking a toll on the 7th Division men, with

96 per cent evacuated sick at some point. This was 22 times as many casualties as in battle.

There was sharp action on the moonlit night of 12/13 December, when about 300 Japanese attacked two 2/25th Battalion companies west of the Evapia River. At about 1.00 am, this large force was spotted approaching, heading mainly towards a platoon supported by a Vickers gun, under Corporal Henry Johnston (MM). The Australians only opened fire with the Vickers and three Bren guns when the attackers were just 50 metres away. This smashed the first enemy attack but also brought a response, not only from the usual rifles and grenades but also some six Nambus and two Woodpeckers. Three members of Johnston's six-man crew were wounded and a spring of the gun was shot away, but the 30-year-old engine driver kept the gun going. This was crucial to repelling the series of assaults the Japanese launched in the first hour, as were the grenades rolled down the steep slopes into these attackers, whose every attempt was rebuffed.

The other 2/25th company was attacked too but inflicted heavy casualties on the 30 or so Japanese in the first rush. Both sides exchanged fire and many grenades. Eventually, five Woodpeckers were in action against the southern company, and communication to the Australian supporting artillery was lost. Corporal Joe O'Brien (MM) led his section bravely, moving among his men and directing their fire. Most were wounded, but he remained in his forward pit and threw dozens of grenades. Ultimately, he too was severely wounded and ordered out. O'Brien was an impressive veteran. During an advance into Merdjayoun, Syria, he had become isolated from his unit, played dead for five hours and sniped at French troops before surviving a bullet hitting a Bren magazine in his shirt pocket. He linked up with Lieutenant Roden Cutler in his Victoria Cross–winning efforts before returning to his unit after three days. A Bren gunner in the Kokoda campaign, O'Brien covered the withdrawal from Ioribaiwa to Imita Ridge, despite being wounded.

After four-and-a-half hours repelling attacks from three sides on 13 December, the companies were low on ammunition and out of communication with their artillery. They reluctantly withdrew, in good order. For 19 casualties, they killed about 100 Japanese. The following day, the Japanese raiders gave up their attack.

Advance on a one-man front: Shaggy Ridge

By then, the 2/16th occupied the Australian toehold on Shaggy Ridge, and on 17 December was ordered to capture the Pimple, a rocky eminence rising steeply about halfway along the crest of Shaggy Ridge. The two companies involved were then to exploit 400 metres north, where there were three more humps. The attackers would have excellent artillery and air support, but the task was formidable. General Vasey's orders for the attack included the typical comment: 'The 7th Division will advance on a one-man front. Anyone disobeying this order will break his bloody neck.'

The attack commenced at 9.00 am on 27 December. In places, the leading company, under Captain Ron Christian (MC), could only negotiate the steep incline on their hands and knees. The Japanese, fully alert, were concealed in pillboxes and foxholes. A shower of grenades from one well-sited pillbox wounded two leaders on the left and halted their section. Corporal Merv Hall (DCM) advanced alone to the pillbox entrance, where he shot dead a Japanese in the doorway. A second Japanese appeared with a knife. Hall's gun had jammed but he downed the Japanese with the butt of his Owen before throwing a grenade into the bunker, ending all resistance there. Hall sustained a penetrating gunshot wound to the left lower eyelid and the left temporal region. A photograph shows him with a bandage around his head, being led away to treatment. Hall's platoon established a footing on the ridge, despite having to negotiate friendly artillery fire and smashed vegetation. There was hand-to-hand fighting for every foxhole. An hour into the attack, the Pimple and a second pimple had been captured. Artillery support, comprising 3368 shells in just two hours, was crucial. A team under Lieutenant Johnnie Pearson (MC), the forward observer, did expert and brave work. He followed

Corporal Merv Hall can still raise a smile while lying wounded on Shaggy Ridge in December 1943. He had just been wounded while silencing an enemy pillbox.
AWM 062295

the first platoon on the ridge and provided accurate fire support in this dangerous location for four days. Pearson had led a detachment of artillerymen who jumped with American forces at Nadzab, in September, and entered Dumpu with the infantry in October. When the platoon commander he was accompanying as forward observer at Balikpapan on 1 July 1945 was wounded, the energetic and dashing Pearson took over, only to be killed by machine-gun fire.

After the second pimple fell, three Australians who charged the next obstacle, a rock-made bunker, were wounded, and although more than 100 grenades were thrown at this bunker, it could not be taken that day. The second company, under Captain Vivian Anderson (MID), advanced and consolidated. Overnight they dug trenches and a track to allow a less dangerous approach to the bunker. Engineers produced makeshift blockbuster bombs for the foremost troops, who used them at 8.30 am on 28 December to kill the brave Japanese officer and private in the bunker who had delayed the advance.

Meanwhile, Lieutenant Jack Scott (MC) led a wide encircling movement through thick timber that took four hours but enabled his platoon to launch a flank attack on the third pimple. At Scott's instruction, Platoon Sergeant Jack Longman (MM), an unflappable soldier whose nickname 'Springy' reflected his athleticism, took a small section carrying only Owens, spare magazines and grenades in an assault intended to allow the rest of the platoon to attack further left, where the slope was easier but more exposed. They had machine-gun support and some cover from smoke rounds, but Longman's section's task was perilous when they clambered forward at noon. Longman had to fire his Owen one-handed as he pulled himself up over the ledge. He then put a grenade with a two-second fuse through the embrasure of the bunker there. The assault then went through. Eyewitnesses marvelled at the efforts of Scott's platoon, one man seeing Scott standing silhouetted against the sky as he gave directions, even after he grabbed his shoulder and staggered at the impact of a bullet. He was wounded again the following day but remained on duty. Scott was 6 feet tall, a farmer from Katanning, and obviously tough: he had been wounded three times before, during the Syrian (back and side), Kokoda (thigh) and Gona (eyebrow and arm) campaigns.

With the third pimple captured, Lieutenant Sam McCaughey's platoon took the fourth, 150 metres away, and Shaggy Ridge's highest point. The defenders were dug into the side of the ridge here, and the Australians dropped blast bombs and grenades into their dugouts. A Japanese mountain gun fired sporadically on the 2/16th's forward positions over the next few days, and one tree burst killed McCaughey, after whom the fourth pimple was subsequently named.

More heroics at Shaggy Ridge

Early in the new year, the 21st and 25th brigades were relieved by the 18th and 15th brigades respectively. Vasey now planned to capture Kankiryo Saddle, followed by a march towards the north coast. Accordingly, plans were formulated to send the 2/9th Battalion along its one weapon pit wide front on Shaggy Ridge, while the 2/10th advanced to its right, and the 2/12th made the main thrust on the left towards the Protheros (two high features called Prothero 1 and Prothero 2) and Kankiryo Saddle. Unlike its sister brigades, the 18th had never fought in mountainous terrain.

On 20 January 1944, the 2/10th advanced to Cam's Saddle. It subsequently met stiff resistance but achieved its goal of diverting Japanese attention from the 2/12th, which advanced to Canning's Saddle unobserved. Then, on 21 January, the 2/9th's advance commenced. The difficulty of supplying troops on the razorback ridge had led the Australians to abandon the second to fourth pimples (Intermediate Pimple, Green Sniper's Pimple and McCaughey's Knoll), so they had to be recaptured. Intermediate Pimple soon fell, but fighting for Green Sniper's Pimple was fierce. The attacking company came under machine-gun and grenade attack. Ominously, a 75mm mountain gun at Prothero 1 bombarded them. Those killed included the company commander, whose body rolled down the mountainside. Lieutenant Ernest Stephenson (MC) arrived to assume command of the company, which his citation says was 'badly shaken'. Stephenson, a Norfolk Islander, showed 'calm courage and forceful leadership'. By 6.00 pm, after a day of severe enemy fire and two counterattacks, the Australians were consolidating on Green Sniper's Pimple. For five hours, Sergeant Hylton Henricksen (MM) directed mortar fire from an exposed location under fire. He ceased for only five minutes, when a shell knocked him unconscious, and later when he dug out his brave orderly, Private Leslie Scheuber, who had been buried by a shell. The 2/9th men sustained 24 casualties that day, most from the mountain gun. More would have fallen if not for events on the 2/12th front.

At 9.20 am, the 2/12th began crossing the start-line for a silent attack on Prothero 1, but the ground was so steep they had to use ropes. The sole approach was via a steep razorback ridge, and artillery was only to be called upon if surprise was lost. About 100 metres below the summit, the forward scouts encountered two Japanese. They killed one, the other fled. He had no time to detonate a demolition charge set up on the approach but did get back to the crew of the 75mm gun that had been blasting the 2/9th from its bunker for two hours. Lieutenant Yo Baba, the gun commander, now ordered the gun dismantled, turned around and reassembled to fire through the bunker's back door. Japanese rifle fire downed several advancing Australians, but only when the survivors were just 30 metres from the bunker did someone spot Japanese movement and call out, 'There are the yellow bastards!' Just then the gun opened fire. Firing out the rear door, its ability to depress and traverse was limited, so its crew fired – at 12 rounds per minute – into the thick tree covering. Huge pieces of shrapnel inflicted horrific wounds on the Australians nearest the gun. Lieutenant Charlie Braithwaite (MID) was ordered to seize the gun by direct assault. Japanese small arms halted an advance via a route covered by the mountain gun. During Braithwaite's second attempt, in the late afternoon, Corporal 'Nugget' Robinson headed for the bunker door, firing his Bren from the hip. A mate saw the back of Robinson's shirt popping out as machine-gun bullets hit and felled the brave gunner. The platoon sergeant, Don McCulloch, threw a blast bomb at the bunker. The massive explosion apparently stunned the defenders, enabling Robinson's number two, Private Richard Lugge (MM), to pick up the Bren. He leapt to within two metres of the entrance and onto his stomach, from where he opened fire. Lugge silenced the gunners, then rolled to his side and followed Braithwaite's direction to engage another pillbox, killing and wounding the machine gunners inside. The remainder of the platoon then finished the bunker's occupants with grenades. Sixteen dead crewmen were found inside. While Lugge, a big Queensland drover, and Braithwaite, a Queensland farmer, received the official credit, McCulloch was also crucial.

In taking the linchpin of the Japanese Shaggy Ridge defences on 21 January, the 2/12th suffered nearly 60 casualties. Many of the wounded lay in the rain and cold overnight. Japanese infiltrators were abroad too. The stoicism of the Australian wounded was exemplified by Private 'Tex' Parnell, who on being told that his arm wound necessitated amputation, said, 'Okay Doc, whip it off'. He had it removed on Prothero 1 before spending a grim night there. The young South Australian miner died the following day, reportedly from shock, exposure and the ordeal of walking down the ridge. When alive he had often been in trouble with the authorities, but his last hours attracted much respect from his mates.

During the mountain gun bombardment, John Palmer (MM), the battalion stretcher-bearer sergeant, evacuated two men under shell fire just 40 metres from the gun. He disregarded enemy fire in supervising the extricating of all the wounded, and on this night supervised the care of 23 stretcher cases. Later he assisted ambulance-men in evacuating the wounded down the precipitous Prothero Track. Throughout these operations he was suffering severely from malaria.

The main Japanese force on Shaggy Ridge still held more than 3 kilometres of the feature, but Australians were closing in on three sides. To their east, the 2/10th was just 1500 metres from their key defences on Kankiryo Saddle.

Early on 22 January, the 2/12th continued advancing, Captain Kevin 'KB' Thomas (MC) in the lead. Japanese were seen running from the opening bombardment. Thomas, a regular soldier from Ulverstone, had an unusual means of encouraging his men: he blew a whistle, at times holding a cane in one hand and a revolver in the other. As he did so early that morning, one of his men, Private Len Bugg (DCM), reportedly called out crude advice as to where Thomas could shove his whistle. The men advanced cheering and firing. Snipers delayed the advance, but Bugg, discarding pouches that caught fire, charged forward firing his Bren and killing a machine-gun crew. Prothero 2 was secured, with 45 Japanese killed. Thomas led with great bravery, standing in the open under fire and shouting directions such as 'Get that bastard, there's another'. He had been Mentioned in Despatches in Tobruk and would serve in Korea.

After Prothero 2 fell, the 2/12th advance continued until stopped by machine-gun fire within binoculars-view of the 2/9th. The lead company of the 2/9th seized McCaughey's Knoll from the seemingly impossible western direction, using ropes and powerful artillery support. The 2/10th also made excellent progress along Faria Ridge.

On 22 January, Private Ron Baggaley (MM) of the 2/10th was a platoon runner when his unit was halted at barbed wire positions on Faria Ridge. He not only carried messages under fire but also crawled out to a man wounded just 20 metres from the enemy. The position was hazardous – his helmet was shot off by a machine gun, and it was impossible to move. He stayed with this man, tending his wounds until dark when he assisted him to medical aid. Private Howard Bloffwitch (MM) distinguished himself the following day when his platoon commander and platoon sergeant were both wounded. Bloffwitch, an unemployed labourer on enlistment, took command of the platoon, organising their defence and, when ordered to withdraw, remaining behind and covering their retreat and the evacuation of casualties. Bloffwitch was in constant trouble for going AWL or deserting. He was court-martialled three times and spent considerable time in military prison. His brother Ray was Mentioned in Despatches for his service with the 2/48th at Alamein, where he was wounded.

On 23 January, two forlorn Japanese counterattacks were repulsed, weak opposition overcome, and patrols of the 2/9th and 2/12th met on Shaggy Ridge, thus signalling its capture. Kankiryo Saddle soon followed. The enemy had decided to make a last-ditch stand on the 1500-metre-high Crater Hill, northeast of Kankiryo. The Australians chose to besiege rather than assault the well-entrenched Japanese. Two thousand artillery shells fell on them on 27–28 January. On 31 January, a 2/9th patrol advanced well into the Japanese positions. When the patrol was stalled by Japanese hurling grenades from a ledge, Acting Corporal Mervyn Berrell (MM) found a position from which he could silence them with his Bren. One hundred metres on, the patrol was halted again, but Berrell took up position beside the track and took on targets indicated to him by his section commander. Though fired on intermittently, he stayed in this exposed position for one and a half hours, killing two snipers and two LMG crews. He was eventually seriously wounded, and though in great pain, carried the gun and magazines to a comrade, who repelled a counterattack that immediately followed. Mervyn's older brother Frank had been killed with the 2/9th at Buna. On 1 February, Australians found that the Japanese had abandoned Crater Hill, leaving two mountain guns and many corpses and graves.

From Kankiryo Saddle to the coast

In mid-February, the 15th Brigade relieved the 18th and in March advanced to renew contact with the retreating Japanese. The terrain between Kankiryo Saddle and the coast, just 30 kilometres away in a straight line, but three times as long on foot, was daunting: steep and rough, covered with rainforest. It rained heavily most days, necessitating corduroying every track. On 14 March, the 57th/60th Battalion reached Yokopi, the head of a motor road the Japanese had built from Bogadjim. Seven members died in two ambushes that month. Sergeant Jack 'Shirley' Temple (MM) made a lone reconnaissance, which gave invaluable information on the dominating 3800 Feature, and Lieutenant Herb 'Walkabout' Atkinson (MC) led a platoon attack that surprised and annihilated the garrison.

On 21 March Australians contacted American troops who had landed east of Bogadjim. Lieutenant Don Brewster (MC) of the 58th/59th Battalion played a key role here, leading a small patrol through enemy territory amidst great privation. When Japanese marines attacked or stumbled upon the platoon of Lieutenant Max Berman (MC) near Yaula on the night of 31 March – 1 April, this regular soldier kept his head despite being out of communication with company headquarters. By the time the Japanese left the scene, they had sustained about 40 casualties, the Australians none. On 26 March, near Barum, some 20 Japanese marines brandishing long knives engaged 58th/59th men in a five-hour clash, much of it at night. A section under Corporal Henry Tremellen (MM) bore the brunt. He moved around his weapon pits in the open. At one stage a Bren had to be moved to repel a new attack. Moving across the skyline, Tremellen took the Bren in his left hand, with two magazines in his right. A Japanese infiltrator attacked Tremellen, who felled him with the magazines.

On 13 April, the 57th/60th Battalion took Bogadjim, with Atkinson again in the lead. He was ably supported by Sergeant Leonard Dick (MM), who often led sub-groups of Atkinson's force and who during the crossing of the Gogol River shot two large crocodiles. On 24 April, a mixed patrol of members of the 57th/60th and 30th battalions entered Madang unopposed.

So the Huon Peninsula was secured. Between September 1943 and August 1944, the Australians lost about 1100 men killed and 2500 wounded. The Japanese lost approximately 35 000 dead in New Guinea from April 1943 to August 1944.

CHAPTER 19

BOUGAINVILLE: THROUGH MUD AND BLOOD TO VICTORY

In 1944, the American component of General MacArthur's forces in the South-West Pacific came to outnumber the Australian. About one-third of the Americans held defensive lines around bases in New Guinea, Bougainville and New Britain. To free these six divisions for operations elsewhere, especially the Philippines, it was agreed that four Australian divisions would replace them. Consequently, in October and November 1944, Australian troops relieved the American garrisons on Bougainville, at Aitape in New Guinea and on New Britain. The Japanese garrisons of these areas were isolated from virtually all outside help. Their American opponents had been content to defend a small perimeter around the airfields and otherwise maintain a tacit truce. However, the Australian senior commanders were determined that their troops would be more aggressive in all three places. They would push the enemy back into restricted areas and, with few troops and even fewer casualties, would destroy the Japanese, ultimately annihilating any remnants with the help of 'native' troops. This approach and its consequences have been controversial ever since. What is uncontested is that the Australian Army fought effectively in all three places, and that individual soldiers fought bravely there, all too often at great personal cost.

When the Australians set up headquarters at Torokina on Bougainville, they estimated enemy strength at 18 000. In fact, it

AUSTRALIAN HEROES OF WORLD WAR II

Bougainville

was about 40 000, many more than the Australian force comprising the 3rd Division and two independent brigades. In accordance with Australia's aggressive approach in the final campaigns, they launched three offensives, in the south, north and centre.

The southern drive

The main Australian advance, led by the 29th Brigade in mid-December 1944, headed southward from Torokina along a narrow coastal plain crossed by many rivers and swamps. Perpetually wet and muddy conditions characterised this campaign. The objective was Buin, the main Japanese base on Bougainville. There were patrol clashes, but for weeks the advance proceeded smoothly. After the Australians took Mawaraka on 17 January 1945, the 7th Brigade took over the advance about halfway between Torokina and Buin. On 5 March, the 25th Battalion easily pushed Japanese forces off a knoll near the meeting of the Puriata River and the Buin Road. The Japanese shelled the area the following day, wounding Private Carl Slater (MID), who remained at his post until relieved. This area became known as Slater's Knoll. The 20-year-old Tasmanian textile worker was the only casualty inflicted by some 600 shells the Japanese fired into the area in March.

That month, though, the Japanese fought back more resolutely near Slater's Knoll. They were well dug in on the Buin Road just a few hundred metres away, and when the 25th Battalion sought to resume the advance, Japanese forces surrounded one company and attacked it for three days before the Australians withdrew. On 19 March, the 25th pushed down the road again, with artillery, mortar and machine-gun support. Two platoons under Lieutenant Dick Jefferies (DSO) encountered a complex of pillboxes at a road junction. After a two-hour firefight in which the Australians employed a PIAT (British counterpart of the bazooka), Jefferies decided to attack with his 35 men against some 15 Japanese. He ordered his men to fix bayonets, which had to be borrowed from another company. Nearby companies were ordered to make as much noise as possible for encouragement and, covered by Vickers MMG fire and with Jefferies leading, his men advanced 25 metres before the enemy responded. On the Australians' left flank, Japanese rifle fire and grenade fragments struck Bren gunner Private Bob Layt (MM). His left leg broken and his right thigh damaged, he could not get up. Nevertheless, from a prone position Layt killed the Japanese in pits immediately ahead. Despite great pain, he threw a grenade into a bunker that was holding up the attack and then gave covering fire to his advancing section. Layt was hospitalised for five months but recovered sufficiently to join the Victory March Contingent in England in 1946. While trying to pick up a Bren dropped by one of his gunners, Lieutenant Jefferies was thrown back by the blast of a Japanese grenade. He reluctantly gave up command, which went to Lieutenant Joe Chesterton (MID). Jefferies and other casualties were tended by RMO Captain Jim Aiken (MC), who personally went forward under fire and retrieved many of the 17 wounded.

After 45 minutes of fighting, the Japanese withdrew to defences down the road. On 22 March, the 25th attacked and cleared these positions following an aerial and artillery bombardment. Corporal Reg Rattey (VC) walked ahead of his section, firing his Bren from the hip to suppress the enemy gunners and then dropping grenades when he reached the weapon pits. He knocked out three bunkers and killed seven occupants. Later he silenced a Woodpecker holding up the advance.

On 27 March, a large-scale Japanese offensive began, striking the 25th Battalion, which was stretched along the Buin Road – now a morass – from Tokinotu to their headquarters on Slater's Knoll, with support units further back. Soon after the telephone line from HQ to the rear echelon went dead at about 8 pm, some 100 shrieking Japanese launched a bayonet charge on Slater's. With fields of fire cleared, booby traps set and Vickers guns in position, the Australians repulsed that charge and two more from different directions.

The 9th Battalion, further north, faced a similarly strong and fierce bayonet charge on the night of the 28th. For no loss, they killed 23. A Japanese captured the next day said that his regiment (800–900 strong) was planning bigger attacks.

Early on 30 March, Japanese attacked Lieutenant Chesterton's company on the Buin Road. Fifteen of Chesterton's men were out patrolling, leaving barely 30 to face four attacks. Every man was needed in his pit, and the company stretcher-bearer, Acting Corporal Ted Rooney (MM), had to deal with the wounded alone. He went from pit to pit under heavy fire, keeping the lightly wounded going with bandages and dragging the badly wounded to shelter. The 30-year-old shearer had already been credited with carrying out four men under fire on 19 March. During the fourth attack, the Japanese penetrated the perimeter. With most of his men casualties, Chesterton decided he must withdraw. The wounded were brought out safely. Among the covering party of Chesterton and five others was Private Irwin Thornberry (MM), who with his Bren had already helped disperse two Banzai attacks. With the Japanese just 20 metres behind them, the rearguard reached the next company under Captain Bob McInnes (MC). He now commanded 85 men.

They endured five attacks from 3.45 pm onwards. Using a Vickers, rifles and Owens, the Australians drove off all five. They inflicted heavy casualties, but some of their own were wounded and their ammunition, food and water were dwindling fast. Sergeant Cec Townsley (MM) was commanding the Vickers section when in the first attack a mortar fragment inflicted a bad arm wound. Once bandaged up, he returned to the fray, directing fire, carrying reserve ammunition and holding the belt boxes while the gun traversed. Most of his crew were wounded too, but Private Sid White stayed with Townsley throughout. When Townsley was evacuated, after 36 hours, this pastoral worker from Roma required a blood transfusion.

Another Roma man, Private Gordon Edwards (MM), had retreated with Chesterton's company and was assisting the wounded in the absence of trained stretcher-bearers. When Townsley left the Vickers for treatment to his arm, Edwards noted that it was unmanned and in danger of being captured. He went to the gun, single-handedly killed several enemy and, though wounded, fired it until Townsley and White returned. Even then, Edwards helped crew the gun.

The attacks hit hard in the sector held by Lance-Sergeant Errol Jorgensen (MM) and his section, but he directed his unit's fire and brought up weapons and ammunition to engage dug-in Japanese. He was eventually wounded in the left shoulder. Nevertheless, when his Bren gunner was seriously wounded, Jorgensen took over the gun and used it to halt an enemy bayonet charge just metres from his position. Jorgensen, a Toowoomba plasterer, had shown great courage at Milne Bay, where as part of a three-man rearguard at Turnbull Airstrip he narrowly escaped death from the Japanese, from strafing RAAF aircraft and a 'friendly' minefield.

Twelve Japanese died trying to silence Townsley's Vickers that night. Japanese were probing elsewhere on the 25th Battalion front too, including Slater's Knoll. Help arrived in the form of three Matilda tanks of the 2/4th Armoured Regiment. After being dragged across water obstacles by a brave but unidentified bulldozer driver, the tanks and accompanying infantry reached McInnes' men on the afternoon of 31 March. Low on ammunition and under attack from fresh troops, the Australian infantry were close to being overrun. They were as surprised as the Japanese to see these heaven-sent behemoths, and indeed Jorgensen prepared the PIAT in case the tanks were Japanese. A newspaper report said the Australians sang 'Waltzing Matilda' on seeing the tanks arrive, but the battalion commander was surely correct to dismiss this invention and declare 'the situation was far too serious for singing'. The Matildas went straight for the Japanese positions, using their weapons and tracks to add more corpses to the dozens scattered around: nearly 100 were found subsequently just 30 metres from the Australian defences. The Japanese survivors eventually fled and the tanks pushed on to Chesterton's former position. The day brought a terrible twist for the Australians when Japanese forces ambushed a 'jeep train', six jeeps towed by a bulldozer and escorted by ten men sent forward to collect the wounded. Driving the lead jeep was Private Stan

'Stumpy' McGrath, a 30-year-old pig grader from Toowoomba. He lost his left hand to enemy fire, but fired back with his Owen, expending two magazines, before he was hit again and killed. His sacrifice bought precious time for others to reach a ditch, where they returned fire. Craftsman Alfred Oliver (MM), of the armoured regiment workshops, took cover just metres from the Japanese forces. When a relief party approached, including tanks, Oliver emerged from his hiding place to shout a warning to the Australians. Japanese automatic fire then struck him in the groin and leg, but the relief force repelled the Japanese. As darkness fell, the tanks had to stay in position. Oliver and other wounded spent 14 hours on the backs of the tanks before they could be treated.

Between 30 March and 1 April, eight Australians were killed, 58 wounded, and 130 Japanese confirmed dead. Combative Japanese were still in the surrounding jungle, and the Australians on Slater's Knoll had already endured three months of nearly continuous frontline service.

On 5 April, in heavy rain and darkness, Japanese crept forward and, after cutting the telephone line to the knoll, launched wave after wave of attacks. The supporting Australian artillery and Vickers guns mowed down attackers until they lay in heaps. A stalemate ensued until two tanks came forward and winkled the Japanese from their positions.

One tank commander, Corporal Clarence Hockey (MM), sustained a fractured jaw, but still directed his Matilda's fire to great effect. Only two hours after he had been hit did he permit his radio operator to inform the troop leader of the painful wound. Hockey, a junior constable in Adelaide before enlistment, was left with facial scars.

With the danger at Slater's Knoll seemingly over, Lieutenant Syd Giles, commanding an attached platoon of the 5th Field Company, led 10 volunteers onto the battlefield to search bodies, but a sniper shot him and a sergeant in the head, killing both. A few weeks earlier, Giles, a civil engineer, had designed and overseen the building of a 100-metre-long bridge over the Puriata River. In the fighting that followed it would carry 500 vehicles a day. It was renamed Giles Bridge in his honour. This was one of many tasks the intrepid engineers had been fulfilling since December 1944. Giles was one of three brothers killed in the war.

The Japanese losses at Slater's Knoll were so heavy that bulldozers were needed to bury them: nearly 300 were interred in mass graves. In the previous week, some 650 Australians had inflicted severe casualties on more than 3300 Japanese.

On 17 April, the 15th Brigade took up the advance towards Buin. That morning, the lead battalion, the 24th, became entangled in fighting near the crossing of Dawe's Creek. Captain Stuart Graham (MC) personally led his company against enemy positions located in thick jungle. Late in the afternoon, Graham and his men secured the crossing. They withstood a counterattack that night and, after seizing and consolidating more high ground on 18 April, repelled another counterattack. Graham, a highly intelligent 24-year-old regular soldier, had topped his graduation class at Duntroon in 1940 and seen action with the British 7th Armoured Division in North Africa and Italy, where he was wounded at Salerno. In the Bougainville campaign he was wounded too, hit in the foot by a sniper's bullet in June. In a stellar postwar career, Graham rose to major-general, served as Deputy Chief of the General Staff and, during the Vietnam War, commanded the 1st Australian Task Force.

On 18 April, Lance-Corporal Fred Rossborough (MM) was on the right flank just 10 metres from the enemy. When his platoon commander and two other men became pinned down, Rossborough called out to the Japanese, drawing their fire. The pinned men escaped, and the platoon commander directed the capture of the strongpoint. Rossborough never forgot the look of relief his mate Jack showed on seeing him return from the bush. A month later, Rossborough's mates saved his life by constructing a makeshift stretcher for him after he was shot in the hip and lung while patrolling.

During the 24th's subsequent advance, Corporal Allen Nott (DCM) led a patrol nearly 3000 metres behind Japanese lines to Hiru Hiru, gleaning valuable information. This young trapper from

Rutherglen was credited with killing ten Japanese in ambushes and fighting patrols. An outstanding leader, Nott never sustained a single casualty on a patrol.

As the advance continued, the determined Japanese began employing anti-tank landmines, setting defences back from the road so that the tanks could not hit them without making a detour, and positioning artillery pieces in ambush positions. On 5 May, the 24th Battalion was advancing when the lead tank, under Sergeant Royce Whatley (MM), suffered a machine-gun stoppage. The crew could neither clear the gun from inside nor risk getting out to follow the procedure of pushing a cleaning rod down the barrel, so they decided to undo it from its mounting and pull it inside the tank. Wireless operator Corporal Frank Clark was doing that – carefully, as the gun was red hot – when a concealed 75mm gun opened fire just 20 metres away. A shell struck the small aperture created when the machine gun was removed. Shrapnel hit Clark, blowing his eye out, and knocked out or shook the driver and gunner. Whatley grabbed a bandage from his field pack and wrapped it around Clark's head. Whatley thought someone had thrown a grenade into the tank, but, ignoring the danger of further attack, the 30-year-old Bendigo plasterer followed his instinct to look after his crewmate. He opened the top of the turret, climbed out and pulled Clark up behind him. Mystified as to why the Japanese did not shoot at them, he carried Clark back to squadron headquarters. By now, infantry on both sides were exchanging fire near the tank, but Whatley returned through it to his vehicle. This gave a boost to the Australian infantry: Whatley heard someone say 'Let's go'. A second tank arrived and knocked out the field gun. The supporting Japanese infantry withdrew. Whatley was wounded 17 days later but remained on duty. The loss of several men in his troop killed and wounded affected him, though, and at one point he was withdrawn for a rest.

On the night of 5–6 May, the Japanese fired some 160 shells into the 24th Battalion area. The following morning, about 100 Japanese attacked the forward company on the Buin Road. A bitter two-and-a-half-hour battle ensued, involving tanks and men. Private Laurie

Barnes (DCM), a Footscray meat worker, was a Bren gunner in a forward post east of the road. As the Japanese launched what his citation called 'a traditional fanatical bayonet charge', Barnes held fire until they were less than 15 metres away, then mowed them down. The attackers reformed and charged again but Barnes repeated the same tactics with the same result. He also eliminated several tree snipers. By the time the Japanese retreated, 13 lay dead in front of Barnes's post. Forty-five other Japanese fell in this action. The Australians crossed the Hongorai River unopposed, but the 24th had sustained 120 casualties in three weeks.

Beyond the crossing, Australian patrols encountered strong Japanese resistance. Four Australians were hit on one 8 May patrol, including 19-year-old Private Frank McLennan (MM). The six-foot-tall Wodonga butcher was a forward scout when a bullet fractured his left femur. His patrol mates could not find him and withdrew, so after applying his own bandage and swallowing sulphanilamide tablets, he began dragging himself out. Four Japanese soon approached for the kill, but he lay still before opening fire from 10 metres. Three fell to his Owen, the fourth fled. Then, using the Owen as a crutch, McLennan crawled painfully on. One night he slept close to Japanese positions and made notes of the dispositions. He narrowly avoided discovery by three groups of Japanese. Only after two days did he obtain a drink, using a wide leaf as a cup. On 11 May, having crawled nearly three kilometres, he was discovered by a friendly patrol and carried in. His notes proved useful for the artillery. McLennan spent the next four-and-a-half years in hospital recovering from his wound.

Parallel to the 24th Battalion's advance, the 57th/60th Battalion progressed on a track further inland. The 2/8th Commando Squadron manoeuvred still further north, gathering valuable intelligence. On 21 April, for example, three commandos were ordered to gather information on enemy movement on the Tiger Road, and given the difficult task of capturing a prisoner. After going some 1800 metres, they lay concealed for five hours, just a few metres from the road. Japanese movement along it was constant and the leader, Trooper Gordon Kemp (MM), recorded seeing 200 troops. Eventually, a lone

Japanese approached, armed with a submachine gun. Kemp jumped on the man and stunned him with a Bren magazine. The patrol brought their prisoner to base.

An eight-man patrol of the 24th Battalion struck trouble near the Hongorai River on 13 May when about 50 well-armed Japanese surprised them, killing the leader. Laurence Barnes, who had used his Bren so effectively the previous week, again helped the defence, but the men were pinned down and one lay wounded by a Japanese machine gun set up behind the Australians. After several attempts had nearly cost him his life, Lance-Corporal Owen O'Connor (DCM) crawled to the wounded man via a circuitous route, dressed his wounds and then assisted a second casualty. He and Barnes then gave covering fire as, on O'Connor's orders, others of the patrol withdrew. When Barnes was almost out of ammunition, O'Connor sent him back. A 20-year-old Sydney trainee butcher, O'Connor risked betraying his position several times by calling to a wounded man that he would not leave him behind. He was about to help this man to the rear when three Japanese came at him with fixed bayonets. Turning his Owen on them, he killed two and wounded the other. O'Connor half-walked, half-dragged his wounded comrade to safety and covered the withdrawal of another man. A newspaper report said that O'Connor was still too young to be shaving, but had now earned the nickname 'Okey'.

On 20 May, the 24th Battalion led a major thrust across the Hongorai River. It had tank and air support, and by 22 May occupied Egan's Ridge, the linchpin of the Japanese defences on the Hongorai. The Australians named the ridge for Lieutenant Clyde Egan (Bar to MC), who had patrolled there on 15 May, and who participated in the ridge's capture. Egan, whose reserved and nervous nature raised doubts about him in officer training at Duntroon in 1941, had already won a Military Cross in New Guinea, where he had been a fine leader at Salamaua and in 1944 led a dangerous patrol into the Finisterre Range to clear it of Japanese who had been murdering locals. Before the war he had been a farm hand and CMF corporal at Glen Innes.

At Egan's Ridge, the Australians found the Buin Road sown with mines and the surrounding scrub booby-trapped. Casualties were sustained and the advance was delayed. A brave bomb disposal squad accidentally detonated a booby trap, which killed two and seriously wounded their commander, thus putting the unit out of action. Lieutenant Jack Syrett (GM), Pioneer Officer of the 24th Battalion, had taken a bomb disposal course and now took over. He and Sergeant Jack 'Cracker' Knight (GM), also of the Pioneer Platoon, had a mine detector, but soon discovered that it could not detect 75mm shells laid by the Japanese as anti-tank mines. Syrett then used a bayonet to find mines, while Knight worked separately with the mine detector, which could find bundles of 81mm mortar bombs set as booby traps connected to trip wires. Syrett dug up 20 of these traps. Between them they also lifted more than a dozen standard Japanese landmines. On 24 May, Syrett was examining suspicious-looking vines when a booby trap exploded, wounding him in the lower back, thumb and elbow, and necessitating his evacuation. By clearing three minefields, Syrett and Knight secured the area for an advance. Vehicles were using the road by 22 May.

On 2 June, Corporal Biri (MM) of the 1st PIB was sent with three men to a location near the Sunin River where 12 Japanese were reportedly constructing an ambush position. On arriving, Biri made a lone assault on the Japanese, shooting one dead with his Owen. The survivors sought to outflank the Papuans, but Biri, calling out challenges and abuse and not even taking cover, blocked every potential attack with accurate fire. When his Owen jammed, Biri took up a rifle. Spotting a Japanese running to a Nambu, Biri calmly shot the gunner in the head. The surviving Japanese fled.

That day, the main advance continued but again encountered mines and booby traps. The 7th Bomb Disposal Platoon was tasked with clearing them. The first sight the Japanese had of the advancing Australians was often one of this unit's men prodding with a bayonet, a tank rolling close behind him. On 2 June, Lieutenant Bill Woodward (DSO) was the bomb disposal officer with the leading company of the 58th/59th Battalion. He moved ahead of the forward troops on the Buin Road, and while under fire from three enemy machine guns, located and 'deloused' four mines and 23 booby traps. Later, after booby traps caused heavy casualties, he went forward under fire and cleared the road and surrounds for 140 metres forward of the Australian troops and right up to the enemy wire. He cleared two mines and over 20 booby traps, two of which he accidentally detonated. Though shaken each time, he completed another solo advance and clearing routine. By the operation's end he had rendered six mines and 63 booby traps inoperable. Lieutenant Woodward's Distinguished Service Order was an exceptional award for a junior officer.

Captain Ted Griff (MC) was approaching the west bank of the Hari River with the spearhead company of the 58th/59th on 8 June when the Japanese counterattacked in strength. Rain had rendered the Australians' wireless sets unserviceable, though after heating them over a fire they obtained intermittent contact. Superbly turned out Japanese marines launched some seven attacks, but all were repulsed with heavy loss. Griff was wounded when the advance resumed. This fine officer had learnt hard jungle warfare lessons with the maligned 58th/59th in New Guinea, where he had been Mentioned in Despatches. After the war he served with distinction in Korea and Vietnam, rising to colonel.

The 57th/60th and 58th/59th battalions, with tank, artillery and air support, crossed the Hari River in mid-June. Mines were an ever-present danger and the road a quagmire. The Japanese were defending strongly and nowhere was safe from their raids. On 22 June, for example, the handful of men holding the perimeter of a company that had sent out patrols were suddenly mortared and attacked by up to 100 determined Japanese. In nearly two hours of fighting, the Japanese came within metres of posts held by the cooks under Sergeant Allan Erbs. The Japanese left 18 dead behind and inflicted no casualties.

In late June, the 29th Brigade took the lead, advancing towards the Mivo River. It was only about 25 kilometres from Buin, but heavy rains flooded the rivers and twice led to postponement of the

Mivo crossing. Daring patrols crossed the river in the meantime, often leading to clashes. On 7 July, for instance, Private Frank Kane (DCM) of the 15th Battalion was forward scout on a patrol that encountered 15 Japanese. He killed the first three with his Owen while under fire from a Nambu less than 30 metres away. Rather than seek cover, Kane coolly positioned the other scouts and directed the patrol's fire, which felled another four Japanese. Two days later he led his section in killing five Japanese. Kane was seriously wounded but commanded and encouraged his men until he lost consciousness. He died of his wounds the following day.

For three weeks from 11 July, heavy rains halted operations. More than 500 millimetres fell that month, rendering the Buin Road virtually unusable at the front. Engineers performed wonders to maintain roads and bridges, and with Japanese forces still roaming, this was dangerous work: on 7 August, seven sappers were killed and as many wounded in a Japanese ambush. Two days earlier, Sergeant Horace Brown (GM), who commanded a detachment building a 55-metre Bailey bridge over the Hongorai River, was forced into unusual action. In the early morning, he spotted two Japanese on the bridge. He fired his Owen, and they fled into the semi-darkness. Looking along the bridge, Brown then discerned a small light. Rushing to investigate, he realised that among the double-storey steelwork, the Japanese had placed a demolition charge with a fuse burning. He removed the charge from the steelwork and took it down to the bridge deck. Recognising the danger to nearby sappers, he carried the charge to a place where he could throw it clear. Within two seconds of him throwing it, the charge exploded. The bridge and its construction workers were unharmed. Brown was a 32-year-old bridge carpenter from Brisbane.

News of the dropping of the atomic bombs on Hiroshima and Nagasaki and the fast-approaching end of hostilities led to orders for long-range and fighting patrols to cease. On 14 August, news came from an ANGAU local of numerous Japanese wanting to surrender near Hanung. Corporal Geai (DCM) was sent out with a PIB section to investigate. On the way, they encountered three

Japanese with hands raised. Geai and the ANGAU man advanced to accept their surrender, but when just a few metres distant, Geai spotted a hidden Japanese LMG and crew covering the track, and other armed Japanese moving to his left. Recognising a trap, Geai ordered his men to take cover and opened fire. He knocked out the Nambu crew and took their weapon, but by now enemy mortar, rifle and automatic fire was hitting the Papuans. Machine-gun bullets struck Geai in the arm and hand, but he rushed forward and single-handedly killed seven Japanese with his Owen. Though hit again, in the leg, he continued engaging the enemy and drawing their fire. Eventually he extricated his section. It was appropriate that a PIB soldier should win an award on the last day of fighting in the war with Japan, just as another Papuan, Katue, had won one on the first night of fighting in Papua.

Advance into northern Bougainville

Like the southern front on Bougainville, the northern sector saw a coastal advance, but with smaller forces engaged. The 31st/51st Battalion, advancing north, first met serious opposition about 65 kilometres from Torokina and just 24 kilometres from the Bonis peninsula, at the island's northern tip. It clashed with Japanese holding Tsimba Ridge, which had trenches and pillboxes stretching nearly 150 metres among its vegetation. A 31st/51st company under Captain Alwyn 'Blue' Shilton (MC) was sent 550 metres inland from Tsimba and across the Genga River to attack Tsimba from the north. For six days the Japanese repeatedly attacked and bombarded this bridgehead. In their fiercest attack, on 29 January, they broke through one sector of the perimeter. Machine-gun fire killed three Australians and wounded several, while the Japanese commander inflicted sword wounds on others, including two Bren gunners. Shilton rushed to this sector and restored the position, bringing up troops from a rear platoon, and directing Vickers fire onto the enemy machine guns. Then, taking a small reserve, he launched a flanking counterattack that surprised the Japanese and led their few survivors to withdraw. Shilton had fought in Libya and Syria with the 2/5th Battalion before being allocated, like other junior AIF officers, to a militia battalion to give these units the benefit of their battle experience. At the Genga River bridgehead, the allocation paid off for Shilton's men. One tip, as Japanese moved around them each night, was for his men not to give away their positions by firing. Instead, they were to use grenades, and he raised eyebrows at headquarters when he sent a message asking for 200 more. The grenades arrived. He later wondered at his 'stupidity' in heading into danger during his counterattack, but acknowledged that had his experience and training not kicked in, and his men not fought so well, the bridgehead would have been overrun.

Lieutenant Jim Forbes (MC), an FOO with the 2nd Mountain Battery, also contributed to the defence. From an observation post in a tree he called down defensive fire from the battery's 75mm guns. This was especially dangerous work during the 29 January attack, when enemy artillery, mortars and snipers threatened. He showed similar cool courage on 14 February. Unable to see in the jungle, he waded out to sea and directed artillery fire from a position open to enemy view. His father had won a Military Cross in World War I and his brother would do the same in Korea. Forbes had a distinguished postwar political career, including a stint as Minister for the Army.

The Australian defence of the Genga bridgehead did not affect the Japanese hold on Tsimba Ridge. On 6 February, a 31st/51st company captured it with a set-piece attack, supported by 500 shells and bombs from the mountain battery and heavy mortars.

On 21 February, the 31st/51st was relieved by the 26th Battalion under Lieutenant-Colonel Callinan, a veteran of Timor. His tactics of outflanking the Japanese, cutting their lines of communication and making amphibious landings behind them succeeded brilliantly, and by 28 March, Japanese resistance on the Soraken Peninsula had ended. Carrying out those tactics with poor maps in difficult terrain required excellent leadership. Captain Keith Coleman (MC) proved a driving and courageous company commander. One advance he led cut the main coastal track and resulted in the Japanese abandoning more than a kilometre of ground and three artillery pieces. Little wonder that this 24-year-old regular soldier rose to colonel in the postwar Army.

On 10 March, Australian forces took Taiof Island, killing or capturing its garrison. The island had invaluable views of the west coast, and on 13 March, a small party from the 26th Battalion Mortar and Machine Gun platoons landed there under Sergeant Matthew Bright (MM). Thanks to his energetic leadership, by nightfall the group had carried heavy wireless equipment, stores and ammunition through mangrove swamps to the top of a 365-metre-high observation post.

The next morning, they were in communication with headquarters and began burying and salvaging enemy equipment. The Japanese had left some locals in charge, but Bright, a fine organiser, took control and obtained food supplies and assistance. The Japanese wanted the island back, and on 26 March landed an advance party. Though informed that this force was large, Bright immediately marched to attack. He set an ambush and, after allowing the Japanese leading scout to pass, his group opened fire and killed the rest of the advance party. He then chased and killed the Japanese scout. No more Japanese landed after this.

The 26th Battalion was relieved on 4 April, but a week later, one of its men performed an extraordinary deed. Japanese artillery scored two direct hits on an ammunition dump containing more than 1000 artillery and mortar rounds. When a call was made for help, Private James Calder (GM), who was at the RAP, grabbed a stretcher and, calling for assistance from those nearby, ran to an injured man just 20 metres from the dump. While mortar bombs exploded around them, Calder put the man on the stretcher and helped carry him out. He twice returned to the RAP, just 150 metres from the explosions, to obtain morphia and plasma.

When the 26th and part of the 31st/51st battalions returned to the front in May, they encountered relatively fresh Japanese naval troops, who fought hard and used harassing tactics against the tiring

Australians. On 22 and 27 May, Captain Syd Searles (MC) of the 26th led a successful defence against 'banzai' attacks, including one made under cover of smoke. Each time this Queensland clerk moved around the perimeter using his Owen. In 16 days his company advanced nearly 1500 metres. By June, though, the 26th Battalion was down to half-strength.

To speed up progress, it was decided to land a reinforced company – 190 men – of the 31st/51st behind Japanese lines at Porton Plantation. The planning was rushed and overly optimistic. When early on 8 June the two attacking waves came in to land, they were nearly 300 metres too far north (beyond damaged jetties that could have been useful) and their landing craft became grounded on a coral reef. The infantrymen had to walk ashore, but dug in and established a U-shaped perimeter up to 150 metres inland. Ten minutes after the second wave landed, Japanese machine guns opened fire.

Two landing craft carrying vital support weapons, ammunition and supplies became stranded on the reef. Heavy fire prevented them from being unloaded. Lieutenant Pete Spark (MC), a regular soldier and artilleryman, found none of the expected landmarks when he came ashore in the second wave, but by 6 am was calling in accurate fire from 4th Field Regiment guns at Soraken. Under his direction his supporting battery fired 3700 rounds over the next two days. Spark had escaped captivity in Crete and reached Egypt six months later. He had been wounded on Bougainville in December, returned to duty and would remain on duty when wounded again at Porton. The artillery fire he called in blew away foliage to reveal enemy defences, but though it could suppress enemy machine guns temporarily, it did not destroy the emplacements. An arc of Japanese pillboxes and trenches confronted the Australians, and Japanese reinforcements were arriving rapidly. The Australians sent out patrols, but it was perilous work. Lieutenant Noel Smith, Mentioned in Despatches as a sergeant with the 2/17th in the Middle East, led a ten-man patrol eastwards. Within 45 metres they saw Japanese movement, exchanged fire with a machine gun, and spotted an ambush set up ahead. As the patrol withdrew it met more Japanese and, under heavy fire, Smith ordered everyone back to the perimeter. One group of three got back after seven hours, four others reached the Australian main force at Ratsua. A machine-gun bullet struck Smith in the wrist, nearly severing it, and he lay wounded, eventually becoming delirious. In a lucid moment he ordered more men to head for Ratsua to bring help. Private Ernest Duck, Smith's 20-year-old batman, chose to stay with his stricken officer. Neither man was seen again.

Three Japanese with a Nambu crawled to within 10 metres of the Australian left flank and opened fire. From the foremost weapon pit, Private Ken Ward (DCM) threw a grenade at the gunners, then climbed out and ran towards them. He shot all three and disabled their gun. Four Japanese now attacked the 19-year-old Western Australian process worker from a flank, but he shot one, then took cover and killed the other three. Later, when an Australian on a nearby listening post was wounded, Ward crawled forward under fire and dragged him to help.

By day's end, the Australians at Porton were not advancing, but holding on against about 250 Japanese. Attempts to land reinforcements and supplies that night failed and orders came the following morning for the force to withdraw on the night of 9/10 June.

The Japanese harassed the defenders throughout the night of 8/9 June and launched a full-scale attack the next morning. The Australians held off that assault and others through the day, helped by friendly artillery fire and aircraft. In the late afternoon, three landing craft arrived to evacuate the troops. Thanks largely to artillery fire directed by Spark, the defenders boarded the landing craft. One drove away once it was full, but the other two were so overloaded they became stuck. An Australian artillery smoke canister landed on one stranded vessel and set alight boxes tied to the top of the engine. Despite intense small arms fire coming towards the craft, Ken Ward risked exposing himself to it and tried to pick up the canister. It was too hot, burning his hands, but he overcame the pain to cut loose the boxes with his bayonet and kick them overboard. Ward would later serve in Korea and marry a Japanese woman. Lieutenant Spark helped men get aboard these landing craft, and for five hours called in fire from one, though he was repeatedly struck by fragments thrown up by enemy fire.

As a machine gunner, Sapper Harold Burrell (MM) of the 42nd Landing Craft Company came under fire when his vessel approached the beachhead. The aft gunner was killed almost immediately, but Burrell continued firing his Browning machine gun until out of ammunition. He then walked, despite enemy fire, to the aft gun and used it until the forward gun was reloaded and he could return to it. Burrell silenced three enemy machine guns. In the meantime, he rescued a wounded soldier from the water.

The tide enabled one of the two stranded landing craft to leave at 10.40 pm, but the remaining vessel had been holed by coral and was half full of water. It was also full of men: 60, including 12 wounded. Japanese swam out to make suicide attacks on these unfortunates. Early on 11 June, three Australian wooden and canvas assault boats reached the landing craft, under cover of heavy artillery fire. Lieutenant Arthur Graham (MC) of the 16th Field Company commanded these boats. Though wounded in the shoulder by shrapnel, and then in the stomach and arm by small arms fire, Graham reached the stranded vessel and brought back 5–12 men. One of his crew, Corporal Maurice Draper (MM) was also wounded in the arm but helped the terribly weakened men on the landing craft to safety. Draper, who volunteered for this rescue mission, had already given outstanding assistance to the infantry at Tsimba Ridge and elsewhere. This tragic Porton action cost the Australians 26 killed, the Japanese about the same.

Lieutenant 'Blue' Reiter (MC), who was prominent in a bayonet charge in Crete, was outstanding again at Porton. As a lieutenant with the 31st/51st, he proved an exceptional patrol leader, and the battalion dubbed one attack he led 'the raid on Reiter's Ridge'. At Porton, Reiter's platoon held the southern flank of the perimeter against all attacks. He was evacuated on the night of 9/10 June, but then, despite being physically and mentally exhausted, volunteered immediately to return to Porton to extricate the men on the stranded landing craft. He rescued eight men swimming near that beached vessel. Following the Porton operation, the company involved was just 31 strong. The company commander, Captain Clyde Downs (MID), died during the fighting, and Reiter was appointed to replace him in preference to more senior officers.

On 20 June, the 23rd Brigade took over with orders to contain the Japanese on the Bonis Peninsula. On 23 July, the 8th Battalion, fighting its first campaign, attacked and took Commo Ridge, near Buoi Plantation. On 24 July, after a heavy bombardment two platoons attacked a series of bunkers called Base 5. Machine-gun fire pinned down the Australians. Though wounded twice in the left arm and once in the thigh, 20-year-old Private Frank Partridge (VC) now took the initiative. He picked up a Bren from a dead gunner and rushed towards a bunker, calling on its occupants to come out and fight. He passed the Bren to another man, then threw a smoke grenade into the bunker and entered. He killed the surviving defender with a knife. Australians helped him clear another bunker before blood loss forced him to stop. He insisted on walking out. Partridge was the youngest Australian recipient of the Victoria Cross in the war, as well as the last, and the only militiaman to receive that coveted award. He was extraordinary in other ways: rising from a dirt-floor farmhouse after the war, he educated himself and won the famed quiz show 'Pick-a-Box' before dying in a car accident aged just 39. His achievements at 'Part Ridge', as Base 5 was known, were part of a group effort. Private Edgar Uebergang (MM) was a stretcher-bearer who carried the platoon's wounded officer to safety then went forward on three more occasions, each time rescuing a wounded man. When the patrol withdrew, Uebergang took a leading role. By 5 August, the Japanese had abandoned the 60 bunkers on Part Ridge.

Aggressive patrolling in central Bougainville

In central Bougainville, the 9th Battalion relieved the Americans on the Numa Numa trail, which followed steep terrain and was difficult to supply. Nevertheless, the Australians attacked almost immediately, capturing Little George Hill on 29 November 1944. Lieutenant Jack Deacon (MC) was wounded but continued to lead the platoon that seized the position by advancing in pairs, one man covering each enemy post with fire while the other used grenades in a flank attack.

This tactic also worked on Arty Hill on 18 December, but it was a tough proposition negotiating the slippery surface of a nearby razorback ridge, devoid of cover after months of shelling and with Japanese throwing grenades and firing from covered weapon pits. Sergeant Duncan Allan (MID) led the attack on the right flank and reached the top of the ridge. The young sawmiller shot dead a Japanese machine gunner before being killed. The 26th Battalion then led the advance and captured Pearl Ridge in hard fighting on 30 December. The Japanese reinforced the area, and Australian resources were directed elsewhere, so the Australians in the central sector had to be content with aggressive patrolling. Over 14 weeks the Australians killed about 250 Japanese for the loss of just four dead. This reflected the expertise of the junior officers, such as the 26th's Lieutenant Arthur Chambers (MC), who led the largely untried other ranks. A feature where he led an attack on 7 January that destroyed enemy defences and diverted enemy reinforcements was named Chambers Knoll. He later led 12 men against 40 Japanese ensconced in nearby defences, causing havoc before withdrawing. In March, Lieutenant Len Goodwin (MC) of the 55th/53rd led a 15-strong long-range patrol tasked with causing mayhem. On the second day, they surprised an outpost, killing six occupants. Two days later, on encountering an enemy bivouac area of 25 men, Goodwin placed his men around the perimeter and gave them individual targets: 15 Japanese were killed before LMG fire forced the patrol to retreat. Goodwin, a Canberra transport driver, led other successful long-range patrols, never sustaining any casualties and accounting for 26 of the 107 Japanese killed by his battalion's patrols.

The 7th Battalion arrived in the central sector in June and was permitted to advance more aggressively than its predecessors. It took several hills, and by war's end was patrolling deep into enemy

Lieutenant Jack Deacon (second from left) having his wounded jaw dressed at the 9th Battalion RAP on 29 November 1944, during or soon after the attack on Little George Hill. When Deacon left the Army in December 1945, he still had grenade splinters in his face and a lip wound.
AWM 077320

territory. The battalion commander, Lieutenant-Colonel Harry Dunkley (DSO) was 'a fighting officer', cool under fire and a fine tactician. A bullet seared his cheek as a memento of one company attack that he led personally. He killed several Japanese and once described the fighting as a combination of mud wrestling, rugby and murder. The 33-year-old schoolteacher had won a Military Cross as a lieutenant with the 2/6th at Bardia and had been Mentioned in Despatches as a major at Salamaua.

Behind the lines

The Army's conventional operations on Bougainville received invaluable support, especially information, from Australians of the Allied Intelligence Bureau (AIB) operating behind enemy lines. Many were members of the Navy or Air Force, but others were soldiers, using wireless sets and employing local 'native' help. An outstanding Army man performing guerrilla work was Lieutenant Gerald McPhee (MC), who as early as July 1943 undertook solo patrols in northern Bougainville, using a radio to give intelligence updates as Japanese sought to hunt down his party. He assisted the American force that landed on the island and then, from November 1944, delivered information to the Australians by wireless, and for over two years he performed 'continuous acts of bravery'.

Sergeant John Wigley (MM) operated in a group of three whites and 'native' supporters from November 1944. Wigley helped plan an attack on Japanese troops based at Teopasino Plantation in February 1945. He spent three days reconnoitring enemy camps and then led locals, armed mainly with axes and bows and arrows, in attacking Japanese doing physical training exercises on 27 February. Every Japanese died in this surprise attack. Other assaults culminated in 54 Japanese deaths for only two wounded locals. Wigley, a Sydney timber worker, also led locals in patrols that harassed the Japanese and gathered valuable information. He was awarded a US Silver Star for his work with the Americans.

AIB soldiers Sergeant Keith Warner (MM) and Corporal Ben White (DCM) achieved remarkable results in 1944-45. Constantly on the move, they did not remove their boots for more than a month in early 1945. At one point Warner, a 38-year-old grazier, led about 100 ill-armed locals who, after a successful ambush, conducted a nine-week siege of 25 Japanese in a southern village. When word came in January 1945 that 100 Japanese had left Buin to relieve their compatriots, White was ordered to intercept. The 33-year-old lime burner took more than 200 locals who ambushed the Japanese in a gorge. These locals used a few Japanese rifles, their own weapons and heavy stones they rolled down onto a relief party, who fled and took to the jungle. White's party pursued and virtually annihilated them. Eighty-five Japanese were killed that day for just one wounded local. Another Japanese relief party, supported by a mobile 20mm gun, reached the garrison after three weeks but also suffered heavily in ambushes. White's citation stated that he personally killed five Japanese in combat, and called him an 'intrepid and splendid jungle fighter'. As we have seen, this term applied to many Australians who fought on Bougainville.

INTERLUDE 4
HEROIC RESCUERS

Nearly 70 of the heroes – about 10 per cent of the men discussed in this book – won recognition for saving the lives of others. Some were famous, like 'Weary' Dunlop and 'Bull' Allen. Dunlop was, of course, a doctor, as were many others, especially RMOs, who risked their lives to tend to others. They included Victor Brand in Malaya, Bill Campbell at the Alamein Blockhouse, John Connell on the Kokoda Track, Victor Sampson at Buna and Owen Williams at Aitape–Wewak. 'Bull' Allen was one of more than 20 stretcher-bearers named here, and there were innumerable other brave ones. At the height of the battle of El Alamein, the war diary of the 2/48th Battalion, the war's most decorated Australian battalion, praised the 'magnificent and gallant' stretcher-bearers, who were generally 'the only people above the surface of the ground which was continuously swept with fire'.[1] In desert and jungle, men like Arthur Williams (Malaya), Tom Langford (Alamein) and Tom Fletcher (Kokoda) won the admiration of others for doing remarkable work. Each of those three lost his life in the process. The intermediaries between the RMOs and stretcher-bearers in an infantry battalion were the RAP sergeants, and the inherently risky and self-sacrificing work of Sergeants Wally Tuit in Tobruk, Pasquale Robino at Pabu and John Palmer at Prothero 1, and Corporal Roland Duncan at Gona, undoubtedly saved lives. Five chaplains are cited for their brave work tending to the wounded. In keeping with the Christian principle of loving self-sacrifice, Tom Gard, Eric Seatree, Jimmy James, Hugh Ballard and Ben Holt all risked their lives to save others. Holt lost his life.

There were other soldiers who unofficially took it upon themselves to be rescuers: men like Private Ron Claffey, who saved 30 casualties in his bullet-ridden truck at Tel el Eisa, and Lance-Bombardier Gordon McAllister, who rescued nine men from the raging Danmap River.

Then there were the numerous leaders and soldiers who, in the course of some other brave deed, rescued wounded men. They included: Lieutenant Kevin Power, a formidable fighting soldier who in the Kokoda campaign led three attacks to save wounded men on one patrol, then carried out two men during an attack on a heavily defended knoll in 1943; Lieutenant Bill MacIntosh, whose rescue of one of his men under fire was just one of numerous exploits that earned him two medals; Sapper Harold Burrell, who silenced three enemy machine guns from an exposed position on a landing craft but also managed to rescue a wounded man from the water; and Sergeant Harry Bell, who won medals in the desert and jungle for destroying enemy machine guns, but also twice saved his platoon commander from imminent death.

It seems that those who were there to rescue fellow soldiers in their hour of need generally won more fulsome praise than those who killed enemies, though that is of course impossible to measure.

CHAPTER 20

NEW GUINEA: FROM AITAPE TO WEWAK

Before the 6th Australian Division took over the Aitape–Wewak area in October–November 1944, the American garrison held a small perimeter around Aitape airfield and harbour, with two outposts. These Americans had little contact with the Japanese, whose forces in the area numbered 35 000 men, though the Allies believed the number was 24 000. General Blamey wanted to give his elite 6th Division a substantial task after a long period of inactivity – more than three years for some units. The main roles allotted to it were to protect Aitape, support ANGAU and AIB units, and, most importantly, destroy Japanese forces in the area. The Australians were outnumbered but far better equipped and supplied than their enemies, for whom food shortages were a huge problem. The Australians had naval and especially air support, but knew that their campaign was a low Allied priority. They knew too that the strategic value of the operations was dubious, but, as the official historian later acknowledged, in each attack, veterans and young soldiers 'performed deeds of fine gallantry'.

Uncertainty about the future deployment of the 6th Division limited planning in this campaign, but as it gradually became apparent that the 6th would not be needed elsewhere, the goal became the capture of Wewak by means of parallel advances along the narrow coastal strip and the Torricelli Mountains.

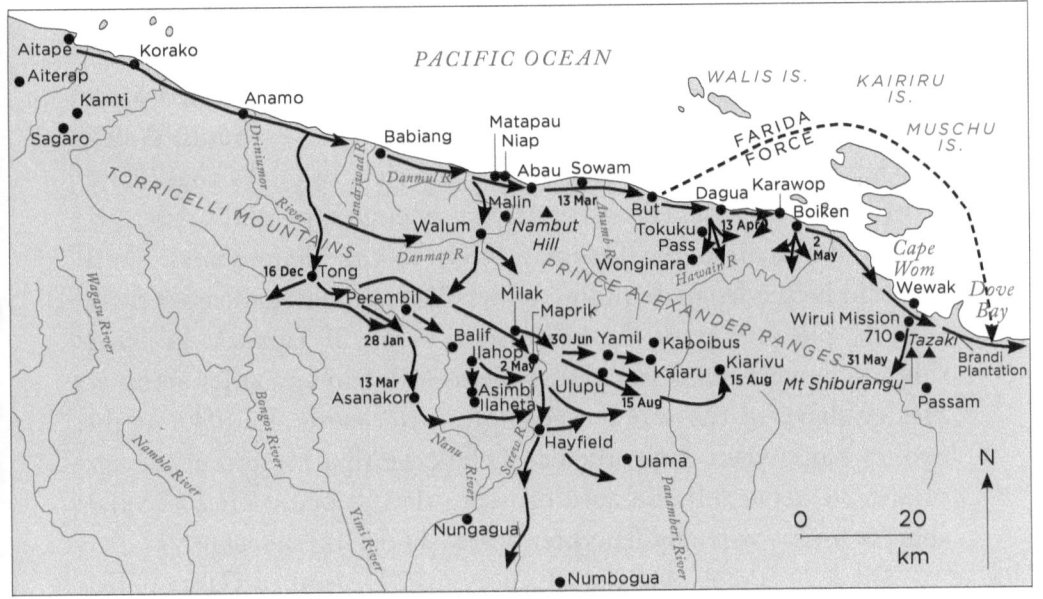

Aitape–Wewak

The terrain was better than in earlier jungle campaigns, but men still had to carry their homes on their backs, enduring heat, rain, hills and illness. The first combat unit to arrive, the 2/6th Cavalry (Commando) Regiment, was ordered beyond the American perimeter to the Danmap River on 2 November. It found evidence of cannibalism among the Japanese and by the end of November had killed 73.

Early in December, the 19th Brigade took over the coastal advance. The 2/4th Battalion led, crossing the Danmap and pushing the Japanese back some 6 kilometres. A platoon under Lieutenant Don Healey (MC) achieved a striking success on 21 December. After five days in an outpost across the Danmap, the platoon was short of food and water and at a low physical ebb. A relief party from the 2/11th was on the way, but the section sent to usher them across the Danmap at the 'Knife Ford' stumbled on a group of Japanese. The Australians shot several, and when Healey arrived with another section, an intense firefight ensued. Private Terry Paff (MID), alone on the extreme right flank, saw a Japanese LMG firing at a section from the flank, and promptly shot the gunner and four riflemen with his Owen. This saved Australian lives. Paff was himself killed while on the riverbank. This dairy farmer from Bulbach, New South Wales, was reportedly recommended for a Victoria Cross. As the 2/11th relief party approached and with the enemy apparently defeated, Healey moved into the Danmap River to call them across. Only then did he see Japanese hiding under the riverbank and shoot three with his pistol. Among the possessions of the 28 Japanese killed in this action were items from Australians killed in an earlier ambush. Healey survived the war but struggled afterwards. In 1949, at the Sydney bank where he worked as a clerk, he shot himself at the age of just 28, reportedly because of depression at being forced to live apart from his wife and daughter due to a housing shortage.

The 2/11th took over the advance on 22 December. Captain Ted Royce (MC) commanded a company attacked by about 35 Japanese at Matapau village on 2 January 1945. The Australians killed six and drove them off. Royce, a Western Australian accountant, served throughout the 2/11th's campaigns and had escaped from Crete.

Lieutenant James Birrell (MC) took six men of the Royal Papuan Constabulary on a patrol: they killed four Japanese and brought back valuable information. Birrell was a member of ANGAU, for which Captain Bob Cole set up a remarkable system of hundreds of locals as 'sentries', who sent invaluable information about the entire area of Japanese operations, as well as killing at least 359 Japanese. Cole, a prewar patrol officer in New Guinea, himself received a Military Cross for an outstanding patrol in Hollandia (Dutch New Guinea) from March to May 1944. The patrol, comprising four Europeans and eight local police, covered 280 kilometres (most of it Japanese-controlled), protected two Dutch patrols, helped the Americans after they landed in the area and killed 52 enemy.

The brigade's third battalion, the 2/8th, advanced on an inland route through the foothills of the Torricellis. By 8 January it was occupying Malin village, which the Japanese sent a large force to recapture. Lieutenant Alex Turnbull (MC) led his platoon in three

When 150 Japanese surrounded 40 Australians at Milak village in March 1945, these three men were crucial in its successful defence. Lieutenant Ken Perkins (centre) received an MC for his 'conspicuous gallantry and courage' in the intense five-day siege. Corporal Tony Gannan, at left, did crucial work commanding a mortar crew. Lieutenant Neil Redmond, who turned 23 during the siege, was later killed in action.
KEITH JOHNSTON AND 6TH DIV CAV REGT

successful patrols against these attackers. On 19 January, a 100-minute engagement against 20 of these Japanese on Long Ridge saw nine Japanese killed and four Australians wounded. Turnbull, a regular soldier, was wounded but remained on duty in terrain so rugged that carrier pigeons were used to send written signals to brigade headquarters. Skilful patrolling was a hallmark of the Australians' efforts here, including those of the commando squadron that was on the 2/8th's flank. Mortality among forward scouts was high, so the role was usually rotated. However, Trooper Charles Olsen (MID) of the 2/9th Cavalry Commando Squadron insisted on permanently holding this position. Using an Owen, he had the squadron's highest tally of kills.

The 16th Brigade relieved the 19th in late January but soon afterwards the coastal advance was temporarily halted when torrential rain washed away seven bridges, including one over the Danmap. Eleven Australians drowned in the river. Lieutenant Fred Williams and Bombardier Charles Pitts of the 2/2nd Field Regiment were swept down the river after holding onto trees and logs for hours on the night of 27/28 January. Completely exhausted and clinging to a tree about 100 metres from the nearest bank of the raging torrent, they had little hope. Suddenly, they saw a light on the bank and a soldier coming towards them. That man wore a belt connecting him to the bank but he had to negotiate underwater obstacles, logs travelling past and falling timber. As the soldier neared, Williams recognised him as Lance-Bombardier Gordon McAllister (GM), who helped him back to the riverbank. No sooner was Williams in safe hands than McAllister went back for Pitts. They were just metres from the tree Pitts had been clinging to when it crashed into the Danmap and was swept away. They were not the only two lives that McAllister saved that night using his belt improvised from signal wire. He repeatedly went out to rescue men, and eventually took off his belt to give it to an exhausted soldier who was dragged ashore. McAllister then narrowly escaped drowning but made it ashore, completely exhausted. This prewar truck driver rescued nine men in more than three hours.

The 2/1st led the coastal advance when it resumed, and on 30 January a platoon under Lieutenant John Haydon (MID) fended off a fierce attack on a knoll at the western end of Nambut Hill, which overlooked a particularly narrow coastal strip. For five hours 30 Japanese tried to drive back Haydon's men with small arms and explosives. They were repulsed from this feature that the Australians dubbed 'Haydon's Knoll'. Only after three weeks' fighting, with air support, was Nambut Hill, a cornerstone of the Japanese defence, taken on 18 February.

Sergeant Bob Graham (MM) and Sergeant-Major Roy 'Vic' Hall (DCM) took leading roles on 17 February when three Japanese LMGs pinned down a patrol, killing two and wounding four. Three casualties lay on open ground, unable to move. Graham was nearby with a water-carrying party and, conferring with his platoon commander, put two Bren gunners in place astride the track, preliminary to reconnoitring forward. One of the gunners was shot immediately, at which point Graham calmly carried out his body and went after the shooter. He swapped his rifle for an Owen gun and disappeared for a few minutes before returning to the officer and proclaiming, 'One more for Valhalla'. Graham then re-entered the jungle. Hall, the company sergeant-major, now arrived, and on hearing of the situation, crawled down the slope towards Graham. Helped by supporting fire from Graham's section, they extracted one wounded man under fire. The enemy was on a ridge so narrow only three men could advance at a time, with slopes too steep to allow outflanking. Hall, Graham and Lance-Corporal Ernest Mould proceeded along this ridge, throwing grenades and firing. They killed eight Japanese and drove off the others. Hall was slightly wounded, but Mould (in his first campaign) was killed. Hall and Graham brought out the other two wounded with their weapons, still under fire. Fourteen dead Japanese were later found among 22 weapon pits in this area. Hall was a 31-year-old Queensland miner and Graham was a NSW farmer often in trouble with Army authority.

While the 2/1st were clearing Nambut Hill, the 2/3rd Battalion, on the inland coastal route, won several fights on Long Ridge. On

1 February, Private John Perry (MID), a 20-year-old forward scout for two platoons sent along the ridge, surprised and silently killed a Japanese sentry with a machete before reporting the presence of 30 Japanese in a nearby camp. Commanding the platoons was Lieutenant Gilbert Cory (MC), who had been outstanding at Eora Creek in 1942. He now sent Lieutenant Stuart Weir (MC) and his platoon to attack the Japanese camp, which sat atop a plateau. Though shot through the shoulder early in the attack, Weir led his men in capturing their allotted sector. He jumped into one LMG pit, killed the gunner and turned the weapon on the enemy with deadly effect. He then led the men on, bringing the Nambu with him and repeatedly firing effective bursts into the defenders. Weir, a 22-year-old regular soldier, had a distinguished postwar military career, which included commanding a company in the Korean War, 1 RAR in the Malayan Emergency and 1st Australian Task Force in Vietnam. He retired as a brigadier.

Weir's platoon became pinned down on Long Ridge. Cory sent in the second platoon, under Lieutenant Ken Pope, but Pope was killed soon after joining Weir in a Japanese foxhole. Cory's force withdrew after dark, short of ammunition.

The 16th Brigade pushed on, and by 21 March had seized the But and Dagua airfields. Weeks of heavy fighting on the high ground inland from Dagua followed and then an advance to the Hawain River. The 19th Brigade relieved the 16th in early May.

The inland advance

The 17th Brigade, with the 2/5th Battalion in the vanguard, had in the meantime advanced into and south of the Torricellis from a base at Tong. The battalion's first contact was on 27 December, when a four- or five-man patrol under Lieutenant Adrian 'Stump' Doneley (MC) clashed with over 20 Japanese. On seeing the enemy approach, Doneley ordered his men into improvised ambush positions, from which they held their fire until the Japanese were just 5 metres away. Fifteen enemies fell dead, another five wounded. Doneley was himself wounded in the face by grenade fragments but remained on duty. Three days later, Doneley led a patrol in a charge, killing five men personally before the enemy fled. By 8 March, when the recommendation for Doneley's Military Cross was made, his citation said he had led 15 patrols and personally killed 15 Japanese, thus earning the status of 'a legend' within his battalion. Doneley had been Mentioned in Despatches as a lance-sergeant with the 2/15th in Tobruk. His 2/5th platoon suffered no casualties in New Guinea until 20 January, when he was among the wounded but again stayed on duty. On 6 June, the 27-year-old Queensland grazier's luck ran out. He had recently heard of the death of his brother Austin with the 2/7th in the same campaign and now led his platoon to capture a hill near Ulupu. After hearing the sounds of a firefight, the platoons behind saw a member of Doneley's platoon staggering back in tears and yelling, 'They got the Stump'. Doneley's mate, Captain Lin Cameron, for once showed emotion and had to be prevented from going forward recklessly.

Cameron won a Bar to his Military Cross at Perembil, a settlement atop a razorback ridge and overlooked by Japanese defences. Cameron ordered the men in immediately after a bombing run, and they found and occupied weapon pits that the Japanese had temporarily abandoned. During one of several enemy counterattacks, Private Bert Escreet (MM) distinguished himself. Though caught in open ground and wounded in the face, chest and arm, the 30-year-old farm labourer brought his Bren into action and kept firing until the enemy fell back, leaving 19 dead. Escreet's wounds ended his military career.

Another 30-year-old Victorian farm worker, Sergeant Charlie Thorn (DCM), led the rush into Perembil. His most outstanding feat came though the following month on 23 February, when Cameron's company was attacked for four hours from three sides by about 120 Japanese at Malahun. When Cameron decided to send out fighting patrols for help and to clear the front, Thorn volunteered to lead one. Thorn then guided his dozen men in a flank attack into the midst of

In January 1945, Private Bert Escreet (pictured here in New Guinea in 1943), lay badly wounded in the face, chest and arm on open ground near Perembil, New Guinea, but he held off an enemy attack with his Bren gun.
AWM 015377

the enemy, killing many and destroying LMGs. When the enemy attention became too intense, Thorn moved behind the Japanese and launched another attack, which forced them to withdraw.

Corporal Ray Dunlop (DCM) was another outstanding patroller for the 2/5th, leading with great courage at least 12 fighting patrols, most of them long, arduous and hazardous. Twice this despatch clerk from Fitzroy resolved dangerous situations through his cool leadership – once repelling a counterattack and another time extricating a patrol pinned down under machine-gun fire.

By late January, the 2/5th had cleared the enemy from a 260-square-kilometre area. The inland advance had just one aircraft in support. In late February, the brigade and commandos advanced on the strong Japanese base at Maprik. Lieutenant Jim Milton (MC) took the lead in a bloody fight at Bombita village on 18 February. Before the action, Milton had crawled to within 5 metres of enemy positions, which he pinpointed before returning to brief his platoon. They attacked about 40 well-ensconced Japanese for at least three hours, after which the Japanese left the field and ten dead. Milton, a 34-year-old caterer from Bendigo, was credited with six killed, using grenades and a rifle. In mid-July, he and his company commander Lin Cameron complained so forcefully about the lack of reinforcements, artillery support and rest their company had been receiving that both were temporarily relieved of command. Milton commanded the company after Cameron fell ill, during which time more artillery support and reinforcements arrived. When the 2/5th was relieved in late February, it had killed 376 Japanese for the loss of seven dead in a 24-kilometre advance.

Some 2000 Japanese retreated south into garden areas, where they threatened the Australian flank. Major David Hay (DSO) and a 2/6th Battalion company pushed them east. On 13 March, 150 Japanese attacked 40 commandos in an isolated forward position at Milak and a five-day siege followed. Under Lieutenant Ken Perkins (MC), the group held off numerous day and night attacks on their weapon pits in a relatively open 45 by 65-metre area. An attached mortar crew under Lieutenant Tony Gannan provided crucial support, some of it with unconventional fire just 30 metres from the mortar. It was an epic defence, recognised only in the award to Perkins, a 30-year-old mail officer who had risen through the ranks. When the Japanese retreated, they left a third of their force dead.

Sergeant John 'Smoky' Hedderman (DCM), who had won a Military Medal in 1943 in New Guinea, was again a cool and courageous commander of 2/6th Battalion patrols and assaults. Early in an attack on 25–30 Japanese defending Gwanginan on 30 March, he sowed confusion among the enemy by calling to imaginary platoons on his left and right, even though this drew fire towards him. When the leading section became pinned down, Hedderman brought to bear 2-inch mortar and EY rifle fire to suppress the enemy and allow his men to advance. Later, when one of his men was severely wounded, Hedderman crawled forward under machine-gun fire to within 10 metres of enemy foxholes, even though two rounds pierced his clothing. He then killed two Japanese with grenades and dragged and carried the casualty from apparently certain death to safety. Hedderman returned to the fight, and when a section commander was killed, he took over that section and directed covering fire to enable the whole platoon to fall back. Hedderman was commissioned lieutenant in August. He went into the postwar building industry as a works supervisor before dying of chronic alcoholism in 1986, aged 70. In describing a patrol that he undertook on Anzac Day 1945, the official historian called him 'the ubiquitous Sergeant Hedderman'.

By April, the Australians were ready to attack Maprik. Lieutenant Lionel Bowden (MC) of the 2/7th Battalion was ordered on 20 April to secure the dominating position there, called House Tamboran. To maximise surprise, he took his platoon across the steepest ground, covered with long pit-pit grass, then rushed the Japanese positions. Bowden threw a grenade at a weapon pit, but it failed to explode. He hurled a second grenade, but the defenders threw it back. He held a third grenade for two extra seconds before throwing it: this time the two plucky defenders were killed. Despite continuous, intense Japanese small arms fire, Bowden's platoon gained the high ground. He was wounded here, as he was again in late May, but remained on duty both times. Lieutenant Reg Saunders, in his first campaign as a platoon commander, led a valuable flanking manoeuvre during the fight for Maprik. By 22 April, the Australians held that base.

Take But!

They were pushing forward on the coastal sector too. The 2/3rd Machine Gun Battalion was ordered to convert to the role of infantry, a difficult task given that some machine gunners were not equipped with rifles. They managed well, their work typified by Lieutenant Henry MacFie (MC), a young Tasmanian bank clerk who led a company attack on Arohemi on 8 March. It was grim work, and by day's end they had not taken all objectives. MacFie's citation says that when the company commander 'lost control' of his company the following morning, MacFie took over and showed initiative, courage and determination in driving off the enemy. Twenty-five Japanese were killed. MacFie was throwing a grenade when, in the rain and mud, it slipped from his hand and landed in long grass among his own troops. He picked it out of the tangle and threw it in the air, where it exploded harmlessly. Standing just 5 feet 5 inches tall, MacFie had joined the militia as an 18-year-old in 1937.

On 2 March, two 2/2nd Battalion forward scouts were ambushed and killed as their unit moved parallel to the machine gun battalion and nearer the shoreline. On moving forward to investigate, the platoon commander and an NCO were also killed. Taking charge, Sergeant Jack Carnell (MID) led four men around the enemy, killed or wounded three and then charged back down the track and killed another. Carnell, a Geelong construction worker, had earlier campaigned with the 39th Battalion.

Japanese defences appeared thin in front of But, site of an airfield and a jetty that the Australians could use to leap forward rather than wait for a road extension to be built. On 14 March, a 2/2nd Battalion company advanced to seize But quickly and initially faced little opposition. The following day they struck a formidable Japanese position, which inflicted casualties and halted the Australians. Japanese defences here included bunkers sited on rising ground and made from sand-filled petrol drums and coconut logs. The open beach lay on one side, an open grassy area on the other. After 400 rounds of supporting artillery fire on 16 March, two 2/2nd platoons launched an attack that culminated in a bayonet charge. When the left-hand platoon was held up on the coastal track by Japanese firing from foxholes and four bunkers just 15 metres away, Lance-Corporal Sam Stubbs (DCM) found a way forward and directed his section's fire into the slits of the two foremost bunkers. Then, with his men providing covering fire, he rushed those bunkers, throwing in grenades that killed four occupants. He moved on to the next two bunkers, firing his Owen into the weapon slits and calling his men forward. He shot dead three more Japanese before moving on to the track and covering his platoon as it consolidated. When he received his Distinguished Conduct Medal in 1947, Stubbs was working as a Canberra taxi driver.

Working towards Wewak

On 17 March, the 2/2nd took But, which became a thriving base. General Blamey arrived two days later and approved an advance over the remaining 30 kilometres to Wewak. He also allotted landing craft and warships to the task. Many Japanese had retreated into the hills south of But, where they threatened the flank of the advance on Wewak. The 2/2nd was sent to clear them from the area, and this brought tough fighting, particularly around the Tokuku Pass. On 24 March, Lieutenant Hugh Jackson's platoon met some 30 Japanese on the Wonginara Track – a Japanese lifeline from the coast to the mountains – and Jackson was severely wounded. A company stretcher-bearer, Private Ernest Morris (MM), took the lead here. Though himself hit in the leg, this Queensland farm worker tended

Jackson's (and probably another man's) wounds and shielded him with his own body before dragging the officer to safety. Only after dark and the arrival of reinforcements could the attackers be extricated.

A famous clash occurred on 25 March, after the leading platoon advancing on one narrow ridge near Dagua became pinned down, its commander wounded. Lieutenant Bert Chowne (VC), commanding the reserve platoon, then took the initiative. This skilled and seemingly fearless leader ran up the steep track and knocked out two machine guns with grenades. Then, firing his submachine gun from the hip, he led his platoon in a charge that seized the next 50 metres, but at the cost of his life. Chowne was posthumously awarded the Victoria Cross, the 6th Division's first. That the award came so late to this elite formation reflected excessive parsimony in the division's senior officers.

Chowne's platoon charge was not the end of the assault on the ridge. Another platoon, under Lieutenant Ken Ferguson (MID), continued the advance. Ferguson was wounded but remained on duty. Private Dick McClelland (MM), from Chowne's platoon, joined them, carrying a Bren he had picked up when the gunner had been severely wounded. McLelland, a 33-year-old Bondi storeman, ran back for two more Bren magazines and then provided covering fire as Ferguson's platoon and a third one that came up took the knoll.

A key to the track from Dagua (which fell on 21 March) to Wonginara Mission was a height that the Australians called 'Jap Knoll', part of the 1410 Feature. In preparation for his company's attack – the battalion's fourth attempt to seize the knoll – Lieutenant Noel Park (DSO) spent 1 April reconnoitring enemy positions. This involved climbing a near-vertical slope and working to within 10 metres of the enemy's foxholes. At the end of the day he returned to his company commander with a plan of attack. On 2 April, aircraft and artillery bombarded the position and an infantry party was placed to provide supporting fire. Park led two platoons in the operation, directing each man up the 20-metre cliff. Once they were assembled at the top, he personally led these men as they went forward, yelling and with fixed bayonets.

Sergeant Max Finlayson (MM) went ahead at a crucial moment, throwing grenades that killed two Japanese in foxholes. He was wounded in the shoulder and fell, but recovered and resumed the lead. He threw more grenades, and with his Owen shot dead a Japanese running from a foxhole. In this key fight, the Australians lost two killed, the Japanese 26. Finlayson, a farm hand from Ulmarra, New South Wales, who was unemployed on enlistment, would in June be promoted to lieutenant but would also be hospitalised with 'anxiety state' in August. Park, a jackeroo from nearby Manilla, received a Distinguished Service Order for his fine work at 'Jap Knoll': a rare honour for a lieutenant. He rose to lieutenant-colonel in the postwar CMF and represented Tamworth in the NSW parliament.

Firing a machine gun on 2 April, two Japanese hidden in a camouflaged weapon pit under a fallen tree were able to wound four Australians leading the advance. Private Alexander Webb (MM) ran forward, leapt across the tree and killed both. He then turned and fired on two other enemy pits sited further back, thus allowing his section to push on. Standing over 6 feet tall, Webb was a NSW farmer and had several times been in trouble with the authorities since enlisting: a court martial had found him guilty in 1943 of 'using insubordinate language to a superior officer'. He was wounded in an accident with a grenade the day after the 2 April fight, and left the Army later that year with 'anxiety state'. On 5 April, Tokuku Pass fell to 2/2nd and 2/3rd battalion troops coming from both sides.

During its advance, the 2/3rd Battalion received news from locals that a Japanese divisional headquarters and its commanding general were just east of Wonginara Mission. Two companies were sent on 2 April to capture this headquarters. Lieutenant Jim Copeman (MC), who won a Military Medal in Syria, commanded the leading platoon, which he manoeuvred undetected to within 10 metres of the enemy's defences. Calling on his men, he then led a charge up a steep incline against the Japanese positions. Even when the enemy opened fire, Copeman stood at his full height, directing the assault of the two forward sections and then leading his reserve section in a decisive assault. Five Japanese officers were among the 28 enemy

Lieutenant Jim Copeman (left) and Private Ken Colbert after returning from patrol in the Torricellis in April 1945. Copeman earned a Military Cross that month, while Colbert earned the Distinguished Conduct Medal in June.
AWM 090443

soldiers killed around the headquarters, but the general escaped. This ended Japanese resistance around Wonginara.

Hayfield heroes

After the fall of Maprik, an airstrip built to the south, 'Hayfield', began receiving transport aircraft, thus allowing troops and heavy equipment to be brought in. A road was constructed to and beyond Maprik. In the subsequent May–June advance, the 2/6th Battalion's Sergeant Jack Daniel (DCM) was outstanding. Prior to an attack on Wombak 2, he led reconnaissance patrols to gather vital preliminary information. In the attack itself on 15 May, this laconic shearer from Holbrook commanded the flanking section, which captured vital ground. In aggressive patrols in the aftermath, he went into the enemy's main defences, killing four Japanese. Before an attack on a similarly strong position at Dombuir on 2 June, he led a five-and-a-half-hour patrol, killing a sentry on the track and a sniper, and then another three enemies during the main assault. Daniel commanded a platoon for most of the campaign and later paid tribute to his men. 'I got recognition, which I'm sure should have been credited to the fine band of fellows I had with me', he said, before naming ten of them from four states. In June 1943, Daniel had won a Military Medal with the same platoon at Nassau Bay, where in protecting American signallers and infantry he killed two Japanese with grenades, stalked and killed a sniper and braved heavy fire to carry a wounded Australian to safety. As a younger soldier he had been in trouble several times for being AWL (1940, 1941 and 1943); had failed a course on artillery instruction; been hospitalised with enteritis in the Middle East, dengue in New Guinea, malaria in Australia; and twice suffered accidental injuries. He also rose from private to sergeant and was selected for the London Victory March Contingent in 1946. His decorations had to be replaced at his own cost after being destroyed by fire in 1952.

Sergeant Jack Daniel DCM, MM was a laconic shearer who despite much ill-health proved an outstanding leader and patroller.
AWM 018695

Gunners of the 2/1st Anti-Tank Regiment were formed into an infantry company under Captain Clifford Johnson (MC) to protect Hayfield and patrol far to the south. Around 17 May, Johnson took a fighting patrol to confront 20 Japanese who were reportedly advancing on Hayfield. After making a reconnaissance, he took the patrol within 15 metres of the village where the Japanese were based and ordered an attack. His artillerymen-turned-infantrymen initially lacked confidence but Johnson's encouragement, direction and personal courage inspired them to push on, employing a frontage about 50 metres wide. When at one point an enemy LMG opened up, wounding two men, Johnson used his Owen to kill the two crewmen and silence their Nambu. As darkness came on, he ordered a withdrawal, though he personally moved further into the village, where he set fire to huts to destroy any enemy equipment they contained. Johnson's bravery had been apparent in Greece, where after commanding anti-tank guns at Tempe, he escaped German imprisonment and returned to Turkey. A member of the regular Army, he finished his career a major in 1966.

Johnson led another attack on 24 May, this time on 37 Japanese defending two positions at Mikau. Just before the main attack was due to go in before dawn, an Owen discharged accidentally, so the main attack force formed a defensive perimeter. However, the secondary assault force took the Owen shot as a signal to attack, and did so. Potential disaster was averted thanks largely to fine work with a Bren by Gunner Harry Kitching (MM), who first dashed into a large hut and wiped out the enemy firing from it and then moved forward through heavy bush to locate and kill a Japanese sniper. With the supporting party having taken its objective, the main body then attacked. It too was successful, finding 30 abandoned packs and rifles. When fire from three enemy strongpoints slowed the advance, Bombardier Frank Reed (MM) rushed forward alone and quickly silenced two by killing the occupants with grenades and his Owen. Calling on his men, he then led the attack on the third strongpoint, which had inflicted casualties on his section, and destroyed it. On

3 June, enemy rifle fire killed Reed, a labourer from Yass, six days before headquarters approved his award.

Warriors at Wewak

The coastal advance continued with hard fighting in enervating conditions. Heat, rain, hills and disease were again constants, though newly issued camp stretchers and half-tent shelters made life easier. A Japanese mortar killed five 2/1st Battalion men on 15 April in the Karawop plantation. The next day, the battalion was ordered to take a feature overlooking the plantation. The leading platoon came under fire, but after Australian artillery shelled the peak, a section moved up the spur to reach the top. In doing so, they entered a cut fire lane, down which a Woodpecker started shooting. Several Australians were hit, one fatally. Private Harry Bartholomew (MM) quickly stepped into the open and, firing his Bren from the hip, stormed the gun. He shot dead the gunner, after which the rest of the crew fled. Bartholomew's ammunition was now exhausted, but he manned the Woodpecker and turned it on the retreating Japanese, killing one and wounding another. The platoon reached its objective. Bartholomew, a young Sydney moulder, had often been in trouble with the authorities for misdemeanours such as not cleaning his rifle, absence without leave, losing equipment and not appearing on parade. He was also often evacuated ill but proved his worth on this day.

With tank support, the 16th Brigade crossed the Hawain River on 27 April. For the loss of 85 dead, its battalions had killed 909 Japanese. The 19th Brigade now took over the advance, with orders to proceed to Cape Wom, and from there attack Wewak, the main goal of the campaign, from the west. At the same time, Australian troops would make an amphibious landing some 15 kilometres east of Wewak as part of a 623-strong 'Farida Force', formed expressly for this operation. The offensive would receive support from nearly all

Private Harry Bartholomew, MM, had often been in trouble for minor misdemeanours. In April 1945, he used his Bren gun and a captured Japanese machine gun to help seize Japanese high ground near Karawop.
AWM 091176

the 6th Division's artillery. The 2/4th Battalion faced no organised opposition on the way to Wewak, which it attacked before dawn on 10 May with artillery and tank support. The main Japanese forces were retreating from Wewak, but a strong rearguard remained. The normally restrained official history called the Australians' work of that morning 'brilliant', and a large part of the credit went to Captain Geoff Hawke (MC), who commanded the leading company. He expected fire from a known enemy machine-gun post soon after crossing the start-line (a series of masked torches), but as he moved forward with his troops, he arranged for one of his own machine guns to silence it. When the company reached open ground, it again came under fire from another machine gun in a bunker. Hawke led a charge that overran this emplacement. Enemy artillery fire caused casualties among the Australians, but with support from two tanks, Hawke led his men through these explosions to their objective, a knoll at the neck of Wewak Point. Hawke, a 31-year-old accountant from Inverell, was a veteran of all the battalion's campaigns, and his marksmanship had won him the nickname 'Hawkeye'.

Lieutenant Kim McMaster (MC) of the 2/4th Armoured Regiment was a ground controller accompanying the three Matilda tanks of the leading troop on foot. Using a walkie-talkie he directed them along the steep, bomb-cratered track. It was touch and go whether the 'old girls' would make it to the high ground from which to support the infantry. McMaster then speedily directed the Matildas' fire against any opposition. Five other members of the regiment helped in this ground control work that day, their squadron's first large-scale action of the war. One of them, Sergeant Angus 'Mac' Walker (MID), controlled a troop that took on and knocked out a 20mm gun, a Woodpecker and a Nambu and killed six Japanese. When his walkie-talkie stopped working, Walker used a telephone on the tank's rear. That broke down too, so he ended up on the tank, directing it via the pistol port.

By 8 am the Australians had taken Wewak Point, and then turned to clear Japanese from surrounding tunnels, caves and bunkers. More than 100 were killed, many of them blown up in caves from which they would not surrender. The Australians lost just two killed and captured Wewak Airfield the following day, killing another 80 Japanese in the process.

To the west, at Yarabos, Japanese ambushed a patrol of the 2/1st Anti-Tank Regiment from the front and flank, killing three and wounding the commander and all NCOs except one. That man was Sergeant Jim Leitch (MM), a short 31-year-old labourer from Yackandandah. He was also a veteran member of the 2/8th Battalion, who had impressed during training courses and been attached to the Anti-Tank Regiment to help as an infantry instructor. He now came into his own, taking command of the patrol, reorganising it and leading it in a charge that broke through the ambush. For ten hours the patrol was in enemy territory, contacting the Japanese on four separate occasions. Locals provided carriers and guides to help them home, but it was largely thanks to Leitch's cool courage and leadership that the patrol, including the wounded, returned safely. A later patrol sent to find the Australian dead confirmed that Leitch's party had killed 21 Japanese.

Further south, the 2/11th Battalion, while seeking to block the Japanese retreat from Wewak, moved through a swamp towards dominating hills. They fought their hardest battle of the campaign at the 710 Feature on 15 May. Forty Japanese of the 51st Airborne Battalion were determined to hold this jungle-clad position and had four fast-firing aircraft machine guns to supplement their Woodpecker and two Nambus. The initial attack foundered, but after a second round of artillery fire, the Australians attacked again. Despite extremely heavy enemy fire, Corporal Humphrey McLennan (MID) and his section were able to crawl forward and gain a foothold on the feature, from where they could suppress the posts holding up the rest of his platoon. At heavy cost, three platoons occupied the feature. After 30 minutes of bloody fighting, they were on top of the 710 Feature. Four men had been killed, 18 wounded – about one-third of the attacking force. The Japanese then launched a Banzai charge from a neighbouring knoll, led by an officer wielding a sword and carrying a shotgun. He was hit immediately by many shots, and the other 15 or so attackers were all killed within a minute. For the many wounded Australians who needed to be stretchered to medical attention, a 12-hour carry down steep slopes followed. Captain Colin Bayly (MC) commanded the attack on the 710 Feature. The planning, organisation, direction of the battle and personal courage of this Perth accountant won widespread admiration. In the first, unsuccessful assault, 38-year-old Private Hugh Grant (MM) distinguished himself by leaving cover to rescue a Bren gunner hit by enemy machine-gun fire. The position was under enemy observation, but having rescued his mate, the Scottish-born Grant went forward again and recovered the Bren. During the successful assault, Grant received a gunshot wound to the neck. When taken to safety he refused medical aid, instead helping to make stretchers for the more seriously wounded until he collapsed.

On 11 May, Farida Force, based mainly on the 6th Division Cavalry Regiment, landed east of Wewak and marched west. At Wewak, 19th Brigade troops were embroiled in hard fighting at Wirui Mission, a steep kunai-covered hill nearly 100 metres high and overlooking the airfield. Supported by tanks, the 2/4th Battalion attacked on 14 May. The approach was only wide enough for one tank at a time, and as the first approached the foremost enemy position, a Japanese machine-gun crew in a nearby pit opened fire, hitting the commander of the leading infantry section. The tank commander could not see three Japanese moving forward from the pit with land mines, hoping to immobilise the lead tank. Thinking quickly, Private William Burton (MM) took charge, leading the section to the pit and killing the tank-attack party before they could detonate their mines. The 2/4th captured the hill's eastern slopes and summit that day, but Japanese continued firing from three bunkers on the north-western slopes.

The next day, as a 2/4th Battalion company advanced on these bunkers, several men were hit and the leading section became pinned down. Just 50 metres from the bunkers, Private Ted Kenna (VC) stood up in the kunai, in full view of enemy machine gunners, and fired his Bren at them. Eventually he called for a rifle, with which he was a superb shot, and silenced the enemy post with four rounds. Then, taking the Bren again, he eliminated a second post about 65 metres away. Another remarkable effort was that of Captain Phil 'Blah' Smith (MC). He commanded the company tasked with capturing the hill. He skilfully used artillery support to enable his men to advance close to the barrage, so they sustained few casualties. He risked his life by intentionally exposing himself to enemy machine-gun fire to locate their positions and bring down supporting fire. By war's end, the 31-year-old former oil company representative was one of only two of the 2/4th's original members still in the battalion. He was also awarded an MBE in 1943 and was Mentioned in Despatches. The 2/4th's RMO, Captain Owen Williams (MBE), had a policy of working as far forward as possible to help the wounded, going to them rather than waiting for them to be brought to him. This policy saved at least one life on 15 May. On 3 July, Williams was shot dead after rushing to the aid of a young reinforcement following an ambush. Williams' death saddened his entire battalion.

When a tank knocked out the third and last post at the Wirui Mission on 15 May, the 2/4th and 2/11th forces met, having secured the Wewak coastal plain. The 2/8th Battalion now took Boram village and on 22 May linked with Farida Force. That force's advance had met relatively light resistance. On 22 May, though, Acting Sergeant Don Warren (MM) of the 2/9th Cavalry Commando Squadron demonstrated exceptional courage when his unit attacked an enemy-occupied knoll near Brandi Plantation. He insisted on being the forward scout whenever his section patrolled – a fact reflected in the MID he received for this campaign – and now went alone to within 5 metres of enemy positions before killing two defenders with grenades and forcing the survivors to retreat. On 23 May, during another attack, he crawled forward under fire and made a lone assault on the crew of a 20mm gun. Using grenades, he killed four and the remainder fled. Warren, a Queenslander, had turned 21 the previous week.

On 24 May, as the 2/4th patrolled near Koigin, Private Randy

Duvanel (DCM) was forward scout. Formerly a member of the 2/22nd Battalion, he had escaped from Rabaul nursing a hatred of the Japanese. While moving ahead of the patrol he came under fire from six enemies. Without calling for help, Duvanel attacked them, killing or wounding five. The sixth fled. Later the patrol entered Koigin village, where members of Duvanel's section began cutting Japanese signal wires. Suddenly, three Japanese charged at them with fixed bayonets. Again, Duvanel took the initiative, intercepting and killing all three.

After conquering Feature 710, the 2/11th continued its dangerous and gruelling advance through the mountains, especially around Feature 770. On 22 May, they attempted to clear a Japanese pocket near Klewalin village, sending one platoon along the track towards it and another around behind it. The lead section of the flanking platoon was halted by Japanese firing two machine guns and rifles from well-concealed foxholes. Sergeant Pat Fogarty (DCM), a 38-year-old locomotive fireman, stepped forward and engaged this group with his Owen from a standing position, killing two and preventing the others from firing accurately. After 15 minutes, a flamethrower arrived and overcame the last resistance. Fogarty's platoon continued its advance. In subsequent fighting he received a perforating gunshot wound to the left arm and fractured ulna from a Nambu round. Fogarty refused to be evacuated until his men were safe and then made his own way back. When discharged from the Army on medical grounds in July 1946, Fogarty was described as having scars across his stomach and back, missing two fingers on his right hand (presumably prewar), and no fewer than seven medical conditions!

Private Jimmy Gilpin (MM) was in Fogarty's platoon on 22 May. He relished being forward scout and, like Fogarty, seemed at home in the jungle. When Fogarty's section first struck trouble, Gilpin's section had still not made contact, but the young millhand took it upon himself to move to the flank and crawl up to the enemy defences. From there he killed four Japanese. When the attack was held up later that day, again he moved out alone, crawled to within 2 metres of the enemy and killed six more, including a machine-gun crew. Gilpin, who stood just 5 feet 5½ inches tall, then reconnoitred the area, obtaining information that allowed accurate shelling. By late afternoon, the Japanese had abandoned their defences. Over subsequent days, the 2/11th drove them from other strongpoints, including Feature 770.

Final shots

The campaign entered its final stage at the end of May. The Japanese had lost all their coastal bases and retreated inland to the mountains. To their west was the 17th Brigade, to their north the rest of the 6th Division. Nevertheless, the Japanese were still organised, determined and holding eminently defensible positions.

The 17th Brigade was encountering more elaborate mountain defences. For more than a month there was a shortage of bombs for the supporting aircraft, but artillery, aircraft and the newly arrived 2nd New Guinea Battalion assisted the brigade to drive the Japanese from successive features. An important battle occurred on 8 July at Ulupu, a pivot of the Japanese defence and an area the defenders had been told to defend to the death. Tunnels connected its many weapon pits, pillboxes and bunkers. Key roles in the attack fell to two platoon commanders, Lieutenants Bruce McDonald (MC) and Ken Newton (MC). Both had joined the 2/5th Battalion just three weeks earlier, having graduated from the Royal Military College, Duntroon, the previous December. McDonald, commanding the lead platoon, moved ahead and destroyed two pillboxes with grenades. When his platoon was held up by a concealed machine gun, he crawled across the open towards it. Though wounded, the 20-year-old silenced the gun with grenades. McDonald had a distinguished postwar military career, serving in Korea, Malaya and Vietnam and rising to major-general. Just as McDonald's career could have been cut short at Ulupu, so could Newton's, for he too crossed open ground towards an enemy machine gun. A Woodpecker in a bunker was holding up the attack, and he charged it, firing his Owen until he had killed the crew. When Newton was wounded, Sergeant Jim Regan (MM) took his place. In the build-up to the attack, Regan had led a patrol that killed about ten Japanese. He had also been an outstandingly efficient and devoted Bren gunner at Mount Tambu in 1943. Now, with most leaders around him wounded, Regan pressed home the final attacks that left 28 enemy dead and their main positions occupied. On 12 July, a firefight lasting five or six hours was required to end the enemy's organised resistance in the area. Private Tom Smith (DCM) destroyed the occupants of several weapon pits and killed a Nambu crew who were delaying the advance. Smith, a Sydney machinist, had already impressed mightily on a patrol of 4 July, when he had silenced an enemy pillbox with grenades and, firing in the open, shot dead the defenders of two other strongpoints. He had been hospitalised with a hand injury just two months earlier. This was his first campaign. He was promoted to lance-corporal on 13 July, one of the new generation of soldiers stepping forward in these final campaigns. A high proportion of the few remaining older soldiers were becoming battle casualties.

After Ulupu fell, the 17th Brigade advanced rapidly. The 2nd New Guinea Battalion constantly harassed the Japanese further south, killing up to 30 a day. Corporal Diti (GM) achieved a remarkable feat on 23 June. During torrential rains, four white members of the battalion became marooned on a truck in the middle of a rising river. Diti saw one swept away to his death but was not deterred from rushing into the torrent and bringing an NCO to safety through the flood. He went back twice more, each time bringing in a soldier. On the third trip, Diti and his helpless charge were twice struck by debris and swept downstream, but they made it ashore. This battalion's heaviest engagement occurred on 30 July at Ulama. A preliminary airstrike killed 21 Japanese but the survivors fought hard. A Japanese machine-gun crew soon killed a platoon sergeant and seriously wounded another man in the lead platoon, which became pinned down. The platoon commander, Lieutenant Gordon Stewart (MC), crawled forward and threw a grenade at the machine gun, which then swung around at him. He silenced it with two more grenades.

The advance continued but enemy fire soon wounded another officer, who fell in open ground covered by a Nambu. Stewart again went forward, under fire, and dragged the officer into a bomb crater. Finding his field dressing inadequate to dress the wound, Stewart carried his fellow officer to shelter and treatment. Stewart, a 31-year-old bank officer from Beecroft, then rejoined the attack.

Clifford Johnson led his anti-tank men in another highly successful attack on 28 July, when he spearheaded a 27-strong fighting patrol in a charge on unsuspecting Japanese in a fortified village, Jama. About ten Japanese died in the first rush, Johnson himself wreaking havoc with a Bren. By the time the Australians withdrew, they had lost four dead – including their second-in-command, Lieutenant John Storrie – and two wounded, but they had killed 32 Japanese.

By 8 August, the 17th Brigade had captured a major base at Kiarivu. The Japanese strength in the ranges, it was later discovered, was twice that of the Australians who were pushing them back so effectively.

The main body of the 6th Division had also been embroiled in mountain fighting, south of Wewak. On 1–2 June, the 2/3rd Battalion attacked a dominant height, Hill 910. When Captain John McCrackan (MC) and Corporal Ken Colbert (DCM) reconnoitred the defences on 1 June, they came under fire from 11 enemy positions, including three concealed bunkers commanding the main track. The following day, McCrackan received a bad leg wound while directing his platoons, but the 36-year-old Kokoda veteran remained on duty. Colbert personally charged one bunker, wiping out its machine-gun crew garrison with his Owen and then directing his section in silencing another bunker.

When the leading section commander and three of his men fell wounded in the fight for Hill 910, stretcher-bearer Private Chris Batten (DCM) went to them. Though grazed by bullets, he dressed their wounds and supervised their evacuation on a two-and-a-half-hour carry. Several men owed their lives to this 5-foot-3-inches-tall labourer from Redfern. They included another section commander who, on 6 May, lay wounded in a position exposed to enemy fire during a patrol. It appeared impossible to reach him without being hit, but Batten calmly dressed his wounds and carried him to safety. Behind the lines, Batten had several times been in trouble, especially for being AWL.

Shiburangu and Tazaki

The 19th Brigade was assigned the capture of two crucial heights, Mount Tazaki and Mount Shiburangu, which dominated the routes into the mountains and where the Japanese had placed battalion-strength rearguards. The ground was unsuited to tanks, and approaches to both features were along razorback ridges punctuated by knolls held by Japanese armed with heavy machine guns – often from damaged aircraft. The advancing Australians could call upon powerful artillery and air support, though this did not deter the surviving Japanese from fighting back.

The 2/8th was ordered to capture Mount Shiburangu, which first necessitated the seizure of features called Hill 1 and Hill 2. At Hill 1, Private Bill Bassula (MM) played a leading part. Bassula was one of five sons of Greek immigrants. After enlisting at 18 he had been charged with at least 15 offences, been court-martialled and acquired the nickname 'Wicked Will'. On 11 June he was one of five in the leading section advancing up the steep Hill 1. When this section reached the top, fire from an enemy post wounded three and pinned the survivors. Bassula ran through this fire and silenced the post. He then directed a second section to cover the rest of the platoon as it manoeuvred to eliminate another strongpoint. In capturing Hill 1, the Australians killed 33 Japanese. It then took a five-hour battle to clear Hill 2.

On 27 June, the attack went in on Mount Shiburangu, preceded by a 3000-round artillery bombardment and heavy air attack. Machine-gun fire pinned down two of the three leading platoons, but the third, under Lieutenant Jim Trethowan (MC), effected a flanking manoeuvre via a deep re-entrant. After climbing 100 metres up an exposed 60-degree slope, they surprised the enemy from the rear, capturing a Woodpecker in the first bunker before it could open fire. Within an hour of beginning their climb, they were on top of Mount Shiburangu, having captured all but one position. They threw seven grenades into this surviving bunker, but before dying, its three inmates inflicted the platoon's one fatality, Private Mick Smith. Trethowan, a 32-year-old farmhand from Donnybrook, had been lucky: three bullets had pierced his clothing, a fourth his hat. The Australians captured at least 20 and as many as 50 bunkers on Mount Shiburangu.

The 2/4th Battalion began its assault on Mount Tazaki on 22 June. Two days later they had taken its main crest, but Japanese continued to fight in the surrounding area. Sergeant Bill Wells (DCM), one of the few originals still in the 2/4th, repeatedly exposed himself to enemy fire here to pinpoint enemy machine guns; he also killed many Japanese.

Selby Dean, who had won a Distinguished Conduct Medal at Heraklion and was now a lieutenant, was wounded in the thigh while fending off one of many Japanese night raids. In that fight on 7 July, the battalion sustained its last fatal casualty of the war, Lance-Corporal Frank Hood. The 30-year-old construction foreman had just returned from hospital, where he had been recovering from a wound. He was given the option of staying with the company rather than going out to Dean's platoon position but decided to go as an extra man to keep guard. Hood represented the countless Australian soldiers whose self-sacrifice received no official recognition.

The 16th Brigade relieved the 19th in late July. On 4 August, the 2/2nd Battalion sought to capture Rindogim, a village situated on a narrow ridge rising 150 metres above the surrounding country and approachable only by a track following a steep narrow spur. The leading platoon had climbed some 30 metres when concealed Japanese opened fire with rifles and machine guns. The platoon sergeant, Allan Donnet (DCM), was bringing up the rear, but as soon as the enemy opened fire, on his own initiative he moved forward. Seeing that the platoon commander and foremost section were pinned down, he ordered the reserve section to a flank, where they could suppress the enemy. He then made a lone charge at the enemy, hurling grenades into their foxholes and firing repeated bursts from his Owen. After Donnet killed four Japanese, the remaining 25 or so turned and ran. He then called his platoon to follow him, and although his calls attracted enemy fire, they reached a knoll that dominated Rindogim village. Lieutenant Alex Lochhead, who had won a Military Medal early in the Kokoda fighting, took his platoon forward and captured the village. Donnet, who turned 24 that day, was on enlistment a 'farmer's assistant' from Gulargambone. He was frequently evacuated ill with influenza, scarlet fever, ancylostomiasis (hookworm infection) and especially malaria. He later named his farm after Rindogim.

The battalions of the 6th Division were now at only about half-strength in riflemen. They were also short of officers. In this long, physically demanding and stressful campaign, the Australians sustained about 450 killed, the Japanese about 9000! The Japanese also lost 7700 square kilometres to the Australians. The men of the 6th Division and their military and political masters had doubted the necessity of the campaign, making the courage of the Australians who risked everything pushing forward over awful terrain against a tenacious enemy even more remarkable.

CHAPTER 21

NEW BRITAIN: THE FEW IMPRISON THE MANY

In October 1944, the 5th Australian Division began arriving on New Britain to relieve the 40th American Division based at the island's western end. The main Japanese forces were concentrated in the Gazelle Peninsula at the eastern end and especially at Rabaul, Japan's chief base in the South Pacific. In the mountainous land between these forces, Australians of the AIB, assisted by patrols of locals, were already fighting a guerrilla war.

Japanese strength was estimated at 38 000 but was actually about 93 000. In mid-1944, Captain Basil Fairfax-Ross (MID) was given command of AIB forces on the south coast and ordered to clear the Japanese all the way from the enemy's westernmost outpost at Montagu Bay to Henry Reid Bay, 150 kilometres away at the neck of the Gazelle Peninsula. In addition, he was to contain the Japanese within that peninsula, to gather intelligence, aid downed airmen, and win and maintain the support of the 'natives' – demanding tasks for a force comprising just five officers, ten Australian NCOs and 140 armed locals. Fairfax-Ross, or 'Fax', was a wise choice. The intelligent and articulate 34-year-old had worked as a plantation inspector at Rabaul, and served with the 2/12th Battalion in the Middle East. After transferring to field intelligence work, he served behind enemy lines on the New Guinea mainland in 1943, where he was wounded. For his work on New Britain he would be twice Mentioned in Despatches and receive the American Medal of Freedom.

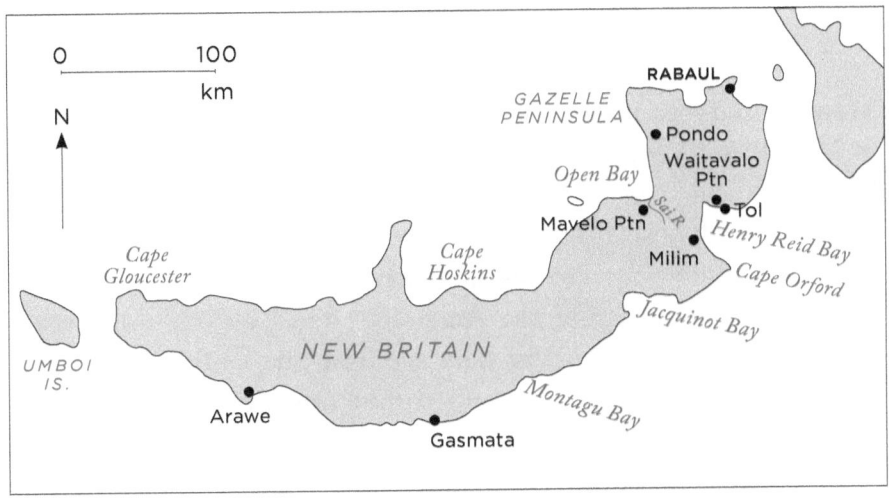

New Britain

One of his able NCOs was Sergeant John Gilmore (DCM), who at the outbreak of war worked on his family's plantation in New Britain. In February 1944, he led a patrol of 14 'natives' 50 kilometres into the island's north around Pondo, despite the area being occupied by the enemy and by hostile locals who had betrayed other whites to the Japanese. Though hunted by numerous patrols and surrounded, Gilmore's skilful bushcraft enabled him to escape into the mountains to the south-east. In that area in March 1944, though suffering starvation, the six-foot-tall Gilmore led a party that rescued an airman downed near Cape Orford. They carried him to safety across precipitous, enemy-patrolled terrain. By April 1945, Gilmore was a lieutenant.

On 4 November 1944, when the Australian 5th Division's 6th Brigade landed at Jacquinot Bay, Fairfax-Ross and his men could reflect proudly that there were no Japanese forces on the coast south of Henry Reid Bay.

The 5th Division takes on five divisions

Between October 1944 and February 1945, the 5th Division arrived in New Britain, with all landing at Jacquinot Bay except the 36th Battalion, which went to Cape Hoskins on the north coast and patrolled assiduously for the next seven months. In the meantime, the equivalent of five Japanese divisions took no action, merely standing idle at Rabaul. Ironically, the Australian division's role was largely to limit the movement of the Japanese from the Gazelle Peninsula, while gathering information and eliminating as many as possible with harassing patrols and advances.

On the south coast, the Australians progressed rapidly, and in late February were ordered to capture the Waitavalo–Tol area. Australians had been massacred there in 1942. The 19th Battalion, fighting its first campaign, crossed the wide and fast-flowing Wulwut River and then fought for successive hills in the rainforest. On 6 March, a company under Captain Darcy Stainlay (MC) captured Cake Hill. Stainlay was a lieutenant with the notorious 53rd Battalion in Papua in 1942 – a fact omitted in the official history's biography – and served with the 2/3rd Battalion before joining the 19th in late 1943. This secretary from Murwillumbah had brought his company to a high level of training, and having no second-in-command on New Britain, was constantly with the foremost troops on patrol and during advances.

Artillery support from the 2/14th Field Regiment helped substantially at Cake Hill, but thereafter the dense rainforest made it hard to direct effectively. The Japanese used mortars, which had registered all the tracks along which the Australians were advancing and were hidden in caves that made it hard for the Australian artillery to hit them. Some of these mortars had been modified to fire 150mm shells.

On 10 March, there was a hard fight over what became known as Young's Hill. When Japanese machine-gun fire pinned down the lead platoon, Lieutenant Ray Young (MC) led his platoon to the flank. As they prepared to attack, machine-gun fire and grenades were directed at Young's men too, inflicting casualties. A grenade wounded Young in the right chest and forearm, but he led the men forward, personally grenading enemy posts on the way. His platoon killed several Japanese, captured one Woodpecker and two Nambus, and enabled the company to seize the position. Though in great pain, Young stayed with his men as the position was consolidated. In the end, this tall 31-year-old insurance agent from Tweed Heads had to be ordered out by his company commander. He was hospitalised for nearly two months.

After Young's Hill was captured, Young's platoon was relieved and the rest of the company advanced along a narrow saddle towards a nearby knoll. Two platoons became pinned down by fire they estimated as coming from seven machine guns. The third platoon, though, under Lieutenant Lionel Perry (MC), continued unobserved on the right. It swept the Japanese from a previously unknown position (later called Perry's Knoll) and then drove the enemy from the defences holding up their company. Like Young and others in the 19th, 32-year-old Perry had earlier served in the Darwin Infantry Battalion.

The Japanese lost 13 dead in the fights for Young's Hill and Perry's Knoll and another 25 in a forlorn charge against the latter position that evening. Throughout that day, Major Adam Armstrong (MC, MID) commanded the company that seized Young's and Perry's with skill, energy and courage. His company sustained 23 casualties that day, and the companies that took their place suffered losses from mortars. By 13 March, the surviving Japanese in the area had retreated to Bacon's Hill, and the 14th/32nd Battalion relieved the 19th for the purpose of assaulting that feature.

Two companies of the 14th/32nd attacked at 10 am on 16 March. Heavy fire halted one company, but a platoon under Lieutenant John Pugh (MC) avoided enemy detection for most of the day and advanced north of Bacon's Hill. Pugh, a short Melbourne insurance clerk, took over the company when its commander was wounded. According to his citation, Pugh 'penetrated into an enemy kitchen and shot the cook', a most unusual incident.

On 17 March, in pouring rain, the two companies, now under Captain Reg Jack (MID), again attacked the 180-metre-high morass that was Bacon's Hill. In this action, Jack seemed to lead a charmed life, as at times he lay in the open directing his men while heavy mortar bombs landed all around. Pugh was seen leading and encouraging his men too. Sergeant Royce Abbey (DCM) was commanding a platoon in the absence of its wounded officer, and when enemy automatic fire halted his men, Abbey went forward alone and found a position from which his Brens could neutralise it, before calling the men forward section by section and directing their fire. This Melbourne clerk repeated this routine later in the attack and personally killed at least two defenders. He was commissioned in September. After the war, Abbey was a successful businessman and philanthropist, President of International Rotary (1988–89), Officer of the Order of Australia (1988) and Victorian of the Year (1989). Through his efforts and those around him on Bacon's Hill on 17 March 1945, 30 Japanese defenders fled the double-pronged Australian attack, which cost the Australians 23 casualties.

On 18 March, a few enemy positions remained in the area. Japanese mortar fire intensified, probably as they were firing off what ammunition remained. More than 80 rounds fell along the one precipitous track that carried the infantry and artillery signal lines, which were severed. Gunners Bob Allan (MM) and Keith Millstead (MM) went out to the lines and, under this terrible pre-registered fire, repaired the repeated breaks. This enabled artillery to be brought to bear on the mortars. Allan, a pastry cook, and Millstead, a factory worker, both from Melbourne, had each been in trouble for three military misdemeanours, especially for going AWL. Corporal Bill Martin (MM) and his section were advancing up one spur when three enemy strongposts suddenly fired on them. Yelling 'They can't do that to me!', Martin jumped up, firing his Owen and throwing grenades. He drove the Japanese out of their three strongpoints, killing five before a grenade wounded him in the left eye. He would eventually lose the eye, but the Melbourne textile worker's one-man assault opened a gap through which the final attack on Bacon's Hill was launched. That afternoon, the hill was clear. The Japanese abandoned the Waitavalo–Tol area. Four months of patrolling followed, as the 5th Division had completed its main task of moving to the neck of the Gazelle Peninsula. It had lost 42 killed and 122 wounded, and counted 206 Japanese dead. As Long put it, one understrength Australian division imprisoned an entire Japanese army in Rabaul.

CHAPTER 22

BORNEO I: TARAKAN AND NORTH BORNEO

While operations on Bougainville, New Britain and at Aitape–Wewak were conducted to free American troops for operations elsewhere, General MacArthur stated that I Australian Corps (7th and 9th divisions) would be engaged in the main Allied advance. Australians long expected MacArthur to employ this corps in the Philippines, but early in 1945, he persuaded Australian civil and military leaders to accept that these elite troops should take Borneo. The 9th Division would capture Tarakan Island in Dutch Borneo and the Brunei Bay area of British (North) Borneo, while the 7th Division would take Balikpapan in Dutch Borneo. The strategic and political justifications for these operations, far from the decisive battles near Japan, were dubious, but many 9th and 7th division soldiers were sick of training on the Atherton Tablelands in Queensland. The island of Morotai, in the Moluccas, served as a base and launchpad for all three operations.

Tragic heroes of Tarakan

The capture of Tarakan Island was allocated to a brigade group based on the 26th Brigade. The landings were planned for 1 May 1945, 'P-Day'. Tarakan is 24 kilometres long and 18 kilometres wide, and constantly hot and humid. Just one bay – Lingkas Bay – was suitable

Borneo I: Tarakan and North Borneo

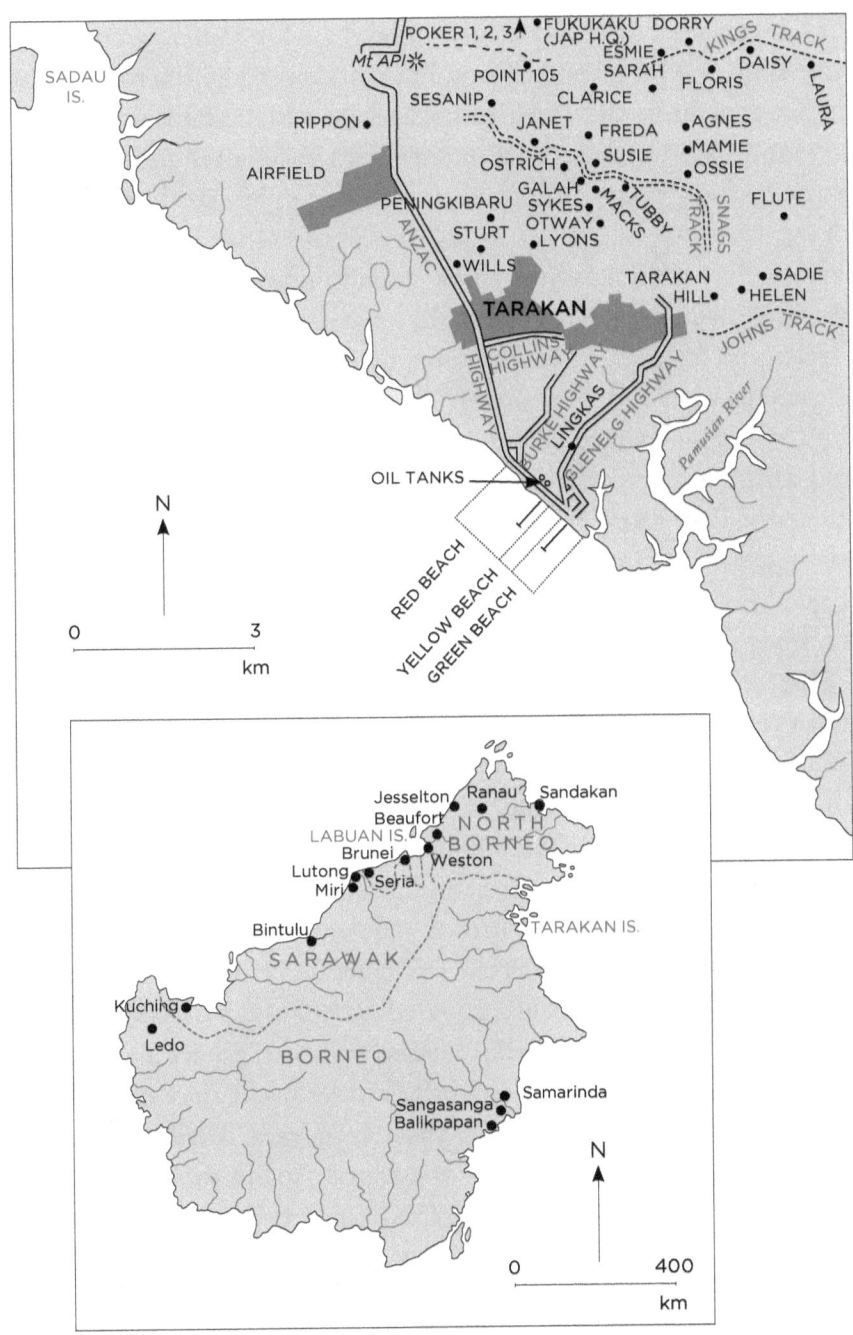

Borneo and Tarakan

for a large-scale landing, and the island's 2200 Japanese defenders were mainly concentrated around the airstrip and numerous inland jungle-clad hills and steep gullies. They had erected obstacles to any landing, stretching 150 metres from the shore, and including barbed wire, wooden posts and steel rails. On 30 April, following a heavy naval bombardment, detachments of 2/13th Field Company sappers left their landing ships in amphibious craft and began blowing 20-metre-wide gaps at the three beaches (designated Red, Green and Yellow). Fire from supporting artillery and ships kept the enemy's heads down, and aircraft laid an effective smokescreen, but the engineers faced a nerve-racking task. Working in morning and afternoon waves, they needed 780 explosive charges to clear the gaps. Primacord wire linked the charges laid on the obstacles so that each gap could be blown in one blast. The smokescreen limited Japanese interference to sporadic rifle and mortar shots, but mud bogged landing vehicles and slowed the sappers' movements. Lance-Sergeant John Nixon (MM) commanded a six-man demolition team set down late and at the wrong position on Red Beach. At 12.35 pm, after 75 minutes working in waist-deep mud, and under fire, they blew a gap, but were running nearly 30 minutes late and four steel rails remained uncut. Nixon's team was ordered to withdraw and to make a second attempt at 3 pm, but, doubtful that they could get back through the mud in time, he received permission to stay and finish the job. Mud had ruined their matches and fuse lighters, so Nixon struggled ashore and walked along the Japanese-held beach to a pier. At the end of the jetty he received fresh supplies from a landing craft. He returned the same way to the obstacles, then blew and signposted his gap. The landing craft tasked to evacuate his team was bogged, so he took them back along the pier and hailed another landing craft. Nixon had received a Commendation Card for gallantry at Alamein. A cabinet maker by trade, he had at times been a carpenter and bricklayer in the Army. He spent seven days in a detention barracks in England in 1940, apparently for disobeying an order, and his rank as an NCO went up and down.

Another demolition team, under Lance-Corporal RC 'Mick' Mace (MM), completed its tasks at Green Beach within 35 minutes. They then travelled by landing craft to help a team struggling to reach their objectives in the Yellow Beach mud. Mace tried to carry a line to an obstacle so he could secure it and enable the sappers to drag themselves forward, but he found himself shoulder-deep in quicksand-like slime and had to be dragged back 25 metres. Undaunted, he took his landing craft – despite enemy fire – to the pier and, after leading his team to the beach, approached the obstacles from that side. To return to the landing craft, he and his men had to lie flat on the mud and drag themselves to it with a line. Mace later said of this day, 'When you're a leading light, if you fall down on the job, everyone else does'. As a result, 'you've got to appear a bit blasé, even if you're sh---ing yourself'. Mace served in Malaya in the 1950s, when he received a British Empire Medal, and Vietnam in the 1970s. After retiring, he had to sell his medals to support his ailing wife.

Remarkably, the engineers sustained no casualties preparing the way for the landings of 1 May. Preceded by a tremendous bombardment, the landings faced no opposition on the beaches. The 2/23rd and 2/48th battalions pushed inland, followed by the 2/24th. As the 2/23rd moved beyond Tank Knoll, site of damaged oil tanks, they first entered thick vegetation then an open area a kilometre from the beach. Here their forward scout was shot dead and fire from a pillbox halted the leading company. When the company commander was wounded, Lieutenant Alan Head (MC) took charge. Tarakan was this former militia officer's first campaign. One of Head's best soldiers was Corporal Noel 'Nuts' Coventry, veteran of Alamein and Mentioned in Despatches in New Guinea. Determined to take this pillbox, after one failed attempt, Coventry and others threw grenades into it, killing 19 Japanese. Coventry inspired his company, but two days later he died from a sniper shot to the head.

The Australians had by the end of 1 May established a perimeter 1800 metres deep and 2500 metres wide. However, groups of Japanese remained hidden in the jungle within, and it was unsafe for support units on the beach to move far inland. The narrow, muddy beach and its few roads became chaotic.

On 2 May, the 2/24th attacked towards the main objective on Tarakan, the airstrip. The plan was to take it that day, but determined Japanese used natural and man-made defences to delay the Australians. The first obstacle was 'Wills', a fortified ridge overlooking 'Anzac Highway', a road running from Lingkas to the airfield.

A 2/24th company sought to capture this treeless 'feature', but some 20 Japanese in a concrete pillbox, a trench system and two large underground bunkers fought back. When his platoon commander was wounded, Sergeant Stanley 'Lofty' Wallis (MM), a 6-foot-tall 34-year-old labourer from Mildura and veteran of all the unit's campaigns, took over. A section leader was hit, but Private Edwin 'Snowy' Rodwell (MM), who had been in trouble with authorities at times and was in his first campaign, took the lead in silencing the pillbox with his Bren and grenades. By 8.35 am, Wallis's men had taken all of Wills except a large underground bunker, where the weapon slits could not be grenaded. A flamethrower was brought up, manned by Lieutenant Harry Freame. His father, also Harry Freame, had at Gallipoli won a Distinguished Conduct Medal and a reputation as an outstanding scout. After serving in the militia, joining the AIF and becoming a sergeant in the Provost Corps, in 1944 young Freame qualified as an officer at Duntroon and was sent to the 2/24th. He was just 5 feet 6 inches tall but weighed 190 pounds. He fired a long burst from the flamethrower through one slit. A screaming Japanese was killed fleeing the bunker. Other Japanese fired and threw grenades but could not stop Freame. More bursts ignited a huge explosion within the bunker, which then collapsed. Eleven dead Japanese lay inside. Freame never left Tarakan either: he died on 8 May when a Japanese infiltrator threw a fused shell into a hospital ward where Freame was resting after urgent dental treatment.

The 2/24th captured more ground on 2 May, but mines and machine-gun fire thwarted progress up the road. By nightfall, the airstrip was still Japanese.

The next morning, Captain Geoff Travis (MC) led his company against Airstrip Ridge. They had tank support, but mines and enemy fire stymied the advance and the Japanese set alight oil in ditches lining the highway. Travis moved in front of the tanks, directing their fire against Japanese pillboxes. Defying enemy machine-gun fire, snipers, and a 25mm anti-aircraft gun firing at close range, Travis led a platoon up the steep sides of the ridge. By 3.30 pm, the Australians controlled Airstrip Ridge. Travis, a 38-year-old station manager from Deniliquin, was an original of the 2/24th. The entire battalion was shocked to hear on 10 May that he had died while assisting tanks.

The fall of Airstrip Ridge on 3 May did not give the Australians the airstrip. Later that day, another 2/24th company advanced diagonally across the airfield towards Rippon Ridge, commanding the north-eastern end, but mines, machine guns and an artillery piece killed or wounded 12 and the unit withdrew.

Japanese firing from a feature further east called Peningkibaru were prohibiting Australian movement on the 'Anzac Highway', so a company was sent to silence them. On the razorback ridge overlooking the road, the Australians encountered eight bunkers and many foxholes, interconnected by 230 metres of trenches. The lead platoon took the first bunker in deadly fighting that involved a flamethrower bravely employed by Corporal Mal Good. Lieutenant Gerry Stretch (MC) led his platoon through that bunker and along the one-man wide trench. To maximise his firepower, he gathered the Owen gunners at the front, followed by the Bren gunners. Their intense firepower expedited the advance, until ammunition shortage and fouling of the guns in the oily ditches took effect. A fellow Western Australian farmer, Private Col Farmer (MM), supported Stretch. Farmer's was the last Bren still operating, and he used it to clear a bunker. As he pushed on, the weapon was shot from his hands. Though his left hand was now useless, he helped a wounded comrade to the rear.

Stretch was now the spearhead of a one-man front, and when he called for ammunition, the defenders launched a counterattack.

On 3 May 1945, Captain Geoff Travis (right) led his platoon in an advance on Tarakan while evading enemy machine-gun fire, snipers and this anti-aircraft gun, which reportedly fired 11 000 rounds. He is showing the gun to General Sir Thomas Blamey. Travis, a 38-year-old station manager, served in all the 2/24th Battalion's campaigns, but was killed in action on 10 May.
AWM 089776

Horatius-like, Stretch held them for a while, even though they looked to him like giants, and when the wounded had been gathered, the Australians withdrew. While Stretch held off the Japanese, Corporal Rex 'Dr Hackem' King (MM), the company's beloved senior stretcher-bearer, tended and evacuated the wounded. Later in the campaign, 36-year-old King would be wounded himself, reportedly in the backside, but stay on duty till all others were saved. A letter in his service record from his son, a Vietnam veteran, notes that King, a former schoolteacher, died poor in 1988.

When Stretch's platoon retreated, the platoon at the first bunker halted the counterattackers. Corporal Arthur 'Baldy' Wilson (MM) and his section bore the brunt of a fight lasting two hours. Wilson occupied exposed positions to help repel the attack and manned the Bren when his gunner was wounded.

On 5 May, the 2/24th found Rippon Ridge abandoned. The Australian flag was raised on the airfield, signifying that the brigade had achieved its main objective. The Japanese still held strongposts overlooking the airfield and town, and the Australians were ordered to take these positions and destroy Japanese forces in south Tarakan, thereby preventing the unlikely scenario of the enemy recapturing the airstrip.

In the attack on the airstrip, Corporal Noel Pearce (MM) of the 2/9th Armoured Regiment commanded the lead tank. His Matilda was often under fire, but he repeatedly dismounted to locate enemy positions and direct accurate fire. Late on 4 May, hearing of the losses in the advance across the airfield, he drove urgent medical supplies and water to a forward company and evacuated 12 wounded on his tank. He then repeated the journey and brought out another 17 casualties. This necessitated travelling the hazardous road in dusk and darkness, and he guided the tank on foot throughout. Pearce, who had enlisted in Burnie, Tasmania, in 1941 as a 19-year-old student teacher, was wounded in the buttock on 22 May and hospitalised for 38 days.

The advance fell behind schedule at the airfield and elsewhere because of strong Japanese resistance and the prevalence of mines and booby traps. By 4 May, the sappers and a small RAAF bomb disposal squad had disarmed more than 300 landmines and modified depth-charges, aerial bombs and booby traps. Engineers were needed to accompany infantry and tanks. Lieutenant Roland Brazier (MC) led a 2/13th Field Company platoon that cleared beach obstacles on 30 April, then lifted mines, 'deloused' booby traps, destroyed enemy tunnels and hideouts and repaired bomb craters. On 6 May, when tanks were held up on Snags Track, he took three men with hand tools to clear a detour. Brazier succeeded, though two of his men were wounded. Thanks largely to the sappers, only one tank was lost on Tarakan, when a mine lifted a Matilda into the air and turned it upside down on 9 May. The crew walked away uninjured.

On 5 May, another sapper, Corporal Joseph North (GM) of the Beach Group Engineers, responded when a truck carrying petrol near a pier caught fire. Men in the truck were badly burned and the fire spread to the oil-soaked ground. Several tons of explosives were stacked less than two metres away and thousands of gallons of oil just 15 metres distant. Rather than run, North organised a human chain, himself closest to the fire, and passed the boxes of explosives (the first few of which were alight) away from danger. He stayed until the fire had been isolated. North was a 40-year-old engine driver from Innisfail, Queensland.

On 3 May, the 2/23rd Battalion made brave but unsuccessful frontal attacks on Tarakan Hill, which dominated the ground 1000 metres around it. It repulsed a Japanese bayonet charge. A patrol got behind the enemy on Hospital Spur, and leading scout Private 'Dutchy' Holland (MM) surprised and killed three Japanese in foxholes. This enabled a platoon to advance 550 metres. Holland, fighting his first battle, then volunteered to take a message to company headquarters. He killed two more enemy on the way. Holland, who had often been in disciplinary trouble, was wounded on 8 May.

The 2/4th Commando Squadron was brought in to tackle Tarakan Hill. After two days of nasty and costly fighting they succeeded. The heavily wooded hill's defences, including numerous tunnels and pillboxes, were overcome with the aid of aircraft, artillery, tanks, a

PIAT and gelignite. Trooper Kevin 'Brolga' O'Regan (MM) was with the leading section in the first attack, which was ordered to seize a bridge and adjacent strongpoints on the way to the hill. The 6-feet-3-inch-tall Queensland station hand considered this 'bloody suicide', but went ahead. As soon as the Australians left cover, machine guns and rifles opened up from the hill. Their officer was killed and others hit, but O'Regan, Lance-Corporal Ken Moss and Trooper Frank Beatty managed to cross the bridge. Using grenades, they silenced one machine gun 20 metres beyond the creek and were attacking another in a pillbox when Beatty was hit in the stomach and elbow. All three crawled to a bunker, where they were under fire from the hill, the pillbox and tree snipers. Trooper Anthony Buntman bandaged up Beatty, probably saving his life, before himself being killed by a machine-gun burst. O'Regan then fell back on Beatty, his scalp grazed by a sniper bullet. When he recovered, Japanese grenades were being rolled towards them from a pillbox higher up and one entered the crater. The Australians tried to throw it back, but it exploded above them. 'That euchred us', Beatty recalled later, for the grenade showered them with steel fragments. Moss's thumb was almost severed and he was temporarily blinded. O'Regan was wounded in the left eye and head. Almost out of ammunition, O'Regan recognised that the commandos had to retreat. This Queensland station hand picked up Moss and carried him out, across the creek and open ground to safety. O'Regan and Beatty died in the 1980s, both from causes related to their wounds on that day.

The capture of Tarakan Hill opened the way to Snag's Track, running northwest into the heart of the Japanese defences at Fukukaku. Meanwhile, the 2/48th Battalion was advancing left towards a major objective codenamed 'Sykes'. On 5 May, Japanese tried hurling 75mm shells at the supporting Matilda tanks but had no luck and were killed. Lieutenant Tom Derrick's platoon occupied 'Otway' as a preliminary to the main attack on 6 May. This was the bloodiest day for the 2/48th on Tarakan. The only approach to Sykes was up a slippery, precipitous slope. Sergeant Glyn Pope (DCM) took his platoon within 50 metres of the top of Sykes before enemy fire and grenades forced them to halt. They pushed on though and were near the crest when a shower of grenades and fused 75mm shells drove them back. Pope, a 33-year-old Tobruk veteran, reorganised his men at the foot of the hill and made a second ascent. Machine-gun and rifle fire, as well as grenades, forced another short withdrawal, but a third attack took them to the summit. Pope sustained bomb and bullet wounds to the chest and leg but destroyed three posts. When his rifle was struck and damaged, he fought on with grenades. His platoon was eventually only eight strong and was forced off the crest by a counterattack, but the Australians regained it. Pope continued until he blacked out and had to be evacuated. He would recover, just as he had after three weeks in hospital from serious leg and arm wounds at Alamein. The first Australian to reach the summit of Sykes was Private Roy Toohey. The young station hand was shot in the abdomen and died of his wounds the following day. He too had survived an earlier wound, in New Guinea. Six of Pope's men died battling for Sykes.

When Pope was evacuated, Lieutenant Ken Allen (MC) was sent from company headquarters to take his place. He arrived just in time to command the remnant of Pope's platoon and some company headquarters personnel as they defended against a 60-man 'Banzai' charge. A grenade duel ensued, but the Australians' height advantage permitted them to roll theirs down on the attackers, who were halted. Allen, a 30-year-old Adelaide insurance inspector, was wounded twice by grenade fragments, but he too threw grenades, and his leadership was crucial. By day's end three platoons had secure possession of Sykes. Allen had received a Commander-in-Chief's Card for his efforts at Alamein, where he was wounded in the thigh and arm.

When the rest of Pope's platoon had been forced off Sykes' peak, Private Arthur Waters (MM) moved forward and, in view of the enemy, hurled numerous grenades into their positions on the reverse slopes. His grenades ran out, but he went back and obtained a 2-inch mortar. Setting this up on the top of the slope, he used airbursts in the trees to kill enemy snipers. Later he obtained more grenades, which

Wounded in the chest and leg on Sykes, Tarakan, Sergeant Glyn Pope (right) receives assistance to safety from Private John Higgins.
AWM 089473

he again took forward and threw until he received a bullet wound to the cheek and was evacuated. It was Waters' first campaign, but not the first Military Medal in the family: his father William had earned one in France in June 1918. Remarkably, Arthur's younger brother John would also earn a Military Medal at Tarakan, on 20 May, when as a forward scout he ignored two successive wounds and pushed back an enemy ambush force. In civilian life, the brothers worked on their father's dairy farm at Burekup, Western Australia.

Private Tom 'Tubby' Taylor (MM) used his rifle and grenades in the initial seizure of Sykes. When the platoon was down to eight men and defending, he took an Owen from a wounded comrade. On running out of magazines he took a Bren and continued fighting until wounded in the head. Officially, Taylor seems to have been a stretcher-bearer, and during the action pulled several wounded men to safety. His hat was shot off as he sought to help one casualty.

On 8 May, the 2/4th Commando Squadron was advancing along Snags Track when the leading scouts were wounded. Sergeant Arthur 'Punchy' Hanson (MM), commanding an attached 3-inch mortar detachment, went to the front and telephoned in covering fire that enabled them to be extricated. He did the same when another man was wounded, only to be hit himself. Hanson remained on duty and at one point dashed forward 40 metres to bring in another casualty. Later, the leading section became pinned down: once again Hanson, a slaughterman from Geelong, went forward and called in mortar fire, this time just 25 metres from his own position. The section was able to withdraw.

On 9 May, three 2/23rd men patrolling towards Snags Track were shot down at the head of the column and lay wounded. Private Norm Dingle (MM), a Bren gunner, advanced and took up position on the track where, with the Bren on his knee, he could engage the enemy while the wounded were evacuated. When his ammunition ran out, the Queensland stockman obtained more from the dead and wounded nearby. By the time the two closest casualties had been pulled out, Dingle had been wounded three times. Lieutenant Stanley Smith (MC) went out alone to rescue the third casualty.

Machine-gun fire wounded him severely in the elbow, but he stayed with the wounded man until certain he was dead and then directed the platoon's withdrawal. At a forward dressing station, his damaged arm was amputated. Smith had enlisted in the ranks in 1941 as a horticultural labourer from Mildura. By war's end he was an officer with a Military Cross, a wife and a two-year-old daughter.

On 9 May, the 2/24th relieved the 2/23rd. That day, Lieutenant Ray Walker (MC) led his platoon on a long-range patrol to Djoeta village and pushed the Japanese out after a skirmish. This would have seemed unlikely on 3 May when, during the advance across the airfield, his platoon had detonated two enormous explosions, which lifted some of the men in the air amidst huge wooden beams. Many were downed, but Walker got them up and marching on. On 13 May, he led a small patrol that found an alternative route – later called 'Walker's Track' – to the oilfields, and in subsequent days obtained vital information on the Poker feature (including Poker 1, 2 and 3). He only stopped after sustaining a severe arm wound while reconnoitring another feature on 23 May.

The 2/3rd Pioneer Battalion was ordered to advance along John's Track to the mouth of the Amal River. This proved difficult, mainly because of two strongly defended hills, 'Helen' and 'Sadie'. The Pioneers first attacked Helen on 7 May, but were still trying on 12 May, when Corporal John Mackey (VC) commanded the leading section. He silenced three posts, the first with a bayonet, the second with grenades, and the third with a submachine gun. He was killed at the third. The only approach to the Japanese posts was along a ridge wide enough for just two men at a time. Lance-Corporal Arthur 'Yorkie' Riedy (DCM) was with Mackey during this charge. Riedy killed two Japanese in the first post, gave covering fire as Mackey charged the second and threw a grenade through its firing slit, and it was his borrowed Owen that Mackey used on the last post. When Mackey fell, Riedy tried to save him, only to find him dead. Riedy was eventually wounded and evacuated. He was a farm worker from Queensland and Mackey a baker from New South Wales.

By the time the Helen feature fell on 15 May, 20 Pioneers had been killed and 66 wounded. Japanese casualties exceeded 200. Over 7000 artillery shells and 4000 mortar bombs were expended on the feature, with napalm decisive in forcing a Japanese retreat. Airpower was used increasingly to support the advance.

The Pioneers reached the coast on 16 May, while other battalions tackled a series of ridges with the aim of surrounding Fukukaku. Despite maximum use of airpower and artillery, losses mounted daily. For example, on 19 May, Corporal Timothy 'Curly' Ryan, who had won a Military Medal with the 2/48th at Sattelberg, was killed between the 'Clarice' and 'Freda' features. Tom Derrick, his platoon commander, considered Ryan 'a marvellous soldier', and the best NCO in the 2/48th. On 22 May, Derrick's platoon and another seized Knoll 2 on the Freda feature. The hand-to-hand fighting here was some of the most intense of the campaign. Private Walter How (MM) was fighting his first campaign, but the Western Australian gardener's enthusiasm was such that several times that day his platoon commander, Lieutenant Wally Walker, ordered him not to get too far ahead of his section. A pillbox was inflicting casualties on the Australians advancing on the right. It looked impossible to progress there, but How advanced up a slope towards the pillbox, firing his Owen as he went and, once in range, throwing grenades. Eventually he fell wounded in the neck but had killed the enemy machine gunner. The remaining defenders abandoned the pillbox. A veteran of all the battalion's campaigns, Private Wally Fennell (MM) was also to the fore – literally. He often went ahead of his section to within five or ten metres of the enemy, determining exactly what the Australians were facing and how best to proceed. At one point, an LMG opened fire from a flank, pinning down his section. Fennell got up and, although his mates were unable to provide covering fire, silenced the post with his Owen. Fennell was often in trouble with authority – he had been reverted to the ranks from corporal for 'conduct to the prejudice of good order and military discipline' in 1944 – but was also a superb fighting soldier, as the wounds he sustained on two separate occasions at Alamein and his close friendship with Derrick suggest. Like Derrick, he hailed from

Berri. By war's end, Fennell would be a lance-sergeant. Knoll 2 fell late that day and the Australians took up positions there. At about 3 am that night, fire from a bunker higher up on Knoll 3 (the main Freda feature) hit ten Australians, including Derrick. He succumbed to his wounds on 24 May. News of the death of this famous fighting soldier was painful to all Australians on Tarakan, and many beyond. This winner of the Victoria Cross and Distinguished Conduct Medal was a national hero, and but for his insistence would not have been allowed to undertake this campaign, his fourth.

The fusillade that hit Derrick heralded a determined Japanese counterattack. It was held off, but with ammunition low and large numbers of wounded, the company commander, Captain Oswald 'Os' Gooden (MC), reluctantly ordered a withdrawal. Gooden had enlisted as a private in 1940 and been wounded at Tel el Eisa. By now, only four of his section commanders were still standing. Some 40 Japanese had been killed. Stretcher-bearer Ernest 'Squizzy' Taylor (MM) worked throughout 23 May at Freda. The wounded lay where they fell, often close to enemy positions, until stretcher-bearers reached them. When one section leader, Corporal George Pearce, fell badly wounded on the track in front of a pillbox, Taylor's platoon commander tried to stop him from going out on what seemed a suicidal rescue mission. Taylor crossed the track, though, crawled to Pearce and calmly bandaged his wounds. He tried to drag Pearce back but the enemy fire, which holed his hat, was so heavy he had to give up. He returned to Pearce two hours later when the Australians had advanced further. Taylor, a Melbourne butcher, was in his first campaign.

From the landing at Tarakan, Lance-Sergeant Gordon Groux (MM) commanded a section of 2/13th Field Company engineers supporting a troop of Matilda tanks. This section was the first to discover mines on Tarakan. Groux had bomb disposal training, and went forward alone to examine and neutralise the mines before allowing his section to touch them. He also organised the night defence of the tanks and twice helped fight off night infiltration raids. On 8/9 May, to support a tank attack due at first light, he voluntarily led a mine lifting party, in stockinged feet, up Snags Track until discovered by an enemy patrol. He was unharmed then, but on 23 May, he was neutralising a new type of enemy device when it exploded. He was dangerously wounded. His right arm was amputated and he lost two fingers on his left hand. He had also been wounded at Alamein. The Melbourne labourer's citation noted Groux's 'cheerful courage under the most dangerous circumstances'.

After a stunning aerial, artillery and mortar bombardment, the 2/48th took Freda on 25 May. The 'Droop' feature was also blasted before the 2/24th captured it on 26 May. The next day, following another bombing strike, the 2/24th encountered an enemy strongpost, and sent a section to outflank it. Private Keith Christmass (DCM), a Western Australian chaff cutter who had just turned 20, led the attack along a razorback track. He had earlier been in trouble for minor offences, and on 4 May was evacuated for four days with exhaustion and abdominal pain. Now, when he was about 15 metres from the strongpost, a Japanese rifle bullet hit him in the chest. He fell, but rose up and fired his Owen, killing one Japanese, then charged and killed another. A serious arm wound stopped him from firing again, but before he was evacuated he told his section commander all he knew of the enemy positions. Christmass died of his wounds on 31 May.

On 2 June, the 2/24th assaulted Poker 3, to which the only approach was a two-man-wide razorback spur. Tunnels and foxholes extended 100 metres away from it. Within metres of advancing, four of the leading section were hit. Corporal Les Beale (DCM) led his section past them until halted by grenades and small arms fire. He continued alone, located the Japanese positions and threw grenades at a machine-gun post before returning and siting two Brens to provide effective fire. When his platoon commander and the remaining section leader were hit, Beale took over the whole platoon. He sited a third Bren and, covered by these LMGs' fire and by phosphorous grenade smoke he threw at the enemy, he personally led a charge. The Australians seized the position, killing 13 enemy. Beale was wounded twice, but when another platoon arrived to take up the attack, he then led its forward section, firing a Bren from the hip and gaining another 200 metres. Beale was just 22 years old. He had been in trouble with the authorities four times in camp, but risked all in battle. Early in this action, grenade fragments had wounded him in the leg and arm and rendered him partially deaf. In New Guinea in 1943, Beale had been wounded in both arms, and would be hit again on 21 June, sustaining shrapnel wounds that necessitated weeks of treatment.

Organised Japanese resistance ended on 21 June. The Australians lost 225 killed on Tarakan, the Japanese about 1500. Nearly 700 Australians were wounded. Plans to use the damaged airfield as a base did not eventuate. The Australians had fought with great courage and skill for little strategic reward.

North Borneo: Bravery at Labuan and Beaufort

While the 26th Brigade was in the last stages of its Tarakan operations, the 9th Division's other two brigades and many supporting troops landed in North Borneo. Their main tasks were to secure the Brunei Bay area, where an advanced fleet base could be established, and to recapture the oilfields. On 10 June, the 20th Brigade landed on Muara Island and on the south side of Brunei Bay at Brunei Bluff, while the 24th Brigade landed on Labuan Island off the northern end of the bay. These landings were unopposed.

The 20th Brigade advanced rapidly against only slight resistance. By 16 June, the lead battalion, the 2/17th, had advanced 120 kilometres and inflicted more than 100 casualties for just 16 of its own. At Seria, the battalion found that the Japanese had set the oil wells ablaze. The 2/3rd Field Company's Lieutenant Edward Underwood (MBE), who had already done fine work locating mines and preventing the destruction of a key bridge, now personally directed and participated in extinguishing the fires at Seria. For over two months, with help from Dutch and American experts and local labourers and tradesmen, this 30-year-old chemical engineer and his platoon employed various means, including beating the fires out, turning off valves and using water, mud and steam.

By the time the fires were out, the fighting in the 20th Brigade area was over. On 20 June, the 2/13th Battalion made another landing at Lutong and advanced to Miri. There were patrol clashes along the road leading south, but the enemy withdrew at most points of contact. The coastal strip and its immediate hinterland were captured, but foot and riverine patrols went out. A rare confrontation occurred on 7 July, when Sergeant Frank Power (MM) and four other patrollers from the 2/15th Battalion surprised up to 30 Japanese in a swamp near Limbang. The Australians opened fire and hit many before a few Japanese reached cover and fired back. Power's men were running short of ammunition and retreated, but counted about 20 dead for no loss. Power, a Queensland sheep station overseer, had earlier been a truck driver at Alamein, where enemy fire damaged his vehicle. He also impressed with his long-distance grenade-throwing at Kumawa in 1943 and killed two Japanese in another patrol in this campaign.

On 27 July, Corporal Charlie Lemaire (MM) of the 2/17th was returning to base with his section and a few indigenous locals (known to the Australians as 'Dyaks') after a reconnaissance patrol when eight Japanese ambushed them. The Australians were moving along a narrow track in tall swamp grass when the Japanese opened fire from a flank. This fire killed one Dyak, wounded an Australian and shattered a third man's rifle. Any movement attracted fire, but Lemaire moved so that he could direct his section better and locate the enemy. Suddenly, three Japanese emerged from the grass, charging. Lemaire killed one, an officer, from three metres. A Bren felled another, and the third was speared by a Dyak tending the wounded man. Lance-Corporal Joseph Giffen helped the Australian casualty too, but then disappeared from view. The enemy fire intensified, though its source remained unclear. Lemaire withdrew his men through a swamp, but stayed himself to try to find Giffen. His calls drew enemy fire on him, and when he began to pull back, covering his men's retreat, he encountered and shot another Japanese at point-blank range. Giffen's body was found days later.

The 24th Brigade faced more resistance than the 20th in North Borneo. On the island of Labuan, it soon occupied Labuan town and the airfield on 10 June, but the 2/28th on the left met increasing opposition. When its forward troops reached a canal 30 metres wide and 1.5 metres deep, they came under heavy rifle fire from high ground ahead. A bridge had been demolished but infantry could cross it. Lieutenant Danny Woodward and his platoon were crossing when a volley of rifle fire hit five men. Only one section made it across the bridge, and they were pinned down. Two tanks came up, and Sergeant Bob Hayes guided them to the bridge and directed their fire until he was killed. The tanks enabled several platoons to cross. Private Bob Walters (DCM) was in the right-hand platoon, which came under enfilade fire from the thickly wooded slopes as it advanced. He was sent left to obtain support from another platoon, and then guided a section into position for a flank attack. As the attack began, the section leader and three others were hit. Walters gathered as much Owen ammunition as he could and made a single-handed attack. He killed five Japanese in a strongpost and dispersed the survivors. Walters continued advancing, throwing grenades after his ammunition ran out. Even when a bullet fractured his leg he crawled on, shouting directions to the platoon. Eighteen dead were later counted around the post he had stormed, most of them credited to Walters, an English-born miner from Reedy, Western Australia. He had enlisted in the militia as Walton, absconded from his unit and joined the AIF in March 1942 under his real surname. He had been wounded in the shoulder in New Guinea. His lone assault on 10 June was reportedly inspired when a mate was wounded. In crossing the canal and seizing the high ground, the battalion sustained 16 casualties.

On 12 June, one company of the 2/28th supported by three tanks of the 2/9th Armoured Regiment was probing along a track, the infantry pointing out targets to the Matildas. Suddenly, they came under Woodpecker and rifle fire. In a day of hard fighting, the troop commander, Lieutenant Churchill Avern (MC), twice dismounted from his tank to liaise with the infantry. A Japanese officer carrying a bag of explosives bravely charged Avern's Matilda, but was shot dead, and engineers discovered a 250-pound aerial bomb planted just 15 centimetres from Avern's right track. By day's end, the tanks and infantry had reached MacArthur Road, and it was apparent that the Japanese had retreated into a stronghold, about 1100 metres by 550 metres and now dubbed 'the Pocket'. Soon it was the sole enemy position on Labuan. After six days of heavy artillery, air and naval bombardment, on 16 June, Australian tanks and infantry of the 2/28th and the 2/11th Commando Squadron sought to take the Pocket by assault. They approached it along a bottleneck entrance and soon sustained heavy casualties. Two chaplains did brave work. Padre Hugh Ballard (MC) of the 2/11th Commandos responded to a call for stretcher-bearers, organising a group of seven and personally helping to carry. The 34-year-old Congregational minister from Renmark was under fire throughout, and at one point a bearer helping him carry a wounded man was hit by a sniper. Ballard moved both men to cover behind a tank and then, to enable the evacuation of the wounded, pointed out the location of the enemy to the tank crew, who destroyed it. Padre Ben Holt of the 2/28th, who had been Mentioned in Despatches for his tireless stretcher-bearing in New Guinea, was doing the same selfless work here when he was mortally wounded.

Trooper Ron Bradbrook (MM), a tank driver, was in action from 9 am until 3.30 pm, when he had to withdraw to replenish ammunition. Thirty minutes later he returned to support a platoon attack. His crew commander ordered him to drive through a thick patch of jungle to a fire position on the other side. The crew soon discovered that the jungle patch was heavily mined. The supporting infantry had now turned left and was out of contact. Bradbrook skilfully negotiated the minefield and reached the fire position, from which it supported the infantry. By 6.30 pm, ammunition was almost out and the commander ordered a withdrawal. As Bradbrook manoeuvred, enemy troops made a suicide attack on the tank with a bomb or mine. It exploded on the left front of the tank, jamming the turret, damaging the hull top, jamming the driver's hatch

Trooper Ron Bradbrook (in the foreground) pictured driving a Matilda tank on Morotai Island in May 1945. The following month he showed extraordinary courage on Labuan, safely negotiating his tank through an enemy minefield and a suicide bomb attack.
AWM 092425

in a half-open position and destroying a starting motor fuse box. Shrapnel splash wounded Bradbrook in the back and shoulders, but he kept the engines running and drove back through the minefield to the Australian lines. When the engines were turned off there, they could not be restarted. Had Bradbrook allowed them to stop earlier, the vehicle and its crew might have been lost. Avern had to render another tank inoperable that day, on which he also directed a third Matilda's withdrawal under fire. On 19 June, Avern, carrying a portable wireless, acted as liaison officer with the infantry, even though his own troop was not engaged. He was moving forward to obtain better observation when machine-gun fire struck his hip. After months in hospital he recovered sufficiently to begin studying law, and became associate to a judge. However, in October 1952 he died as a result of his war wounds, aged just 31.

By 21 June, there were about 250 Japanese alive in the Pocket. At 4.30 am, some 50 of them infiltrated through the swamps and raided the Australian base area at Labuan town. Many Allied troops were sleeping at the time, and some Americans of the 593rd Engineer Boat and Shore Regiment were killed or wounded. Infiltrators attacked the 2/1st Docks Operating Company lines, where Sergeant Eric Antill (MM), a 35-year-old haulage contractor from Wagga Wagga, organised the defence. The raiders had at least one machine gun and grenades, Antill's men only rifles, but the Australians held off the attackers for two hours till daylight. Then Antill organised a group to finish off the remaining raiders facing him.

That day, the Pocket's last defenders were overrun. Four hundred Japanese were killed or captured on Labuan; the Australians lost 34 killed.

On 17 June, the 2/32nd Battalion landed unopposed on the Borneo mainland, at Weston. Two days later, on 19 June, the 2/43rd Battalion and 2/11th Commando Squadron disembarked at Mempakul and pushed rapidly inland. By 26 June, the Australians were in position to attack Beaufort, an important communications centre. About 1000 Japanese were defending it, but unlike the Australians, they had no air or artillery support. Beaufort sat on the swampy northern bank of the Padas River, with jungle-clad features rising on three sides. On 27 June, the 2/43rd overcame strong resistance to seize high ground north of the town, thus blocking the main Japanese escape route. However, one Australian company, under Captain Merv Glover (MC), became surrounded and over the next 30 hours faced a horrible ordeal: at least five counterattacks, many in the dark and involving hand-to-hand combat in tropical rain with hordes of mosquitoes and knee-deep mud. Lieutenant Bill Keane (MC), a recently arrived 22-year-old platoon commander, had led his men on to the objective in heavy rain and failing light. They then came under fire from a feature above them, but Keane coolly moved from man to man, encouraging them to persevere. When one man was seriously wounded, Keane left cover with a stretcher-bearer to rescue him, and then dug him a pit in which to shelter. One of Keane's Bren gunners, Private Richard Heffernan (MM), had knelt in the open to support his platoon when they stormed the high ground. During the enemy counterattacks, he received a shrapnel wound to the right shoulder, but continued to stand up and sweep the enemy with fire, seemingly oblivious to the grenades exploding around him. Heffernan had been in trouble with the authorities more than once, and would be again: in February 1946 he travelled illegally from Morotai to Australia and was fined and retained in the Army until August. Borneo was his first campaign.

Like Heffernan, Private Dudley 'Pongo' Kotz (MM), was prominent in the attack. As a No. 2 Bren gunner, he kept up ammunition to the gun but also shot several enemies with his rifle. Then, in defence, with one enemy group just 20 metres away, he calmly rose to his feet and fired his rifle so accurately that three fell dead and the rest fled. During one counterattack, Corporal George Cleeland (MM) positioned himself in a shallow weapon pit in front of his section and, firing his Bren from a standing position, cut down numerous attackers. Later he killed some as close as 15 metres away, despite constant enemy rifle fire and grenade explosions. Glover, the 35-year-old Tasmanian schoolmaster commanding these men, was wounded in the leg during the attack, but led it aggressively and then, hobbling around his platoons, organised the defence calmly and with sound judgment. He had also been wounded at Alamein, commanding the 2/43rd's Carrier Platoon.

The 2/43rd's other companies worked hard on 27–28 June too. Private Ian Kelly (MM), of an adjacent company, was digging in alone on the flank of his platoon when a group of Japanese attacked him. Almost immediately he was shot in the leg, but he returned fire with his Owen. A sword-wielding Japanese severely wounded him on the arm and shoulder, but Kelly fought on alone with one hand. Eventually, his opponents fled, leaving six dead. Kelly, a farmer from Adaminaby, New South Wales, had served on the Kokoda Track with the 3rd Battalion. He had been accepted into the Army despite having lost three toes in a prewar woodchopping accident.

Another company was advancing towards Glover's early on 28 June when the forward scout was wounded and the lead platoon halted by Japanese defending camouflaged weapon pits along the track. Bren gunner Private Tom Starcevich (VC) now took the initiative and advanced. Seemingly impervious to enemy fire, he eliminated four posts in succession. Starcevich, who had been wounded at Ruin Ridge in 1942, was the only one of the 9th Division's seven Victoria Cross winners to survive the war, but it was a near-run thing.

Despite Starcevich's efforts, his company could not link up with Glover's that day as it found a steep ravine blocking its path. On the morning of 29 June, two companies joined Glover's and the last Japanese in Beaufort were killed or forced out. The 2/43rd lost 13 killed in the fighting, the Japanese over 100. By 12 July, the 2/32nd had occupied Papar, thereby completing the brigade's task of securing Brunei Bay.

Australian special forces operated in large numbers in the interior of British Borneo. Captain Eric Edmeades (MC), of Z Special Unit, ensured that the Japanese retreating from Brunei suffered heavily at the hands of his force of about 200 Dyaks. This 24-year-old South Australian clerk's force accounted for 200 Japanese at Patengoa and then another 134 near the Padas River. Some of these poor Japanese committed suicide in despair.

In the North Borneo operations, 114 Australians were killed while the Japanese lost at least 1234. As these operations came to a close, the last Australian landings in Borneo began at Balikpapan.

CHAPTER 23

BORNEO II: BALIKPAPAN

The last major Australian operation of the war was the campaign at Balikpapan, a great oil port on the south-east coast boasting seven piers, an oil refinery and about 40 storage tanks. The operation had unprecedented air, naval and artillery support. The Australian force comprised 21 000 men of the 7th Division, together with 12 000 other personnel. Facing them were 3900 Japanese troops, with a further 2100 Japanese and Formosan (Taiwanese) workers who were potential fighters. Their defences constituted many trenches, tunnels, concrete bunkers and strongposts. The defenders also manned approximately 112 coastal, dual-purpose and anti-aircraft guns.

During June 1945, up to 200 bombers a day hit the defences, and naval vessels bombarded them with 23 000 shells. General Edward Milford, commanding the 7th Division, landed his troops at Klandasan, where the enemy defences were strongest. He reasoned that the enormous firepower available at the outset would negate these and give the Australians a firm base for a quick and relatively bloodless campaign. After landing, the 18th Brigade would march north towards Balikpapan town while the 21st Brigade would march east to seize the two airfields at Sepinggang and Manggar.

The landing, 'F-Day', occurred on 1 July, with the spectacular sight of smoke rising high above the town and oil tanks bursting into flames. Battalions were landed on the wrong beaches, but they faced no opposition and pushed inland over relatively open country. Units from both brigades soon reached the motor roads: 'Vasey Highway'

Borneo II: Balikpapan

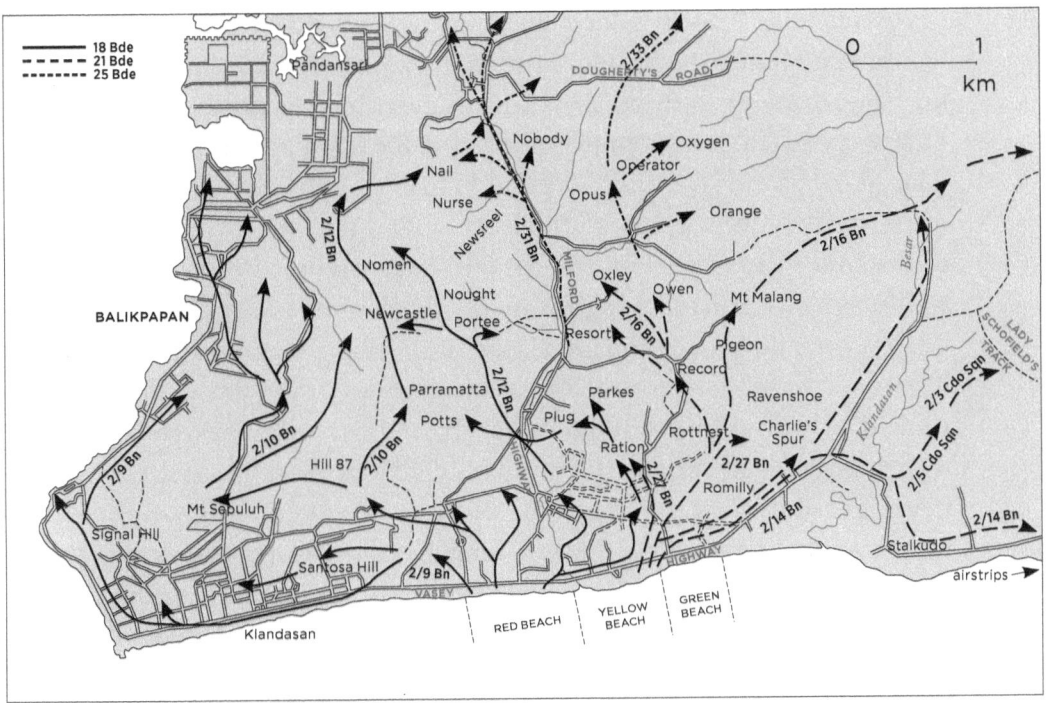

Balikpapan

on the coast and 'Milford Highway' inland. On the right, the 21st Brigade's leading battalion, the 2/27th, reached the first objectives with little opposition. The 2/16th then pressed on towards Mount Malang, a dominating feature that the Japanese would not give up without a fight. The Australians attacked it in the late afternoon, with artillery, mortar and machine-gun support. They also employed a flamethrower. Lieutenant Lance Armstrong (MID) commanded the leading platoon aggressively and effectively until he was killed just 10 metres short of the top. This commercial traveller from Coolamon had previously served with the 3rd Battalion on the Kokoda Track. On leaving for the shore in a landing craft that morning, he had called to the battalion chaplain, 'See you on Malang Hill tonight'. Planners had allotted five days to the capture of Malang, but it fell on the first day. Captain Ron Christian, whose company seized the feature, won a Bar to the Military Cross he had earned at Kokoda.

After the 2/14th seized its objective with ease, the 2/5th Commando Squadron passed through. It suddenly came under heavy fire from anti-aircraft guns, machine guns, snipers and mortars. Four were killed and seven wounded. The RMO, Captain Raymond 'Doc' Allsopp (MID), and Corporal Frank McKeown went forward to assist. They were helping a casualty onto a stretcher when bursts of machine-gun fire killed the casualty and wounded Allsopp and McKeown. After bandaging his own thigh wound, Allsopp tended McKeown's wounded arm and sent him back. Allsopp need not have gone forward: one story says an erroneous message – 'doctor wanted' – had summoned him rather than his stretcher-bearers. His wife had died in childbirth in April 1943 (13 months after their marriage) and he was bitter, reportedly to the point of saying he would win a Victoria Cross or not come home. Allsopp now treated men on the spot. Eventually, a Japanese grenade landed near him, inflicting a mortal wound to the temple. Allsopp was credited with saving at least three lives during the hour in which he was at the front. The 30-year-old medical practitioner from Wollongong was unsuccessfully recommended for a Victoria Cross.

One platoon of the 2/12th, under Lieutenant Lance Kent (MC), became separated from its battalion at the landing. Kent took the initiative of seizing an important feature called Portee, even though it was well beyond the original objectives. When Japanese forces advanced on this height, Kent's men drove them off, killing 36. The Japanese suffered further rebuffs when they launched more attacks on Portee that night. Kent, a teacher at Newington College, Sydney, was 6 feet 3 inches tall and fighting his first campaign. His platoon sergeant, Frank Manson (MM), personally accounted for nine enemy attackers. Manson, a labourer from Railton, Tasmania, was 37 years old and a veteran of Greece, Tobruk and New Guinea. Private Reg Fletcher (MM), also of the 2/12th, was in a section sent to destroy a nest of snipers. Moving to the flank of the section, he located one sniper and, despite enemy fire, killed him from just five metres. He then spotted the main enemy group near a building 50 metres away. Moving towards them rapidly, he dodged enemy grenades before throwing his own and killing three Japanese with his rifle at close range. He felled three more as they fled while cutting off the retreat of another six who died at his section's hands. Fletcher, a former station hand from Bingara, had earlier been in a mountain battery, trained as a parachutist and been in trouble a couple of times, including once for being insubordinate to an officer.

The 2/10th Battalion, to the left of the 2/12th, had the crucial task of seizing the Parramatta feature, which dominated the landing beach area. Lieutenant Albert Sullivan (MC) contributed substantially to this advance when his platoon seized the lower slopes of Hill 87, in front of Parramatta. Sullivan leapt into an enemy-occupied trench and killed three with his rifle and bayonet. Naval guns, 25-pounders, tanks and heavy mortars were allotted to the 2/10th's support, but by the time the battalion was ready to advance on Parramatta, the naval guns had been reassigned, the 25-pounders' wirelesses were jammed and the tanks were bogged. Nevertheless, the attack proceeded. By skilful manoeuvre, Lieutenant Alan McDougall (MC) took the leading platoon within 50 metres of the crest of Hill 87, though intense enemy fire from Parramatta and a ridge called 'The Island' killed five of his men and wounded seven. Another platoon moved to his left and seized Green Spur, where Lance-Corporal John Copping accounted for six of 16 Japanese killed. Four of his platoon mates died here. Corporal Bill Symons (MM), commanding the leading section, managed to move his men forward through the fusillade in leaps and bounds, helped by the courage of Private Clifford Abel (MID), who used a Bren to subdue one post and then an Owen to cover the advance, even after he was severely wounded in the arm. Symons, a clerk from Port Augusta, stood just 5 feet 5 inches tall. He used a rifle grenade at one point to kill five Japanese in a troublesome strongpoint. Later, Symons' section and the adjacent one had lost their Brens to enemy fire and were down to nine men between them. The arrival in the late morning of two Matildas proved decisive: they helped destroy isolated enemy posts, and when they rumbled over the crest, Japanese firing on Hill 87 ceased. Major Edward Ryrie (MID), second-in-command of the 1st Armoured Regiment, calmly moved around on foot, reconnoitring for the tanks. Ryrie, a solicitor from Tottenham, New South Wales, had been an outstanding trainee who rose from lieutenant to major in two years. He would die in action nine days later.

On 1 July, the attack on Parramatta began at 1.20 pm and Ryrie went ahead of the leading tank and leading infantry section. There were now six tanks up, a battery of 25-pounders and a 6-pounder gun. Within an hour, Parramatta was in Australian hands, thanks largely to flamethrower tanks and infantry flamethrowers. Two 2/10th men prominent in this fighting were Private John Semler (MM) and his section commander, Corporal Arthur 'Snowy' Evans (DCM). Semler's flamethrower malfunctioned early in the action on Hill 87, and he was walking back when he encountered two Japanese emerging from a tunnel. Using a rifle from a dead comrade, he killed both. After rejoining his section, Evans took Semler to neutralise an enemy post firing on them from a pit containing a coastal defence gun. Between them, they shot all ten occupants. At another point, while the section was sheltering in a bomb crater from enemy fire, Semler stood up – he was 5 feet 11 inches tall - and, firing a Bren from the shoulder, shot down four Japanese. Semler turned 40 four weeks later. Evans was similarly involved in a series of remarkable incidents. During the mopping up on Hill 87, a grenade thrown from a bunker wounded another NCO in the back. Evans advanced alone on the bunker, firing at its weapon slit and then finishing it with a grenade thrown from three metres. He and his section shot four more Japanese in the advance on Parramatta and then went on patrol towards the Newcastle feature. Evans shot a Japanese lying alongside the track with an LMG and, after killing several more Japanese and destroying an occupied hut, they seized Newcastle and held it until the rest of the platoon came up. Evans, an Adelaide labourer serving in his third campaign, sent what the battalion history calls 'a somewhat cheeky message' to the company commander announcing his success.

The Australians' successes on 1 July assured them of victory at Balikpapan, but much hard fighting lay ahead. The 2/10th killed

40 infiltrators that night. On 2 July, the 2/14th Battalion captured the Sepinggang Airstrip without a fight and on 3 July, the 2/10th occupied Balikpapan town. By now, 17 000 Australians were ashore. Australian engineers were doing vital work: during the campaign, they disarmed more than 8000 mines and booby traps and helped to destroy 110 tunnels and pillboxes. At the landing, Lance-Corporal Ray Clarke (MM) of the 2/6th Field Company was attached to the 2/27th Battalion. When one 2/27th platoon became held up by fire from a tunnel near the beachhead, Clarke was ordered to block the tunnel with a demolition charge. He went to the very mouth of the tunnel and destroyed it. He then came under fire from a second tunnel, prompting him to take a second charge to it. Seventeen enemy dead were later counted in these tunnels. Clarke, a 30-year-old Sydney bricklayer, never learnt of his award. Within weeks of the end of the war, he died when he accidentally fell during bridge repairs on Borneo.

On 2 July, three Japanese aerial bombs deployed as booby traps were found within 6 metres of a burning hut and 30 metres from a Japanese ammunition dump. Sapper Bert Foley (GM) of the 1st Bomb Disposal Platoon recognised the danger and went forward, removing the bombs and preventing casualties. Foley's platoon commander, Lieutenant John Liddy (MC), was recognised for his brave work under fire, working with tanks and infantry and supervising his men in neutralising nearly 5000 mines, bombs and booby traps. Liddy, a 39-year-old train examiner from Melbourne, who had enlisted with the rank of Fitter, had served on Tarakan too, where he had remained on duty after being wounded in the foot by a grenade fragment. He also received a US Bronze Star Medal.

Encounters on the Milford Highway

The 25th Brigade took the lead in the advance along Milford Highway from 3 July. The Japanese offered firm resistance. When fire from two pillboxes halted the 2/31st's advance, Sergeant Guss

Campbell (MM) moved alone to the right flank, then rushed at them. Heavy fire from four enemy in one pillbox and three in the next could not stop this Western Australian farm worker: he killed them all with grenades and rifle fire. The 2/33rd, advancing to the 2/31st's right, captured four significant features but suffered heavy casualties among the log emplacements and weapon pits that dotted the hill called Oxygen. Here, Private Athol Martin (MM) ignored severe pain and loss of blood from a wound to make a lone charge, in which he killed the occupants of a machine-gun post with grenades and his Owen. Though wounded a second time, he kept fighting until the feature was taken. New Zealand-born Martin was officially 20, but probably only 18. Four others involved in the battalion's heavy fighting that day were recommended unsuccessfully for Military Medals, though Captain Phil Curry (MC) – a tall, 31-year-old Sydney grocer – was rewarded for the 'extraordinary bushcraft' and 'rare initiative' he displayed in guiding his company in an encircling movement through dangerous country to attack the enemy from behind on 3 July. Lance-Corporal Bob Freeman (MM) was also recognised: he became a byword for skilful patrolling, and his actions included recovering the body of his platoon commander and locating an enemy 75mm gun that was subsequently destroyed. On 19 July, he killed one enemy on patrol before being severely wounded in the face. Even then he brought back useful information. However, Freeman had a remarkable record of absence without leave: over five separate occasions from 1940 to 1943, he was absent or in detention for a total of 537 days. He also went AWL at least five times in 1944. Other misdemeanours included escaping while under arrest, resisting arrest, giving a false number and name, and creating a disturbance in a ship's hospital. Freeman completed his service with 'facial palsy'.

The menacing hills of Manggar

On 4 July, the 2/14th approached the last major objective of the eastern advance: Manggar. It occupied the airstrip without a fight, but late in the morning, the situation changed dramatically when, from the hills, Japanese coastal and 75mm artillery as well as mortars and 20mm quick-firing guns opened fire. The guns concentrated on the airfield control tower and bridge over the Manggar River, and soon eight Australians were killed or wounded. Lieutenant Graham Thorp (MC) of the 1st Naval Bombardment Group was in the control tower, which was hit several times, damaging three of its legs. He stayed at his post, though, calling in fire from a destroyer, the USS *Eaton*, which temporarily subdued the Japanese guns. The following day, Thorp continued his valuable work from the rickety tower, which was dubbed 'Thorp's Tower'. This Sydney architect also served in Greece and New Guinea.

The naval fire was useful but not decisive against the steel-shuttered doors of the enemy guns, which on 5 July rapidly knocked out three Matildas brought forward to combat them. A 6-pounder gun from the 2/2nd Tank Attack Regiment was brought up and from 1100 metres disabled one coastal gun with six direct hits: the names of its brave crew seem to be lost to history. That night, a 25-pounder gun of the 2/5th Field Regiment was brought up to the bridge so it could fire from close range in daylight. Sergeant Kelvin 'Kelly' Palmer (MM), a Sydney ironworker, was selected to command the gun because of his experience manning a similar direct-fire gun at Buna. Palmer's crew opened fire at dawn, silencing two guns – a 155mm and a 75mm – with 150 rounds. The 155mm gun was later found to be loaded and aimed at 'Palmer's Gun'. His crew comprised ten volunteers, two of whom were wounded in a duel with an enemy 20mm gun firing from a concrete pillbox. The gunners were withdrawn rather than continue this one-sided gunfight. The following morning, after a barricade had been built around Palmer's Gun, it knocked out two 20-mm guns, including its nemesis from the previous day.

With the war's end in sight, senior Australian commanders were keen to avoid pointless casualties and to use heavy firepower wherever possible. A 13-strong fighting patrol under Lieutenant Frank Doyle (MID) was sent on 6 July to capture the big guns on what came to be known as Waites' Knoll after one of the men killed attacking it. Naval, field and anti-aircraft artillery, mortars and aircraft were used to support this tiny group. After 90 minutes of jungle-bashing, the Australians got within 50 metres of the first emplacement and charged it, throwing grenades and firing. Two 2/6th Field Company engineers, sappers Theodore Scholz and Leo Ryan (MM), were accompanying the patrol with explosive charges – they had done the same on an unsuccessful patrol the previous night. Now Scholz was killed, as was Lance-Corporal Harry Waites, a brave 32-year-old veteran who had picked up the charge in the hope of using it. On his own initiative, Ryan then grabbed the charge, raced forward under fire, and threw it into the gun pit. Soon afterwards he noticed thick wires leading from an enemy position. Warning others in the patrol to take cover, he cut the wires with a shovel. These wires were attached to aerial bombs: had they been pulled, the bombs would have exploded. Ryan, who had occasionally been in trouble with Army authority, was a blacksmith's striker from Bondi.

Records do not show whether the charge that Ryan hurled had an effect, though a 'big explosion' and a gun still burning fiercely that night are mentioned in an official account. It appears, though, that two other men were largely responsible for clearing the Japanese from the two coastal gun emplacements encountered by Doyle's patrol. One was Corporal Harry Lynch (MID), who was first to reach one coastal gun emplacement. Lynch, a soldier often in disciplinary trouble, had his finest hour as he hurled grenades into and sat atop the emplacement to cover the approach of his section. Private John Sullivan (MID), another soldier with a substantial disciplinary record, had been lead scout in the march to the guns. Now he ran some 80 metres across the enemy front to reach the second gun, on which he made a lone attack with phosphorous grenades. When the enemy ran, the New South Wales station hand followed them,

Corporal Harry Lynch (second from the left in the back row) and Lieutenant Frank Doyle (third from the left in the same row) took leading roles in the capture of this and another coastal gun emplacement at Waites' Knoll, Balikpapan, in July 1945.
AWM 110975

shooting down several from a standing position. About 50 Japanese fled these emplacements.

Doyle now consolidated the position. It seemed miraculous that he had survived this attack. He had enlisted as a private, and done great service with the 2/6th in the Middle East and New Guinea, where he had been wounded in the neck, arms and head when a 'friendly' 2-inch mortar bomb exploded near him accidentally on 21 July 1943. On 22 July 1945, on the eve of leaving the front for early discharge from the Army, this cement worker from Kew would be mortally wounded by the accidental discharge of an Owen. On the night of 6 July, he was reinforced, but the company was nearly overrun as they fought from water-filled trenches against heavy counterattacks. When a standing patrol in front of the company was withdrawn, two men on a flank were left behind. Private Allan Leeson (MID), a Bren gunner, and his No. 2, Private Arthur Hamilton (MID), held their position and killed eight Japanese. Hamilton was wounded the following day. Private Hubert Hill (DCM), a Western Australian truck driver, manned a sector that bore the brunt of the four attacks. Ammunition shortages were a problem that night, and during the final attack, the Bren gunner was away obtaining ammunition. Hill used his Owen and the Bren alternately until both guns jammed in the wet conditions. When three spear-wielding Japanese attacked him, he shot down two and held off the third with one hand while he fixed the Bren stoppage. Eventually he shot the spearman. Nine dead Japanese lay in front of Hill's position the next morning, though other casualties had been carried out.

The following night brought more fierce Japanese counter-attacks, but this time the defenders had accurate and heavy artillery support, called down by Lieutenant Norm Ham (MC), FOO from the 2/5th Field Regiment. Captain Bob Thompson (MID) directed the defence of Waites', even though he had been wounded by mortar fire before arriving. The veteran Thompson, commissioned in the field during the Kokoda campaign and Mentioned in Despatches for the Ramu Valley campaign, continued virtually without sleep for two days. Another man very short on sleep was Sapper Ryan, mentioned earlier, who after his heroics with the demolition charge and aerial bomb was serving as an infantryman, though virtually without sleep since 5 July. The company was relieved on 8 July. By dusk on 9 July, when the Japanese were forced from their last strongholds in the Manggar area, some twelve thousand 25-pounder rounds and 5000 naval shells (5-inch) had been fired and 120 tons of bombs (including napalm) dropped in support of the 2/14th Battalion in six days.

The capture of Manggar airfield meant the key objectives of the Balikpapan campaign had been obtained. The two Japanese battalions defending the coastal area had been virtually annihilated, but the third battalion was still fighting hard against the Australian advance along the Milford Highway.

Caution and courage on the inland advance

As on the coast, the Australians advancing inland proceeded cautiously, seeking to maximise the use of supporting arms to minimise casualties, and by 9 July, the Japanese had fallen back 5 kilometres on the highway. Thick bush now replaced open country. The 2/31st Battalion was in the vanguard when, on the evening of 9 July, Japanese used remote control to explode five 500-kilo bombs lying on the road. Three Australians were killed and 17 dazed, and then Japanese machine guns opened fire on them. The explosion threw Corporal John Mullins (MM), a section commander, nearly 5 metres off the road, but he got up and returned to the highway. Two of his men lay dead, others wounded and stunned, and the area was swept by fire. Nevertheless, he carried out a wounded man and shepherded the bewildered remainder to safety. He later returned to locate and retrieve another wounded man. Most of the platoon was hospitalised with bomb blast, but Mullins remained on duty despite suffering severe shock. He was a tractor driver from Tully, Queensland.

During the advance on 10 July, a flamethrower tank and a 2/31st platoon moved to the right of the road, up a track, and engaged a group of enemy bunkers. The tank flamed and silenced two bunkers but was then unable to advance. Warrant-Officer Ron Willson (MM) was in the lead section of infantry when a Japanese officer emerged from the bushes 10 metres away, brandishing a sword. The Bren gunner's weapon jammed, and Willson shot the officer in the head. 'That is my sword!' was Willson's laconic comment. The section then attacked enemy weapon pits and log emplacements. Willson destroyed three pits and their occupants and continued to advance even after being wounded in the head by a grenade. The war diary stated he personally accounted for seven Japanese. This 31-year-old farm worker from Kangaroo Island was using a rifle and bayonet. He and his section also captured a powerful naval gun.

The next objective was a steep, heavily wooded knoll called 'Coke', which a 2/31st company seemed to be occupying with ease when fire erupted from Japanese entrenched among trees and fallen logs. Major Ryrie of the tanks was among those killed. The leading platoon suffered heavy losses on the road, and another platoon was sent to help. Three of its men were hit. Lance-Corporal Ernest Cooper (MID), a former lance-sergeant with the elite 1st Parachute Battalion, gathered five men and advanced to the logs. He disposed of two Japanese who appeared, before ordering the group to drop haversacks and fix bayonets. With more Australians arriving, Cooper sent two men to locate a machine gun that had inflicted many casualties. When the leading scout, Private John Blunden, fell, Cooper ran to try to help, only to find Blunden dead at the feet of a Japanese. Cooper bayoneted this enemy and, taking Blunden's Owen, killed another four. He then held his ground until ordered to withdraw. As the 2/31st history says, why Cooper received no medal is a mystery. This postman from Frankston had spent much of his Army service in postal units.

The Australians wounded in this ambush lay mainly in an area some 5 metres by 20 metres. The forward tank, having exhausted its flamethrower fuel, took back some wounded, and another tank came forward. Private Hugh Douglass (MM), a 39-year-old storeman at battalion headquarters, now volunteered to help. He went down the road, ignoring innumerable bullets, and carried out two casualties. Then, on the back of another tank, he returned to the scene, where he tended more wounded and assisted them onto this tank. When the tank departed, he remained to tend wounded, still under fire. Ten Japanese appeared about 50 metres from the stricken men, but Douglass held them off with a casualty's Owen until the tank had evacuated all the wounded. A war correspondent reported that '[m]agnificently he alone broke up the enemy drive and those who watched him agree that he saved the lives of four of our wounded'. Word of 'Angel' Douglass's selfless actions spread quickly throughout the battalion. So did appreciation of an unnamed Salvation Army officer (possibly Aub Hall), who carried coffee around the weapon pits.

While Douglass covered the tank departing with his wounded, another Matilda, under Acting Corporal Leslie Murdock (MID), a farmer from Warooka, South Australia, fired until its main gun's high-explosive ammunition had run out and its machine gun was damaged and reduced to firing single shots. At 5.50 pm, Murdock received orders to withdraw and to pass an order to the infantry to do the same. He dismounted the tank under fire, informed the infantry, and directed the placement of four more wounded on the tank. Two of his own crew had also been wounded. The Australians lost 18 killed and 23 wounded at Coke before withdrawing.

On 14 July, the 2/25th relieved the 2/31st and pushed forward. On the night of 15/16 July, 40 to 50 Japanese used the cover of heavy rain and a moonless night to approach very close to a company holding the 'Calm' feature and then attack. One Australian was wounded with a sword. The fight lasted all night and left 13 Japanese and four Australians dead. Most of the Japanese dead were attributed to Lance-Corporal Ron Grigg (DCM), a station hand from Wagga Wagga, whose section faced the heaviest attacks. He moved among the men, encouraging and directing them. At one point, he advanced alone to a log being used by Japanese for cover. Holding his grenades after pulling the pins, he threw them over the log with just a second remaining before the explosions: the effect was devastating. The next morning, Australian reinforcements drove off the attackers. Another enemy attack on the wet night of 17/18 July saw three Australians and 53 Japanese killed in fighting that lasted from dawn until 8.30 am.

On 20 July, Lieutenant Jack Raward (MID) was sent with a patrol to destroy a pillbox on the highway some 300 metres away from the 2/25th's perimeter. This proved to be harder than expected, but success was achieved through Raward's skilful division of his group into two, and by the expert and daring use of a flamethrower by Corporal Colin Ford (MID).

Patrols were now the main means of advance. 'Hit hard. Get no casualties' was the instruction of one 20 July patrol. When the Australians reached the line of Pope's Track on 22 July, the campaign was effectively over. Patrolling continued, with the 18th Brigade securing the western shores of Balikpapan Bay and patrolling inland. The 2/9th Battalion's Lance-Corporal Colin McKinlay (MM), a 45-year-old grazier from Inverell, led daring patrols on foot and by prahu (Malay boat) along and on the Riko River. One of his ambushes sank a Japanese launch and captured a motorboat and five Japanese. On 26 July, McKinlay was badly wounded in the hand and lower leg by friendly fire but reached home with valuable information. Earlier in the war, while serving with the 7th Division Cavalry Regiment in Papua, he had been lucky to survive being accidentally shot in the abdomen. He had also survived scrub typhus in 1944.

The inland advance along the Milford Highway had been the costliest part of the Balikpapan operation, which in total cost 229 Australian lives. More than 2000 Japanese were killed. As these numbers suggest, the Australians achieved their objectives, a success due largely to the courage of their frontline troops.

CONCLUSION

While advancing at Balikpapan in the last days of the war, Australian troops found the bodies of local men and women murdered and mutilated by Japanese soldiers near the coastal Vasey Highway. This was one of several large groups of civilians found slaughtered, including 16 decapitated Indonesians on the Milford Highway, and these discoveries embittered the Australians. Similarly, in the Aitape-Wewak campaign, a machine-gun battalion officer wrote that the repeated evidence of Japanese atrocities markedly affected the men's morale, causing them to fight with more determination to kill Japanese.[1] This provides part of the answer as to why Australians fought with such resolve and bravery. So does the fact that they volunteered to fight. Commanders of British and American armies in World War II often bemoaned the relative decline since World War I in the willingness of troops to carry out orders likely to lead to their deaths.[2] Australian volunteers were probably more ready to follow such orders – Alamein and Gona come to mind.

It is said that evil triumphs when good men do nothing. In war, the something that good men do necessarily includes bloody violence. This book's pages abound with stories of what might be called butchery in the service of a noble cause. Some of these brave men did not kill, such as stretcher-bearers and doctors who saved lives, but most either killed or directed killing. The famous American combat officer Dick Winters talked of units depending on a rare breed of 'killers', men who 'instinctively wage war without restraint and without regard for their personal safety'.[3] Such men feature in this book but did not predominate among Australian combat units, even though most members had volunteered to fight.

Australians loved using sporting metaphors for warfare: talking, for instance, about a 'game', comparing themselves to enemies as in a boxing match and discussing whether opponents had fought 'fair'. Yet many Australian acts listed above were not committed in a sporting fashion, and indeed, the nature of war means most could not be. Moreover, doing good was not the only motive for these men. Or rather, when performing their heroic deeds they were not primarily concerned with winning the war for the Allies or even with protecting Australia. The vast majority never recorded what motivated them, but some were clearly fighting to save their mates, or to avenge them, or took the initiative because of their training or a desire to win a medal, or just instinct. Esprit de corps was a factor too. A minority were men with psychological problems, who probably enjoyed the thrill of the fight or even found excitement in killing.

A high proportion of the men in these chapters were leaders, whether as officers, NCOs or even privates. No doubt some of them consciously sought to gain awards by their actions – and in some cases probably worried or angered subordinates in doing so. Yet it is remarkable how many leaders selflessly risked their own lives to achieve a military objective – even if based on unrealistic orders from above – or to protect or rescue their men. As mentioned, being brave for a few minutes of intense combat, especially in hand-to-hand fighting, was no guarantee of an ability to lead on a continuing basis, but many leaders won deserved promotion because of courageous command in battle.

Another prominent group discussed above were Bren gunners, men given a pivotal responsibility within their units to provide firepower. That responsibility, the type of man it attracted and probably the loyalty that weapon induced in its users, all contributed to the overrepresentation of Bren gunners among medal winners. It is relevant that the American military analyst SLA Marshall argued that in the US Army, men armed with the Browning Automatic Rifle (or BAR) – a weapon with a similar tactical role to the Bren – were more likely to fire than those with rifles.[4]

The Bren gun exemplifies the fact that courage alone cannot win wars. Effective weapons are significant too, as are effective tactics, sound leadership (not just courage) at all levels, adequate supplies and air support.

Australia was fortunate to have those qualities in most campaigns, and to be on the winning side for most of the war. More medals were awarded in victorious campaigns. Some soldiers fought in multiple campaigns and became better soldiers, though winning a medal put an extra burden on the winners, who were expected to be brave thereafter. Corporal Don McKay won a Military Medal with the 39th Battalion on the Kokoda Track, where he took his section to reinforce the hard-pressed front, then moved from post to post while under fire to bolster that section when it took losses. At the time, he felt he was just doing his job. While fighting at Gona, months later, he was told that he had been awarded that Military Medal. His immediate reply was, 'Christ. They'll expect me to be brave.' This premonition proved correct.[5] As the British and American armies knew, even the bravest soldiers could only go to the well so many times before the stress caught up with them. Although men like 'Tex' Weston, 'Diver' Derrick and 'Teddy' Bear were brave in several campaigns, this book also contains poignant stories of Australians who performed courageous deeds and were seeming rocks in their units but later suffered mental health issues, such as 'Bull' Allen, who was discharged from the Army with anxiety state and temporarily lost the power of speech. New men – fresh blood, one might say – came forward in each campaign to prove themselves. Often, these new men, for example in the 2/10th at Balikpapan, were former militiamen, a group once derided as too scared to join AIF units. Being young and naïve helped some men take risks that more hard-bitten veterans avoided.[6]

Many soldiers in this book were labourers and farmers, accustomed to hard lives working with their hands. Perhaps they found it easier than others to fight. Some were probably motivated by a desire for recognition that would improve their lot after the war. How most men described here fared after 1945 is beyond this book's scope, though as mentioned, many signed on for more military service. Others struggled to cope. Don McKay of the 39th was stressed even before the war ended. After the Kokoda campaign, he struggled to sleep and was always on guard. In a 2003 interview, he stated that because of recurring fear, he had not slept more than two hours straight ever since. Horton McLachlan, whose deeds in Operation Bulimba stand out even in this book of remarkable actions, also battled postwar demons. In the 1980s, aged 67, he wrote: 'I would not go to another war after the way I've been treated since'. As mentioned, he also cited being unable to forget bayonetting men and bashing out another's brains to stay alive and protect his unit.[7] For many of the soldiers described in this book, the war and especially their medal-winning feats represented a high point of their lives. The oft-mentioned anti-climax of a postwar life must have applied with extra force to many of these men, and I have researched one who spent much of the remainder drinking at a local RSL. I once met a veteran of Borneo who told me that in Army training he had been taught to ignore a crucial tenet drummed into him since childhood: 'Thou shall not kill'. He had killed in 1945, then found it hard to meet the expectation on returning to civilian life that he would forget about that carnage. The same feeling haunted some men in this book.

The deeds had to be done, and the soldiers who courageously performed them should be remembered as contributing to victory in a 'good war'. An Australian report on the battle of Alamein concluded: 'Throughout this report there has been little mention of the determination and outstanding gallantry of the troops – the operations speak for themselves'.[8] In fact, merely telling of the operations or battles is not enough. In war, and especially in great battles, there are so many brave acts that the deeds of courageous individuals pass unnoticed all too easily. Examples of gallantry among Australian troops need to be chronicled if they are to be remembered.

ACKNOWLEDGEMENTS

The digital resources of the Australian War Memorial, the National Archives of Australia and the National Archives of the United Kingdom have been indispensable to the writing of this book, and I gratefully acknowledge the work of those wonderful organisations.

As ever, my friend Peter Stanley offered wise counsel at various critical points.

Grateful thanks to Elspeth Menzies for taking on this book, and to the whole professional team at NewSouth Publishing, especially Emma Hutchinson and Joumana Awad. Luke Causby produced another evocative cover and Gabriella Sterio was a most helpful copyeditor. Josephine Pajor-Markus did a phenomenal job meeting my many requests concerning the maps.

Bryce Abraham of the Australian War Memorial generously shared his detailed knowledge of the honours and awards system. He directed me to his excellent PhD on the topic and provided a crucial tip as to where to find obscure citations.

Paul Mishura, brilliant Scotch College archivist, also gave me help and advice about searching for biographical information. Other Scotch College friends, Frank Maguire, Peter Riley, Sherril Schultz and Narelle Sheezel gave valuable assistance, especially on illustrations.

Many thanks also to Karl James, Leigh Mulgrave, Wes Olson, Jason Plumbridge and Mike Rosel. As always, my dear wife Deborah gave me essential support.

BIBLIOGRAPHY

Government and Army documents

Australian Army Journal

Langtry, JO, 'Man-the-weapon', March 1966, <researchcentre.army.gov.au/sites/default/files/aaj_202_mar_1966.pdf>.

Sweeting, AJ, *'Australia's Pearl Harbour' [Review]*, April 1967, <researchcentre.army.gov.au/sites/default/files/aaj_215_apr_1967_0.pdf>.

Australian Government Defence Honours and Awards Appeals Tribunal

'Report of the inquiry into recognition for Far East prisoners of war who were killed while escaping or following recapture', November 2015, <defence-honours-tribunal.gov.au/wp-content/uploads/2019/11/FEPOW-II-Inquiry-Report.pdf>.

Australian War Memorial

AWM 52

War Diaries (Class 8) of these battalions: 2/2nd, 2/6th, 2/7th, 2/8th, 2/18th, 2/24th, 2/25th, 2/28th, 2/31st, 14/32nd, 19th

AWM 54

527/6/9, 26 Bde Report on Operations, Oct–Nov 1942.

Collections

Interview with Vic Knight, <www.awm.gov.au/collection/C87931>.

'Warrant Officer Class 2 Tapioli', <www.awm.gov.au/collection/P11072133>.

Private Records

PR84/035, Lt-Col. H. Dunkley, letter 28 August 1945

PR87/066, Pte A. Murnane, 2/21 Bn, diary

PR89/165, Pte J. Armstrong, 2/21 Bn, diary

Commonwealth of Australia Gazette

Awards for Timor campaign notice, 2019, <www.gg.gov.au/sites/default/files/2019-07/Sparrow%20Force%20Six.pdf>.

National Archives of Australia

B883 service files. I have consulted over 300 files in this category. They are listed in the notes to the relevant chapters. For example, the service file of SX1708 Ron Willson, who won the Military Medal at Balikpapan, is mentioned in the notes of chapter 23. All soldiers whose files are listed in the chapters are also in the index.

B884 PN417 Matpi.

B2455, Howes RA 2918.

M1415, 329, Personal Papers of Prime Minister Curtin, Correspondence 'S', including Sgt John Smith MM.

Bibliography

The National Archives (United Kingdom)
WO 373/27/417 Recommendations for Honours and Awards for Gallant and Distinguished Service. I have consulted over 190 files in this subseries. As with the B883 service files, they are listed in the notes to the relevant chapters, under 'UK Recommendations', and all soldiers whose WO 373 files are listed there are also in the index. Sometimes these files have been used in addition to the B883 files where, for example, the citation is missing or illegible in the Australian file.

Published works

Official histories
Dexter, David, *The New Guinea Offensives*, Australian War Memorial, Canberra, 1961.
Long, Gavin, *Greece, Crete and Syria*, Collins/Australian War Memorial, Sydney, 1986.
— *The Final Campaigns*, Australian War Memorial, Canberra, 1963.
— *The Six Years War*, Australian War Memorial, Canberra, 1973.
— *To Benghazi*, Collins/Australian War Memorial, Sydney, 1986.
Maughan, Barton, *Tobruk and El Alamein*, Australian War Memorial, Canberra, 1966.
McCarthy, Dudley, *South-West Pacific Area – First Year: Kokoda to Wau*, Australian War Memorial, Canberra, 1959.
Wigmore, Lionel, *The Japanese Thrust*, Australian War Memorial, Canberra, 1957.

Unit histories
2/2nd Field Regiment, *Action Front: Official History of the 2/2nd Field Regiment*, Co-Creations Pty Ltd, Melbourne, 2006.
Allard, Jim, *Tank Tracks: The War History of the 2/4th Australian Armoured Regimental Group*, Halstead Press, Sydney, 1953
Allchin, Frank, *Purple and Blue: The History of the 2/10th Battalion, A.I.F.*, Griffin Press, Adelaide, 1958.
Anderson, JA & Jackett, JGT (eds.), *Mud and Sand: the Official War History of the 2/3 Pioneer Battalion A.I.F.*, 2/3rd Pioneer Battalion Association, Sydney, 1955.
Argent, JNL, *'Target Tank'. The History of the 2/3rd Australian Anti-Tank Regiment, 9th Division, AIF*, Cumberland Newspapers, Parramatta, 1957.
Austin, Ron, *Let Enemies Beware! 'Caveant Hostes': The History of the 2/15th Battalion, 1940–1945*, 2/15th Battalion and Slouch Hat Publications, McCrae, 1995.
Bellair, John, *From Snow to Jungle: A History of the 2/3rd Australian Machine Gun Battalion*, Allen & Unwin, Sydney, 1996.
Bentley, Arthur, *The Second Eighth*, 2/8 Battalion Association, Melbourne, 1984.
Bilney, Keith, *14/32 Australian Infantry Battalion A.I.F. 1940 – 1945*, 14/32 Australian Infantry Battalion A.I.F. Association, Victoria, 1994.
Bishop, Les, *The Thunder of the Guns! A History of 2/3 Australian Field Regiment*, 2/3 Australian Field Regiment Association, Sydney, 1998.
Blair, Ron, *A Young Man's War: A History of the 37th/52nd Australian Infantry Battalion in World War Two*, 37/52 Australian Infantry Battalion Association, Melbourne, 1992.
Bolger, William & Littlewood, JG, *The Fiery Phoenix: The Story of the 2/7 Australian Infantry Battalion 1939–46*, 2/7 Battalion Association, Parkdale, 1983.
Brigg, Stan & Brigg, Les, *Ike's Marines: The 36th Australian Infantry Battalion*, The 36th Battalion, Sydney, 1967.

Burns, John, *The Brown and Blue Diamond at War: The Story of the 2/27th Battalion A.I.F.*, 2/27th Battalion Ex-Servicemen's Association, Adelaide, 1960.

Christensen, George, *That's the Way It Was: The History of the 24th Australian Infantry Battalion (A.I.F.) 1939-1945*, 24th Battalion (A.I.F.) Association, Melbourne, 1982.

Christie, Robert W & Christie, Robert (eds.), *A History of the 2/29 Battalion – 8th Australian Division AIF*, Enterprise Press, Sale, 1983.

Clift, Ken, *War Dance: A Story of the 2/3 Aust. Inf. Bn.*, PM Fowler and 2/3rd Battalion Association, Kingsgrove, 1980.

Combe, Gordon, Ligertwood, Frank & Gilchrist, Tom, *The Second 43rd*, Second 43rd Battalion AIF Club, Adelaide, 1972.

Corfield, Robin S, *Hold Hard, Cobbers: The Story of the 57th and 60th and 57/60th Australian Army Infantry Battalion, 1912-1990*, 57/60th Battalion (AIF) Association, Glenhuntly, 1991.

Crooks, William, *The Footsoldiers: The Story of the 2/33rd Australian Infantry Battalion, A.I.F. in the War of 1939–45*, Printcraft Press, Brookvale, 1971.

Dickens, Gordon, *Never Late: The 2/9th Australian Infantry Battalion 1939–1945*, Australian Military History Publications, Loftus, 2005.

Doneley, Bob, *Toowoomba to Torokina: The 25th Battalion in Peace and War, 1918–45*, Big Sky Publishing, Newport, 2012.

Draydon, Allan W, *Men of Courage: A History of 2/25 Australian Infantry Battalion 1940–1945*, 2/25 Australian Infantry Battalion Association, Chermside, 2000.

Elliott, Di & Silver, Lynette, *A History of 2/18th Infantry Battalion AIF*, 2/18th Battalion (AIF) Association, Pennant Hills, 2006.

Fearnside, Geoffrey Harry (ed.), *Bayonets Abroad: A History of the 2/13th Battalion A.I.F. in the Second World War*, Waite and Bull, Sydney, 1953.

Finkemeyer, Colin, *It Happened to Us*, Australian War Memorial, Canberra, 2015.

Givney, EC (ed.), *The First at War: The Story of the 2/1st Australian Infantry Battalion 1939–45*, Association of First Infantry Battalions, Earlwood, 1987.

Glenn, John G, *Tobruk to Tarakan: The Story of the 2/48th Battalion A.I.F.*, Rigby, Adelaide, 1960.

Graeme-Evans, Alex, *Of Storms and Rainbows: The Story of the Men of the 2/12th Battalion, Volume 1*, Southern Holdings, Hobart, 1989.

— *Of Storms and Rainbows: The Story of the Men of the 2/12the Battalion, Volume 2*, 12th Battalion Association, Hobart, 1991.

Hamlyn-Harris, Geoffrey, *Through Mud and Blood to Victory*, 2/31 Australian Infantry Battalion AIF Association (NSW), Newport, 1999.

Handel, Paul, *Dust, Sand and Jungle: A History of Australian Armour 1927 to 1948*, RAAC Memorial and Army Tank Museum, Puckapunyal, 2003.

— *The Vital Factor: A History of 2/6th Australian Armoured Regiment 1941–46*, Australian Military History Publications, Loftus, 2004.

Harrison, Courtney T, *Ambon: Island of Mist*, TW & CT Harrison, North Geelong, 1988.

Hay, David, *Nothing Over Us: The Story of the 2/6th Australian Infantry Battalion*, Australian War Memorial, Canberra, 1984.

Henry, RL, *The Story of the 2/4th Field Regiment*, Merrion Press, Melbourne, 1950.

Henning, Peter, *Doomed Battalion: the Australian 2/40 Battalion*, Allen & Unwin, St Leonards, 1995.

Jesser, Peter, 'The Papuan Infantry Battalion: A Brief History – Part 2', PIB NGIB HQ PIR Association, (n.d.), <www.soldierspng.com/?page_id=3730>.

Laffin, John, *Forever Forward: The Story of the 2/31st Infantry Battalion*, 2/31st Australian Infantry Battalion Association, Newport, 1994.

Johnson, Carl, *Mud Over Blood: Stories from the 39th Infantry Battalion*, History House, Melbourne, 2006

Macfarlan, Graeme, *Etched in Green: The History of the 22nd Australian Infantry Battalion 1939–1946*, 22nd Australian Infantry Battalion Association, Melbourne, 1961.

Magarry, WR, *The Battalion Story: 2/26th Battalion, 8th Division, A.I.F.*, W.R. Magarry, Jindalee, Qld, 1994.

Masel, Philip, *The Second 28th*, 2/28th Battalion and 24th Anti-Tank Coy, Perth, 1961.

Mathews, Russell, *Militia Battalion at War: The History of the 58/59th Australian Infantry Battalion in the Second World War*, 58/59th Battalion Association, Sydney, 1961.

McAllester, JC, *Men of the 2/14 Battalion*, 2/14 Battalion Association, Melbourne, 1990.

Mitchell, James, *Men at War: A Social History of the 2/2nd Pioneer Battalion*, Hardie Grant, Melbourne, 2023.

Newton, Reginald & McGuiness, Peter (eds), *The Grim Glory: The Official History of 2/19 Battalion AIF*, 3rd edition, 1/19 RNSWR Association, Sydney, 2006.

Oakes, Bill, *Muzzle Blast: Six Years of War with the 2/2 Australian Machine Gun Battalion, A.I.F.*, 2/2 Machine Gun Battalion War History Committee, Sydney, 1980.

O'Brien, John W, *Guns and Gunners: The Story of the 2/5th Australian Field Regiment*, Angus and Robertson, Sydney, 1950.

O'Leary, Shawn, *To the Green Fields Beyond: The Story of 6th Division Cavalry Commandos*, Wilke Group, Zillmere, 1975.

Olson, Wes, *Battalion into Battle: The Unit History of the 2/11th Australian Infantry Battalion 1939–1945*, Wesley Olson, Hilton, 2012.

Parsons, Max, *Gunfire! A History of the 2/12 Australian Field Regiment*, Globe Press, Cheltenham, 1991.

Penfold, AW, Bayliss, WC, Crispin, KE, *Galleghan's Greyhounds: The Story of the 2/30th Australian Infantry Battalion*, 2/30 Bn AIF Association, Sydney, 1979.

Pike, P et al, *'What We Have … We Hold!': A History of the 2/17 Australian Infantry Battalion*, 2nd edn, Australian Military History Publications, Loftus, 1998.

Pirie, AA, *Commando Double Black: An Historical Narrative of the 2/5th Australian Independent Company, Later the 2/5th Cavalry Commando Squadron, 1942–1945*, 2/5th Commando Trust, Sydney, 1993.

Russell, WB, *The Second Fourteenth Battalion*, Angus and Robertson, Sydney, 1949.

Serle, RP (ed.), *The Second Twenty-Fourth*, The Jacaranda Press, Brisbane, 1963.

Share, Pat (ed.), *Mud and Blood: 'Albury's Own' Second Twenty-Third Australian Infantry Battalion*, Heritage Book Publications, Frankston, 1978.

Share, Pat & Keating, Allan (eds), *Roll Call of the Second Twenty-Third Australian Infantry Battalion, 1940–1945*, 2/23rd Australian Infantry Battalion Association, Blackburn, 1994.

Sinclair, James, *To Find a Path: The Life and Times of the Royal Pacific Islands Regiment, Volume 1*, Boolarong Publications, Brisbane, 1990.

Trigellis-Smith, Syd, *All the King's Enemies: A History of the 2/5th Australian Infantry Battalion*, Headquarters Training Command, Georges Heights, 1994.
— *Britain to Borneo: A History of 2/32 Australian Infantry Battalion*, 2/32 Australian Infantry Battalion Association, Sydney, 1993.
— *The Purple Devils: The 2/6 Australian Commando Squadron*, 2/6 Commando Squadron Association, Melbourne, 1992.
Unit History Editorial Committee, *White Over Green: The 2/4th Infantry Battalion*, Angus and Robertson, Sydney, 1963.
Uren, Malcolm, *1,000 Men at War: The Story of the 2/16th Battalion, A.I.F.*, John Burridge, Swanbourne, 1988.
Wall, Don, *Singapore and Beyond: The Story of the Men of the 2/20 Battalion*, 2/20 Battalion Association, Netley, 1985.
Ward-Harvey, Ken, *The Sappers' War: With 9 Aust. Div. Engineers 1939–1945*, Sakoga, Newcastle, 1992.
Watt, Jim, *The 61st Battalion*, Australian Military History Publications, Loftus, 2001.
Wick, S, *Purple Over Green, The History of the 2/2 Australian Infantry Battalion*, 2/2 Aust. Inf. Bn Association, Guildford, 1978.

Other published works

Barker, Theo, *Signals: A History of the Royal Australian Corps of Signals 1788–1947*, Royal Australian Corps of Signals Committee, Canberra, 1987.
Barrett, John, *We Were There: Australian Soldiers of World War II Tell Their Stories*, Viking, Ringwood, 1987.
Beaumont, Joan, *Gull Force, survival and leadership in captivity 1941–1945*, Allen & Unwin, Sydney, 1988.
Bradley, Phillip, *Battle for Wau*, Cambridge University Press, Port Melbourne, 2008.
— *D-Day New Guinea*, Allen & Unwin, Sydney, 2019.
— *Hell's Battlefield: The Australians in New Guinea in World War II*, Allen & Unwin, Sydney, 2012.
— *On Shaggy Ridge*, Allen & Unwin, Sydney, 2004.
— *The Battle for Shaggy Ridge*, Allen & Unwin, Sydney, 2021.
— *To Salamaua*, Cambridge University Press, Port Melbourne, 2010
— *Wau 1942-1943*, Army History Unit, Canberra, 2010.
Brown, George A, *For Distinguished Conduct in the Field: The Register of the Distinguished Conduct Medal 1939–1992*, Naval & Military Press, Milton Keynes, 2006.
Brown, Wayne, *Blue: The Remarkable Exploits of 'Blue' Reiter M.C., M.M., MID 1939–1945*, Wayne Brown, Warana, 2006.
Brune, Peter, *Those Ragged Bloody Heroes: From the Kokoda Trail to Gona Beach 1942*, Allen & Unwin, Sydney, 1991.
Burness, Peter, 'Heroes of Tobruk', Australian War Memorial, 2010, <www.awm.gov.au/wartime/86/article-one>.
Clift, Ken, *The Saga of a Sig*, KCD Publications, Randwick, 1972.
Coates, John, *Bravery Above Blunder: The 9th Australian Division at Finschhafen, Sattelberg and Sio*, Oxford University Press, Melbourne, 1993.
Davidson, Audrey, *Porton: A Deadly Trap*, Boolarong Press, Moorooka, 2006.

Bibliography

Dawes, Allan, *'Soldier Superb': The Australian Fights in New Guinea*, FH Johnston Publishing Co., Sydney, 1944.
Farrell, Brian & Pratten, Garth, *Malaya 1942*, Army History Unit, Canberra, 2009.
Gamble, Bruce, *Invasion Rabaul: The Epic Story of Lark Force, the Forgotten Garrison, January–July 1942*, Zenith Press, Minneapolis, 2014.
Gullett, Henry ('Jo'), *Not as a Duty Only: An Infantryman's War*, Melbourne University Press, Carlton, 1984.
Handel, Paul, *Dust, Sand & Jungle: A History of Australian Armour During Training and Operations, 1927–1948*, RAAC Memorial and Army Tank Museum, Puckapunyal, 2003.
Hartley, Francis John, *Sanananda Interlude*, The Book Depot, Melbourne, 1949.
Hastings, Max, *Warriors: Portraits from the Battlefield*, Vintage Books, New York, 2007.
Heckmann, Wolf, *Rommel's War in Africa*, Smithmark, New York, 1995.
Horner, David, *The Gunners: A History of Australian Artillery*, Allen & Unwin, Sydney, 1995.
Hunter, Claire & Walker, Isabelle, 'A Day in the Life', *Wartime*, Issue 95, Winter 2021.
Hurrell, Albert Lloyd, *Hurrell's Way: An Autobiography*, Crawford House, Belair, 2006.
James, Karl, *Double Diamonds: Australian Commandos in the Pacific War 1941–45*, NewSouth Publishing, Sydney, 2016.
— *The Hard Slog: Australians in the Bougainville Campaign, 1944-45*, Cambridge University Press, Port Melbourne, 2012.
Johnston, Mark, *An Australian Band of Brothers*, NewSouth Publishing, Sydney, 2018.
— *Anzacs in the Middle East*, Cambridge University Press, Melbourne, 2012
— *Derrick VC in His Own Words*, NewSouth Publishing, Sydney, 2021
— *Stretcher-bearers: Saving Australians from Gallipoli to Kokoda*, Cambridge University Press, Melbourne, 2015.
— *That Magnificent 9th*, Allen & Unwin, Sydney, 2002.
— *The Australian Army*, Osprey, Oxford, 2007.
— *The Japanese Advance 1941–1942*, published by Department of Veterans' Affairs, Canberra, 2007.
— *The Proud 6th*, Cambridge University Press, Melbourne, 2008
— *The Silent 7th*, Allen & Unwin, Sydney, 2005.
Johnston, Mark & Stanley, Peter, *Alamein: The Australian Story*, Oxford University Press, South Melbourne, 2002.
Joyce, Ken, *As I Saw it: From Tobruk to Tarakan 1940–1945*, Ken Joyce, Australia, 2002.
Kennett, Lee, *G.I.: The American Soldier in World War II*, Charles Scribner's Sons, New York, 1987.
Legg, Frank, *War Correspondent*, Rigby, Adelaide, 1964.
Lindsay, Neville, *Equal to the Task: The Royal Australian Army Service Corps*, Historia Productions, Kenmore, 1991.
Lindsay, Patrick (dir.), *Kokoda: The Bloody Track* [documentary], Australian Army, 1992.
Mayo, Linda, *Bloody Buna*, New English Library, London, 1975.
McAllester, Jim & Trigellis-Smith, Syd, *Largely a Gamble: Australians in Syria June–July 1941*, Headquarters Training Command, Sydney, 1995.
McNicoll, Ronald, *The Royal Australian Engineers 1919 to 1945: Teeth and Tail, Volume 3*, Corps Committee of the Royal Australian Engineers, Canberra, 1982.
Mehan, Russell, *An Unrewarded Hero: The Alan Haddy Story*, Russell Mehan, Carine, 2000.

Powell, Alan, *The Third Force: ANGAU's New Guinea War 1942–46*, Oxford University Press, Melbourne, 2003.
Smith, Alan H, *Battle Winners: Australian Artillery in the Western Desert 1940–1942*, Barrallier Books, Geelong, 2014.
Stanley, Peter, *Tarakan: An Australian Tragedy*, Allen & Unwin, Sydney, 1997.
Steward, HD, *Recollections of a Regimental Medical Officer*, Melbourne University Press, Melbourne, 1983.
Torrent, Andrew, *A 'Day' in the Army*, South West Printing, Bunbury, 1980.
Warren, Alan, *Singapore 1942: Britain's greatest defeat*, Hardie Grant, Melbourne, 2002.
Williams, FDG, *Slam: The Influence of S.L.A. Marshall on the United States Army*, Center of Military History, Washington, 1999.
Williams, Peter, *The Kokoda Campaign 1942: myth and reality*, Cambridge University Press, Port Melbourne, 2012.
Wilmot, Chester, *Tobruk 1941*, Angus and Robertson, Sydney, 1945.
Wilson, Neil, 'Mud-covered decoys', *Herald Sun*, 11 June 2005, p. 90.
Winters, Dick, *Beyond Band of Brothers*, Ebury Press, London, 2011.

Australians at War Film Archive

Interviews
Ray Brown, <australiansatwarfilmarchive.unsw.edu.au/archive/2547-ray-brown>.
Pat Lawry, <australiansatwarfilmarchive.unsw.edu.au/archive/122-patrick-lawry>.
Don McKay, <australiansatwarfilmarchive.unsw.edu.au/archive/343>.
Ron Plater, <australiansatwarfilmarchive.unsw.edu.au/archive/htmlTranscript/1507>.
Frederick Rossborough, <australiansatwarfilmarchive.unsw.edu.au/archive/1835>.
Alwyn Shilton, <https://australiansatwarfilmarchive.unsw.edu.au/archive/243>.
Bede Tongs, <australiansatwarfilmarchive.unsw.edu.au/archive/1151>.
Royce Whatley, <australiansatwarfilmarchive.unsw.edu.au/archive/636>.

Australian Dictionary of Biography

Bou, Jean, 'Alexander John Taylor', <adb.anu.edu.au/biography/taylor-alexander-john-15687>.
Burness, Peter, 'Russell Melton (Bill) McCure', <adb.anu.edu.au/biography/mccure-russell-melton--bill-15058>.
Crawley, Rhys, 'Clyde Joseina Egan', <adb.anu.edu.au/biography/egan-clyde-joseina-18060>.
Falk, Barbara, 'Albert Gordon (Bon) Austin', <adb.anu.edu.au/biography/austin-albert-gordon-bon-12156>.
Grant, Ian, 'Gilbert Ernest Cory', <adb.anu.edu.au/biography/cory-gilbert-ernest-9831>.
Hall, Robert, 'Timothy Hughes', <adb.anu.edu.au/biography/hughes-timothy-10567>.
Hodges, Ian, 'John William Hedderman', <adb.anu.edu.au/biography/hedderman-john-william-12615/text22725>.
Johnston, Mark, 'Bell, Harry James', <adb.anu.edu.au/biography/bell-harry-james-12192/text21857>.

Lewis, DC, 'Basil Edward Fairfax-Ross', <adb.anu.edu.au/biography/fairfaxross-basil-edward-12476>.
Powell, Alan, 'Robert Kerr McLaren', <adb.anu.edu.au/biography/mclaren-robert-kerr-11001>.
Staunton, Anthony, 'Cecil Hamilton (Jim) Cawthorne', <adb.anu.edu.au/biography/cawthorne-cecil-hamilton-jim-12300>.

Newspaper articles (Trove)

'Abbott Convicted of Casino Murder', *Sydney Morning Herald*, 30 November 1951.
'Cut Off in the New Guinea Jungle', *The Bunyip*, 26 February 1943.
'D.C.M. FOR SWIMMER', *The Daily News* (Perth, WA), 28 January 1944, p. 7.
'D.C.M. Man Returns to Leeton', *The Murrumbidgee Irrigator*, 1 May 1942, p. 3.
'D.C.M. Presented to Canberra Man', *Newcastle Morning Herald and Miners' Advocate*, 31 July 1947, p. 2.
'Death of Lt. Lance Armstrong', *Mudgee Guardian and North-Western Representative*, 30 August 1945, p. 10.
'Decorated Men Meet', *The Daily News* (Perth, WA), 9 February 1944.
'Hero's Date With Death', *Truth*, 10 July 1949, p. 2.
'Honours to Eighth Division P.O.W.s', *The Sydney Morning Herald*, 7 March 1947, p. 5.
'McLennan Managed to Get Back to His Lines Again', *Goulburn Evening Post*, 22 May 1945, p. 1.
'Military Cross', *Mount Barker and Denmark Record*, 23 March 1944, p. 1.
'Motor Tragedy in Moree', *Warialda Standard and Northern Districts' Advertiser*, 22 August 1949.
'Obituary: Mr Byron Dawes', *Canberra Times*, 12 October 1977.
'Obituary: Mr Churchill Avern', *The Inverell Times*, 10 October 1952, p. 4.
'Sergeants Beck and Smith', *The Bulletin*, 10 November 1943, p. 7.
'So O'Connor Got The Name "Okey"', *News* (Adelaide), 26 June 1945, p. 2.
'Soldiers Awarded George Medal', *Daily Examiner* (Grafton), 22 October 1945, p. 6.
'Welcome to Soldiers at Timboon', *Camperdown Chronicle*, 13 October 1944.
'Wicked Will of the 6th', *The Daily News*, 18 September 1945, p. 1.
'W/O F. P. Bingham', *Advocate* (Burnie), 14 August 1945.
'Wounded, But Dodged Japs For Four Days', *The Argus*, 21 May 1945, p. 16.

Other websites

2/2 Pioneer Battalion, <www.2nd2ndpioneerbattalion.com/>.
2/4th Machine-Gun Battalion, <2nd4thmgb.com.au/about/>.
2/20th Battalion, <secondtwentieth.org.au/pages/>.
2/30th Battalion, <www.230battalion.org.au/>.
Mishura, Paul, Obituary of William Chevily Woodward, *Great Scot*, December 2011, <www.scotch.vic.edu.au/greatscot/2011decGS/76a.htm>.

Theses

Abraham, Bryce, 'Valore Australis: Constructions of Australian Military Heroism from Sudan to Vietnam, 1885–1975' [PhD thesis], University of Newcastle, 2019, <ogma.newcastle.edu.au/vital/access/manager/Repository/uon:36329?view=null&f0=sm_mimeType%3A%22application%2Fpdf%22&f1=sm_type%3A%22thesis%22&sort=ss_dateNormalized+asc%2Csort_ss_title+asc&f2=sm_date%3A%222020%22&f3=sm_creator%3A%22Abraham%2C+Bryce+Scott%22 >.

Unpublished sources

Jones, AA, 'A Volunteer's Story', 1988. Donor: AA Jones

NOTES

I set out to limit the number of notes in this book. Nevertheless, it is based on a very large amount of research. The narrative of events relies heavily on the seven volumes in the Army series of the official history, *Australia in the War of 1939–1945*. These volumes also include information on most of those who won medals. The published battalion histories contain details of many of those individuals as well as citations for some of their medals. Indispensable to the content of the book are the service records of the individuals discussed. Where these had not yet been digitised by the National Archives of Australia at the time of writing, I often turned to the 'Recommendations for military honours and awards 1935–1990' on the website of the National Archives of the United Kingdom. I have also made much use of newspapers available at the excellent Trove website. Below is a list of the main sources used in each chapter, divided into official histories, unit histories, other secondary sources and archival records, especially service records held at the National Archives of Australia (NAA), recommendations for awards on the UK National Archives website (UK Recommendations) and newspaper articles on the Trove website. The sources appear roughly in the order in which they were used within each chapter. Unless otherwise noted, all quotations are from the official histories or individual citations. I used numbered notes for the Introduction, Interludes and Conclusion.

Introduction
1 Calculated from the Australian War Memorial website's Honours and Awards pages.
2 National Archives (UK), WO 373/45/284, 'Recommendation for Award for Rose, Allan'.
3 AWM52 8/3/6/32, 2/6 Bn WD, 25 April, 16 and 17 June 1945.

4 Torrent, *A Day in the Army*, p. 70. Rose is mentioned in chapter 16.
5 Alan Avery (MM) in the 1992 documentary *Kokoda: The Bloody Track*.
6 Combe et al, *The Second 43rd*, p. 243.
7 Barrett, *We Were There*, p. 223.
8 Torrent, p. 70.
9 James, *Double Diamonds*, p. 83.
10 Gullett, *Not as a Duty Only*, p. 115.
11 Gullett, p. 114.
12 Christensen, *That's The Way It Was*, p. 243.
13 Long, *Final Campaigns*, p. 581n. The battalion was more generous in the war's last months.
14 Gullett, p. 114.
15 Sweeting, 'Book review', *Australian Army Journal*, April 1967, pp. 57–58.
16 Gullett, p. 114.
17 Quoted in Kennett, *GI*, pp. 702–704.
18 Caption to AWM ART26993.
19 Quoted in Barrett, pp. 228–229.
20 Quoted in Barrett, pp. 223–224.
21 Langtry, 'Man-the-weapon', *Australian Army Journal*, March 1966, p. 6.
22 Hastings, *Warriors*, p. xxiii.
23 Pte 'Osty' Ostberg in Austin, *Let Enemies Beware*, p. 95.
24 Information provided by Bryce Abraham.

Chapter 1 Baptism at Bardia
Archival: NAA B883: NX2233 Abbott, NX4293 Pickett, VX8452 Symington, VX3680 Morse, VX1367 Cantelo
UK Recommendations: Rankin, Vickery
Trove: 'Abbott Convicted of Casino murder', *Sydney Morning Herald*
Official: Long, *To Benghazi*
Unit: Givney, *First at War* (2/1st Bn); Trigellis-Smith, *All the King's Enemies* (2/5th Bn) Wick, *Purple Over Green* (2/2nd Bn)
Secondary: Johnston, *Proud 6th*; McNicoll, *Royal Australian* Engineers; Clift, *The Saga of a Sig*
Other: Orma Jean (Hildebrand) Warner, <www.wikitree.com/wiki/Hildebrand-1034> (Abbott)

Chapter 2 The advance to Benghazi
Archival: NAA B883: VX9024 Neall, QX6083 Ryan, VX31716 Berry
UK Recommendations: MacDougal, Stenning, McQuillan, Diffey
Official: Long, *To Benghazi*
Unit: Clift, *War Dance* (2/3rd Bn); Bentley, *The Second Eighth*; Unit History Committee, *White Over Green* (2/4th Bn); O'Leary, *To the Green Fields Beyond* (6th Div Cav); Olsen, *Battalion into Battle* (2/11th); Dickens, *Never Late* (2/9th Bn)
Secondary: Barker, *Signals*; Johnston, *Proud 6th* and *Silent 7th*

Chapter 3 Tobruk: Holding the thin Red Line
Archival: NAA B883: NX12222 Handley, NX16216 Dunbar, NX23052 McElroy, SX7272 Spavin, WX7959 Aston, QX6940 Christsen, QX2687 AJ Taylor, QX1399 Hobson, VX24598 Courtney

Notes

UK Recommendations: Mackell, Cook, Noyes
Official: Maughan, *Tobruk and El Alamein*
Unit: Fearnside, *Bayonets Abroad* (2/13th Bn); Glenn, *Tobruk to Tarakan* (2/48th Bn); Serle, *The Second Twenty-Fourth*; Share, *Mud and Blood* (2/23rd Bn); Combe et al, *The Second 43rd*; Masel, *The Second 28th*, including 24th Anti-Tank Company; Allchin, *Purple and Blue* (2/10th Bn)
Secondary: Johnston, *That Magnificent 9th* and *An Australian Band of Brothers*; Wilmot, *Tobruk 1941*; Heckmann, *Rommel's War*; Bou, 'Taylor, Alexander John'.
Other: Pte Harry Frazer, 2/24 Bn, letter 23 June 1941, MJC (Rosel)

Chapter 4 Mission impossible: The campaign in Greece
Archival: NAA B883: NX2389 Lacey, VX1912 Craig, VX17880 Killalea, VX587 Anderson
UK Recommendations: Duncan, Lacey, Hiddins, FE Harris
Official: Long, *To Benghazi* and Long, *Greece, Crete and Syria*
Unit: Bentley, *The Second Eighth*; Bishop, *Thunder of the Guns* (2/3 Fd Regt); Wick, *Purple Over Green*; Lindsay, *Equal to the Task*; 2/2nd Field Regiment, *Action Front*
Secondary: Johnston, *Proud 6th*; Barker, *Signals*
Other: Laybourne Smith, letters 1941, MJC

Chapter 5 Island of doomed heroes: Crete
Archival: NAA B883: WX1005 Mulgrave, NX2470 H Johnston, WX788 Johnson, WX1944 Richards, WX9 Fitzhardinge, WX981 Bradfield; AWM54, 253/1/10, Sgt H Thomas, 2/7 Bn, diary May 1941
Trove: 'DCM Man Returns to Leeton', *The Murrumbidgee Irrigator* (Swanson)
Official: Long, *Greece, Crete and Syria*
Unit: Bolger & Littlewood, *Fiery Phoenix* (2/7th Bn); Unit History Committee, *White Over Green*; Olsen, *Battalion into Battle*; Givney, *First at War*
Secondary: Johnston, *Stretcher-bearers*, *Proud 6th* and *Fighting the Enemy*; Brown, *Blue*
Other: Interview with Pat Lawry

Chapter 6 Tobruk: Besieging the besiegers
Archival: NAA B883: QX8348 Smithers, VX48694 Malloch, QX2047 N Russell, SX5399 Cawthorne, WX3404 Coppock, SX5547 Quinn, NX20944 Perkins; AWM 3DRL/3825, Butler, 2/23 Bn, diary 1941
UK Recommendations: Hunt, Cawthorne
Official: Maughan, *Tobruk and El Alamein*
Unit: Share, *Mud and Blood*; Glenn, *Tobruk to Tarakan*; Fearnside, *Bayonets Abroad*; Combe et al, *The Second 43rd*; Masel, *The Second 28th*; Ward-Harvey, *Sappers' War*; Graeme-Evans, *Of Storms and Rainbows*, Volume 1 (2/12th Bn)
Secondary: Johnston, *That Magnificent 9th* and *An Australian Band of Brothers*; Staunton, 'Cawthorne'; McNicoll, *Royal Australian Engineers*

Interlude 1 The language of heroism
1   Clift, *War Dance*, p. vi.
2   Maughan, *Tobruk and El Alamein*, p. 12.
3   Dexter, *The New Guinea Offensives*, p. 677.
4   Clift, p. v.

Chapter 7 The unsung heroes of the Syrian campaign
Archival: NAA B2455: Howes RA 2918 and B883 SX3404 Howes, QX6190 Bolton, NX12174 Gall, NX4314 Atkinson, NX4597 Donoghue, QX1352 Gesch, VX17772 Avery, VX42260 Shannon, NX5398 Mackay, VX16232 Warburton
UK Recommendations: Bright, V Thomas, C Smith, Melvaine, W Ferguson, M Groundwater, Jeffrey, Sims, Lee, Smith
Official: Long, *Greece, Crete and Syria.*
Unit: Uren, *1,000 Men at War* (2/16th Bn); Henry, *Story of the 2/4th Field Regiment*; Burns, *The Brown and Blue Diamond at War* (2/27th Bn); O'Leary, *To the Green Fields Beyond*; Crooks, *Footsoldiers* (2/33rd Bn); Laffin, *Forever Forward* (2/31st Bn); Clift, *War Dance*; Russell, *Second Fourteenth Battalion*; Mitchell, *Men at War* (2/2nd Pnr Bn)
Secondary: Johnston, *Silent 7th*; McAllester & Trigellis-Smith, *Largely a Gamble* (including decorations total); Mehan, *An Unrewarded Hero: The Alan Haddy Story*; McNicoll, *Royal Australian Engineers*
Other: Hunter & Walker, 'A Day in the Life'

Chapter 8 The Japanese onslaught: Malaya and Singapore
Archival: NAA B883: VX39136 Wedlick, VX39085 Brand, VX32772 Benoit, QX13802 Easton, QX11509 Parker, NX34879 Vernon, VX38307 Reid
UK Recommendations: Wankey, D Phillips, Bingham, Magarry
Official: Wigmore, *The Japanese Thrust*
Unit: Penfold, *Galleghan's Greyhounds* (2/30th Bn); McCure in Finkemeyer, *It Happened to Us* (4th AT Regt); Christie, *History of the 2/29 Battalion;* Newton, *The Grim Glory of the 2/19 Battalion AIF*; Wall, *Singapore and Beyond* (2/20th Bn); Elliott & Silver, *A History of 2/18th*; Magarry, *The Battalion Story* (2/26th Bn)
Secondary: Johnston, *Japanese Advance*; Warren, *Britain's Greatest Defeat*; Farrell & Pratten, *Malaya*; Horner, *Gunners*; Burness, 'McCure'
Other: 2/30th Battalion A.I.F Association, <www.230battalion.org.au>; 2/4th Machine Gun Battalion Ex-Members Association, <2nd4thmgb.com.au/story/d-company-no-13-platoon-lim-chu-kang-road-8th-february-1942/>; Korean War Online, <www.koreanwaronline.com/history/oz/Charlie/Derrington.htm>

Chapter 9 Doomed battalions: New Britain, Ambon, Timor and Java
Archival: NAA B883: VX8370 Appel, VX19233 Mitchell; AWM PR89/165, Pte J. Armstrong, 2/21 Bn, diary; PR87/066, Pte A. Murnane, 2/21 Bn, diary/memoir 1 Feb 1942
Official: Wigmore, *The Japanese Thrust*
Unit: Harrison, *Ambon* (2/21st); Henning, *Doomed Battalion* (2/40th); Bellair, *From Snow to Jungle* (2/3rd MG); Mitchell, *Men at War*
Secondary: Johnston, *Japanese Advance*; Beaumont, *Gull Force*
Other: 'Hero of Ambon', <www.awm.gov.au/articles/blog/hero-of-ambon>; caption to AWM133887 and 124976; 2019 awards for Timor campaign, <www.gg.gov.au/sites/default/files/2019-07/Sparrow%20Force%20Six.pdf>; Inquiry into Recognition for Far East Prisoners of War, <defence-honours-tribunal.gov.au/wp-content/uploads/2019/11/FEPOW-II-Inquiry-Report.pdf>

Chapter 10 Return to the Desert: Egypt
Archival: NAA B883: SX9328 Bell, SX8466 Haynes, SX7244 Ramsdale, NX25805 Roberts, VX42774 Fyffe, SX5282 Dean, VX42434 Hughes, SX10570 Ashby, QX5495 Else, QX3000 Patrick, QX5634 McLachlan; AWM 2/32 Bn WD, July–August 1942 (Langford)
UK Recommendations: Hinson, McMahon, Williams, Bryant, Kinghorn, Knight, Cotterill, Brandrick, Masterson, Maddocks, Manning, Cameron, Bambling, McLachlan, Baggaley
Trove: 'Motor Tragedy near Moree', *Warialda Standard and Northern Districts' Advertiser*
Official: Maughan, *Tobruk and El Alamein*
Unit: Share, *Mud and Blood*; Oakes, *Muzzle Blast* (2/2nd MG Bn); Argent, 'Target Tank' (2/3rd AT Regt); Serle, *Second Twenty-Fourth*; Austin, *Let Enemies Beware* (2/15th Bn)
Secondary: Johnston, *Australian Band of Brothers*, *Magnificent 9th* and *Derrick VC in His Own Words*; Johnston & Stanley, *Alamein: The Australian Story*
Other: Interview with Vic Knight; Abraham, 'Valore Australis' [PhD thesis] (Neuendorf)

Interlude 2 The warriors' weapons
1   Jones, *Volunteer's Story*, p. 246.
2   Dawes, *Soldier Superb*, p. 20.
3   Givney, *First at War*, pp. 317–318.
4   Christie, *A History of the 2/29 Battalion*, p. 69.

Chapter 11 Kokoda: The first clashes
Archival: NAA B883: VX100098 McClean, V42272 Pyke, VX8452 Symington, VX103150 Smythe; NAA B884: V5493 Cowey
UK Recommendations: O'Neill
Official: McCarthy, *SWPA First Year*
Unit: Johnson, *Mud Over Blood* (39th Bn)
Secondary: Williams, *The Kokoda Campaign*
Other: Interview with Don McKay

Chapter 12 Milne Bay: Breaking the Japanese spell
Archival: NAA B883: SX9891 Kotz, SX10515 Abraham, TX500137 [sic] Holmyard, QX54580 Baumann, QX1254 Paterson, VX20960 Marriott
UK recommendations: Irwin
Official: McCarthy, *SWPA First Year*
Unit: Doneley, *Toowoomba to Torokina* (25th Bn); Allchin, *Purple and Blue*; Graeme-Evans, *Of Storms and Rainbows*, Volume 2; Dickens, *Never Late*
Secondary: Mayo, *Bloody Buna*

Chapter 13 Kokoda: Fighting retreat, fighting return
Archival: NAA B883: VX15241 McCallum, NX40507 Fletcher, WX4227 Maidment (under Thornton), VX52829 Pearce, SX4984 Zanker, WX4210 Moloney, NX2642 McCloy, NX34302 Leaney, NX47465 Stewart, NX7864 Cory, NGX18 AL Hurrell, QX12408 Redgrave

UK Recommendations: Preece, Tongs, Catterns, Pett, O'Donnell, Stoddart, Shearwin
Official: McCarthy, *SWPA First Year*
Unit: McAllester, *Men of the 2/14th*; Russell, *Second Fourteenth*; Burns, *The Brown and Blue Diamond at War*; Draydon, *Men of Courage* (2/25th Bn); Crooks, *Footsoldiers*; Givney, *First at War*; Laffin, *Forever Forward* (2/31st)
Secondary: Williams, *Kokoda*
Other: Lindsay (dir.), *Kokoda: The Bloody Track*; 'Cut Off in the New Guinea Jungle', *The Bunyip*; Hamlyn-Harris, *Through Mud and Blood*

Chapter 14 El Alamein: The decisive battle
Archival: NAA B883: VX10064 Broadhurst, QX19122 Stevenson, WX11512 Greatorex, NX21416 Harris, NX18260 Easter, NX13746 Cortis, NX21473 Bentley, NX16920 Taylor, WX5057 Wallder, VX31716 Berry, VX34703 J Anderson, VX27602 Cameron, QX8109 V Anderson, QX4060 MacDonald, NX4031 Davidson, SX7410 Ranford, VX56822 O'Brien, SX8897 Hare, SX5093 Joy; A471 51258 [O'Brien court martial]
UK Recommendations: Rodriguez, Kennedy, Albrecht, J Anderson, Menzies, McAllister, Seatree, James, Dingwall
Trove: 'W/O F. P. Bingham', *Advocate* (Burnie)
Official: Maughan, *Tobruk and El Alamein*
Unit: Serle, *Second Twenty-Fourth*; Fearnside, *Bayonets Abroad*; Argent, *Target Tank*; Glenn, *Tobruk to Tarakan*; Share, *Mud and Blood*; Austin, *Let Enemies Beware*; Anderson & Jackett, *Mud and Sand* (2/3rd Pioneer Bn), Combe, *Second 43rd*
Secondary: Johnston & Stanley, *Alamein: The Australian Story*; Johnston, *Australian Band of Brothers*; Smith, *Battle Winners*
Other: Joyce, *As I Saw It*

Chapter 15 The Beachhead Battles: Gona, Buna and Sanananda
Archival: NAA B883: NX7423 Mulally, VX12331 Duncan, VX120253 Edgell, WX4274 Thompson, VX14647 Dougherty, VX13894 Crilly, VX106080 Ellis, VX100096 Gartner, VX5449 Taylor, QX2163 MacIntosh, QX11632 Thomas, QX3097 Jesse, SX929 McAuliffe, SX1570 Hughes, SX911 Duffy, SX8790 Brandon, QX21910 Dyne, VX39414 Sampson, QX3787 Hudson, NX68372 Albanese, NX11538 Ledden, NX68683 Soltan, QX1253 Forster, V230062 Butler, NX15895 Morton, NX90672 Burgess, NX43691 Lynn, SX22130 Saint; AWM52 8/3/7, 'Report on Carrier Operation in the Cape Endaiadere Area'
UK Recommendations: Soltan, Murphy, Dalby, Plater, Blair, Oxlade, Hooke, McInnes
Official: McCarthy, *SWPA First Year*
Unit: Russell, *Second Fourteenth*; Dickens, *Never Late*; Allchin, *Purple and Blue*; Graeme Evans, *Of Storms and Rainbows, Volume 2*; Givney, *First at War*; Brigg, *Ike's Marines* (36th Bn); Handel, *Vital Factor* (2/6th Armd Regt)
Secondary: Johnston, *Silent 7th* and *Proud 6th*; Bradley, *Hell's Battlefield*; Mehan, *Unrewarded Hero*; Hall, 'Hughes'
Other: Interview with Ron Plater; Hamlyn-Harris, *Through Mud and Blood*; Steward, *Recollections*; Hartley, *Sanananda Interlude*

Notes

Chapter 16 Wau–Salamaua: Heroism in the hills
Archival: NAA B883: VX4456 St John, VX38792 Gray, VX4740 Walker, VX2525 Gibbons, VX1017 Reeve, VX3347 Cameron, VX5660 Tatterson, PX191 Hall, VX41023 Looker, PN3 Farr, VX54565 Smith, VX12728 Hedderman, NX113462 Roach, SX20339 Moss, WX11335 McEvoy, VX105917 Wellings, TX708 Walters, QX54772 Miles, VX4838 Naismith, QX56274 Deal, Q31503 Sallaway, QX31091 Troughton, VX17556 Frawley; NAA M1415 329 'Death of VX3491 Sgt John Smith MM'
UK Recommendations: Walker, Cameron, Waters, Bowen, Ehava brothers, A Smith, Ryan, Exton, G Smith, Moss, Warfe, Proby, Laver, Barnett, Frawley
Official: McCarthy, *SWPA First Year*; Dexter, *New Guinea Offensives*
Unit: Hay, *Nothing Over Us*; Jesser, 'The Papuan Infantry Battalion'; Mathews, *Militia Battalion at War* (58th/59th Bn)
Secondary: Johnston, *Proud 6th* and *Stretcher-Bearers*; Bradley, *Hell's Battlefield*; Bradley, *Wau*; Bradley, *To Salamaua*; Hodges, 'Hedderman'

Chapter 17 By air, sea and land: Lae and the Huon Peninsula
Archival: NAA B883: VX7410 Lawrie, WX500547 Crouchley, WX5557 Brooks, NX134066 Jaggar, NX57501 Childs, QX17700 Brockhurst, QX26271 Richards, VX11589 Copp (Cullen), NX14353 R Groundwater, VX4310 A Scott, QX8529 Fink, QX14730 Guilfoyle, WX13372 Nankiville
UK Recommendations: Lawrie, Fairlie, Schram, May, Pope, Starmer, Grant, Rolfe, Crawford
Trove: 'Welcome to Soldiers At Timboon', *Camperdown Chronicle*; 'Decorated Men Meet', *The Daily News* (Perth, WA); '"D.C.M. for Swimmer' and 'Decorated Men Meet', *The Daily News* (Perth, WA)
Official: Dexter, *New Guinea Offensives*
Unit: Draydon, *Men of Courage*; Fearnside, *Bayonets Abroad*; Share, *Mud and Blood*; Keating, *Roll Call* (2/23rd Bn); Trigellis-Smith, *Britain to Borneo* (2/32nd Bn); Crooks, *Footsoldiers*; Parsons, *Gunfire* (2/12th Fd Regt); Masel, *The Second 28th*
Secondary: Bradley, *D-Day New Guinea*; Coates, *Bravery Above Blunder*; Johnston, *Australian Band of Brothers*; Torrent, *A Day in the Army*; Johnston, 'Bell, Harry James'

Chapter 18 To Sattelberg and Shaggy Ridge
Archival: NAA B883: VX54281 Balderstone, NX15984 Dawes, WX10241 Leary, WX9926 Keley, VX105949 Deslandes, VX72101 Drew, WX5607 Scott, VX36233 Green, SX1071 Bloffwitch, VX141681 Tremellen
UK Recommendations: Morphett, Barry, Robino, McNee, Hamilton, Bear, Pearson, Stirling, Berrell, Temple, Atkinson,
Trove: 'Sergeants Beck and Smith', *The Bulletin*; 'Military Cross', *Mount Barker and Denmark Record* (Scott); 'Obituary: Mr Byron Dawes', *Canberra Times*.
Official: Dexter, *New Guinea Offensives*
Unit: Trigellis-Smith, *Purple Devils* (2/6 Cdo); Austin, *Let Enemies Beware*; Fearnside, *Bayonets Abroad*; Trigellis-Smith, *Britain to Borneo*; Share, *Mud and Blood*; Keating, *Roll Call*; Blair, *Young Man's War* (37th/52nd Bn), Macfarlan, *Etched in Green* (22nd Bn); Burns, *The Brown and Blue Diamond at War*; Draydon, *Men of Courage*; Dickens, *Never Late*; Graeme-Evans, *Storms and Rainbows*, Volume 1; Corfield, *Hold Hard, Cobbers* (57th/60th Bn); Mathews, *Militia Battalion at War*

Secondary: Bradley, *On Shaggy Ridge*; Bradley, *Battle For Shaggy Ridge*; James, *Double Diamonds*; Johnston, *Derrick VC in His Own Words*; Johnston, *Australian Band of Brothers*
Other: Jones, *Volunteer's Story*

Chapter 19 Bougainville: Through mud and blood to victory
Archival: AWM PR84/035, Lt-Col. H. Dunkley, letter 28 August 1945; NAA B883: NX153358 Layt, Q111747 Jorgensen, SX14615 Hockey, VX103648 Whatley, VX93416 McLennan, NX208094 O'Connor, NX150794 Syrett, QX40532 Brown, QX36511 Searles, NX14999 N Smith, NX179453 Duck, VX4024 Reiter, VX104330 Chambers, NX151510 McPhee, NX71415 Wigley
UK Recommendations: Oliver, S Graham, Nott, Rossborough, Barnes, Kemp, Egan, Biri, Woodward, Langtry, Kane, Shilton, Bright, Calder, Spark, Burrell, A Graham, Draper, Uebergang, Deacon, Goodwin, White
Trove: 'McLennan Managed to Get Back to His Lines Again', *Goulburn Evening Post*; 'So O'Connor Got The Name "Okey"', *Adelaide News*
Official: Long, *Final Campaigns*
Unit: Doneley, *Toowoomba to Torokina*; Christensen, *That's the Way It Was* (24th Bn); Mathews, *Militia Battalion at War*
Secondary: James, *Hard Slog*; McNicoll, *Royal Australian Engineers*; Crawley, 'Egan, Clyde Joseina'; Obituary of William Chevily Woodward, *Great Scot*, December 2011; Jesser, 'The Papuan Infantry Battalion'; Davidson, *Porton: A Deadly Trap*
Other: Interviews with Frederick Rossborough, Royce Whatley and Alwyn Shilton

Interlude 4 Heroic rescuers
1   In Johnston, *Stretcher-bearers*, p. 217.

Chapter 20 New Guinea: From Aitape to Wewak
Archival: NAA B883: WX248 Royce, NGX46 Cole, DX174 McAllister, NX73070 Graham, QX38356 Hall, NX7864 Cory, VX12728 Hedderman, SX4240 Bowden, TX1766 Macfie, NX2323 Finlayson, NX21119 Webb, VX501799 Daniel, NX68854 Reed, NX78416 Bartholomew, VX6526 Leitch, WX1932 Grant, WX11396 Fogarty, WX12639 Gilpin, NX173075 Smith, NX128778 McCrackan, NX126254 Batten, WX14930 Bassula; NX42848 Donnet; AWM52, 8/3/2, 2/2nd Bn War Diary, March 1945; AWM52, 8/3/8, 2/8th Bn War Diary, June 1945
UK Recommendations: Birrell, Turnbull, Weir, Stubbs, Morris, McLelland, Park, Copeman, Daniel, Johnson, Kitching, McMaster, Burton, Warren, McDonald, Newton, Stewart, Colbert, Batten, Bassula, Trethowan
Trove: 'Hero's Date With Death', *Truth* (Healey); 'DCM Presented To Canberra Man', *Newcastle Morning Herald and Miners' Advocate* (Stubbs); 'Wicked Will of the 6th', *The Daily News* (Bassula)
Official: Long, *Final Campaigns*
Unit: Unit History Committee, *White Over Green*; O'Leary, *To the Green Fields Beyond*; Givney, *First at War*; Trigellis-Smith, *All the King's Enemies*; Wick, *Purple Over Green*; Allard, *Tank Tracks* (2/4th Armoured Regiment); Hay, *Nothing Over Us*; Sinclair, *To Find a Path* (Royal Pacific Islands Regiment); Clift, *War Dance*; Bentley, *The Second Eighth*
Secondary: Johnston, *Proud 6th*; Powell, *Third Force*; Handel, *Dust, Sand and Jungle*

Notes

Chapter 21 New Britain: The few imprison the many
Archival: NAA B883: NGX12 Gilmore, NX127371 Stainlay, QX48766 Young, QX50510 Perry, VX111035 Armstrong, VX117017 Pugh, VX113314 Abbey, VX64986 Allan, VX25139 Millstead, VX73557 Martin; AWM52 8/3/53/13, 14/32 War Diary, 16 March 1945
Official: Long, *Final Campaigns* and *Six Years War*
Unit: Bilney, *14/32 Australian Infantry Battalion A.I.F*
Secondary: Lewis, 'Fairfax-Ross, Basil Edward (1910–1984)'
Other: Royce Abbey Award and Scholarship, <www.royceabbey.com>

Chapter 22 Borneo I: Tarakan and North Borneo
Archival: NAA B883: NX13142 Nixon, VX39988 Head, VX30968 Wallis, NX177991 Freame, WX9506 Stretch, WX35631 Farmer, VX11616 King, TX5755 Pearce, NX194034 Holland, QX500604 O'Regan, SX6915 Pope, SX14298 Toohey, SX12498 Allen, WX28395 Waters, VX71785 Hanson, QX32908 Dingle, VX55120 S Smith, WX26495 How, SX6832 Fennell, SX9377 Gooden, VX117486 E Taylor, VX23442 Groux, WX22774 Christmass, VX63991 Beale, NX65985 Lemaire, WX21015 Walters, SX22714 Ballard, VX65728 Bradbrook, TX2910 Glover, SX19630 Heffernan, NX178209 Kelly, SX11095 Edmeades; AWM52, 8/3/24, 2/24th Battalion War Diary April–May 1945, pp. 181–183 (account of Wills action)
UK Recommendations: Mace, Wilson, T Taylor, R Walker, Riedy, Underwood, Power, Avern, Keane, Kotz, Cleeland
Trove: 'OBITUARY: Mr Churchill Avern', *The Inverell Times*
Official: Long, *Final Campaigns*
Unit: Share, *Mud and Blood*; Keating, *Roll Call*; Serle, *Second Twenty-Fourth*; Glenn, *Tobruk to Tarakan*; Lambert, *Commando* (2/4th Cdo Sqn); Austin, *Let Enemies Beware*; Chivas, 'The Canal' in Masel, *Second 28th*; Combe et al, *Second 43rd*
Secondary: Johnston, *Magnificent 9th*; Wilson, 'Mud-Covered Decoys', *Herald Sun*; Stanley, *Tarakan*; McNicoll, *Royal Australian Engineers*; Ward-Harvey, *Sapper's War*; Johnston, *Derrick VC in His Own Words*; Johnston, *Australian Band of Brothers*
Other: Legg, *War Correspondent*

Chapter 23 Borneo II: Balikpapan
Archival: NAA B883: NX137809 Kent, TX1238 Manson, NX110368 Fletcher, SX11003 McDougall, SX20021 Copping, SX20342 Symons, NX564 Ryrie, WX20219 Semler, SX10404 Evans, VX57908 Liddy, WX2066 Campbell, NX32658 Curry, VX11935 Freeman, NX58197 Thorp, VX16572 Doyle, NX66110 L Ryan, VX13168 H Lynch, WX12808 Hill, QX6500 Ham, QX15555 Mullins, SX1708 Willson, VX13988 Cooper, SX17203 Murdock, NX114055 Raward, NX20981 McKinlay; AWM52 8/3/25 – 2/25 Infantry Battalion, 15 July 1945; AWM52 8/3/31, 2/31 Bn WD, 10 July 1945
UK Recommendations: Douglass, McKinlay
Official: Long, *Final Campaigns*
Unit: Pirie, *Commando Double Black* (2/5th Cdo Sqn); Graeme-Evans, *Of Storms and Rainbows, Volume 2*; Allchin, *Purple and Blue*; Crooks, *Footsoldiers*; O'Brien, *Guns and Gunners* (2/5th Fd Regt); Russell, *Second Fourteenth*; Laffin, *Forever Forward*; Draydon, *Men of Courage*

Conclusion
1 Long, *Final Campaigns*, pp. 342, 522, 539n.
2 Hastings, *Warriors*, p. xiv.
3 Winters, *Beyond Band of Brothers*, p. 94.
4 Williams, 'Slam', p. 59.
5 Interview with Don Mackay.
6 Hastings, p. xxii.
7 Barrett, *We Were There*, pp. 228–229.
8 AWM, 26 Bde Report on Operations Oct–Nov 1942, 'General Conclusions and Lessons'.

INDEX

References to units in brackets are to the units to which those individuals belonged while discussed in the book

42nd Street, Crete 58, 59, 67
710 Feature (map p. 345) 366–67
770 Feature 369–70

Abbey, Royce (14/32 Bn) 380
Abbott, Bill (2/2 Bn) 15
Abbotts, Frank (2/30 Bn) 106
Abel, Clifford (2/10 Bn) 411
Abraham, Bert (2/10 Bn) 177
Absence Without Leave 6
Acreman, Keith (101 Anti-Tank Regt) 180
Ahioma (map p. 176) 175
Aiken, Jim (25 Bn) 320
Aitape (map p. 345) 317, 344
Aitape-Wewak campaign 2, 167, 344–75, 382
Alamein, El (map p. 141) 8, 37, 40, 74, 78, 141–64, 167, 168, 199–216, 244, 272, 274, 275, 278, 281, 282, 291, 292, 293, 294, 295, 314, 342, 384, 392, 396, 398, 400, 406, 423, 426
Albanese, Ralph 'Bees Knees' (2/1 Bn) 235, 236
Albrecht, Kingsley 'King' (2/48 Bn) 167–68, 204
Allan, Bob (2/14 Fd Regt) 380
Allan, Duncan (9 Bn) 338
Allen, Arthur 'Tubby' (Australian general) 194
Allen, Dick (2/10 Bn) 243
Allen, Ken (2/48 Bn) 392
Allen, Les 'Bull' (2/5 Bn) 252, 264–65, 342
Allied Intelligence Bureau (AIB) 340–41, 344, 376

Allsopp, Raymond 'Doc' (2/5 Cdo Sqn) 410
Amboga River 220
Ambon (map p. 129) 128–30
Ambush Knoll (map p. 248) 261, 269
American awards to Australians 4, 139, 172, 227, 264, 340, 376, 413
American Army 138, 226–27, 233–34, 237, 240–41, 256, 258, 260, 264, 266, 277, 310, 316, 317, 340, 344, 346, 360, 376, 382, 404, 423, 424, 425
    40th Division 376
    593rd Engineer Boat and Shore Regiment 404
Anderson, Charles (2/19 Bn) 110–13
Anderson, Graham 'GG' (2/23 Bn) *71*
Anderson, Jimmy (2/24 Bn) 166, 205, 212–13
Anderson, John (2/2 Fd Regt) 53–54
Anderson, Kitchener 'Kitch' (2/28 Bn) 75
Anderson, Vincent 'Bill' (2/15 Bn) 206–07
Anderson, Vivian (2/16 Bn) 310
Annear, Gordon (2/24 Bn) 155
Antill, Eric (2/1 Docks Operating Coy) 404
Anzac Day 1, 133, 181, 354
Apex Hill, Crete 59–60
Appel, Ernest 'Pip' (2/22 Bn) 125–27
Armstrong, Adam (19 Bn) 379
Armstrong, James 'Dummy' (2/40 Bn) 132
Armstrong, Lance (2/16 Bn) 409
Arty Hill (map p. 318) 338
Ashby, Herb (2/48 Bn) 158
Assheton, Charles (2/20 Bn) 121, 244
Aston, Felix (24 Anti-Tank Coy) 42
Atherton Tablelands 382
Atkinson, Bill (2/16 Bn) 223–24
Atkinson, Clarence (2/3 Bn) 95, 167

Atkinson, Herb 'Walkabout' (57/60 Bn) 315, 316
Atkinson, Jack (2/23 Bn) 7, 272–74
Auchinleck, Claude (British general) 154
Austin, Albert 'Bunny' (2/24 Bn) 155, 156
Australian army, 8
  organisation of
  corps **I** 46, 382; **Anzac** 49, 52
  divisions **3rd** 253, 319; **5th** 276, 376–81; **6th** 5, 12–22, 23–32, 33, 46–54, 55, 97, 140, 344–75; **7th** 12, 83–101, 140, 174, 194, 270, 277–79, 288–90, 301–-15, 382, 408; **8th** 12, 102–139; **9th** 5, 12, 33–45, 140–64, 199–216, 270, 274–77, 279–80, 286–87, 288, 291, 382, 399, 406
  forces **Anderson Force** 114; **Blackforce** 133–34, 136; **Eastforce** 107, 115; **Farida Force** 363, 367, 368; **Gull Force** 128–30; **Kanga Force** 169, 247, 249, 253; **Lark Force** 125–28; **Lustre Force** 46, 54; **Mackay Force** 46; **Maroubra Force** 174, 188; **Merrett Force** 122; **Sparrow Force** 130–33; **Westforce** 104, 111; **'Z' Special** 99, 139, 406
  armour and cavalry **Armoured Division** 230; **1st Armd Regt** 412; **1st Tank Bn** 287; **6th Div Cav Regt** 21, 29, 31–32, 88, 100, 226; **7th Div Cav Regt** 422; **9th Div Cav Regt**; **2/4th Armd Regt** 88, 322, 325, 365, 367; **2/6th Armd Regt** 229–33, 240–42; **2/9th Armd Regt** 389, 401; **2/6th Cav (Cdo) Regt** 345; **2/7th Cav Regt** 238–41
  artillery 20, 50, 277; **8th Light Anti-Aircraft Bty** 45; **2/1st Anti-Tank Regt** 362, 366, 372; **2/2nd Tank Attack Regt** 415; **2/3rd Anti-Tank Regt** 149–50, 160–61, 203, 215; **2/4th Anti-Tank Regt** 106, 107; **101 Anti-Tank Regt** 180; **24 Anti-Tank Coy** 42; **26 Anti-Tank Coy** 41–42; **2/1st Field Regt** 22; **2/2nd**

Field Regt 53, 348; **2/3rd Field Regt** 48, 57, 66–67; **2/4th Field Regt** 85, 86; **2/5th Field Regt** 415, 418; **2/7th Field Regt**; **2/8th Field Regt** 148; **2/10th Field Regt** 115–16, 138; **2/12th Field Regt** 281; **2/14th Field Regt** 378; **2/15th Field Regt** 112–13, 119; **4th Fd Regt** 334; **2nd Mtn Bty** 332; **1st Naval Bombardment Group** 415; **65th Bty** 112–13
independent companies and commando squadrons **2/2nd Ind Coy** 133; **2/3rd Ind Coy** 253, 260, 269; **2/4th Ind Coy** 276 ; **2/5th Ind Coy** 169–70, 249; **2/6th Ind Coy** 4, 288–290; **2/4th Cdo Sqn** 390-91, 394; **2/5th Cdo Sqn** 410; **2/8th Cdo Sqn** 326–27; **2/9th Cdo Sqn** 348, 368; **2/10th Cdo Sqn** 353–54; **2/11th Cdo Sqn** 402, 404
infantry brigades; **4th** 298–99; **7th** 175, 319; **8th** 299; **15th** 268, 311, 315, 324; **16th** 14–15, 21, 23, 46, 191, 192, 194, 237, 348, 350, 363, 374; **17th** 17–18, 97, 99, 247, 253, 267, 350, 370-71, 372; **18th** 35, 42, 65, 77, 175, 229, 230, 234, 241, 242–3, 311, 315, 408, 422; **19th** 24-27, 29, 44, 345, 350, 363; **20th** 33, 201, 202, 208, 280, 283, 286, 291, 299, 399-400; **21st** 83, 174, 190, 218, 220, 223, 301, 306, 311, 408–09; **22nd** 107, 116, 119, 120, 123; **24th** 35, 154, 158, 200, 215–16, 286, 291, 294, 297, 399, 401; **25th** 85, 88–89, 101, 190, 191, 194, 198, 217, 218-19, 301, 306, 311, 413; **26th** 33, 81, 154, 204, 215, 287, 291, 295, 382, 399; **27th** 104, 119, 122; **29th** 267–69, 319, 329; **30th** 238, 240
engineers 20, 23, 277, 293, 330, 413; **1 Bomb Disposal Pl** 413; **7 Bomb Disposal Pl** 328–29; **2/1st Docks Operating Coy** 404; **2/2nd Fd Coy** 20-21; **2/3rd Fd Coy** 199, 200, 399–400; **2/5th Fd Coy** 90; **2/6th Fd Coy** 413, 416; **2/7th Fd Coy**

140; **2/13th Fd Coy** 77, 164, 200, 384, 390, 397; **7th Fd Coy** 330; **16th Fd Coy** 336; **2/1st Fortress Engrs** 130–31; **42nd Landing Craft Coy** 336; **Beach Group Engrs** 390

infantry battalions 244; **2/1st** 14, 21, 23, 56–57, 61–63, 65, 192–93, 196, 212, 235–37, 349, 363, 367, 373; **2/2nd** 5, 14–15, 17, 23, 49–50, 65, 223, 225, 355–56, 358, 374–75; **2/3rd** 15–17, 23, 24, 91–95, 97, 99–100, 191, 192, 194, 349–50, 358-60, 372-73, 378; **2/4th** 27, 46, 56, 60, 345-47, 365, 367, 368–69, 374 ; **2/5th** 18–20, 90, 97, 99–100, 226, 247–52, 261, 272, 332, 350–53, 370 ; **2/6th** 2-3, 21, 247–51, 256, 258, 260, 266, 268, 340, 353, 354, 360, 418; **2/7th** 18, 57–59, 226-27, 250, 253, 256, 265, 267, 269, 351, 354-55; **2/8th** 25–27, 30, 46, 48, 57, 59, 226, 346, 348, 366, 368, 373-74; **2/9th** 31–32, 44, 181–82, 209, 229–30, 232-33, 237, 241–42, 256, 311–13, 314–15, 422; **2/10th** 42, 177, 179, 231–33, 311, 313, 314, 409, 411–13, 425; **2/11th** 29–30, 56, 61, 62, 63, 66, 67–69, 345, 346, 366, 368, 369–70; **2/12th** 73, 180–83, 233, 241–43, 311–14, 376, 410-11; **2/13th** 5, 33–34, 75, 78-79, 202-03, 206, 281, 283, 285, 291, 400; **2/14th** 81, 96, 98–99, 174, 185–88, 190, 218, 220, 222, 225, 226, 301, 303, 409, 410, 413, 415, 419; **2/15th** 70, 161, 162–64, 200, 201, 206-07, 210, 280, 281, 282–83, 290, 351, 400; **2/16th** 85, 98, 174, 187, 188, 190, 218, 220–21, 223–24, 308, 311, 409; **2/17th** 35–37, 199, 201, 202–03, 206, 283, 284, 292, 334, 399, 400; **2/18th** 115–17, 120, 123, 138; **2/19th** 107, 110, 113, 114, 115, 119; **2/20th** 115, 119, 120, 121, 137–38; **2/21st** 128–30; **2/22nd** 104, 125–28, 369; **2/23rd** 38, 40, 41, 70–73, 148, 151–52, 154–55, 157, 207, 270, *273*, 296–97, 385, 390, 394–95; **2/24th** 41–42, *71*, 81, 142–44, 148, 154-57, 200, 205, 208-09, 211–13, 296–97, 385–89, 395, 398; **2/25th** 95, 190, 217, 277, 280, 307, 421, 422; **2/26th** 116, 118–19, 121; **2/27th** 86–87, 98–99, 188, 189–90, 218, 220, 223–24, 226, 301, 305–06, 409, 413 ; **2/28th** 66, 75–77, 158–61, 215–16, 274–76, 286–87, 295, 401, 402; **2/29th** 107, 110–14, 123; **2/30th** 104–06, 114–15; **2/31st** 66, 88–89, 96, 101, 190, 195–96, *197*, 217, 218, 239, 279–80, 409, 413–14, 419–20; **2/32nd** 37, 152–53, 158, 208–11, 214–15, 278–79, 287, 294–95, 297, 404, 406; **2/33rd** 88–89, 90, 91, 95–96, 190–91, 217–19, 279, 409, 414; **2/40th** 130–32; **2/43rd** 3–4, 40, 74, 75–7, 78, 140–42, 152–53, 158, 160, 215–16, 284, 295–96, 404–06; **2/48th** 38, 42, 73, 142–45, 148, 150, 154, 157–58, 204–05, 208–09, 211–13, 214, 292–93, 314, 342, 385, 391–92, 396, 398; **3rd** 191, 218, 409; **7th** 338–39; **8th** 337; **9th** 181, 320–21, 337–39; **11th** 106; **14th/32nd** 379–80; **15th** 267–68, 330; **19th** 378; **22nd** 280, 298, 299; **24th** 146, 243, 254, 276–77; **25th** 176, 179, 319–20, 322; **26th** 133, 332–34, 338; **29th/46th** 298; **30th** 316; **31st/51st** 331–32; **36th** 238, 240, 378; **37th/52nd** 298–99; **39th** 171–74, 185–86, 218, 220, 223–26, 355, 425, 426; **42nd** 267, 269; **47th** 183–84, 268–69; **49th** 237–38, 240; **53rd** 174, 185, 237, 378; **55th/53rd** 237–38, 240, 338; **57th/60th** 315–16, 326–27, 329; **58th/59th** 260, 265–67, 316, 328–29; **61st** 175–77, *178*, 179; **Darwin Inf** 379; **1st New Guinea (NGIB)** 225, 258; **2nd New Guinea (NGIB)** 252, 269, 370–72; **New Guinea Volunteer Rifles** 169–70; **Papuan Infantry Battalion (PIB)** 171, 255, 258,

299, 328, 330–31; **'Special Reserve Bn'** 122; **X Bn** 122
machine gun battalions **2/2nd** 146, 149, 151, 158–59; **2/3rd** 136, 355; **2/4th** 120, 122
pioneer battalions **2/1st Pnr** 66; **2/2nd Pnr** 96, 97, 98, 100, 134–36; **2/3rd Pnr** 67, 208–09, 213–14, 395–96
Australian New Guinea Administrative Unit (ANGAU) 180, 188, 255, 330–31, 344, 346
medical units **2/3rd Fd Amb** 294; **2/5th Fd Amb** 183; **2/7th Fd Amb** 55–56
ordnance **2/10th Ord Wksps** 138
provost companies; **7th** 50
Service Corps 52
Signals 23; **8th Div** 113, 121; **9th Div** 145, 208

Australian Imperial Force
  First 22
  Second 49, 169, 227
Avern, Churchill (2/9 Armd Regt) 401–02, 404
Avery, Alan (2/14 Bn) 3, 96–97, 185, 437n
Ayre, Gordon (58/59 Bn) 244, 265

Babau (map p. 131) 130–32
Bacon's Hill 379–80
Badarane (map p. 84) 89, 101
Baggaley, Harold (2/13 Fd Coy) 164
Baggaley, Ron (2/10 Bn) 314
Bakri (map p. 103) 107–10
Balderstone, Bob (2/6 Ind Coy) 290
Baldwin, Aubrey (22 Bn) 299
Balfe, John (2/17 Bn) 36, 37
Balikpapan (maps pp. 383, 409) 44, 139, 239, 256, 310, 382, 407, 408–22, 423, 425
Ball, John (2/9 Bn) 181–82
Ballard, Hugh (2/11 Cdo Sqn) 402
Bambling, Reg (2/15 Bn) 162–64
Bamess, Ben (2/43 Bn) 296
Bandung (map p. 134) 136
Bar to medal, defined 10
Barclay, Peter (2/1 Bn) 193
Bardia (map p. 16) 12–23, 24, 29, 31, 62, 88, 94, 168, 244, 251, 252, 340

Barnard, Jack (2/23 Bn) 40
Barnes, Frank (2/3 Bn) 94
Barnes, Laurie (24 Bn) 325–27
Barnes, Ron (2/27 Bn) 306
Barnet, Evan (2/6 Armd Regt) 229, 231
Barnett, Arch (2/25 Bn) 190–91
Barnett, Len (47 Bn) 268–69
Barrand, Roy (2/23 Bn) 296
Barratt, Charlie (2/48 Bn) 293
Barrel Hill, or B11 (map p. 141) 208, 210, 214–16
Barry, Jim (2/48 Bn) 293
Bartholomew, Harry (2/1 Bn) 363, *364*
Bassula, Bill (2/8 Bn) 373
Batten, Chris (2/3 Bn) 372–73
Batty, Len (2/48 Bn) 38, *39*
Batu Pahat (map p. 103) 116
Baumann, Lionel (9 Bn) 181
Baxter, Mick (2/7 Bn) 58
Bayly, Colin (2/11 Bn) 367
Beale, Les (2/24 Bn) 398–99
Bear, Lindsay 'Teddy' (2/14 Bn) 303, *304*, 425
Beatty, Frank (2/4 Cdo Sqn) 391
Beaufort (map p. 383) 399, 404–06
Beda Fomm (map p. 13) 31
Bedells, Jack (2/11 Bn) 62
Beecroft, Bob (2/24 Bn) 155
Beer, Ron (2/48 Bn) 73
Beirut (map p. 84) 85, 92, 93, 97
Beit ed Dine (map p. 84) 98–99
Bell, Harry (2/32 Bn) 278–79, 343
Bell, John (2/23 Bn) 151
Bell, Ted (2/24 Bn) 144, 167
Bengari (1 PIB) 299
Benghazi (map p. 13) 30–31, 33
Bennett, Gordon (Australian general) 104, 107, 112, 122
Benoit, Max (8 Div Sigs) 113
Bentley, Allen (2/13 Bn) 203
Beresford, Eric (2/18 Bn) 123
Bergonzoli, Annibale (Italian general) 13
Berhala Island camp and 'Berhala Eight' 138
Berman, Max (58/59 Bn) 316
Berrell, Frank (2/9 Bn) 315
Berrell, Mervyn (2/9 Bn) 315
Berry, Bernard (2/9 Bn) 32
Berry, George (2/24 Bn) 167, 205, 207

Index

Berryman, Frank (Australian general) 267
Bethune, John (58/59 Bn) 267
Beverley, Frank (2/19 Bn) 112
Billet, Basil (2/40 Bn) 132
Bingham, Francis (2/3 Fd Coy) 167, 168, 200–01
Bingham, Geoffrey (8 Div Sigs) 113, 123
Biri (1 PIB) 328
Birrell, James (ANGAU) 346
Bishop, John (2/27 Bn) 306
Bisset, Harold 'Butch' (2/14 Bn) 186
Bitoi Ridge (map p. 248) 258, 260
Black Cat Track (map p. 248) 247
Blackburn, Arthur (Blackforce) 133–34, 136
Blair, Clive (49 Bn) 238
Blamey, Thomas (Australian general) 49, 77, 83, 169, 194, 218, 227, 247, 253, 256, 267, 280, 288, 344, 356, *388*
Bland, Robert (2/30 Bn) 105
Blockhouse, the (map p. 141) 209–210, 213, 214
Bloffwitch, Howard (2/10 Bn) 245, 314
Bloffwitch, Ray (2/48 Bn) 314
Blow, Rex (2/10 Fd Regt) 138–39
Bode, Lance (2/15 Bn) 162
Bogadjim (map p. 289) 301, 315, 316
Bogan, William 'Bluey' (2/33 Bn) 191
Boland, Ted (2/2 Bn) 17
Bolton, David (2/2 Anti-Tank Regt) 91
Bonis Peninsula (map p. 318) 331, 337
Bonner, Ron (2/43 Bn) 296
Borneo (map p. 383) 15, 138, 150, 201, 244, 382–422, 426
Bostock, Bert (53 Bn) 185
Bougainville campaign (map p. 318) 5, 8, 32, 133, 146, 175, 178, 198, 244, 265, 267, 280, 317–41, 382
Boughton, Geoff (2/6 Armd Regt) 242
Bowden, Lionel (2/7 Bn) 354–55
Bowerman, Bill (2/12 Bn) 233
Bowring, Bill (2/29 Bn) 110, 112
Bracegirdle, Barry (2/16 Bn) 85–86
Bradbrook, Ron (2/9 Armd Regt) 402, *403*, 404
Braddon, Russell (2/15 Fd Regt) 113
Bradfield, Ron (2/11 Bn and 2/3 Pnr Bn) 67, *68*

Braithwaite, Charlie (2/12 Bn) 312–13
Brallos (map p. 47) 50, 52–54
Brand, Victor (2/29 Bn) 112, 342
Brandi Plantation (map p. 345) 368
Brandrick, Eric (2/2 MG Bn) 151
Brazier, Roland (2/13 Fd Coy) 390
Breese, Fred (2/30 Bn) 106
Bren gun, as heroes' weapon 165–66, 424–25
Brettingham-Moore, Tim (2/3 MG Bn) 136–37
Brewster, Don (58/59 Bn) 316
Bright, Matthew (26 Bn) 333
British Army 5, 70, 94, 119, 122, 250, 423, 425
    model for Australian Army 8, 12
    Black Watch 60
    Gordon Highlanders 202
    Western Desert Force 13
    2nd Armoured Division 33
    6th Division 101
    7th Armoured Division 27-28, 324
    8th Army 142, 154, 199
    16th Brigade 93
    40th Battalion Royal Tank Regiment 214–15
    70th Division 78
British Commonwealth Occupation Force 195, 260
Broadhurst, Tom (2/3 Fd Coy) 199–200
Brockhurst, Harold (2/25 Bn) 277
Broinowski, Stefan (2/4 Bn) 27
Brooks, John (2/28 Bn) 275
Broun, William 'Tinny' (2/28 Bn) 287
Brown, Claud (2/4 Anti-Tank Regt) 108
Brown, Horace (7 Fd Coy) 330
Brown, Murray (2/10 Bn) 232
Brown, Ray (2/30 Bn) 105
Browning Automatic Rifle (BAR) 424
Bruce, William 'Tubby' (6 Div Sigs) 23–24
Brunei Bay (map p. 383) 382, 399, 406
Bryant, Don (2/48 Bn) 145
Buckingham, Ted (2/23 Bn) 148–49
Buckley, Adrian (2/1 Pnr) 66
Bugg, Len (2/12 Bn) 314
Buin (map p. 318) 319, 324, 329, 341
Buin Road (map p. 318) 319–30
Buisaval Track (map p. 248) 247

Buitenzorg (map p. 134) 133–34, 136
Bulimba, Operation 7, 162–4, 206, 281, 426
Bumi River (map p. 271) 281, 282
Bunga River (map p. 271) 270
Buoi Plantation (map p. 318) 337
Burgess, Jim (2/8 Bn) 25
Burgess, Lionel (55/53 Bn) 241
Burma Railway 112, 132, 136–37
Burns, John (2/27 Bn) 189–90
Burrell, Harold (42 Landing Craft Coy) 336, 343
Burton, William (2/4 Bn) 367
Busu River (map p. 271) 4, 274–76
But (map p. 345) 350, 355–56
Butler, Edward (49 Bn) 238
Butler, Rex (8 Div AASC) 139
Byrne, Leslie (15 Bn) 268

Cake Hill 378
Calder, James (26 Bn) 333
Callinan, Bernard (2/2 Ind Coy and 26 Bn) 133, 332
Cameron, Allan (2/22 Bn and Maroubra Force) 127, 172
Cameron, Angus (2/7 Bn) 227
Cameron, George 'Charlie' (37/52 Bn) 299
Cameron, Fred (2/24 Bn) 205, 212
Cameron, Lin (2/5 Bn) 252, 262–64, 351, 353
Cameron, Richard 'Darky' (2/2 MG Bn) 158–59, 168
Campbell, Bill (2/32 Bn) 210, 342
Campbell, Guss (2/31 Bn) 413–14
Campbell, Ian (2/1 Bn) 61, 63, 65
Campbell, Kenneth (2/33 Bn) 89
Campbell, Ross (2/33 Bn) 89
Cam's Saddle (map p. 302) 311
Canea (map p. 56) 58, 67
Cantelo, Bill (2/2 Fd Coy) 21
Cape Endaiadere (map p. 170) 229–30
Cape Hoskins (map p. 377) 378
Cape Killerton and Cape Killerton Track (map p. 170) 241, 243
Cape Wom (map p. 345) 363
Carey, Paddy (2/27 Bn) 305
Carnell, Jack (2/2 Bn) 355
Carrier Hill (map p. 34) 38, 70
Carson, Arthur (2/3 Bn) 192, 244

Catterns, Basil (2/1 Bn) 193, 235–37
Cawthorne, Jim (2/43 Bn) 74
Chambers, Arthur (26 Bn) 338
Champlong (map p. 131) 130–32
Changi prisoner of war camp 120, 138
Chesterton, Joe (25 Bn) 320–22
Chesworth, George (2/7 Cav Regt) 239
Childs, Fred (24 Bn) 276–77
Chilton, Fred (18 Bde) 65
Chinese guerrillas 108
Chowne, Bert (2/2 Bn) 166, 357
Christian, Ron (2/16 Bn) 308, 409
Christmas Hills (map p. 271) 297
Christmass, Keith (2/24 Bn) 398
Christoff, George (2/30 Bn) 114–15
Churchill, Winston 31, 77, 83
citations for honours and awards 2
Citizen Military Forces *see* militia
Claffey, Ron (2/23 Bn) 155, 343
Clampett, Bob (2/27 Bn) 306
Clark, Frank (2/4 Armd Regt) 325
Clark, Laurie (2/31 Bn) 279
Clarke, Ken (2/23 Bn) 157
Clarke, Michael (2/16 Bn) 187
Clarke, Ray (2/6 Fd Coy) 413
Cleeland, George (2/43 Bn) 405
Clift, Ken (6 Div Sigs) 22, 23–24, 80, 81, 167
Clout, Harry (2/1 Bn) 166
Clowes, Cyril (Australian general) 175
Cobb, Bill (2/15 Bn) 161–62, 168
Cobb, Henry (2/7 Cav Regt) 240
Cochrane, John (2/30 Bn) 105
Cockram, John (2/2 MG Bn) 146
Coke feature 420–21
Colbert, Ken (2/3 Bn) *359*, 372
Cole, Bob (ANGAU) 346
Cole, Rod (42 Bn) 267
Coleman, Keith (26 Bn) 245, 332–33
Collett, Fred (2/30 Bn) 105
Collins, Ron (2/3 Ind Coy) 261
Combe, Gordon (2/43 Bn) 3–4, 284
Connell, John (2/1 Bn) 192, 342
Connell, Ned (2/7 Cav Regt) 239
Connor, Eric (2/28 Bn) 276
Connor, George (2/33 Bn) 88–89, 91
Cook, Frank (2/10 Bn) 42, 44, 243
Cook, Ted (47 Bn) 184
Cooper, Ernest (2/31 Bn) 420

Index

Copeman, Jim (2/3 Bn) 93, 358, *359*
Copping, John (2/10 Bn) 411
Coppock, Harold (2/28 Bn) 75
Cortis, John (2/17 Bn) 202
Cory, Gilbert (2/3 Bn) 194, 350
Cotterill, Richard (2/3 Anti-Tank Regt) 150
Courtney, Ted (8 LAA Bty) *43*, 45
Cousens, Harry (2/15 Bn) 281
Coutts, Len (2/4 Anti-Tank Regt) *109*
Coventry, Noel 'Nuts' (2/23 Bn) 385
Cowey, Jim (39 Bn) 173
Coyle, Geoff 'Punchy' (2/2 Bn) 49–50
Craig, Felix (AASC) 52
Craske, Allen (16 Anti-Tank Coy) 22
Crater Hill (map p. 302) 315
Crawford, Geoff (2/13 Bn)
Crete campaign 21, 30
Crilly, Les (2/14 Bn) 221, *304*
Cristenson, Eric (2/9 Bn) 230
Croft, Ron (2/29 Bn) 114
Crummey, Bill (2/23 Bn) 40
Crystal Creek (map p. 248) 251–52, 264
Cullen, Doug (2/33 Bn) 279
Cullen, Paul (2/1 Bn) 66, 193, 235, 237
Curren, Bill (2/43 Bn) 40, 167
Curry, Phil (2/33 Bn) 414
Curtin, John 264
Curtiss, Grant (2/6 Armd Regt) 231
Cutler, Roden (2/5 Fd Regt) 95, 98, 307
Cutting, the (map p. 141) 148, 151
Cyrenaica (map p. 13) 27, 31, 33, 35

Dagua (map p. 345) 65, 350, 357
Dalby, Hugh (39 Bn) 223, 225–26
Daley, Dan (2/3 Anti-Tank Regt) 154
Damascus (map p. 84) 85, 91–93, 99
Damour (map p. 84) 97–101
Daniel, Jack (2/6 Bn) 360, *361*
Daniels, Ken (2/4 Anti-Tank Regt) *109*
Daniels, Ron (2/48 Bn) 38, *39*
Danmap River (map p. 345) 343, 345–46, 348
   flooding of 348
Dargie, William 7, 171
Davidson, Alex (2/32 Bn) 168, 209
Davies, Stan (2/48 Bn) 293
Dawes, Byron 'Snowy' (2/17 Bn) 167, 291–92

Deacon, Jack (9 Bn) 338, *339*
Deal, Frank 'Shorty' (42 Bn) 245, 267
Dean, Hollister (2/43 Bn) 153
Dean, Selby (2/4 Bn) 60, 374
Deeley, Leo (2/14 Bn) 96–97
de Forest, Percy (2/23 Bn) 296
Dehne, Arthur (2/6 Bn) 268
Deir Mar Jorjos (map p. 84) 99–100
Deniki (map p. 170) 172–74
Derbyshire, Max (2/2 Bn) 65
Derna (map p. 13) 27–30
Derrick, Tom 'Diver' (2/48 Bn) 9, 80, 81, 142, 148, 150, 167, 190, 231, 293, 303, 391, 396–97, 425
Derrington, Norman (2/26 Bn) 118–19
Deschamps, Paul (2/13 Bn) 285
Deslandes, Roy (29/46 Bn) 298
de Vantier, Roy (2/9 Bn) 182
Dexter, Bill (2/6 Bn) 256, 258
Dick, Leonard (57/60 Bn) 316
Diffey, Colin (2/8 Bn) 30–31
Dingle, Norm (2/23 Bn) 394
Dingwall, Len 'Ding' (2/24 Bn) 212
discipline issues among decorated soldiers 6–7, 245
Distinguished Conduct Medal, defined 10
Distinguished Service Order, defined 10
Diti (2 NGIB) 371
Doneley, Adrian 'Stump' (2/5 Bn) 350–51
Doneley, Austin (2/7 Bn) 351
Donoghue, Tim (2/3 Bn) 93–94
Donnet, Allan (2/2 Bn) 374–75
Doolan, Amos (2/30 Bn) 105
Doolan, William (2/21 Bn) 129–30
Doran, John (2/1 Bn) 192–93
Dougherty, Bob (2/14 Bn) 221, *222*, 223
Douglass, Hugh (2/31 Bn) 420–21
Downs, Clyde (31/51 Bn) 337
Doyle, Frank (2/14 Bn) 416, *417*, 418
Draper, Maurice (16 Fd Coy) 336
Drew, Ron 'Kanga' (37/52 Bn) 299
Dridan, Ron (39 Bn) 173, 244
Duffy, Des (2/30 Bn) 104–05
Duffy, Frank (2/10 Bn) 232
Dumas, Harry (2/20 Bn) 120
Dumpu (map p. 289) 288, 290, 301, 310
Dunbar, Alfred 'Shorty' (2/17 Bn) 36

Duncan, Roland (2/31 Bn) 218, 342
Duncan, Wally (2/8 Bn) 48
Dunkley, Harry (2/6 Bn and 7 Bn) 340
Dunlop, Edward 'Weary' (2/2 CCS and No 1 Allied General Hospital) 136–37, 342
Dunlop, Ray (2/5 Bn) 353
Duntroon 224, 324, 327, 370, 386
Dutch East Indies 104, 128
Dutton, Bob (2/13 Bn) 281
Duvanel, Randy (2/4 Bn) 368–69
Dyaks 400, 406
Dyne, Alf (2/12 Bn) 233

East Point 24 (map p. 141) 148, 151, 155, 157
Easter Battle, Tobruk 35–37, 41
Easter, Roy (2/13 Bn) 201–02
Easton, Charles (2/10 Fd Regt) 115–16
Eather, Kenneth (25 Bde) 190
Ed Duda 78
Edgell, Reg (39 Bn) 220, 224
Edmeades, Eric (Z Special Unit) 406
Edmonds, Fred (26 Anti-Tank Coy) 41–42
Edmonds, Stanley 'Shorty' (2/48 Bn) 293
Edmondson, Frank 'Spike' (2/2 Pnr Bn) 135
Edmondson, Jack (2/17 Bn) 35–36
Edwards, Gordon (25 Bn) 321–22
Edwards' Plantation (map p. 271) 279–80
Efogi (map p. 170) 188, 190
Egan, Clyde (24 Bn) 327
Egan's Ridge 327–28
Ehava, John (PIB) 255
Ehava, Gabriel (PIB) 255
Eichelberger, Robert (American general) 226
El Boum (map p. 84) 99
Ellis, Stan (39 Bn) 167, 223, 225–26
Else, Alick (2/15 Bn) 161–62, 291
Else, Cyril (2/15 Bn) 162
Eora Creek (map p. 170) 17, 192–94, 350
Er Regima 33–34, 79
Erbs, Allan (24 Bn) 329
Escapes from captivity 15, 30, 65–69, 137–39
Escreet, Bert (2/5 Bn) 351, *352*
Evans, Arthur 'Snowy' (2/10 Bn) 412

Evans, Bernard (2/23 Bn) 152
Evans, Frank (2/2 Bn) 50
Evapia River (map p. 302) 307
Everett, Wally (2/48 Bn) 293
expectations of medal-winners 425
Exton, Ted (2/6 Bn) 165, 258

Fairfax-Ross, Basil (AIB) 376
Fairlie, Dave (2/23 Bn) 270
Faria Ridge (map p. 302) 314
Faria River (map p. 302) 301
Farmer, Col (2/24 Bn) 387
Farr, Nicholas (PIB) 255
Fennell, Wally (2/48 Bn) 396–97
Ferguson, Bill 'Inky' (2/31 Bn) 96
Ferguson, Ken (2/2 Bn) 357
Fergusson, Maurice (2 Armd Bde) 226
Fergusson, Terence (2/7 Bn) 226–27, 229
Ferres, Bert (2/13 Bn) 78
Fielding, Arthur (2/7 Fd Regt) 160
Fig Orchard (map p. 141) 206
Finisterre Range (map p. 289) 290, 306, 327
Fink, Fred (2/15 Bn) 282
Finlayson, Max (2/2 Bn) 358
Finn, Don (2/7 Bn) 266
Finney, Ron (25 Bn) 179
Finschhafen (map p. 271) 280–86, 288
Fisher, Ray (2/27 Bn) 305–06
Fitzhardinge, John (2/3 Fd Regt) 67
flamethrowers 369, 386, 387, 409, 412, 419–20, 422
Fletcher, Reg (2/12 Bn) 410–11
Fletcher, Tom (2/14 Bn) 186-87, 342
Fogarty, Pat (2/11 Bn) 369
Fogg, Colin (2/9 Bn) 181
Foley, Bert (1 BD Pl) 413
Forbes, Bill (2/48 Bn) 38
Forbes, Jim (2 Mtn Bty) 332
Forbes' Mound (map p. 13) 41
Ford, Colin (2/25 Bn) 422
Forster, Russell (2/9 Bn and 49 Bn) 237
Fortification Point (map p. 289) 299
Franklin, Derrick 'Red' (2/43 Bn) 140
Frawley, Tom (2/7 Bn) 269
Freame, Harry (2/24 Bn) 386
Freda feature (map p. 383) 396–98
Freeman, Bob (2/33 Bn) 414

Index

French, Jack (2/9 Bn) 182
Freyberg, Bernard (New Zealand general) 55, 57, 59, 65
Friend, Percy (2/5 Bn) 263

Gall, John (2/3 Bn) 93
Galleghan, Frederick 'Black Jack' (2/30 Bn) 104, 106
Gallipoli 52, 173, 182, 386
Gama River (map p. 176) 177, 179, 181
Gannan, Tony (2/7 Bn) *347*, 353–54
Gard, Tom (2/43 Bn) 76, 342
Garland, Ron (2/3 Ind Coy) 269
Gartner, Phillip (39 Bn) 168, 225
Garwood, Bert (2/43 Bn) 284
Gazelle Peninsula (map p. 377) 376, 378, 381
Gazzard, Lou (2/24 Bn) 41
Geai (1 PIB) 330–31
Gemas (map p. 103) 104–05
Gemencheh 104, 106
Genga River (map p. 318) 331–32
George Medal, defined 10
German Army and troops
    15th Panzer Division 41
    21 Panzer Division 148
    90th Light Division 208
    Intercept and Intelligence Company 621 143
    SS Adolf Hitler Brigade 46–47
Gesch, Bill (2/33 Bn) 95–96
Giarabub Oasis (map p. 13) 31–32
Gibbons, Neville 'Blue' (2/6 Bn) 251
Giffen, Joseph (2/17 Bn) 400
Gilbert, Lance (2/4 Anti-Tank Regt) 108
Giles, Arthur (2/5 Fd Coy) 90
Giles, Syd (5 Fd Coy) 323–24
Gilmore, John (AIB)
Gilmore, Joseph (39 Bn) 223
Gilmour, Neil (2/23 Bn) 296–97
Gilpin, Jimmy (2/11 Bn) 369–70
Ginzberg, Eli 6–7
Giropa Point (map p. 170) 232–34
Glover, Merv (2/43 Bn) 405–06
Goldman, Maurice (2/3 Bn) 192
Gona (map p. 170) 167, 186, 188, 189, 217–26, 311, 342, 423, 425
Good, Mal (2/24 Bn) 387
Goode, Lindsay (2/48 Bn) 212

Gooden, Oswald 'Os' (2/48 Bn) 397
Goodenough Island (map p. 176) 183–84
Goodview Junction (map p. 248) 261, 267
Goodwin, Len (55/53 Bn) 338
Gorari (map p. 170) 195–96, 198, 237
Gordon, Jack (2/9 Bn) 182
Gordon, Jim (2/31 Bn) 7, 101
Gordon, John (2/43 Bn) 153
Graham, Alan (2/2 Pnr Bn) 135–36
Graham, Arthur (16 Fd Coy) 336
Graham, Bob (2/1 Bn) 349
Graham, Stuart (24 Bn) 324
Graham, Syd (2/6 Ind Coy) 289–90
Grant, Eric (2/43 Bn) 284–85
Grant, Hugh (2/11 Bn) 367
Gratwick, Percy (2/48 Bn) 204–05, 244
Gray, Jamieson (2/6 Bn) 249
Grayson, Arthur (2/43 Bn) 295
Great Depression, the 12, 102
Greatorex, Tony (2/24 Bn) 200, 205
Greece campaign (map p. 47) 15, 17, 20, 25–26, 31, 33, 46–54, 57, 60, 62, 65–69, 91, 92, 168, 174, 227, 362, 410, 415
Green, Charles (2/11 Bn) 66
Green, Dave (2/33 Bn) 279
Greenway, George (2/11 Bn) 67, 69
Griff, Ted (58/59 Bn) 329
Griffin, Ray (2/18 Bn) 123
Griffiths, William (2/5 Bn) 18, 20
Grigg, Ron (2/25 Bn) 421
Groundwater, Murray (2/31 Bn) 96
Groundwater, Ronnie (2/31 Bn) 279
Groux, Gordon (2/13 Fd Coy) 246, 397–98
Guilfoyle, Clem (2/15 Bn) 282
Gullett, Henry 'Jo' (2/6 Bn) 5, 167, 250–51
Gurney, Stan (2/48 Bn) 157–58
Gusika (map p. 271) 286, 294–95, 298

Hackney, Ben (2/29 Bn) 113–14
Haddy, Alan (2/16 Bn) 85, 98, 167, 220, 223
Haddy's Village (map p. 170) 224–25
Hall, Ben (ANGAU) 254
Hall, Merv (2/16 Bn) 308, *309*
Hall, Roy 'Vic' (2/1 Bn) 349
Hallion, Reg (2/6 Ind Coy) 290
Ham, Norm (2/5 Fd Regt) 418

Hamilton, Arthur (2/14 Bn) 418
Hamilton, Herb 'Hammy' (25 Bn) 180
Hamilton, John (29/46 Bn) 298
Hamlyn-Harris, Geoff (2/31 Bn) 218
Hancox, Frank (2/7 Cav Regt) 239
Handley, Ted (2/13 Bn) 33–34
Hanel, Ivan (2/48 Bn) 158
Hansen, Ivan (2/7 Bn) 67
Hanson, Arthur 'Punchy' (2/2 Pnr Bn) 394
Harcourt, Harry (2/6 Ind Coy) 4
Hare, Ivan 'Bunny' (2/43 Bn) 216
Hari River (map p. 318) 329
Harris, Bert (2/6 Ind Coy) 290
Harris, Edwin 'Toby' (2/17 Bn) 201
Harris, Frank (7 Div Prov Coy) 50
Hastings, Max 8
Hawain River (map p. 345) 350, 363
Hawke, Geoff 'Hawkeye' (2/4 Bn) 167, 365
Hay, David (2/6 Bn) 353
Hay, Reg (2/40 Bn) 132
Hayes, Bob (2/28 Bn) 401
Hayfield (map p. 345) 360, 362
Haydon, John (2/1 Bn) 349
Haynes, Bob (2/48 Bn) 144, 167
Head, Alan (2/23 Bn) 385
Head, Harry (2/30 Bn) 105
Head, John (2/28 Bn) 75
Healey, Don (2/4 Bn) 168, 345–46
Heap, Des (2/6 Armd Regt) 242
Hearman, Ben (2/16 Bn) 85
Heath's Plantation (map p. 271) 170
Hedderman, John 'Smoky' (2/6 Bn) 166, *257*, 258, 266, 354
Heffernan, Richard (2/43 Bn) 405
Hele, Ivor 7, 38, 164, 265
Helen feature (map p. 383) 395
'hell ships' 98, 113, 135, 136
Henderson, Neil (2/33 Bn) 95
Hendry, Gordon (2/2 Bn) 14–15
Henricksen, Hylton (2/9 Bn) 312
Henry Reid Bay (map p. 277) 376–77
Heraklion (map p. 56) 55–56, 59–60, 374
Hergenhan, Harold (2/3 Bn) 17
'hero' and other words concerning bravery 8, 80–82
Herring, Edmund (Australian general) 240

Hewitt, Errol (2/24 Bn) 143
Hickey, Kenneth (2/1 Fortress Engrs) 130–31, 244
Higgins, John (2/48 Bn) *393*
Hill 87 (map p. 409) 411
Hill 127 (map p. 103) 123
Hill 209 or Ras el Medauuar (map p. 34) 37, 41–42, 70
Hill 567 99
Hill 1284 96–97
Hill, Hubert (2/14 Bn) 418
Hinson, Jim 'Spud' (2/48 Bn) 143, 145, 146, *147*, 212
Hobson, Bob (2/9 Bn) 44
Hockey, Clarence (2/4 Armd Regt) 323
Holding, Fred (2/28 Bn) 159–60
Holland, Walter 'Dutchy' (2/23 Bn) 390
Holman, Jack (2/24 Bn) 143
Holmyard, Richard (2/12 Bn) 180–81
Holt, Ben 2/28 Bn) 342, 402
Homer and the *Iliad* 1, 199
Homer, Roy (2/20 Bn) 119
Hongorai River (map p. 318) 326–27, 330
Honner, Ralph (2/11 Bn and 39 Bn) 61–62, 174, 224
honours and awards
    parsimony in distributing 5, 132
    system, Australian 1–6, 8, 10, 132, 138
    system, British 5, 8
    types, 10 *see also* Victoria Cross
Hood, Frank (2/4 Bn) 374
Hooke, Peter (2/7 Cav Regt) 238–39
Hordern, Sam (2/7 Cav Regt) 240
Horii, Tomitarō (Japanese general) 198
Hoskins, George (2/2 MG Bn) 159
How, Walter (2/48 Bn) 396
Howes, Richard (2/27 Bn) 86, *87*, 88, 244
Hudson, Enever (2/9 Bn) 167, 234
Huggins' road-block (map p. 170) 237–41
Hughes, Bill (2/24 Bn) 154–55
Hughes, Tim (2/10 Bn) 231–32
Hunt, Geoff (2/13 Bn) 75
Hunt, John (2/1 Bn) 193
Huntley, Neil (2/30 Bn) 105
Hurrell, Les (2/31 Bn) 196
Hurrell, Lloyd (2/31 Bn) 167, 195–96
Hutchinson, Alan (2/23 Bn) 40

Index

Ibbott, Alan (2/19 Bn) 111
Imita Ridge (map p. 170) 190. 307
Indian Army 83, 85, 101, 108, 111–14, 119, 122, 225
   5th Brigade 92
   12th Brigade 121
   44th Brigade 121
   45th Brigade 107, 111–12
Innocent, Robert (2/23 Bn) 272
Ioribaiwa (map p. 170) 188, 190, 307
Isaksson, Zak (2/48 Bn) 37, 38
Isurava (map p. 170) 174, 185–86, 303

Jack, Reg (14/32 Bn) 380
Jacka, Albert 222
Jackson, Don (2/28 Bn) 66
Jackson, George (2/9 Bn) 241–42
Jackson, Hugh (2/2 Bn) 356–57
Jackson, Jimmy 'Lofty' (2/5 Bn) 166, 262–63
Jacquinot Bay (map p. 377) 377–78
Jaggar, Brian (2/4 Ind Coy) 276
James, Edgar 'Jimmy' (2/15 Bn) 210–11, 342
James, Jack (2/7 Cav Regt) 239
James, Oliver (2/12 Bn) 74
James' Perimeter 239–41
Jap Track (map p. 248) 247
Japanese Army 106, 116, 119, 129
   Guards Division 107
Java (map p. 134) 98, 100, 133–37
Jeanes, Mervyn (2/43 Bn) 140, 142
Jebel Mazar (map p. 84) 94–95
Jefferies, Dick (25 Bn) 319–20
Jeffrey, Jim (2/14 Bn) 99
Jemaluang (map p. 103) 116
Jenkins, Claude (2/48 Bn) 37
Jesse, Jim (2/9 Bn) 230, 242
Jezzine (map p. 84) 89–90, 96–97, 101
Jivevaneng (map p. 271) 283–86, 291–92
Johns, Bob (2/27 Bn) 305
Johns' Knoll (map p. 302) 305–06
Johnson, Clifford (2/1 Anti-Tank Regt) 362, 372
Johnson, Henry 'Slim' (2/11 Bn) 62
Johnson, Wal (58/59 Bn) 265
Johnston, Archie (2/12 Bn) 182
Johnston, Henry (2/25 Bn) 307
Johnston, Herbert (2/1 Bn) 61

Johnston, Keith (2/1 Bn) 192
Jones, Allan (2/43 Bn) 270
Jorgensen, Errol (25 Bn) 322
Joy, Fernley 'Alby' (2/43 Bn) 216
Joyce, Ken (2/23 Bn) 168, 207–08
Julius, William (2/15 Fd Regt) 113
jungle warfare 3, 111, 329

Kaiapit (map p. 289) 288–90
Kakakog (map p. 271) 281, 285–86
Kane, Frank (15 Bn) 268, 330
Kankiryo Saddle (map p. 302) 290, 301, 311, 313, 315
Karawop (map p. 345) 363, 364
Kari (PIB) 255
Katika (map p. 271) 281, 283, 286–87, 295, 297
Katue (1 PIB) 171, 331
KB Mission (map p. 176) 175–77, 181
Keane, Bill (2/43 Bn) 405
Keley, Merv (2/32 Bn) 294–95
Kelliher, Richard (2/25 Bn) 165, 244, 278
Kelly, Ian (2/43 Bn) 406
Kelly, James (2/23 Bn) 73
Kemp, Gordon (2/8 Cdo Sqn) 326–27
Kemsley, Bill (2/1 Bn) 235
Kenna, Ted (2/4 Bn) 165, 367–68
Kennedy, Nev (22 Bn) 299
Kennedy, Robert (2/48 Bn) 204
Kennett, Lee 6–7
Kent, Lance (2/12 Bn) 245, 410
Kerr, Allan and Leonard (2/3 Pnr Bn) 213–14
Kesteven, Ken 'Pluto' (2/4 Bn) 60
Khalde (map p. 84) 100
Khiam (map p. 84) 88–89, 95
Kiarivu (map p. 345) 372
Kibby, Bill (2/48 Bn) 211
Killalea, Henry (Signal Corps) *51*, 52
Killey, George (2/3 Fd Regt) 48, 57
killing, heroism and 8–9, 423–24, 426
Kimberley, Arch (2/12 Bn) 168, 234
King, Gordon (2/6 Ind Coy) 288, 290
King, John (47 Bn) 184
King, Rex 'Dr Hackem' (2/24 Bn) 389
Kinghorn, Alan (2/8 Fd Regt) 148
Kingsbury, Bruce (2/14 Bn) 165, 185, 303
Kirk, Colin (2/12 Bn) 181–82

Kitching, Harry (2/1 Anti-Tank Regt) 362
Knife Ford 168, 345
Knight, Vic (2/2 MG Bn) 149
Knight, Jack 'Cracker' (24 Bn) 328
Koepang (map p. 131) 130
Koitaki (map p. 170) 218
Kokoda Village and airfield (map p. 170) 171–73, 195
Kokoda campaign 3, 17, 49, 97, 99, 167, 169–74, 185–98, 217, 218, 235, 244, 253, 255, 303, 307, 311, 342, 372, 375, 406, 409, 418, 425, 426
Komiatum (map p. 248) 261, 264, 266
Korean War 119, 149, 291, 314, 329, 332, 335, 350, 370
Kotz, Dudley 'Pongo' (2/43 Bn) 405
Kotz, Jim (2/10 Bn) 167, 177
Kranji River (map p. 103) 121
Kuanko (map p. 271) 296–97
Kudamati (map p. 129) 130
Kumawa 162, 291, 400
Kumusi River (map p. 170) 195, 196, 198, 255

Lababia Ridge (map p. 248) 253–54, 256, 258
Labuan Island (map p. 383) 399, 401–04
Lacey, Allan (2/2 Bn) 49
Lae (map p. 271) 169, 247, 253, 269, 270, 276–80
Lae campaign 4, 167, 244, 270–80
Laha (map p. 129) 128–30
Lakona (map p. 289) 299
Lamb, Donald (2/3 Bn) 92
Langemak Bay (map p. 271) 287
Langford, Tom (2/32 Bn) 153, 294, 342
Langtry, John (24 Bn) 7–8
Larissa (map p. 47) 49, 50
Lavarack, John (Australian general) 35, 37, 89, 97
Laver, Harold (2/6 Bn) 266–67
Lawrie, Don (2/23 Bn) 270, 272, *273*
Lawry, Pat (2/1 Bn) 62
Laybourne Smith, Bill (2/3 Fd Regt) 57, 59
Layt, Bob (25 Bn) 320
leaders, leadership and awards 4, 285, 424

Leahy's Farm (map p. 248) 250
Leaney, Gordon (2/1 Bn) 193–94
Leary, Reg (2/48 Bn) 292
Ledden, Jack (2/1 Bn) 236
Lebanon *see* Syria
Lee, Mert (2/27 Bn) 99, 190
Leeson, Allan (2/14 Bn) 418
Leeson, Herbert 'Curly' (2/32 Bn) 153
Legg, Les (2/24 Bn) 297
Leggatt, William (2/40 Bn) 130–32
Leitch, Jim (2/8 Bn) 366
Lemaire, Frank (2/17 Bn) 400
Leonard, Jack (2/28 Bn) 244, 275
Leuwiliang (map p. 134) 134–35
Libya (map p. 13) 12–22
Liddy, John (1 BD Pl) 413
Lightfoot, Operation 199
Lindsey, Bart (2/48 Bn) 204–05
Lingkas Bay (map p. 383) 382, 386
Litani River (map p. 84) 85
Little George Hill (map p. 318) 338, 339
Littler, Jack (2/25 Bn) 277
Livingstone, Malcolm (2/1 Fortress Engrs) 131
Lochhead, Alex (39 Bn and 2/2 Bn) 375
Locke, Leslie (2/7 Bn) 227
Logan, Edgar (2/7 Bn) 239
Logue, Ron (2/48 Bn) 293
Lokanu Ridge (map p. 248) 268
Loller, Jimmy (2/4 MG Bn) 120
London Gazette 10
Long, Gavin 80
Long Ridge 168, 348–50
Longhurst, Gus (2/2 MG Bn) 146
Longman, Jack 'Springy' (2/16 Bn) 310
Looker, Leslie (24 Bn) 254–55
Ludlow, Joffre (25 Bn) 167, 179
Luff, Percy (2/31 Bn) 89–90, 245
Lugge, Richard (2/12 Bn) 313
Lutong (map p. 383) 400
Lyall, Ken (2/28 Bn) 77, 160
Lynch, Francis (2/12 Bn) 74
Lynch, Harry (2/14 Bn) 416, *417*
Lynn, Ray (2/6 Armd Regt) 242

MacArthur, Douglas (American general) 169, 194, 226, 253, 280, 284, 288, 317, 382
MacDonald, Duncan (2/32 Bn) 209

Index

MacDougal, Bruce (2/3 Bn) 24, 100
Mace, RC 'Mick' (2/13 Fd Coy) 385
MacFie, Henry (2/3 MG Bn) 355
MacGraw, Donald (53 Bn) 185
MacGregor, Alex 'Sandy' (2/28 Bn) 275
MacGregor, Ken (2/6 Armd Regt) 242
MacIntosh, Bill (2/9 Bn) 229–30, 343
Mackay, Hector (2/3 Bn) 100, 244
Mackell, Austin (2/17 Bn) 35–36
Mackey, John (2/3 Pnr Bn) 166–67, 395
Maddern, Peter (2/40 Bn) 132
Maddocks, Jim (2/43 Bn) 158
Maidment, George (2/16 Bn) 167, 187-88
Main, Hugh (2/17 Bn) 283–84
Magarry, Ron (2/26 Bn) 118–19
Makh Khad Ridge (map p. 141) 152-53
Malang, Mount (map p. 409) 409
malaria 15, 175, 196, 212, 217, 221, 224, 226, 230, 232, 241, 278, 306–07, 313, 345, 360, 375
Malayan campaign 102–119
    recommendations for bravery rejected for Malaya and Singapore 105, 120
Malayan Emergency 299, 350, 370, 385
Maleme (map p. 56) 55–57
Malin (map p. 345) 346, 348
Malloch, Ian (2/23 Bn) *71*, 72
Manggar Airfield (map p. 409) 408, 415–19
Manning, Athol (2/7 Fd Regt) 160
Manson, Frank (2/12 Bn) 410
Maprik (map p. 345) 2, 353, 354, 360
Markham Point 276–77
Markham River and Valley (maps pp. 271 and 289) 170, 253, 270, 288–90
Marriott, Roy (2/5 Fd Amb) 183
Marshall, SLA 8, 424
Martin, Athol (2/33 Bn) 414
Martin, Bill (14/32 Bn) 380
Martin, Howard (2/5 Bn) 263
Matpi, William (1 PIB) 299, *300*, 301
Mawaraka (map p. 318) 319
May, Neville (2/28 Bn) 274
Mersa Matruh (map p. 13) 67
McAllister, Gordon (2/2 Fd Regt) 343, 348
McAllister, Tom (9 Div Sigs) 208
McAuliffe, Bill (2/10 Bn) 231
McBroom, Vincent (2/24 Bn) 37

McCallum, Charlie (2/14 Bn) 185–86
McCarter, Lew (2/43 Bn) 76
McCaughey, Sam (2/16 Bn) 311
McCaughey's Knoll (map p. 302) 311, 314
McClean, Doug (39 Bn) 171–72
McCloy, Jim (2/1 Bn) 193, 196, 198, 237
McCluskey, John (2/23 Bn) 155
McCormack, Fred (2/5 Bn) 262
McCrackan, John (2/3 Bn) 372
McCulloch, Don (2/12 Bn) 312–13
McCure, Bill (2/4 Anti-Tank Regt) 107–08, 110
McDonald, Bruce (2/5 Bn) 370
McDougall, Alan (2/10 Bn) 411
McElroy, Bob (2/17 Bn) 37
McEvoy, Keith (2/3 Ind Coy) 261
McGrath, Stan 'Stumpy' (25 Bn) 322–23
McGregor, Ron 'Jockey' (2/2 MG Bn) 159
McIlrick, Alan (2/3 Anti-Tank Regt) 160–61
McInnes, Bob (25 Bn) 321–22
McInnes, Ron (2/9 Bn) 242
McKay, Don (39 Bn) 173, 425, 426
McKeague, Robert 'Butts' (6 Div Sigs) 23–24
McKellar, Reg (2/13 Bn) 291
McKenzie, Charles (2/2 Ind Coy) 133
McKeown, Frank (2/5 Cdo Sqn) 410
McKinley, Colin (7 Div Cav Regt and 2/9 Bn) 244, 422
McLachlan, Horton (2/15 Bn) 7, 163–64, 167, 426
McLaren, Robert (2/10 Ord Wkshps) 138–39
McLelland, Kenneth 'Dick' (2/2 Bn) 357
McLennan, Frank (24 Bn) 244, 326
McLennan, Humphrey (2/11 Bn) 366
McLeod, Eric (2/24 Bn) 212
McMahon, James (2/3 Anti-Tank Regt) 144–45
McMaster, Kim (2/4 Armd Regt) 365
McNamara, Jack (2/24 Bn) 81
McNee, Leonard 'Scotty' (29/46 Bn) 298
McPhee, Duncan (2/27 Bn) 86
McPhee, Gerald (M Special Unit) 340
McQuillan, Vince (6 Div Cav Regt) *28*, 29, 168
McVeigh, Jack (2/16 Bn) 98

Melvaine, Maurice (2/3 Bn) 94–95
Melville, William (2/30 Bn) 106
Mentioned in Despatches, defined 10, 11
Mentiplay, Vic (2/4 MG Bn and Special Bn) 122
Menzies, Bob (2/7 Fd Regt) 206
Menzies, Jack (2/15 Fd Regt) 113
Merdjayoun (map p. 84) 88–91, 95–96, 100, 307
Mersing (Map p. 103) 115
Miethke, Geoffrey (2/10 Bn) 177
Milak (map p. 345) *347*, 353–54
Miles, Cyril (2/5 Bn) 262–63
Milford, Edward (Australian general) 408
Milford Highway (map p. 409) 409, 413, 419, 422, 423
Military Cross, defined 10
Military Medal, defined 10
militia 169
Miller, Jim (2/31 Bn) 66, 196
Miller, Stan (2/1 Bn) 235
Mills, George (6 Div Cav Regt) 29
Mills, Tom (6 Div Cav Regt) 88
Millstead, Keith (2/14 Fd Regt) 380
Milne Bay (map p. 176) 167, 174, 175–84, 217, 229, 233, 241, 322
Milton, Jim (2/5 Bn) 353
Miri (map p. 383) 400
Mitchell, Charles (2/11 Bn) 63
Mitchell, Henry (2/22 Bn) 128
Miteiriya Ridge (map p. 141) 152–53, 161, 158–281
Mivo River (map p. 318) 329–30
Mollard, Bill (2/24 Bn and 2/32 Bn) 154–55, 157, 294
Moloney, Brian 'Blue' (2/16 Bn) 190
Monastir (map p. 47) 46
Montgomery, Bernard (British general) 202, 206, 208, 216
Morgan, Wal (2/3 Bn) 92
Moriarty, Bill (2/1 Bn) 61
Morley, Rufus 'Tich' (2/4 Anti-Tank Regt) 108
Morphett, Hortle (2/48 Bn) 293
Morris, Ernest (2/2 Bn) 356–57
Morse, Bill (2/5 Bn) 18, *19*, 20
Morshead, Leslie (Australian general) 35, 37, 42, 73, 74, 75, 79, 81, 151, 162, 206, 208, 213, 214, 215, 216
Morton, Ham (2/7 Cav Regt) 239–40
Moss, Ken (2/4 Cdo Sqn) 391
Moss, Ron (2/6 Bn) 260
Moten, Murray (17 Bde) 247, 249
Motieau (map p. 176) 181
motivation for heroic acts 423–24, 425
Mould, Ernest (2/1 Bn) 349
Moviavi 255
Muar (map p. 103) 105, 107, 110, 113
Muara Island 399
Mubo (map p. 248) 170, 247, 250, 253, 256, 260–61
Mulally, Neville 'Irish' (2/33 Bn) 217–18, *219*
Mulgrave, Andy (2/11 Bn) 63, *64*, 69, 167
Mulley, Ted (2/3 Pnr Bn) 213–14, 246
Mulligan, Clive (2/30 Bn) 105
Mullins, John (2/31 Bn) 419
Murchison, Allan (2/3 Bn) 94
Murdoch, Murray (2/3 Bn) 93
Murdock, Leslie (2/1 Armd Bde Recon Sqn) 421
Murnane, Alan (2/21 Bn) 129
Murphy, Gordon (2/16 Bn) 220
Mussolini, Benito 12, 13
Myola (map p. 170) 191

Nadzab (map p. 271) 270, 277, 290, 310
Naismith, Allan (2/7 Bn) 167, 266
Nambut Hill (map p. 345) 349
Nankiville, Bert (2/28 Bn) 286–87
Napier (map p. 248) 258
Nason, Clive (2/2 Pnr Bn) 100
Nassau Bay (map p. 248) 256, 258, 360
Nauro (map p. 170) 189
Neall, Oliver 'Oz' (2/8 Bn) 25–26
Nelligan, Philip 'Joe' (2/12 Fd Regt) 281
Neuendorf, Keith (2/23 Bn) 151–52
Newbery, Collin (2/28 Bn) 216
New Britain (maps pp. 126, 377) 125–28, 254, 280, 317, 376–81, 382
Newcastle feature (map p. 409) 412
New Zealand Army 5, 52, 55, 67
    Maori Battalion 58
    New Zealand Division 46
Newton, Ken (2/5 Bn) 370–71
Nithsdale Estate 116

Index

Nixon, John (2/13 Fd Coy) 384
No Man's Land 8, 63, 72, 75, 77, 203, 211, 225, 229, 232
Norman, Hugh (2/28 Bn) 4
Norrie, Edward (2/13 Bn) 201
Norris, Robert (2/15 Bn) 282
North Borneo (map p. 383) 382, 401–07
North, Joseph (Beach Gp Engrs) 244, 390
Nott, Allen (24 Bn) 324–25
Noyes, Bill (2/9 Bn) 44, 238
Numa Numa Trail (map p. 318) 337–38

O'Brien, Joe (2/25 Bn) 167, 307
O'Brien, John (2/24 Bn) 213, 244
Observation Hill 260, 266
O'Connor, Charles (2/13 Bn) 201
O'Connor, Owen (24 Bn) 5, 327
O'Connor, Richard (British general) 13, 23
O'Day, Gerald (2/14 Bn) 96–97
O'Dea, James (2/20 Bn) 137–38
O'Donnell, Morrie (2/31 Bn) 195
official histories, Australian 2, 5, 14, 41, 61, 73, 80–81, 95, 120, 123, 129, 131, 209, 216, 227, 231, 232–33, 252, 274–75, 285, 298, 305, 344, 354, 365, 378
Oivi (map p. 170) 171, 195–96, 198, 237
O'Keefe, Phillip (2/33 Bn) 191
Old Strip, Buna 231
Old Vickers Position (map p. 248) 253, 260, 265–66
Oldfield, Tom (2/8 Bn) 48, 60
Oldfield, Tom (2/29 Bn) 123
Olive Oil Factory (map p. 58) 61–62
Oliver, Alfred (2/4 Armd Regt) 323
Olsen, Charles (2/9 Cav Cdo Sqn) 348
O'Neill, Bill (2/5 Ind Coy) 170
O'Regan, Kevin 'Brolga' (2/4 Cdo Sqn) 245, 391
Orodubi (map p. 248) 260, 261, 267
Ottley, Darrell 'Dal' (2/19 Bn) 119
Otway (map p. 383) 391
Owen Stanley Range (map p. 170) 171
Own, William (39 Bn) 172
Oxlade, Lionel (2/7 Cav Regt) 238–39
Oxygen feature (map p. 409) 414

Pabu (map p. 271) 294–97, 342
Paff, Terry (2/4 Bn) 345–46
Paine, Bob (2/27 Bn) 306
Palandri, Bert (2/7 Fd Amb) 56
Pallier, Nolan 'Nol' (2/14 Bn) 301, 305
Pallier's Hill (map p. 302) 301–03, 305
Palmer, John (2/12 Bn) 313, 342
Palmer, Kelvin 'Kelly' (2/5 Fd Regt) 415
Parbury, Philip (2/3 Bn) 92–3, 100
Parit Sulong (map p. 103) 111–14, 123
  massacre at 114
Park, Noel (2/2 Bn) 357–58
Parker, Terry (2/26 Bn) 118, 119
Parnell, Roy 'Tex' (2/12 Bn) 246, 313
Parr, William 'Snowy' (39 Bn) 172
Parramatta feature (map p. 409) 411–12
Parsons, Charlie (2/4 Anti-Tank Regt) 107, *109*
Partridge, Frank (8 Bn) 165, 244, 337
Patrick, Ron (2/15 Bn) 8, 162
Pearce, George (2/14 Bn) 188
Pearce, George (2/48 Bn) 397
Pearce, Noel (2/9 Armd Regt) 389
Pearl Harbor 104
Pearl Ridge 338
Pearson, John (2/4 Fd Regt) 308, 310
Peel, Edward (2/2 Fd Coy) 20–21
Penfui (map p. 131) 130
Peningkibaru (map p. 383) 388
Percival, Arthur (British general) 107, 112, 116, 119, 121–23
Perembil (map p. 345) 252, 351
Perivolia (map p. 58) 57, 61–62
Perkins, Ken (2/10 Cav Cdo Sqn) *347*, 353–54
Perkins, Les (2/13 Bn) 78
Perry, John (2/3 Bn) 350
Perry, Lionel (19 Bn) 379
Peterson, Bruce (2/7 Bn) 254
Pett, Lester 'Tarzan' (2/3 Bn) 194
Philippines 138–39, 317, 382
Phillips, Doug (2/20 Bn) 121, 246
Pickett, Arthur (2/3 Bn) 17
Pilmer, Laurie (2/28 Bn) 160
Pinios Gorge (map p. 47) 49–50
Pitts, Charles (2/2 Fd Regt) 348
Plater, Ron (39 Bn) 167, 224–25, 245
Pocket, the 402, 404

Poidevin, Gordon (2/24) 41
Point 23 (map p. 141) 142
Point 26 (map p. 141) 142–43
Poker feature (map p. 383) 395, 398
Pollitt, Bill (2/1 Bn) 193
Pope, Howard (2/13 Bn) 281
Pope, Glyn (2/48 Bn) 391–92, *393*
Pope, Ken (2/3 Bn) 350
Port Moresby (map p. 170) 169–71, 193, 218, 249, 255
Portee feature (map p. 409) 410
Porter, Selwyn (2/31 Bn, 30 Bde and Maroubra Force) 89, 188, 240
Porton Plantation (map p. 318) 334–36
posthumous awards 11, 36, 40, 132, 139, 151–52, 157, 172, 185, 211, 227, 249, 357
postwar army careers 27, 36, 72, 90, 119, 149, 195, 291, 314, 324, 329, 335, 350, 358, 370, 426
Potts, Arnold (21 Bde) 174, 185, 188
Power, Frank (2/15 Bn) 400
Power, Kevin (2/33 Bn) 191, 245, 343
Preece, Ron (ANGAU) 188–89
Prigg, Jack (2/5 Bn) 263
Prior, Colin (2/1 Bn) 235
Proby, Lawrence 'Butch' (58/59 Bn) 265
Protheros (map p. 302) 311–14, 342
Pryor, Wally (2/48 Bn) 157
psychological issues in heroes 6–7
Pugh, John (14/32 Bn) 379–80
Purdon, Arthur (2/30 Bn) 107
Puriata River (map p. 318) 319, 323
Pyke, Charles (39 Bn) 167, 172

Quinn, Bob (2/43 Bn) 76

Rabaul (maps pp. 126 and 377) 104, 125–27, 169, 259, 369, 376, 378, 381
Ramsdale, Dick (9 Div Sigs) 145
Ramu Valley (map p. 289) 288, 290, 418
Randolph, Edgar (2/7 Fd Amb) 55–56
Ranford, Robert 'Snowy' (2/48 Bn) 81, 211–12
Rankin, Don (2/1 Bn) 21–22
ranks, defined 11
Ratsua (map p. 318) 335
Rattey, Reg (25 Bn) 165, 320
Rau, Walter (2/4 Fd Regt) 86
Raward, Jack (2/25 Bn) 422

Redgrave, Ernest 'Snow' (2/31 Bn) 196, *197*
Redmond, Neil (2/10 Cdo Sqn) *347*
Reed, Frank (2/1 Anti-Tank Regt) 362–63
Reeve, Eddie (2/5 Bn) 168, 251–52, 261–62
Reeves, Sims (2/32 Bn) 295
Regan, Jim (2/5 Bn) 371
regular army soldiers 60, 122, 191, 224, 245, 272, 279, 284, 299, 314, 316, 324, 333, 334, 348, 350, 362
Reid, Cedric (2/9 Bn) 181
Reid, Harold (2/29 Bn) 123
Reiter, Frank 'Blue' (2/7 Bn and 31/51 Bn) 59, 63–64, 336–37
Retimo (maps pp. 56, 58) 55–59, 61–64, 66–67, 69
Reynolds, Pat (2/19 Bn) 110–11
Rhodesian troops 215
Richards, Billy (2/25) 278
Richards, Harry (2/11 Bn) 66
Richards, Joe (2/2 Pnr Bn) 135
Riedy, Arthur 'Yorkie' (2/3 Pnr Bn) 395
Rindogim 374–75
Ring Contour 25 (map p. 141) 154, 157
Rippon Ridge (map p. 383) 387, 389
Roach, Laurie (2/6 Bn) 258
Roach, Leonard (2/21 Bn) 128
Roberts, Reg (2/3 Anti-Tank Regt) 150
Robertson, John (2/29 Bn) 107–08, 110
Robino, Pasquale (2/3 Fd Amb) 294–95, 342
Robinson, Bert (61 Bn) 175–76, *178*, 180
Robinson, Melven 'Nugget' (2/12 Bn) 312–13
Rodriguez, Tim (2/7 Fd Regt) 203
Rodwell, Edwin 'Snowy' (2/24 Bn) 386
Roff, Norman (2/40 Bn) 131–32
Rommel, Erwin (German general) 33, 36, 37, 41, 42, 45, 70, 140, 142, 144, 149, 152, 154, 199, 202, 206, 208, 210, 214, 215, 216
Ronan, Ray (2/43 Bn) 284
Rooke, Peter (2/28 Bn) 287
Rooney, Ted (25 Bn) 321
Roosevelt Ridge (map p. 248) 261
Rose, Allan (2/6 Bn) 2–3, 268
Rosel, John (2/24 Bn) 41, *71*
Ross, John (2/15 Fd Regt) 113

Index

Rossborough, Fred (24 Bn) 324
Rowe, Lionel (2/31 Bn) 279–80
Royce, Ted (2/11 Bn) 346
Ruin Ridge *see* Miteiriya Ridge
Russell, Bill (2/14 Bn) 81, 99
Russell, Bill (2/7 Bn) 254
Russell, Doug (2/3 Fd Regt) 48–49
Russell, Neil (2/12 Bn) 73–74
Ryan, Geoffrey (2/6 Bn) 2–3
Ryan, James 'Killer' (2/11 Bn) 29–30
Ryan, Leo (2/6 Fd Coy) 416, 418–19
Ryan, Robert (2/6 Bn) 256
Ryan, Timothy 'Curly' (2/48 Bn) 396
Ryan, William (2/2 Pnr Bn) 135
Ryrie, Edward (1 Armd Regt) 411–12, 420

Saaby, John (2/32 Bn) 295
Saggers, Albert (2/4 MG Bn and Special Bn) 122
Saidor (map p. 289) 254
Saint, Murray (2/10 Bn) 243
Salamaua (map p. 248) 169 166, 169, 170, 244, 247–48, 253–55, 258–69, 327, 340
Salient, The (map p. 34) 42, 44–45, 70, 73, 74–77, 237
Sallaway, Ervine (15 Bn) 268
Sampson, Victor (2/12 Bn) 234, 342
Sams, Ernest (2/30 Bn) 105
Sanananda (map p. 170) 44, 217, 231, 234, 235–43, 247
Sandakan (map p. 383) 138
Sanderson, Alex (2/1 Bn) 192
Sanderson, Oswin 'Sandy' (2/7 Cav Regt) 239
Sanderson, Ross (2/13 Bn) 210
Sandover, Ray (2/11 Bn) 63
Sanopa 172
Sattelberg (maps pp. 271 and 289) 283, 286, 291–94, 296, 396
Sargent, Bert (2/14 Bn) 99
Saucer, the 214–16
Saunders, Reg (2/7 Bn) 58, 303, 355
Scanlan, John (2/22 Bn) 125–26
Scarlet Beach (map p. 271) 280–81, 283, 286–87, 291
Schindler, Aub (25 Bn) 179–80
Scholz, Theodore (2/6 Fd Coy) 416
Schram, Alan (2/23 Bn) 270

Schwebel, Albert (2/3 Anti-Tank Regt) 215, 244
Scott, Alan (2/32 Bn) 297
Scott, Alfred (2/31 Bn) 279–80
Scott, Jack (2/16 Bn) 310–11
Scott, William (2/21 Bn) 128, 130
Scott Orr, Walter (2/3 Bn) 92, 244
Scout Hill (map p. 248) 268
Scout Ridge (map p. 248) 268
Searle, John (2/13 Bn) 78
Searles, Syd (26 Bn) 334
Seatree, Eric (2/3 Pnr Bn) 210, 342
Selby, Tom (2/1 Bn) 22
Selmes, Bill (2/2 MG Bn) 146
Semler, John (2/10 Bn) 412
Sepinggang airfield 408, 413
Seria (map p. 383) 399–400
Shaggy Ridge (map p. 302) 167, 288, 301, 306, 308–15
Shannon, Tom (2/2 Pnr Bn) 98, 100, 244
Shattock, Bob (2/5 Bn) 20
Shearwin, John (2/1 Bn) 196
Sherlock, Bill (2/6 Bn) 249
Shiburangu, Mount (map p. 345) 373–74
Shillaker, Bob (2/48 Bn) 205
Shilton, Alwyn 'Blue' (2/5 Bn and 31/51 Bn) 331–32
Sidi Barrani (map p. 13) 13, 27
Silver, Ted 'Heigh-Ho' (2/14 Bn) 303
Simemi Creek 231, 232, 234
Simonson, Don (39 Bn) 167, 173–74
Sims, Charlie (2/27 Bn) 99
Singapore (map p. 103) 99, 102, 104, 106, 112, 116, 119–24
Singaua (map p. 271) 270, 272
Slater, Carl (25 Bn) 319
Slater's Knoll (map p. 318) 319–24
Slim, William (British general) 182
Smith, Allan (2/6 Bn) 245, 256
Smith, Carlyle (2/3 Bn) 93
Smith, Charles (2/5 Bn) 18
Smith, Denis (2/21 Bn) 129–30
Smith, Greig (2/6 Bn) 258
Smith, John (2/5 Bn) 100, 263–64
Smith, Mick (2/8 Bn) 374
Smith, Noel (2/17 Bn and 31/51 Bn) 334–35
Smith, Phil 'Blah' (2/4 Bn) 368
Smith, Stanley (2/23 Bn) 246, 394–95

Smith, Tom (2/8 Fd Regt) 148
Smith, Tom (2/5 Bn) 371
Smithers, Gordon (2/15 Bn) 70, 167, 246
Smythe, Vic (39 Bn) 173
Snags Track (map p. 383) 390, 394, 397–98
Snell, Len (2/15 Bn) 162–64, 282
Snell's Hill (map p. 271) 282
Soltan, Eric (2/1 Bn) 236, 246
Song River (map p. 271) 294, 295, 296
Soputa (map p. 170) 235, 241
South-West Pacific Area 169, 317
Spark, David 'Pete' (4 Fd Regt) 334–36
Spavin, Jack (2/48 Bn) 38, *39*
Spence, Colin 'Col' (2/18 Bn) 116, *117*
Spencer, Don (2/48 Bn) 293
Spencer, George (2/10 Bn) 232–33
Sphakia (map p. 56) 59, 66, 67
Spittle, Cecil (2/3 Anti-Tank Regt) 150
St George-Ryder, Harrowby (2/1 Bn and 55/53 Bn) 198
St John, Ted (2/6 Bn) 249
Stainlay, Darcy (19 Bn) 378
Stanley, Oswald 'Os' (2/25 Bn) 191
Starcevich, Tom (2/43 Bn) 165, 406
Starmer, Lex (2/15 Bn) 282
Steele, Ray (2/15 Fd Regt) 138
Steele, Stan (25 Bn) 176, 179
Stenning, Bill 'Curly' (2/8 Bn) 26, 27
Stephenson, Ernest (2/9 Bn) 311–12
Stevenson, Arthur (2/13 Fd Coy) 200
Stevenson, John (2/3 Bn) 93–94
Stewart, Gordon (2 NG Bn) 371–72
Stewart, James (2/1 Bn) 194
Stewart, Laurie (2/20 Bn) 120
Stoddart, Roy (2/1 Bn) 196
Stokes, Albert 'Taffy' (2/2 Pnr Bn) 100
Storrie, John (2/1 Anti-Tank Regt) 372
Stretch, Gerry (2/24 Bn) 387, 389
stretcher-bearers 342, 423
Stubbs, Sam (2/2 Bn) 167, 356
Suda Bay (map p. 56) 55, 58
Sullivan, Albert (2/10 Bn) 411
Sullivan, John (2/14 Bn) 416, 418
Supercharge, Operation 208, 216
Sutherland, Douglas 'Slogger' (2/48 Bn) 293
Swanson, Ted (2/4 Bn) 60, 245
Sweetapple, Arthur (2/33 Bn) 89
swords, Japanese 105, 114, 116–17, 170, 198, 224, 331, 366, 406, 420, 421
Sykes (map p. 383) 391–94
Symington, Noel (39 Bn) 172–73
Symington, William (2/5 Bn) 18, 244
Symmons, Fred (2/11 Bn) 62
Symons, Bill (2/10 Bn) 168, 411
Syrett, Jack (24 Bn) 328
Syrian campaign (map p. 84) 7, 83–101, 135, 152, 167, 185, 187, 190, 220, 221, 224, 244, 263, 264, 279, 306, 307, 311, 332, 358

Taggart, Colin (2/48 Bn) 204
Taiof Island (map p. 318) 333
Tambu, Mount (map p. 248) 252, 261, 263–67, 371
Tanglin (map p. 103) 123
tanks **Australian** 152, 229–33, 240–42, 287, 291, 292–93, 295, 298, 299, 322–23, 325, 327, 328–29, 363, 365, 367, 368, 388, 390–91, 397, 401–02, 404, 411–13, 415, 420–21; **British** 13, 14, 21, 23, 31, 36–37, 38, 62, 69, 72, 83, 134, 143, 151, 158, 160, 162, 163, 200, 201, 207, 214–15; **German** 34, 35, 37, 41–42, 50, 70, 72, 144–46, 148, 149–51, 153, 154, 160, 200, 204, 214–15, 216, 278; **Italian** 15, 17, 20, 25, 26, 27, 44, 62, 202–03; **Japanese** 104, 106, 107–09, 112, 113, 175, 177, 179, 180; **Vichy French** 83, 88, 90–91
Tapioli (1 PIB) 258, *259*, 260
Tarakan (map p. 383) 81, 167, 382–99, 413
Tarakan airfield (map p. 383) 386, 388–89
Tarakan Hill (map p. 383) 390–91
Tart, Reece (2/15 Bn) 281
Tate, Bertie (2/15 Fd Regt) 113
Tatterson, Vin (2/7 Bn) 253
Taylor, Alexander (2/10 Bn) 44
Taylor, Douglas 'Jock' (2/7 Bn) 226–27, *228*
Taylor, Ernest 'Squizzy' (2/48 Bn) 397
Taylor, John (2/13 Bn) 203
Taylor, Tom 'Tubby' (2/48 Bn) 394
Tazaki, Mount (map p. 345) 373–74
teamwork 4, 8
Tel el Eisa (map p. 141) 38, 142–43, 145, 148–51, 154, 162, 167, 205, 212, 343, 397
Tel el Eisa station (map p. 141) 143

Index

Temple, Jack 'Shirley' (57/60 Bn) 315
Templeton, Sam (39 Bn) 171–72
Templeton's Crossing (map p. 170) 189, 192
Tengah Airfield (map p. 103) 121
Thailand 113, 136
Thomas, Harry (2/7 Bn) 59
Thomas, Kevin 'KB' (2/12 Bn) 313–14
Thomas, Lin (2/43 Bn) 200–01
Thomas, Lloyd (2/15 Bn) 280–81
Thomas, Reg (2/9 Bn) 229–30
Thomas, Viv (2/2 Anti-Tank Regt) 90–91
Thompson, Bob (2/16 Bn) 220–21
Thompson, Bob (2/14 Bn) 418
Thompson's Post (map p. 141) 205, 212
Thorn, Charlie (2/5 Bn) 351, 353
Thornberry, Irwin (25 Bn) 321
Thornton, Clarrie (2/4 Anti-Tank Regt) 107–08
Thorp, Graham (1 Naval Bombardment Group) 415
Till, Jimmy (2/4 MG Bn and Special Bn) 122
Tiller, Bill (2/5 Bn) 261–62, 264
Timor (map p. 131) 130–33, 244, 332
　Portuguese Timor 132–33
Tobruk (map p. 34),
　Australian capture of 23–27, 48, 61
　siege of 8, 32, 33–45, 70–79, 238
Tokinotu (map p. 318) 320
Tokuku Pass (map p. 345) 356, 358
Tol (map p. 377) 127, 381
Toms, Seymour (2/27 Bn) 306
Tong (map p. 345) 350
Tongs, Bede (3 Bn) 191
Toohey, Roy (2/48 Bn) 392
Torokina (map p. 318) 317, 331
Torrent, Andy (2/28 Bn) 3, 4, 168, 275–76
Torricelli Mountains (map p. 345) 344, 346, 350, 359
Townsley, Cec (25 Bn) 321–22
Travis, Geoff (2/24 Bn) 387, *388*
Treacy, Maurice 'Mokka' (2/14 Bn) 186
Tremellen, Henry (58/59 Bn) 316
Trenerry, Rex (2/27 Bn) 306
Trethowan, Jim (2/8 Bn) 373–74
Trevor, Terence (2/30 Bn) 105–06
Treweeke, Fred (2/13 Bn) 201

Trig 29 (map p. 141) 204–06, 208
Trig 33 (map p. 141) 71, 142–44, 149, 150, 206
Tripoli, Libya (map p. 13) 31, 33
Troughton, Herb (15 Bn) 268
trunk road, Malaya 104, 116
Truscott, Les (2/19 Bn) 111
Tsimba and Tsimba Ridge (map p. 318) 331–32, 336
Tuit, Wally (2/43 Bn) 76–77, 342
Turnbull, Alex (2/8 Bn) 346, 348
typical heroes, traits of 244–46

Uebergang, Edgar (8 Bn) 337
Ulupu (map p. 345) 351, 370
Underwood, Edward (2/3 Fd Coy) 399–400
unemployment and heroes 12, 18, 181, 231, 232, 237, 244, 295, 314, 358
units, defined 11
Usau (map p. 131) 132

Varnum, Arnold (2/1 Bn) 236–37
Vasey, George (Australian general) 194–95, 218, 223, 240, 289, 308, 311
Vasey Highway (map p. 409) 408, 423
Vernon, Jack (2/18 Bn) 120–21
Vevi (map p. 47) 25, 48
Vickery, Norman (2/1 Fd Regt) 22
Victoria Cross 1, 4, 7, 9, 10, 36, 52, 65, 81, 98, 101, 165, 185, 357
　ages of winners 244, 337
　candidates who missed out 5, 41, 52, 119, 151–52, 182, 185, 188, 249, 291, 296, 346, 410
　weapons of winners 165, 166
Victory March in London 146, 320, 360
Vietnam War 324, 329, 350, 370, 385, 389
volunteers, Australian soldiers as 6, 12
Vunakanau (map p. 126) 125–27

Wagner, Charles (2/18 Bn) 138, 139
Waitavalo (map p. 377) 127, 378, 381
Waites, Harry (2/14 Bn) 416
Waites' Knoll 416, *417*, 418
Walker, Angus 'Mac' (2/4 Armd Regt) 365
Walker, Ian (2/7 Bn) 227, 250

Walker, James (24 Bn) 277
Walker, Keith (2/7 Bn) 250
Walker, Ray (2/24 Bn) 395
Walker, Wally (2/48 Bn) 396
Walker, William (2/16 Bn) 190
Wallder, Fred (2/3 Anti-Tank Regt) 203, 215
Wallis, Stanley 'Lofty' (2/24 Bn) 386
Walters, Bob (2/28 Bn) 401
Walters, Vernon 'Mick' (2/5 Bn) 261–63, 264
Wandumi (map p. 248) 247, 249
Wankey, Eric (2/4 MG Bn) 120
Warburton, Charlie (2/2 Pnr Bn) 100
Ward, Ken (31/51 Bn) 244, 335
Wareo (map p. 271) 286, 291, 294–98
Warfe, George (2/3 Ind Coy) 260–61
Warner, Keith (AIB) 341
Warren, Don (2/9 Cav Cdo Sqn) 167, 368
Warren, John (25 Bn) 176
Washbrook, Walter 'Swanny' (2/48 Bn) 293
Waterman, Frank (2/28 Bn) 287
Waters, Arthur (2/48 Bn) 167, 392, 394
Waters, John (2/48 Bn) 394
Waters, Len (2/7 Bn) 254
Watt, Arnold (2/6 Bn) 167, 256
Watts, Harry (2/4 Bn) 27
Wau (map p. 248) 167, 168, 247–53, 262, 263
Wavell, Archibald (British general) 13, 33, 35, 83, 154
Wayte, Jack (2/33 Bn) 89
weapons used by heroes 165–168
Webb, Alexander (2/2 Bn) 358
Wedgwood, Claude (2/28 Bn) 286–87
Wedlick, Victor (2/29 Bn) 110
Weeks, Stan (2/14 Bn) 221
Weir, Charles (2/24 Bn) 213
Weir, Dave (2/15 Bn) 163
Weir, Stuart (2/3 Bn) 168, 350
Wellings, Claude (2/3 Ind Coy) 261
Wells, Bill (2/4 Bn) 374
West Point 23 (map p. 141) 162
West Point 24 (map p. 141) 151, 157
Westendorf, Albert (2/6 Ind Coy) 290
Weston 404
Weston, Arthur (2/10 Bn) 243
Weston, Jack 'Tex' (2/48 Bn) 73, 143, 145–46, *147*, 425

Wewak (map p. 345) 167, 344, 356, 363–68, 372
Whatley, Royce (2/4 Armd Regt) 325
Wheatley, Mervyn 'Doc' (2/2 Ind Coy) 133
White, Ben (AIB) 341
White, Clem (2/2 Pnr Bn) 134–35
White, Sid (25 Bn) 321–22
Whitechurch, John 'Bluey' (2/14 Bn) 303–04
Whitehead, Norm 'Boof' (2/6 Armd Regt) 230–31
Whittaker's Bridge (map p. 271) 277–78
Whyte, Jack (2/33 Bn) 89
Wigley, John (M Special Unit) 340
Williams, Arthur (2/19 Bn) 112, 342
Williams, Col (2/48 Bn) 145
Williams, Fred (2/2 Fd Regt) 348
Williams, Len (2/27 Bn) 189
Williams, Owen (2/4 Bn) 342, 368
Willson, Ron (2/31 Bn) 420
Wilson, Arthur 'Baldy' (2/24 Bn) 389
Wilson, Francis 'Joe' (2/20 Bn) 115, 166
Wilson, Henry 'Jumbo' (British general) 83
Wilson, John 'Butch' (2/6 Ind Coy) 290
Winters, Dick 423
Wirui Mission (map p. 345) 367–68
Wonginara Mission (map p. 345) 356–58, 360
Woods, Bill 'Dadda' (2/15 Bn) 291
Woodward, Bill (7 BD Pl) 328–29
Woodward, Danny (2/28 Bn) 401
Wootten, George (Australian general) 31, 286, 291
World War I veterans as World War II heroes 18, 52, 86, 92, 100, 110, 111, 173, 192
Wyatt, Bob (25 Bn) 179
Wylie, Douglas (49 Bn) 238

Yamil (map p. 345) 2
Yaula (map p. 289) 316
Yokopi (map p. 289) 315
Yong Peng (map p. 103) 113–14
Young, Keith (2/13 Fd Coy) 77
Young, Ray (19 Bn) 378–79

Zanker, Alf (2/27 Bn) 189

www.ingramcontent.com/pod-product-compliance
Lightning Source LLC
Chambersburg PA
CBHW051240300426
44114CB00011B/825